Tourism Policy and Planning

Tourism Policy and Planning
Yesterday, Today and Tomorrow

David L. Edgell, Sr
Maria DelMastro Allen
Ginger Smith
Jason R. Swanson

AMSTERDAM • BOSTON • HEIDELBERG • LONDON • NEW YORK • OXFORD
PARIS • SAN DIEGO • SAN FRANCISCO • SINGAPORE • SYDNEY • TOKYO

ELSEVIER

Butterworth-Heinemann is an imprint of Elsevier

Butterworth-Heinemann is an imprint of Elsevier
Linacre House, Jordan Hill, Oxford OX2 8DP, UK
30 Corporate Drive, Suite 400, Burlington, MA 01803, USA

First edition 2008

Notice
No responsibility is assumed by the publisher for any injury and/or damage to persons
or property as a matter of products liability, negligence or otherwise, or from any use
or operation of any methods, products, instructions or ideas contained in the material
herein.

British Library Cataloguing in Publication Data
A catalogue record for this book is available from the British Library

Library of Congress Cataloguing-in-Publication Data
A catalogue record for this book is available from the Library of Congress

ISBN: 978-0-7506-8557-3

For information on all Butterworth-Heinemann publications
visit our web site at books.elsevier.com

Printed and bound in Great Britain
08 09 10   10 9 8 7 6 5 4 3 2 1

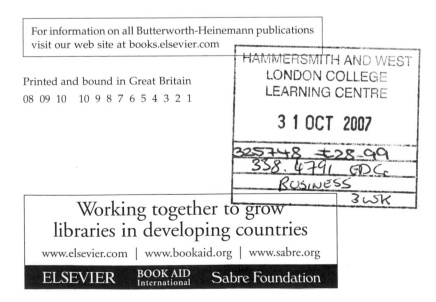

Dedication

This book is dedicated to the men and women who work in the international tourism and hospitality industry; to the destinations and local communities which make tourism possible; to the transportation industry that facilitates travel, and to all those studying for careers in tourism.

and

Edgell – To my grandson, Nathan Lee Edgell, born July 30, 2007
Allen – To my children, Jane McIver and Wm. Kemp
Smith – To my son and daughter, Reli and Nida Parks
Swanson – To my parents, Tom and Mary, and to all the friends and family who have joined me on the porch swing

and

Allen, Smith, Swanson – To our tourism policy and planning mentor – yesterday, today, and tomorrow – Dr. David L. Edgell, Sr.

Contents

Foreword   xiii
Preface   xv
Acknowledgements   xvii

1   Introduction   1
Tourism defined   1
Tourism policy defined   7
Worldwide importance of tourism   9
In the global tourism context   10
New challenges   11
A new look at tourism policy   13
Economic and non-economic benefits   16
Economic and non-economic costs   18
Cooperation/integration   19
Balanced/comprehensive tourism policy   19
Case study 1. Kansas Tourism Opportunities:
    Strategic Overview   22
References   35

2   Tourism policy issues of yesterday   37
Historic perspectives   37
The beginnings of modern tourism policy   42
International tourism policy for the United States   43
The importance of the National Tourism Policy Act of 1981   47
Some reasons for a US tourism policy   49
Case report 2. National Tourism Policy Act of 1981   52
References   62

3   Tourism policy issues for today   63
Introduction and overview   63
Business ethics in a tourism policy issues framework   64
Types of tourism policy evaluation stages   65
    Stage 1. Formative phase tourism policy evaluation   66
    Stage 2. Development phase tourism policy evaluation   67
    Stage 3. Summative phase tourism policy evaluation   68
Importance of tourism policy issues   69
    Tourism, regulation and public policy   69
    Sex tourism   70
    Tourism and health related issues   71

Tourism and safety/security   72
Space travel   73
Agritourism   74
Complexity of tourism policy issues   75
Tourism technologies and information communication   76
Tax legislation   77
International development aid   77
Banking loans and bonds   79
Grants   80
Tourism policy issues, destination management and
   the future – an open-ended conclusion   80
Summary and conclusion   81
Case report 3. World Hotel Link – An ICT (Information and
   Communication Technology) Driven Approach to
   Equitable and Sustainable Tourism   82
Bibliography for case report 3   93

4   **Tourism as a commercial and economic activity**   **97**
Global importance   100
Tourism as an economic development tool   100
Demand side of tourism   105
Supply side of tourism   108
Coopetition   109
Comparative advantage   111
Employment   114
Income   115
Multiplier effect   116
Exporting tourism   118
Economic development   119
Rural tourism in the United States   120
Economics of tourism information   122
Conclusion   122
Case study 4. Sustainable Tourism as an Economic
   Development Strategy Along Coastlines
   (Edited for this publication)   123
References   138

5   **Political and foreign policy implications of tourism**   **141**
Tourism agreements   142
Intergovernmental organizations and regional industry
   associations   143
United Nations World Tourism Organization   144
World Travel and Tourism Council   145
Organisation for Economic Cooperation and Development   146

Organization of American States   147
Asia-Pacific Economic Cooperation   149
Caribbean Tourism Organization   151
Southeast Tourism Society   152
Tourism facilitation   154
Tourism and foreign policy   157
Tourism as a policy for peace   158
A reason to maintain peace   160
Political stability, safety and tourism   160
Mutual trust and respect created by tourism   163
Conclusion   164
Case study 5. Southeast Tourism Policy Council: An
    Emerging Model for Federal Tourism Advocacy   165
References   180

6 **Managing sustainable tourism**   **181**
Sustainable tourism – its essence   183
Current trends in sustainable tourism   186
The natural environment   189
The built environment   190
Global impact   191
Planning first   193
Policy and management strategy   194
Benefits   196
Important precepts   197
The Credo   198
Case study 6. Sustainable Ecotourism: Balancing Preservation
    and Economic Growth (Edited for this publication)   199
References   217

7 **Education and training in tourism**   **219**
Introduction and overview   219
Workforce supply and workplace demand: need for defining
    tourism   221
Defining tourism and hospitality education and training 223
Defining education, training and human
    resource development   225
Factors contributing to the dominant role of the
    hospitality sector   228
Human resources issues for education and training in tourism 231
Need for understanding and reducing misperceptions   231
Need for credibility of post-secondary education
    programmes   233

Need for investment in human resources
in tourism   234
Need for education and training performance standards
and accreditation processes   235
Leadership role of the United Nations World Tourism
Organization   237
UNWTO Education Council of the Affiliate Members   237
UNWTO-Themis Foundation and TedQual Program   237
Need for coordinated education and training infrastructure
for tourism   239
Higher education and training programmes in tourism   240
Hong Kong   240
United States   240
Canada   241
Non-credit tourism training programmes   241
United States   241
Need for vertical and horizontal coordination among key
stakeholders   242
Need to understand the dynamics of a rapidly changing
world and the impact on workforce development   244
Importance of education and training in tourism   245
Case report 7. BEST EN Business Enterprises for Sustainable
Tourism Education Network Curriculum Development
Think Tank Process   247
BEST EN Think Tank V   248
References   254
Supplemental readings   257

8   **Affecting and influencing tourism policy**   **259**
An applied study of tourism policy influences   260
Politicization of the tourism office   261
Misunderstanding of tourism policy   262
Increasing importance of the tourism industry   262
Understanding the public decision-making process   263
Influencing political decisions with information   265
Conflict and compromise   267
Techniques of cost–benefit analysis   269
Step 1: Defining the project and alternatives   269
Step 2: Identifying, measuring, and valuing costs and
benefits of each alternative   270
Step 3: Calculating cost–benefit values   270
Step 4: Presenting the results   273
Influencing political decisions with financial
contributions   274

Conclusion   280
Case study 8. A Cost–Benefit Analysis for Coordinating
    International Visitor Information Collection and
    Distribution in the United States   281
References   295

9   **Strategic tourism planning**   **297**
Defining strategic tourism planning   299
Planning example   302
    Internal analysis   303
    External environmental scan   305
Sustainable tourism's effect on planning   306
Case study 9. Canada: An Effective Tourism Policy   308
References   323

10 **Future world tourism policy issues**   **325**
Safety and security in tourism   326
The impact of the world's economy on tourism   330
Managing sustainable tourism responsibly   331
Tourism policy and strategic planning   334
Utilizing e-commerce tools in tourism   335
    Weblogs   336
    Podcasts   336
    Internet marketing   337
Tourism education and training   338
Emerging tourism markets   340
Quality tourism products and experiences   341
Partnerships and strategic alliances in tourism   344
The impact of health issues/natural disasters/climate change
    on tourism   346
    Health issues and tourism   347
    Effects of natural disasters on tourism   348
    Climate change and tourism   350
Conclusion   353
Case report 10. United Nations World Tourism Organization
    Global Code of Ethics for Tourism   354
References   362

Appendix   **365**
Appendix A. Education and Training in Tourism:
    An Historical View   365
Appendix B. Agreement between the United States of
    America and the United Mexican States on the
    Development and Facilitation of Tourism   383

Appendix C. United States–Canada Free Trade Agreement
    Sectoral Annexes   391
Appendix D. Manila Declaration on World Tourism   395
Appendix E. World Peace Through Tourism – The Columbia
    Charter   401
Appendix F. Traveler Safety and Security Initiative   405

Index   407

Foreword

Influencing public policy is one of the most important activities any industry pursues. Businesses, non-profit organizations and other groups in all industries attempt to influence public policy with the intent to benefit their particular missions, goals and objectives. Since this is true, tourism entities must have a clear awareness of policy in order to compete. Understanding public policy, and how to influence it, is also critical as tourism continues to increase in political, social and economic importance. This book – *Tourism Policy and Planning: Yesterday, Today and Tomorrow* – provides readers throughout the world with a solid foundation for understanding not only what tourism policy is and the benefits of well-formulated tourism policy but also how to influence and implement it.

The public policy process intimidates many tourism professionals. They often feel less knowledgeable about the issues and are unclear how to approach members of the government to discuss important issues. Several tourism industry trade organizations are working together with tourism professionals to reinvigorate a grass roots approach to tourism advocacy as we work to advance tourism's overall agenda. By developing a strong base at the local level, the tourism industry can facilitate a two-way communication process – informing industry members locally and political decision makers at the federal level of the important policy issues affecting tourism and their communities.

The book begins with a detailed historical account of tourism policy in the United States, recounted by those who experienced much of it when it was happening. The lessons learned in the United States have been applied to national tourism policy development in other parts of the world and can continue to be applicable into the future. The final chapter of the book, based on a solid understanding of historical events and the current situation, provides a look into the future of tourism and public policy. The remaining chapters present pertinent issues for today ranging from the politics and economics of tourism to education and managing sustainable tourism.

Particularly important to local destination managers is the discussion on strategic tourism planning. All tourism professionals should read this section to ensure that proper planning is in place considering tourism's increasingly competitive landscape. Equally important is the presentation of affecting and influencing tourism policy through policy analysis and research. With these tools, the tourism industry will be able to compete better for the attention of legislators and policy makers.

Because of the comprehensive treatment of tourism policy and planning, tourism professionals in all sectors of the industry can find this book useful. The structure of the book, which incorporates a wide array of international examples, will appeal to a full spectrum of users including multinational industry organizations, regional trade associations, local destination managers, in addition to graduate and undergraduate students and faculty members in colleges and universities.

Part of what differentiates this book from others in the field of tourism is the combined perspectives of the various co-authors. Dave Edgell's experience as the Acting Under Secretary of Commerce for Travel and Tourism within the US Department of Commerce and as Commissioner of Tourism for the US Virgin Islands supplies a storied history of first-hand tourism policy development. He has lived and breathed tourism policy since 1974, and his footprints are numerous in the development of local, national and international tourism policy. Ginger Smith has worked with countless tourism students as founding Dean of the International School of Tourism and Hotel Management in Puerto Rico, as Associate Dean, College of Professional Studies and Associate Professor of Tourism Studies, School of Business, The George Washington University, and currently as Professor and Academic Chair of Graduate and Undergraduate Studies at New York University's Preston Robert Tisch Center for Hospitality, Tourism and Sports Management. She has been able to use the multiple tourism policy courses she has taught as laboratories for much of the material in this book. The work of Maria Allen, through the Institute for Tourism at East Carolina University, brings a particular concern for the local destination to the book. The seasoned experience is rounded out by the fresh perspective of Jason Swanson, a scholar and leader of tourism's young generation of practitioners and researchers. Undoubtedly, Jason will further develop several topics presented in this book in his research for the next several decades.

The positive implications for enhancing understanding of the need for tourism policy and planning are tremendous. To that end, the book includes a range of scholarly input, applying history to today's situation and looking far into the future to provide a solid foundation for tourism policy as the industry continues to progress.

Bill Hardman, Jr
President and CEO
Southeast Tourism Society

Preface

Tourism policy and planning tend to be coupled in our minds with change. The first decade of the new century is a period of intense and complex interactions involving tourism issues as factors influencing both international institutions and political practices regarding the quality of economic, socio-cultural and environmental policy and planning. The co-authors underscore this integrative viewpoint in this volume and feature similar and differing perspectives through references to the rich foundation of literature provided by an outstanding cadre of our travel and tourism scholar predecessors and contemporaries.

In our writing a book about tourism policy and planning, as well as our teaching, we found disjointed information regarding the study of tourism policy and planning. Aside from co-author David L. Edgell, Sr's earlier foundational texts and several recent and very useful edited volumes, there is no major textbook to provide us with the basics of tourism policy and planning.

By exploring the future of tourism in the context of tourism policy and planning yesterday and today, we hope to offer current and future businesspersons, politicians, managers, students and academics insight into key international trends and issues. The volume is also intended to help prepare national tourism agencies and local destination management organizations in developing policies and planning strategies to increase competitiveness and sustainable resource management.

We are confident that government tourism organizations, politicians and students will find in these pages informative areas assisting them in persevering in their efforts to build more prosperous, just, equitable and democratic societies. International tourism organizations such as the United Nations World Tourism Organization (UNWTO), Organisation for Economic Cooperation and Development (OECD), Organization of American States (OAS), local, state, provincial, regional and national policymakers, and the international academic community will now, we hope, have a basic tourism policy and planning resource volume readily at hand.

Additionally, we view our level of presentation as appropriate for several specific uses. One use is as a text for a one-semester introduction tourism policy and planning course for senior level undergraduate and graduate students in tourism and hospitality management, public policy and public administration, business administration and international affairs, among others. We believe our emphasis on conceptual foundations also makes it attractive as a supplemental text for courses in graduate programs in political science, economics and international relations. At the undergraduate level, we recommend selected chapters – such as the first three and final chapters providing an overview of tourism policy and planning and outline of key related trends and issues – as useful supplements to more commonly used materials introducing students to tourism and hospitality, sport, and event management and administration. In addition, this book has many uses and applications for tourism officials at the local, state, provincial, regional and national levels. Finally, the book is helpful to the general public in understanding the importance and impact of tourism on national and international issues. The chapter case studies and reports and volume appendices provide yet further research, teaching and applied tourism policy and planning resources.

We have organized our approach to the broad subject of tourism policy and planning into 10 chapters, each with a chapter case study report, and appendix where appropriate. The chapter case studies, reports, and appendices present extended examples illustrating how tourism policy analysts have approached policy problems and the results they have been able to achieve. Chapters 1–3 provide an introduction and overview, a look to the past, and a report on key current issues affecting tourism policy and planning. Chapters 4–6 probe various aspects of tourism policy and planning including its role in economic and foreign policy and in sustainable tourism. In Chapters 7–9, the volume focuses in greater depth on the significant role of education and training in tourism and on major external influences on tourism policy and planning, and provides an overview of strategic tourism planning. Chapter 10 broadens the analysis to a look at the role of tourism policy and planning in relation to many of today's contending socio-cultural, economic and environmental issues as they affect our future.

In sum, in this book, we have tried to illuminate past and current examples of tourism policy and planning in meaningful and understandable ways and to propose that policy and planning is central to sound management of international tourism – one of the largest and potentially greatest industries for shaping tomorrow's world.

Acknowledgements

This book is the result of efforts by many individuals and the cooperation of numerous groups and associations over a long period. It is not practical to acknowledge all such contributions. Mentioned below are a few people and organizations for special recognition.

Authors Ginger Smith, Jason Swanson and Maria Allen especially wish to thank David L. Edgell, Sr for his invitation to them to co-author this book. He has contributed to tourism policy for many years. Dave began his career in tourism in 1974 by reviewing US tourism policy and contributing to the development of the United Nations World Tourism Organization under the watchful guidance of Deputy Assistant Secretary of Commerce David N. Parker. You see Dave's footprints in tourism policy in dozens of articles, books, US policy papers, international organization documents and trade in tourism agreements from 1974 to date. He also contributed to the development of the National Tourism Policy Act of 1981 (signed into law by President Ronald Reagan) under the guidance of Secretary of Commerce Malcolm Baldrige, the direction of Ambassador Frederick M. Bush, and in cooperation with John K. Snyder, Jr (and others).

This book is possible because Jane Macdonald, Acquisitions Editor, Elsevier, initiated interest, guided the authors, and kept them on track. She made many helpful suggestions along the way. The authors want to thank Sally North, Senior Commissioning Editor – Hospitality, Tourism and Leisure, Elsevier, for her encouragement. We also want to recognize Lawrence Shanmugaraj, Project Manager, for his patience and guidance through the revisions/editing process and Indexing Specialists (UK) Ltd for completing the index of this book.

A key individual who helped all of the authors in a first edit to improve the book is Marilyn Niemela. She was always available for us. We also appreciate the copy-editing grant provided by the International Institute for Tourism Studies, The George Washington University.

Jane M. Allen, Elke Bielecki, J.R. Gast, Sarah J. Gust, Matt Schuttloffel and Jason Swanson contributed the photographs appearing in this book from some of their travels. Thank you, also, to Wm. Kemp Allen for his assistance in reproducing three of the appendices materials and to Alison Slattery, with a Master of Tourism Administration degree from GW, for providing research assistance throughout the writing process. Special assistance related to applied mathematics for the policy analysis section was provided by Ellen Stryker Peterson.

The authors wish to thank Tom Penney, MBA, MPA, Vice President Planning & Evaluation, Product Development, Emerging Markets, Canadian

Tourism Commission; David N. Parker, President and CEO, American Gas Association; Ambassador Frederick M. Bush, Associate Director, Woodrow Wilson International Center for Scholars; John K. Snyder, Jr, President, Diamond International Galleries; Professor Patrick T. Long, University of Colorado at Boulder; Suzanne D. Cook, PhD, Senior Vice President, Research, Travel Industry Association of America; Dr Kristen Betts, President, Research Strategies International; Sheryl Elliott, Associate Professor of Tourism Studies, and Donald E. Hawkins, Eisenhower Professor of Tourism Policy, The George Washington University; Stanley Selengut, President, Sustainable Development, Inc.; Bill Hardman, President and CEO, Southeast Tourism Society; David L. Edgell, Jr, tourism consultant; Chuck Y. Gee, Dean Emeritus, University of Hawaii at Manoa; James C. Makens, Associate Professor of Management (retired), Wake Forest University; Nancy Del Risco, Senior Research Associate, Center for Tourism Technology, Florida International University; Kurtis M. Ruf, Ruf Strategic Solutions; Jafar Jafari, Editor-in-Chief, Annals of Tourism Research; Francesco Frangialli, Secretary General, United Nations World Tourism Organization; Eduardo Fayos-Solà, Head, Human Resource Development, United Nations World Tourism Organization; Mac Noden, Senior Lecturer of Tourism (retired), Cornell University's School of Hotel Administration; Dr Rob Kwortnik, Assistant Professor of Marketing, Cornell University's School of Hotel Administration; and Drs Gene Brothers and Larry Gustke, Associate Professors of Tourism, along with Dr Lari Jackson at North Carolina State University.

We wish to express our appreciation to the authors (other than the co-authors of the book) of case studies and reports that appear in the book. The case report for Chapter 3 is provided by Zachary Rozga, President, GeoSavvy Development, Cape Town, South Africa. Dr Joseph Flood, Assistant Professor, East Carolina University, was responsible for preparing the case study in Chapter 6. The case report for Chapter 7 on BEST EN (Business Enterprises for Sustainable Travel – Education Network) is provided by Claudia Jurowski, Northern Arizona University (USA) and Abraham Pizam, University of Central Florida (USA) with contributions from Pauline Sheldon (University of Hawaii, USA), Larry Dwyer (University of Western Sydney, Australia), Kristin Lamoureaux (The George Washington University, USA) and Janne J. Liburd (University of Southern Denmark). Dr Sheryl Elliott, Associate Professor, The George Washington University, is co-author of Chapter 7 and the author of the appendix relating to Chapter 7. Tourism consultant Scott Meis and Dr Stephen L.J. Smith, Professor, University of Waterloo were the principal authors of the case study in Chapter 9.

We also owe a debt of gratitude and thanks to our respective families and friends for their patience and understanding of our responsibilities for meeting tight deadlines and for their support and encouragement.

Any errors or omissions are the responsibility of the authors.

1

Introduction

Out of the future that is not yet, into the present that is just beginning, back to the past that no longer is.

St. Augustine

Tourism defined

In this book, the term tourism is used synonymously with all aspects of travel and tourism unless otherwise specified. With respect to international tourism, this text uses the following definitions as recommended by the United Nations World Tourism Organization:

- *Visitor*. Any person visiting a country other than that in which the person usually resides, for any reason other than following an occupation remunerated from within the country visited. This definition covers two classes of visitors: 'tourist' and 'excursionist'.
- *Tourist*. A temporary visitor staying at least 24 hours in the country visited, the purpose of whose journey can be classified under one of the following headings: (a) leisure, recreation, holiday, health, study, religion or sport; and (b) business, family, mission or meeting.

- *Excursionist*. A temporary visitor staying less than 24 hours in the country visited (including travellers on cruises).
- *Tourism*. In terms of balance-of-trade accounting, is defined as travel and transportation and is determined a 'business service' export from the tourism recipient to the tourism generating economy; the entirety of the (tourism) industry.

It can be said that no other industry has a greater self-image problem. Tourism is inherently a complex field difficult to define, resisting comparability within itself and with other industries. Tourism is the practice of travelling and also the business of providing associated products, services and facilities. It is not a single industry but instead an amalgam of industry sectors – a demand force and supply market, a personal experience and a complicated international phenomenon. Tourism incorporates social, cultural and environmental concerns beyond physical development and marketing. It encompasses both supply and demand, more than the sum of marketing and economic development.

Tourism has strong links to cultural and social pursuits, foreign policy initiatives, economic development, environmental goals and sustainable planning. The industry includes the buying, selling and management of services and products (to tourists) that might range from buying hotel rooms to selling souvenirs or managing an airline. To accomplish these complex activities, the tourism industry demands the most creative and innovative managers because tourism represents one of the most perishable of products. If hotel rooms, airline seats, cruise ship births or restaurant tables are not filled daily and repeatedly, the point-of-sale moments to generate revenue from these 'products' are gone forever. There is no opportunity to put such unsold products on sale at a later time, in storage or in inventory (Figure 1.1).

Tourism is also the most wide-ranging industry in the sense that it demands products from other sectors of the economy. For example, the US State of North Carolina's top agricultural exports include leaf tobacco, poultry and poultry products, live animals and meat, cotton and cotton linters and forestry products that supply demand throughout the United States and across the globe. These products are also 'assistance goods' used by the tourism industry. In addition to agricultural products, airplanes must be produced, computer reservation systems developed, steel and concrete manufactured and hotels constructed. There is no other industry in the economy that is linked to so many diverse products and services as is the tourism industry. In order to plan for and provide rational order to such a wide-ranging and dynamic industry, it is necessary to develop policies to assist the decision makers in the management of this complex industry.

According to the US Travel and Tourism Advisory Board (2006), 'It is safe to say that the world is now entering a new golden age for travel

(a)

(b)

Figure 1.1 Tourism is characterized by perishable inventory in the form of cruise ship berths, hotel rooms, and rental cars (Photo: J.R. Gast)

and tourism'. The United Nations World Tourism Organization indicated that the 4.5 per cent growth rate of tourism in 2006 '... exceeded expectations as the tourism sector continued to enjoy above average results...' (2007). Demographic changes, increasing disposable income levels, heightened emphasis on sustainability, greater availability of leisure time, new communication tools and technology, higher levels of education, emerging tourism markets, growth in the supply of facilities and destinations and other supplementary factors are having an impact on the demand for tourism. The supply side of tourism, for the most part, is meeting most tourists' demands.

Tourism Policy and Planning: Yesterday, Today, and Tomorrow addresses the state of current affairs, offers remedies for past mistakes and presents prescriptions to assure positive tourism results for the future growth of tourism. It provides policymakers, planning authorities, local communities, academic scholars, students of tourism and the public a blueprint for understanding the broad ramifications of the tourism industry. The case studies at the end of each chapter refer to situations encountered, a completed project, or important guidelines with respect to tourism issues and policies.

For the tourism industry to be sustainable in the future, it is vital that effective policy and planning take place today. The policymakers, planning officials and stakeholders must identify the emerging trends in tourism and orchestrate new measures that lead to orderly growth and quality products that benefit tourists and communities. Unfortunately, in the past, many governments have not given the tourism industry the same concern given to manufactured goods or other service industries. In part due to the terrorists' attacks on the United States on 11 September 2001, and tragedies elsewhere, this attitude is now changing globally. News of conflicts, terrorism, health concerns, natural disasters and weather conditions in many different countries throughout the world often bring the tourism industry to the forefront. The Severe Acute Respiratory Syndrome (SARS) epidemic and concerns about avian influenza have taken their toll on tourism, along with earthquakes, hurricanes, tsunamis and other disasters. The escalation of petroleum prices, difficulties in the world economy and adjustments to new technologies are affecting the tourism industry in unprecedented ways. This book discusses many of these changes and issues and, in some cases, suggests remedies.

Since the agricultural and industrial revolutions of the nineteenth century, we have measured the wealth of nations almost entirely on the development and exportation of tangible goods: agriculture and livestock, mining and manufacturing; on the construction of infrastructure: highways and dams; and transportation: ocean vessels, railroads, airplanes, buses, automobiles and other vehicles that transport people and assets from place to place around the world. In the twenty-first century, we are deep into the services revolution that is changing the way we live and evaluate the world's wealth and economy. An ever-expanding world of innovation has already provided us with multi-use telephones, e-commerce tools within computer technology, digital cameras, high-definition television and practical applications of satellite technology. In this bright new world, we have found another major growth service sector – sometimes referred to as an 'invisible' or 'intangible' activity: *tourism*. This growing service industry embraces technology in its widespread use of e-commerce tools, for its applications to new products such as space and undersea tourism and for developing new methods of marketing and promotion. The tourism industry has become one of the most dynamic industries throughout the globe as it adapts to technological change, product innovations and new markets. Managing sustainable tourism in today's world adds an important dimension to the growth of the tourism industry. The policies we set for tourism in an ever-changing world will direct the courses of action for the travel and tourism industry in the future. This book is an effort to meet this challenge and provide policy and planning solutions for the orderly growth and development of tourism and add to its sustainability.

The tourism industry's ability to fashion policies and plans for global tourism in the future will depend on solid research to better understand and accept new ideas and concepts as they appear. Such research, conducted in a chaotic world, may hammer out innovative and creative approaches that differ from the traditional guidelines for policy and planning once held by the tourism industry. The policies must be flexible and resilient enough to foster the development of new tourism products and services in a rapidly changing world. A static policy that is firmly in place can be rendered useless or in need of radical remedies, whenever a tragic event or global disturbance occurs, as has been the case in recent years.

The opportunity offered by tourism for future economic, environmental and social benefits will depend on understanding the tourism industry of yesterday, making the best possible decisions today and addressing forward thinking trends for tomorrow. We can define clear plans and policy guidelines now for the future of tourism or let it happen haphazardly and hope for the best. This book provides new information and concepts to help meet the challenge of charting a favourable course for tourism's future.

Tourism policy assembles the planning function and political goals for tourism into a set of guidelines to give us direction as we move ahead. Without such guidance, we might find tourism's future considerably less beneficial than we had hoped. With the information and precepts presented in this book, students, professionals and policymakers will have a set of conceptual tools for understanding the myriad factors that make up the tourism policy and help foster the industry's future growth in positive ways.

In many communities and countries throughout the world, tourism is the most valuable industry. Las Vegas, Nevada – shown in Figure 1.2 – along with Orlando, Florida, and Cancun, Mexico, and similar destinations are cities that would likely be unknown if not for the large numbers of domestic and international tourists visiting their tourism attractions and environment.

Economic changes taking place in China, India and the United States (with almost three billion people, half the world's population) will have major impacts on the global tourism markets of tomorrow. Social–cultural changes in Europe, with borderless tourism crossings and a common currency, are increasing the opportunities for tourism growth. East Asia and the Pacific Rim are experiencing unprecedented growth and change in

Figure 1.2   The Las Vegas strip, created in the desert, is now one of the most visited destinations in the world (Photo: J.R. Gast)

tourism. From the perspective of economic policy, tourism is a vital economic development tool for local communities and national governments, producing income, creating jobs, spawning new businesses, spurring economic development, promoting economic diversification, developing new products and contributing to economic integration. If local and national governments are committed to broad-based tourism policies, tourism will provide its citizens with a higher quality of life while generating sustained economic, environmental and social benefits.

The wellspring of future growth for tourism throughout the world is a commitment to good policy. Governments, private sector and not-for-profit agencies must work cohesively to be the leaders in creating sustainable tourism policy that transcends the economic benefits and embraces environmental and cultural interests as well. This book addresses key ingredients for positive tourism policies and planning that will lead this generation and the next toward a greater quality of life resulting from tourism growth. The aim of this book, then, is to provide government policymakers (at all levels), business leaders, not-for-profit executives, university professors, students, tourism industry managers and the general public with an introduction and examination of important policy and planning issues in tourism.

A look at travel and tourism within this context mandates that policymakers must understand the need for developing wide-ranging strategies, adjusted as conditions fluctuate or mature. Policymakers must be knowledgeable about market trends and flexible enough to adjust strategic plans in the face of rapidly changing market forces. In summary, policymaking within the new tourism horizon must fully encompass the complex nature of tourism and the far-reaching mechanics of its implementation. Tourism policy and planning will drive the appropriate management techniques and tools essential for meeting emerging trends. This transformation must take place in a new world of globalization and competition, in which, at the same time, the world's population and economies are changing. New technology (particularly in communications and transportation), barriers to travel, political relations and many other factors will affect tourism policy and planning in the future.

Tourism policy defined

Merriam-Webster Online Dictionary (2007) has defined *policy* as 'A definite course or method of action selected from among alternatives and in light of given conditions to guide and determine present and future decisions'. The popular tourism textbook *Tourism: Principles, Practices, Philosophies* (Goeldner & Ritchie, 2006) defined tourism policy by stating, 'Tourism policy can be defined as a set of regulations, rules, guidelines, directives, and development/promotion objectives and strategies that provide a framework within which the collective and individual decisions directly affecting long-term tourism development and the daily activities within a destination are taken'. This definition is highly useful in most circumstances. Another useful discussion of tourism policy is contained in a new tourism book titled *Travel and Tourism: An Industry Primer*. Biederman (2007) adds importantly to the definition of tourism policy the following thoughts, 'A tourism policy defines the direction or course of action that a particular country, region, locality or an individual destination plans to take when developing or promoting tourism. The key principle for any tourism policy is that it should ensure that the nation (region or locality) would benefit to the maximum extent possible from the economic and social contributions of tourism. The ultimate objective of a tourism policy is to improve the progress of the nation (region or locality) and the lives of its citizens'.

For purposes of the approach taken in this book, tourism policy will be more broadly defined to include marketing, planning and sustainability. In this context, tourism policy is 'a progressive course of actions, guidelines, directives, principles, and procedures set in an ethical framework that is issues-focused and best represents the intent of a community (or nation) to effectively meet its planning, development, product, service, marketing, and sustainability goals and objectives for the future growth of tourism'. This definition acknowledges the important role marketing, product development and hospitality services play in tourism policy. In addition, the tourism sustainability concept (discussed later) must support the long-term goals in economic, environmental and social development. More importantly, this definition recognizes that tourism policy is 'dynamic' and flexible enough to allow adjustments and refinements as the occasion arises.

This book, with some divergences, utilizes the classic tourism-planning model that includes a 'vision' and 'mission statement'. (See Chapter 9 for detailed explanation.) The vision should be a few words that describe where local or national tourism policy wants to be while the mission statement explains how to get there. The vision and mission statement would be followed by a set of 'goals, objectives, strategies, and tactics', sometimes represented in the form of a 'tree diagram' (Figure 1.3).

Tourism has the potential to engage and change the economic, political, social and ecological dimensions of future lifestyles. Edgell (1990) asserted that '. . . the highest purpose of tourism policy is to integrate the economic, political, cultural, intellectual and economic benefits of tourism cohesively with people, destinations, and countries in order to improve the global quality of life and provide a foundation for peace and prosperity. The political aspects of tourism are interwoven with its economic consequences . . . tourism is not only a continuation of politics but also an integral part of the world's political economy. In short, tourism is, or can be, a tool used not only for economic but for political means'. Fayos-Solà (1996) suggested a more balanced role in tourism policymaking between the private, public and voluntary sectors. He stated, 'The changing nature of the tourism industry, with its move away from mass tourism towards greater market segmentation, use of new technologies, differentiation of the product and adoption of new management styles, demands a change in the substance of governments' tourism policies'. Edgell (1999) went further to say that '. . . The tourism industry will be faced with some difficult challenges over the next several years. Technology, whether in communications information, new aerospace developments, or other fields, will heavily affect the tourism industry. The industry will need to develop effective policies and plans to deal with terrorism and other disruptions to the tourism market'. Goeldner and Ritchie (2006) said, 'Tourism policy

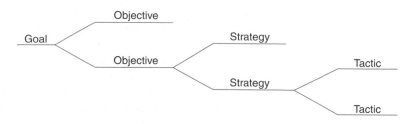

Figure 1.3   Tree diagram: goal-oriented tourism planning

seeks to ensure that visitors are hosted in a way that maximizes the benefits to stakeholders while minimizing the negative effects, costs, and impacts associated with ensuring the success of the destination. In effect, tourism policy seeks to provide high-quality visitor experiences that are profitable to destination stakeholders while ensuring that the destination is not compromised in terms of its environmental, social and cultural integrity'.

The tourism industry is composed of private, public and not-for-profit components interested in tourism development, new products, destination marketing, economic benefits and future sustainability. These tourism interests have broad ramifications on community life and need parameters and guidelines to help define and plan the future direction of tourism policy, ultimately providing quality tourism products and services. Tourism policy should aim to improve the quality of life of the local citizenry at any given destination. A good tourism policy will assist in that process. This book will attempt to identify some of the issues and concerns that tourism policy should address in order to insure a positive sustainable future for the tourism industry.

Local, state/provincial, regional and national governments and other leveraging regional and global organizations such as the United Nations World Tourism Organization and the World Travel and Tourism Council help determine tourism policies that best represent the business environment, local community interests in tourism and governmental structure. Numerous tourism associations and organizations seek to influence tourism policy so that their interests are also included. This aspect of tourism is discussed later in the book with some case study examples.

Worldwide importance of tourism

The twenty-first century is seeing increases in leisure time and income for millions of people. Shorter working hours in some cases, greater individual prosperity, faster and cheaper travel, more destinations to choose from and the impact of advanced technology have all helped to make the leisure and travel industry one of the fastest growing industries in the world. The significance of tourism as a viable source of income and employment, and as a major factor in the balance of payments for many countries has been attracting increasing attention on the part of governments, regional and local authorities and others with an interest in economic development. Furthermore, sustainable tourism concerns for the environment, social conditions and other concepts have entered the decision-making process and will forever change the way tourism grows throughout the world. (This is discussed in some detail with respect to sustainable tourism in Chapter 6.)

New research by the World Travel and Tourism Council (*Navigating the Path Ahead*, 2007) estimates that tourism in 2007 will generate direct and induced employment for approximately 231.2 million people world-wide, or 1 in every 12 jobs. By 2017, it is predicted that employment will be approximately 262.6 million jobs, or 1 in every 12 jobs. According to the report, global tourism in 2007 (both domestic and international) is approximately a US \$7.1 trillion industry that will continue to grow in the future, reaching US \$13.2 trillion in 2017. Equally important is the fact that tourism, as an export, is of critical importance to both industrialized and developing nations. As an economic factor, tourism is growing faster than the rest of the world economy in terms of export, output, value added, capital investment and employment. (See Chapter 4 for a complete discussion of the economics of tourism.)

While tourism has been growing rapidly since World War II and will continue its dynamic growth into the future, this does not mean the indus-try will grow smoothly. As evidenced, there will be occasional structural, economic, political, environmental, social and conceptual impediments in its path. An example of this was the severe decline in travel worldwide at the start of the Persian Gulf War in 1991. Mediterranean destinations, North America and parts of Asia, far from the war zone and Middle East conflicts, were all affected. Coupled with this is the public's and, in some cases, governments' inadequate understanding of the economic, environ-mental and social importance of tourism and low levels of access to current information about tourism affairs. At the same time, however, the global importance of tourism is becoming better understood because, in many geographic areas, tourism is replacing other industries that have tradition-ally been the paramount economic drivers. This, in turn, necessitates better tourism research, policy and planning to support this momentum.

In the global tourism context

As part of the overall growth of services, tourism's recognition as an important sector in the global economy is more frequently accepted. Key multilateral governmental policy organizations such as the United Nations (New York), the United Nations World Tourism Organization (Madrid), the Organisation for Economic Cooperation and Development (Paris), the Organization of American States (Washington, DC), the Asia-Pacific Economic Cooperation (Singapore), the Caribbean Tourism Organization (Barbados) and other international bodies are providing important research reports and data to the tourism industry. One of their shared goals is to link tourism to other sectors of the international economy. The European Community, North America Free Trade Agreement and other regional economic instruments are seeking to break down traditional barriers for conducting tourism services across borders, which will ultimately aid international tourism. The World Travel and Tourism Council (London), the Pacific Asia Travel Association (Bangkok), the Southeast Tourism Society (Atlanta) and other groups representing mainly private interests and some public concerns are already establishing a higher level of cooperation and coalition building to tackle broad policy issues. (See Chapter 5 for more information on these organizations.) These changes indicate increasing recognition of the impact of tourism in the twenty-first century.

The importance of what has happened globally in the tourism policy arena since the terrorists' attacks of 11 September 2001 has been manifested by the movement of the world to better understand the necessary implementation of new safety and security measures. The prognosis for the future growth of tourism is good in spite of the adjustments most nations have had to make to the threat of terrorism. This acknowledgment of forced change distinguishes much of the tourism industry today. Chapter 10 will highlight some of the future tourism trends that need to be addressed within policy and planning.

New challenges

As many heretofore unknown places in the world become better known and accessible, most governments will seek to encourage greater travel to their respective destinations. Many developed and developing countries conduct their national tourism promotions under the aegis of government tourism policy covering research, strategic planning, marketing, coordination, development and training. Often, this process is in conjunction with associations of private sector tourism interests, joint public–private consultative bodies and international and intergovernmental organizations.

The broad range of economic, political, environmental and social implications for tourism on both the domestic and international fronts is yet to be fully realized. One way to focus attention on this need for recognition is to examine the larger role that tourism plays beyond its marketing and promotional goals. Sound tourism policy and planning goes well beyond the marketing and promotion objectives to consider and evaluate its comprehensive effect.

The full scope of domestic and international travel and tourism, therefore, encompasses the output of segments of many industries. The travel 'industry' consumes the output of and creates a far-reaching base of wealth for feeder industries such as agriculture, fishing, food processing, brewing, construction, airports, transportation vehicles, communications equipment and furniture to name a few. In addition, tourist activities make use of the services of other industries, such as insurance, credit cards, advertising, database and niche marketing, the internet and e-commerce tools.

Tourism is an economic activity that provides local destinations, states, provinces, or countries with new sources of income and currency exchange. The impact tourism has on the economy can be tremendous as it creates jobs, reduces unemployment, fosters entrepreneurship, stimulates production of food and local handicrafts, demands effective communications, facilitates cultural exchanges and contributes to a better understanding of the local area, state, province, country and the world at large. The changing dimensions of this expanding industry have introduced the need for a sharper focus when dissecting the economic, cultural, ecological, environmental, social and political consequences of tourism – in brief, the future sustainability of tourism (Figure 1.4).

Over the next several chapters, these aspects of tourism policy and planning are presented and discussed in more detail. With a thorough understanding of tourism's implications, policymakers, planners and business people can better facilitate community involvement in the tourism industry at all levels. The more vested the local community is in the decision-making process, the more likely it is that the future of tourism will create positive economic, environmental and social improvements to the quality of life of the local citizenry and lead to successful sustainability of the area.

Figure 1.4   The island of Majorca, Spain, provides strong economic benefits to the country's tourism industry (Photo: Sarah J. Gust)

A new look at tourism policy

Since the tourism industry is difficult to clearly define because of the involvement of so many different economic sectors, it tends to foster many major policy development challenges. Fundamentally, tourism policy should present a set of guidelines, which, when combined with planning goals, charts a course of action for sound decision-making. Tourism policy, typically fragmented and poorly defined by governments throughout the world, is sometimes difficult to understand. For the past decade, leading tourism thinkers have called for increased attention to the social science aspects of tourism in an effort to continue to improve the quality of life and promote global peace.

Public policy is both a process and a product – the decision-making process and the product of that process. Today, there is recognition that policy should serve not only the government, but also the public's interest in tourism. Policy, when properly applied, is a vehicle for a government to direct and stimulate the tourism industry, as for example through tax policy and research. The actions of public, private and non-profit tourism sectors play an important role in policy determination and, in turn, affect economic and political influence on policy decisions of other tourism-related industries.

Only reliable and comprehensive research on tourism's impacts will lead to good decision-making and policy development. Within the last 10 years, many policy and planning experts have cited the increasing importance of research in tourism, but, historically, research is not an area that governments and the private sector have supported very well. At a minimum, a tourism office's research department should utilize a travel monitoring method and an evaluation system to enhance marketing and promotion initiatives. One way to begin is to research a 'tourism issue', taking it through several of the steps outlined in Figure 1.5. Local, state/provincial, regional and national tourism planners are recognizing the importance of a sound plan, coupled with visionary policies, as they prepare for the future development of tourism.

Arguably, in the past, the bulk of tourism policy and subsequent tourism policy research has focused on the demand side of the equation or on economic and marketing issues, which had led to underestimating other important considerations within the supply side and with respect to tourism development. Marketing a destination, complicated by the difficult supply characteristics of the industry, needs careful planning at the outset. It should operate under a coordinated tourism policy so that the many suppliers and promotion organizations can work well together. Bull, who reported on the state of London, England's tourism policy, studied

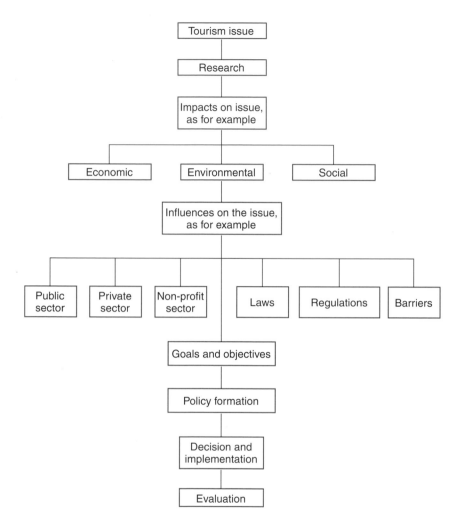

Figure 1.5 Tourism policy formulation: general diagram

this dilemma. Bull (1997) highlighted the challenges associated with the long-term impact of short-term changes in the city's marketing programs and concluded that for long-term sustainability, infrastructural and facility issues needed more attention. One conclusion drawn from this analysis is that tourism is far more than just marketing, and that tourism policy should address a multitude of tourism concerns.

Opponents of tourism often cite the negative impacts an influx of visitors might have on the destination, and there is a need to have a policy that recognizes these concerns, but, of course, the positive impacts should be equally important to policymakers and practitioners. Understanding both positive and negative impacts will lead to practical sustainable tourism development. When the negative impacts on the local environment are addressed, corrected and managed well by the host community, and the positive attributes built upon, tourism becomes an important driving force in community development. The benefits derived from visitors bear repeating: creating new jobs, spawning new businesses, adding new products, generating additional income, promoting economic integration and diversifying the local economy.

Tourism encompasses specialties within industry segments that are not often recognized by policymakers or industry outsiders as tourism demand generators. Today, travelers 'fit' categories. Travel Industry Association of America, in its publication *Domestic Travel Market Report 2005 Edition*, catalogued some of the travel segments including business travel, leisure travel, air and auto travel, solo travel, travel with children, travel that includes social/family events and many others. This organization also takes the practice further by addressing other needs and desires as reported in *The National Parks Traveler*, *Europe Traveler Demand* and *The Minority Traveler*, to name just three. These travelers are looking for specific environments when planning their travels, as in heritage tourism. Figure 1.6 illustrates the heritage of community members in the village of Pisac, Peru. This demand for special tourism activities is important to realize for many areas of the world where tourism is being developed to offset the decline of manufacturing industries, mining and agriculture. A comprehensive tourism policy will encompass all aspects of supply and demand that can be associated with tourism.

Local, state/provincial, regional and national governments should view tourism policy across agencies as it affects various components of the

Figure 1.6 The colorful dress of the village elders in Pisac, Peru, is a prominent feature of heritage tourism (Photo: Matt Schuttloffel)

operating sectors. Tourism influences infrastructure and planning in multiple areas simultaneously. Transportation, zoning and water use are typical areas where the policy crosses functional boundaries. These issues are highly sensitive to local residents and have the potential of greatly affecting tourism. On the other hand, rather than potentially stressing a system, tourism developers could use this information to determine the feasibility of proposed investment in all industry-operating sectors. Included in this policy process should be a survey of the tourism superstructure about quality, quantity and geographic distribution, as well as special events, such as festivals. To be meaningful, this approach should be related to demand for a variety of products to adequately assess the nature of tourism supply needed to reach the market.

Public sector organizations include local, state/provincial government and national tourism offices, tourism departments and other destination management organizations. For the well-being of the destination's citizenry in terms of economic, political, environmental, social and cultural issues, the public sector must play an active role in the development, legislation, financing, planning and policy of the tourism industry. Without this interaction, the legitimacy of certain tourism policies faces numerous barriers. Because of fragmentation inherent among the members of the tourism industry, the government must do more than just set policy – it must also assist in the implementation of the said policy. One country's tourism administration that does a good job in this respect is the Canadian Tourism Commission.

Historically, coordination within governments among different departments in the European nations, the United States and many other countries has been poor. Consequently, tourism has received low priority and has often been overlooked when governments distribute limited resources or when comprehensive policies are developed. A coordinated approach with a full and complementary partnership in tandem with either public and/or private sector organizations will go a long way toward alleviating some of these past problems. As mentioned previously, Canada, through its Canadian Tourism Commission, is one country that recognizes the importance of the public/private partnership in tourism policymaking and marketing. (See Chapter 9 for a discussion of Canadian tourism planning.)

Economic and non-economic benefits

A problem in many countries is that legislators and administrators lack knowledge and understanding of the tourism industry. The positive economic impact of tourism (see Chapter 4) is the best argument presented by practitioners to their policymakers when looking for increased funding and recognition. Logical and documented research on tourism's economic impact can help to lead to better public policy decisions. Youth sports and tourism is an example. Wayne and Riley (2003) relate, 'An important value of accurately estimating the economic impact of sports lies in the ability to use that knowledge to gain financial support for youth leagues from the host community'. Destinations' tourism decisions have focused primarily on the economic benefits of tourism, but destinations are (and should be) expanding their decisions to include social, cultural, environmental and other non-economic concerns.

Tourism development should be in harmony with the socio-cultural, ecological and heritage goals, values and aspirations of the host community. All such community endeavors need consideration, along with economic objectives, to stimulate greater participation in other interests from the stakeholders. Tourism offers many opportunities for members of the host community to participate in cultural and historical attractions and events. Added to the direct economic benefits reaped by local artisans and tourism industry employees are increased pride in the (local) heritage, enhanced self-worth, or global recognition through bringing the world and its cultures to the destination's doorstep. Market demand is now forcing communities to consider a full range of impacts as a means to stay competitive, as illustrated by coastal communities' recognition that visitors come seeking clean beaches and, in many cases, a certain amount of tranquility (Figure 1.7). Klien et al. (2004)

Figure 1.7 Visitors enjoy the quality beaches at the Shangri-La Mactan Island Resort & Spa in Cebu, Philippines (Photo: J.R. Gast)

has noted this by saying, 'The user's willingness to pay is increasing function of beach quality'.

Economic and non-economic costs

While positive economic impacts draw the attention of developers and governments, tourism organizations must recognize the existence of negative economic possibilities when developing the policy. In the United States, two powerful examples can be given. First, new tourism development in local communities (and especially in regions known as 'gateway' or entrance communities to major tourism destinations such as national parks and man-made attractions) may drive up real estate values in proposed areas, making the cost for housing prohibitive to local inhabitants and the labor market servicing the needs of visitors. A second scenario deals with environmental use/overuse, such as the ongoing debates regarding the permissibility of winter snowmobiling in Yosemite National Park in the United States. In the past, very little comprehensive research has been conducted to clearly define best practices for economic, environmental and social impacts on tourism. Today's research advances comprehensive economic, environmental and social impact statements (sometimes required by law) in many cases prior to commencement of local and regional economic development projects. Social impact research may include analysis regarding economic, psychological and environmental impacts, as well as relationships among all three. There is a need for more research and better solutions in this field.

As tourism becomes more widespread throughout the world, knowing the benefits-to-costs ratio enables a tourism organization to invest in attracting and developing the appropriate and optimal market segments and tourism facilities (Frechtling, 1994). The policy should address these issues in a proactive way to achieve an optimum return for all tourism investments and assets. An inadequate capability by destination managers to address negative impacts on their sites can lead to degradation of the tourism destination and a detrimental reputation, hampering both tourists and outside marketing agents.

As cited earlier in this book, tourism is a multi-disciplinary subject that embraces economics, environmental studies, social science, geography, business, history, psychology and many other disciplines. Concerning the psychological aspects of tourism, according to Travel Industry Association of America, only 68 per cent of the US state travel offices conducted such research at least periodically. In the September 2005 issue of *American*

Psychologist, an insightful article by Tracy Berno and Colleen Ward points to the need for more psychological research on tourism. At the conclusion of the article, the authors stated, 'Natural laboratories for the investigation of stress and coping, culture learning, and social identification are found in tourist settings in which tourists' experiences, tourist-host impressions and encounters, and changes in host communities are all novel topics for psychological inquiry. The application of psychological theories for promoting positive results for individuals, communities, and the tourist industry more broadly presents groundbreaking opportunities for health, social, community, and applied psychologists. It also promises innovative outcomes for tourism researchers and contributes to tourism that is both sustainable and beneficial to the people it affects most'.

Cooperation/integration

Stakeholder participation is important when developing tourism policy because of the diversity of organizations and interests involved, from both the public and private sectors. Stakeholders can include local citizens, business owners, public regulatory and land-use departments and offices, public, private and non-profit organizations – all constituencies involved or who ought to be involved in the decision-making process. In the past, tourism and economic development projects and processes overlooked the important role of a wide range of stakeholders. Some recent research on 'coopetition' (discussed in Chapter 4) is lending additional support for greater cooperation in tourism decision-making at all levels. The many organizations involved in promoting tourism and their different objectives make tourism policy difficult to coordinate and implement; therefore, it is important to have an integrated policy.

Balanced/comprehensive tourism policy

Tourism policy should be future-oriented, balanced and comprehensive since it incorporates the interests of the tourism stakeholders. Policy issues need extension beyond those traditionally thought of as tourism, to be inclusive of such related public programs as transportation and water usage. Policymakers should familiarize themselves with all products, not just with those perceived as tourism products. For instance, water management issues are usually a concern of local governments and residents, yet water parks, large golf resorts, aquariums and other tourism infrastructure can consume vast quantities of water. Large free-form swimming pools in resort destinations, as shown in Figure 1.8, are examples of potential drains on a community's water supply if not properly planned and managed.

Therefore, waterworks departments must consider both the tourism industry and the local residents when developing their policy. This is crucial for the industry's long-term success, and not understanding it can lead to a funding organization's focus tied only to promotion or marketing and less to other initiatives of equal importance to tourism development, such as research, product development and environmental, social and economic sustainability. Resources should be earmarked to 'give the tourists the product they want' while taking care to protect and 'extend the sustainability of the product'. (See Figure 1.9.)

Case Study 1 presents a practical example that has both policy and planning overtones; it is an abbreviated version of a draft strategic overview document prepared for the State of Kansas tourism program. While the intent of the strategic overview was not to define a tourism policy, the

Figure 1.8 Poolside revelers in Las Vegas, Nevada, benefit from the city's municipal water supply (Photo: J.R. Gast)

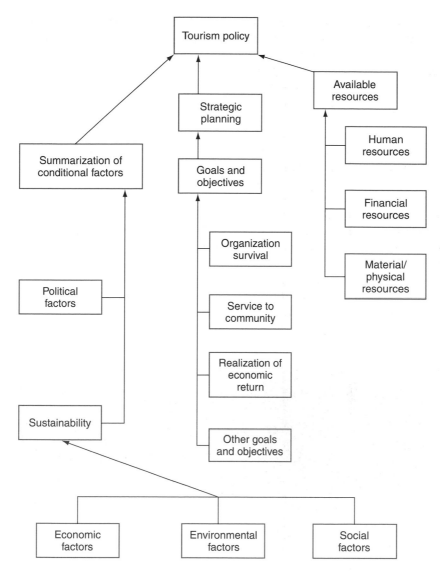

Figure 1.9 Tourism policy development process

results included a number of policy and planning implications. This case study does not purport to represent tourism policy or planning in the State of Kansas. It merely illustrates a few of the steps that might be taken by an entity interested in the broad ramifications of tourism policy.

Case study 1

KANSAS TOURISM OPPORTUNITIES: STRATEGIC OVERVIEW

NOTE: This case study was developed from a longer document titled *Kansas Tourism Opportunities*, prepared by one of the authors of this book, David L. Edgell, Sr, PhD, for the Kansas Travel and Tourism Development Division in 2005. This shortened version (which contains modifications from the original document) illustrates only the research phase necessary to develop a strategic planning document to support changes or modifications in a tourism policy. (While it demonstrates some of the ingredients needed to fashion a state tourism policy based on strategic planning, it is not indicative of the full process for constructing a tourism policy or planning model.) As a guideline for this project, a "Strategic Plan Development Flow Chart" (Figure 1.10) was constructed, but not followed in every detail. (It can be seen at the end of this case study.)

Executive summary

The tourism business is now, perhaps, the largest industry on earth. When strategically well planned and executed, tourism provides an economic stream both into and within a community, and an incentive to preserve the best features a community, or destination, has to offer, from its wildlife habitats, its historic districts, its scenery, to its local culture and heritage. Properly integrated, tourism can provide an improved quality of life for the community. In this particular case study, tourism can also be seen as a major driver for Kansas' new brand image: "Kansas, As Big As You Think".

Tourism impacts greatly on the economy of many communities in Kansas. It can be a valuable industry, producing income, creating jobs, spurring economic development, promoting economic diversification, developing new products, growing more businesses, adding tax revenue and contributing to economic integration. Kansas is also committed to a broad-based tourism product that will provide its citizens with a higher quality of life while it generates sustained environmental benefits for the state. Tourism is heavily dependent on information and communication through traditional systems, effective application of new e-commerce tools and responding to travel trends and niche travel. Transportation modes – motor coaches or trains, airlines and rental cars, recreation vehicles, or (as is most dominant in Kansas) the automobile – present a variety of economic opportunities. Infrastructure, ranging from airports, highways and byways, restaurants and hotels, spas and resorts, bed and breakfast establishments, campgrounds and hunting lodges, Native American casinos, and . . . the list goes on, provide diverse tourism opportunities. Public recreation lands, inclusive of local, state and national parks, are increasingly important in the development of new tourism products. Agritourism, ecotourism, rural tourism, adventure travel, geotourism, historic site visitation and built attractions are all part of the tourism phenomenon. Ultimately, the key to a successful program is an effective and efficient strategic plan that includes a marketing approach and that recognizes the great diversity of the tourism products in Kansas. However, in the eyes of the consumer, the great variety of Kansas tourism may not be well known.

Lest we forget, it is tourists, energized by personal wants and needs, who partake of our tourism products and drive the marketplace. Their common denominator is that they are mobile and that, by definition, they are motivated to leave the place where they reside to visit other places for business or pleasure.

Collectively, pleasure travelers' desires are endless: touring the countryside, viewing panoramic vistas, experiencing wilderness adventures, visiting cultural and historic sites, camping, hiking, hunting, fishing, birdwatching, engaging in sports, attending theatrical or sporting events – all with infinite variations. Today's tourist is looking for tourism products that offer authenticity, variety, flexibility, value and quality. In order to respond to the dynamic changes taking place in the competitive world of tourism, Kansas needed some direction and that is the focus of the case study: "Kansas Tourism Opportunities".

Tourism is a growth industry; and while that growth may, from time to time, show some short-term slowing, the long-term prospects are good. Growth is expected to continue based on continuously rising per capita incomes, lower relative travel costs, increased leisure time, sound promotional strategies, changes in consumers' tastes/preferences toward travel, abundance of recreational opportunities, substantial leisure goods and services, a supply of good facilities and the introduction of new technology. However, to make this happen, sound strategic tourism planning must occur. While the economic aspects are important, planning should also emphasize the site's environmental integrity and the social benefits to the community, especially enhanced human welfare, happiness and quality of life.

The year 2004 served as the Year of Research for Kansas, providing the initiative and direction to begin a significant research program. The year also identified communication, product development and usage of e-commerce tools as rudiments critical to the growth of tourism. Finally, 2004 was the year for beginning to develop a strategic overview to guide growth opportunities for Kansas tourism.

The year 2005 was the Year of Challenge, a time for developing an effective strategy for "growing tourism" to the state, to pursue the image and product of Kansas as a special tourism destination, and to research the critical paths to tourism success for the state. Emphasis was placed on five significant strategic directions:

1. emphasis on brand marketing;
2. marketing applications based on research;
3. better communication;
4. recognition of new products;
5. innovative use of e-commerce tools.

The year 2006 was the Year of Transition, whereby new administrative structures were realized and instituted, with partnership marketing enriched and expanded. It was the year in which the efforts in tourism research, product development and marketing strategies began to show promise and progress. In Kansas, particularly with respect to sustainable tourism, its wide open spaces allow for big things to happen. A rich legacy in Kansas is her people, such as Dwight D. Eisenhower and Amelia Earhart – two persons who have changed the course of history and inspired others to accomplish great deeds. Kansas is building on the strength of its people and a rich heritage and culture.

I. The road to success

Industry-led, market-driven and research-based, the mission of the Kansas Travel and Tourism Development Division (KTTDD) is to increase awareness of and interest in Kansas as a multi-seasonal, protean-experience tourist destination. To achieve this mission, the KTTDD initially set goals, objectives, strategies and tactics, in 2005, some of which follow:

Goals

- Promote the state brand image of "Kansas, As Big As You Think" for "across industry usage", utilizing it to promote tourism products (and other products), and present it as a representative image of the state.
- Expand the comprehensive tourism research initiative begun in 2004 and use it to define and underscore the tourism program, and distribute the research results to all interested parties.
- Foster a broader communication mechanism that educates and provides tourism information internally and externally to the industry, legislature, communities, governmental entities and media.
- Introduce new tourism initiatives, enhance and enrich traditional tourism products and provide an environment for continuance and innovation of tourism product development.
- Better utilize new and innovative e-commerce tools to provide information and to market and promote tourism products.

Objectives

- Sustain a vibrant and profitable Kansas tourism industry.
- Partnership marketing of Kansas as a desirable tourist destination.
- Build on the new Kansas brand image in both the domestic and international tourism market places.
- Assist the Kansas tourism industry to develop products and services that satisfy customer demands.
- Support a cooperative relationship between the private sector, not-for-profit tourism entities and local governments in Kansas with respect to Kansas tourism.
- Use its research capability and in-market staff to provide newly attained information about Kansas tourism and its markets to the private sector, local governments and tourism entities.

Strategies

- Work toward building the brand image as a key tourism tool to help generate the marketing of Kansas tourism products.
- Begin to develop return-on-investment accountability in all of the tourism initiatives.
- Use a long-term marketing approach that is research based, proactive, partnership oriented and aims to introduce new tourism products and initiatives.
- Build a creative budget approach based on "outthinking" versus "outspending" the competition for the tourism dollar. Understand that to be successful in the tourism industry it is important to have fresh thinking, entrepreneurship and innovation even if initially it might be disruptive.
- Recognize that creative Internet marketing in tourism can be the greatest platform of equality.

Tactics

- Work in partnership with the Kansas tourism industry to develop a solid marketing plan.
- Include in the research for a marketing plan a "competitive analysis".
- Perform a SWOT (Strengths, Weaknesses, Opportunities, Threats) analysis on the Kansas tourism program.
- Update regularly a "situation overview" which looks at the current market situation and follows the trends in the tourism industry.
- Review each of the actions regarding public relations, promotions, Internet marketing, events, database marketing, co-op marketing and others to insure accountability.

II. Where the journey begins: economics of tourism explained

The data clearly show that Kansas relies more on automobile travel than most states and was cited by the Automobile Association of America as the least expensive destination. There is no question that tourism is an important contributor to the state's economy. Business and leisure travelers are experiencing the recreational, historic and natural advantages of the state and its facilities. Thanks to strong relationships with travel writers, motor coach tour operators, individual travelers, the international travel community and the Internet, the word about Kansas tourism is becoming better known.

In 2004, Callahan Creek, the Kansas Travel and Tourism Development Division's contract marketing agency, conducted important consumer research for the state. An overview of some of that research shows that approximately half (48 per cent) of those individuals requesting Kansas travel information subsequently visited the state. It is interesting to note that visitors mainly cited vacation/pleasure (42 per cent), passing through (25 per cent) and visiting friends/relatives (19 per cent) as the key reasons for their trip. Historic attractions, a part of "sustainable tourism" as described later, was the most important activity of participation.

Popular leisure activities range from visiting historic attractions to Western/pioneer sites. Important attributes of the vacation destination that Kansas offers are safe/secure destinations, friendly people, good value, restful and relaxing environments, beautiful countryside, unique experiences, friends and family relationships, wide-open spaces, historic attractions and outdoor recreation. Safety and security will continue to be important; culture, arts, history and heritage will become increasingly significant reasons for traveling, and "reality" experiences (what some tourism experts are increasingly referring to as "experiential tourism") are growing in popularity. The study suggests that important opportunities for Kansas (those that are high on travelers' "to-do" lists) include meeting friendly people, seeing beautiful countryside, having a chance to relax, visiting historic attractions and many others.

III. The changing landscape: emerging tourism issues in Kansas

Kansas realizes the need for greater creativity, ingenuity, local and regional "coopetition" (greater *coop*eration amongst local markets to meet the com*petition* from outside markets) and a culture shift that emphasizes intellectual capacity in its tourism marketing strategies. Kansas must be on the cutting edge in terms of the latest trends in tourism (what tourism consumers want in their tourism products) and to determine which Kansas tourism products fulfill that market demand. The research reports prepared by TIA are a good source of tourism trend information. Some recent trends that are particularly relevant to Kansas are discussed below.

Ecotourism is a market trend that Kansas can capitalize on by highlighting more strongly its natural and geographical assets and its abundance of flora and fauna. The Flint Hills region of Kansas, for example, is well-suited for ecotourism. Some work accomplished in 2004–2005 by FERMATA, Inc. (an international nature tourism consulting group), while under contract to KTTDD, details the enormous opportunities for nature and cultural tourism in, and near, the Flint Hills. FERMATA, Inc., stresses the opportunities for ecotourism in conjunction with a relatively new national park, "The Tallgrass Prairie National Preserve", a unique public/private partnership venture. Its mission is to preserve and enhance a nationally significant remnant of the tallgrass prairie ecosystem and the processes that sustain it; preserve and interpret the cultural resources of the Preserve and the heritage associated with the ranch property; and offer opportunities for education, inspiration, and enjoyment through public access to its geological, ecological, scenic and historical features.

The Flint Hills region, including The Tallgrass Prairie National Preserve, is consistent with the new tourism phenomenon generally referred to as "sustainable tourism". In the July/August 2005 issue of the *National Geographic Traveler* (the most read travel magazine), the National Geographic Society's Office of Sustainable Tourism published a rating by a panel of experts of National Parks in Canada and the United States that included The Tallgrass Prairie National Preserve, which received a good rating. In the March/April 2005 issue of *Midwest Living*, a magazine important to Midwest travelers, a section called "30 Things Every Midwesterner Should Experience" refers to The Tallgrass Prairie National Preserve in these words: "Smell the lush stinging wetness of a storm rumbling across a wide-open sky from amid undulating green-golden grasses in the Kansas Flint Hills. This is North America's largest expanse of native tallgrass prairie, and it has an unforgettable sense of place that blends powerful sky, dramatic land and stirring moments". (Author's note: Also of interest is the article "*Splendor of the Grass*" in the April 2007 issue of *National Geographic*. This article says, "The prairie's grip is unbroken in the Flint Hills of Kansas. . . . Much that remains of this once vast ecosystem lies here in the Flint Hills, saved from the plow by stubborn layers of stone jutting rawboned through thin soil . . . . The hard part here in the Flint Hills – and in any of the few remaining patches of native prairie – is learning to see the tallgrass ecosystem for itself . . . . Learn it well enough and you begin to suspect that grasses are what hold this world together.")

A TIA study (sponsored by *Smithsonian Magazine, 2003*) titled *The Historic/Cultural Traveler* identified another major trend in tourism in this way: "Cultural, arts, historic, and heritage activities or events are quite popular among US travelers today. In fact, most US adults (81 per cent) who took at least one trip of 50 miles or more, one way, away from home in the past year included at least one such activity or event while traveling . . . This represents over 118 million adult historic/cultural travelers". Such a trend is another opportunity for Kansas tourism. Kansas is historically and culturally rich, with interesting small towns and communities and many special local museums and art galleries. The Native American history and culture throughout the state offers an abundance of special tourism product opportunities, along with historic themes including life on the prairie, heritage connected to the Civil War, the unique Eisenhower Museum, air and space museums, the birthplace of Amelia Earhart and much more.

Another important TIA study in 2004 of particular relevance to the tourism industry nationally and in Kansas is the *Travelers' Use of the Internet* (TIA). The Internet and electronic commerce tools have become fundamental to marketing tourism throughout the United States. For states like Kansas, the Internet offers some unique opportunities to put little known tourism products and destinations, especially in remote rural areas, before the large market of tourism consumers who peruse the Internet in planning their travel. According to the TIA study, as of July 2004, ". . . over half of American adults age 18 or older (56 per cent) claimed they currently used the Internet, either at home, work/school, or both". The study goes on to say, "Nearly half of travelers use the Internet for travel planning, while three in ten use it to make travel reservations. Not surprisingly, frequent travelers are more likely than infrequent travelers to indicate they use the Internet".

The Internet, good Websites, linkages and effective use of e-mail will be key to the marketing strategies for Kansas tourism. Electronic commerce tools are comparatively inexpensive, effective and efficient communication mechanisms for most communities in Kansas. It will take innovative and creative strategies to link Kansas to the right drivers of tourism throughout the state, region and nation.

Rural tourism in Kansas is another challenge, whether it is overnight vacation camping (the top outdoor recreation adventure activity in the United States), hunting, fishing, bird-watching (the second fastest growing outdoor activity in the United States), following trails, or any other rustic activity. Some new research suggests that hospitality and tourism in rural areas will be a growth opportunity in the future. This research is contained in a report titled *Competitiveness in Rural US Regions: Learning and Research Agenda* by Michael E. Porter, Institute for Strategy and Competitiveness, Harvard Business School, 2004. The report states, "Many experts highlight the common misperception that agriculture is the dominant source of employment and income in rural economies. In fact, agriculture is important in only a small number of rural counties, and its overall impact on rural regions in the US is negligible". The study includes a "Cluster Mapping Project" – clusters consist of related industries within a sector that are prone to co-locate. The traded clusters with the highest absolute level of employment in rural regions were hospitality and tourism, food processing, heavy construction services, automotive, metal manufacturing and business services. The study indicates that "rural tourism" in its broadest sense includes scenic beauty as well as special clusters like the "California Wine Cluster" that includes a "tourism cluster". It is important to note that at this time, agritourism in Kansas offers some very special opportunities and may also offer new tourism "clusters".

The foregoing examples were selected to indicate some of the travel trends and niche markets recently identified as unique growth areas in tourism. There are many other opportunities for product development in Kansas that can be linked with special niche markets. Festivals and special events are popular; Native American casinos attract specific travelers; visits to local, state and national parks continue to grow; and sports and business travel are also important. Clearly, keeping a close watch on trends in tourism is vital to our strategic planning.

Knowing what visitors want

Tourism demand has changed substantially in recent years. Several factors have initiated these changes:

- The emergence of experience-based travel, referred to as "experiential tourism".
- An aging population with more time available for leisure travel.
- A larger amount of disposable income allocated to travel.
- Increasingly accessible travel information via the Internet.
- Popularity of sustainable tourism products.

These changes are forcing a reassessment of how marketing organizations cater to travelers' needs. Kansas must change its emphasis, too.

Clearly, factors affecting the process of and the decision to travel, along with the choice of destination, are changing. More tourists are looking for a specific experience rather than a destination (again, "experiential tourism"). Learning vacations, spas, bird-watching and sustainable tourism products (inclusive of ecotourism, agritourism, adventure tourism, historical, heritage and cultural sites) have grown significantly in the last several years. While not much is available to measure the growth of this trend, tourism publications and promotional literature are already shifting focus in response to this demand.

IV. Taking the right road: opportunities offering strategic advantage

Providing strategic information to the industry

The KTTDD, as a public sector entity in partnership with the private sector, can help drive tourism to and throughout the state. However, the tourism industry of Kansas must take the leadership role in marketing tourism for the state. KTTDD can provide strategic information services that support and assist the decision-making process in the private sector tourism industry. KTTDD needs to provide timely, credible and relevant information that will augment the industry's efforts to market, advertise and promote tourism products. Special programs provided by KTTDD to assist the private sector are given below.

Research program

The Kansas tourism research program is designed to identify trends, interpret markets and track changes in markets, so that policies developed are aimed in the right direction and based on facts rather than on hunches or opinions. The research conducted in Kansas seeks to reduce the risk of unanticipated changes in markets and to keep the marketing and promotion programs current. This effort is an ongoing process that will likely lead to the discovery of additional market opportunities, new products and innovative uses for established destinations.

Target marketing

A major move by KTTDD in 2004 was its contract engagement with Ruf Strategic Solutions (a database target marketing firm) and the subsequent decision to apply the latest techniques in tourism "target marketing", sometimes referred to as "market segmentation" or "niche marketing". Target marketing is a key to a successful tourism marketing program. The basic tenet of target marketing is that few destination areas are universally acceptable and desired by the tourist. Therefore, instead of wasting valuable resources on trying to please all travelers, the Kansas tourism industry should "target" highly identified prospects specifically and cater to their wants and needs. One of the early steps in marketing, then, is to divide the present and potential market on the basis of meaningful characteristics and concentrate marketing, promotion and product development on serving the most likely parts of the market – the target markets. Ruf Strategic Solutions, under contract by KTTDD, is probably the best tourism target marketing firm in the nation. This firm has a system that can profile almost any potential visitor within the United States. Their profile system includes geographic, demographic (age, sex, income, education, etc.), socioeconomic, psychographic and behaviour patterns, in addition to many other characteristics of the potential visitor.

Public relations

Under a contract with Travel Media Relations, Kansas conducts several different types of public relations. This effort has been ongoing for several years and is updated frequently. The media contacts include phone calls, e-mails, follow-up on media leads, press releases, press kits, journalist newsletter and travel writer meetings. Numerous stories about Kansas appeared in magazines, newspapers and electronic media in 2004.

Marketing program

Like its counterparts in the other 49 states, Kansas works hard to market its tourism products. Tourism marketing is similar in many ways to the marketing of other products, but it also possesses some unique traits. Most marketing programs are based on the four Ps of marketing: product, price, place and promotion (which are also relevant to tourism marketing). However, due to the nature of the tourism product, there are six additional Ps – partnership, packaging, programming, positioning, people and planning – that should be integrated. The 2004–2005 marketing of Kansas tourism includes a number of changes and new directions. In addition to traditional marketing efforts, KTTDD is "marketing" the new Kansas brand image, "Kansas, As Big As You Think". To get this message across, to the wide spectrum of audience within Kansas and throughout the United States, will require some innovative marketing and special packaging.

Eye on the horizon: an outlook on the next 4 years

Providing the direction

In Kansas, the key to success is a total team effort. With a very limited budget, the KTTDD has to be selective in choosing activities it can engage in to support the tourism industry in Kansas, and is finding that it must develop, form and participate in joint partnerships with other agencies and the private sector. Nevertheless, the division has taken a key leadership role in conducting the necessary tourism research and proposing product development opportunities and marketing strategies. This puts the KTTDD in a position to "make or break" the efforts for growing tourism in Kansas. Members of the greater private sector in Kansas need to take advantage of the work of the KTTDD as they move on their own agendas. Some of the larger tourism-related corporations, such as Cabela's and the Kansas Speedway, need constant reminders that they, too, are part of the overall tourism strategy for the state, even if they can financially survive with little or no help from the KTTDD. Their cooperation is needed in stimulating other areas of the state, which ultimately will benefit their companies as well.

An obvious key player on the tourism team is the Kansas Department of Transportation. Tourists love maps, depend on good roads and will not find what they are looking for without good signage. However, much of what the Department of Transportation can do depends on a tripartite involvement. First, the community needs to identify the tourism products to be promoted and provide the necessary supply side facilities of good local roads, signage, restrooms and other tourist needs. Secondly, in this process the community needs to work hand-in-glove with the KTTDD and other state agencies. Finally, as the local marketing plan is evolving, other infrastructure players are drawn in, including not only transportation, but sewage, water supply and other facilities.

While inventory, assessment and tourism product development seem fundamental, it is not uncommon for local communities to see marketing or promotion or state financial help as the key to their salvation. The tourism development process takes hard work, local leadership and community endorsement if it is to be successful. While the KTTDD can be helpful in this process, especially in identifying some of the partners needed, it cannot be expected to resolve every tourism issue or problem.

Who sets the tourism policy

The tourism policy formulation is unique to each state. Tourism policy should set the regulations, rules, guidelines, directives and development/promotion objectives and strategies for long-term tourism development. Usually, the governor's office and administration, working together with the state legislature, serve as the architects, budgeters and planners for initiating, implementing and supporting a state's tourism program. But there are many other stakeholders: private citizens, local governments, private businesses, economic, as well as environmental, social, and other groups that must all be involved in the process. Ultimately and ideally, a framework for public/private discussions is created that addresses the important tourism policy questions of taxation, financing, transportation, regulatory practices, environmental practices, human resources, community relationships, technology, marketing practices and the many other aspects of the tourism industry.

Some states develop a "tourism visionary statement" to help describe the policy and in some cases to support a "brand image" of the state. This is usually followed by a "mission statement" that helps chart the direction. The KTTDD, under the present structure, would be the primary implementation agency for Kansas' tourism policy.

A strategic tourism plan

The reason for this strategic overview or "plan", for Kansas, as for any state, is multi-faceted. The socio-economic/environmental benefits from tourism are powerful. Tourism development for the State of Kansas has many positive attributes, especially with respect to its particular combination of natural, scenic, historical, archaeological, cultural and heritage attractions. As already established herein, tourism is a growth industry, and while growth may show some slowing in the short term, the long-term prospects are good, with expected growth based on continuously rising per capita incomes, lower travel costs, increased leisure time and changes in consumers' tastes and preferences toward travel, recreation and leisure goods and services. While tourism has many positive attributes for a community, it should not be regarded as a panacea for all the area's development problems. Arguments for developing and promoting tourism in Kansas include the following:

1. It provides employment opportunities, both skilled and unskilled, because it is a labor-intensive industry.
2. It increases income.
3. It adds new products.
4. It provides special opportunities for spawning new businesses, especially small ones.
5. It helps to diversify the local economy.
6. It tends to be one of the most compatible economic development activities.
7. It requires the development of an infrastructure that will also help stimulate local commerce and industry.
8. It reinforces preservation of heritage and tradition.
9. It justifies environmental protection and improvement.
10. It increases governmental revenues.
11. It creates a favourable image for the destination.
12. It provides tourist and recreational facilities that may be used by a local population who could not otherwise afford to develop such facilities.
13. It offers a showcase to promote social tourism interests in history, heritage and culture of the local area.
14. It can be developed with local products and resources.
15. It broadens educational and cultural horizons and improves feeling of self-worth.
16. It spreads development.
17. It has a high multiplier impact.
18. It provides opportunities for improving the quality of life of the local citizens.

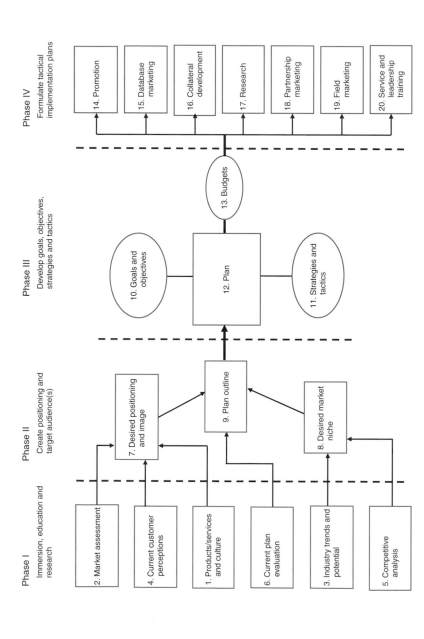

Figure 1.10 Strategic plan development flow chart

Note: This chart was designed by David L. Edgell, Sr. to illustrate to communities a possible planning tool in developing a strategic plan.

References

Biederman, Paul S., Jun Lai, Jukka M. Laitamaki, Hannah R. Messerli, Peter D. Nyheim and Stanley C. Plog. (2007). *Travel and Tourism: An Industry Primer*. Pearson Education, Inc., Upper Saddle River, NJ.

Berno, Tracy and Colleen Ward. (2005). Innocence Abroad – A Pocket Guide to Psychological Research on Tourism. *American Psychologist*, **60**(6), 593–600.

Bull, P. (1997). Tourism in London: Policy Changes and Planning Problems. *Regional Studies*, **31**(1), 82–85.

Callahan Creek. (2004). Kansas Travel and Tourism 2004 Consumer Research Overview, Lawrence, KS.

Edgell, Sr, David L. (1990). *Charting a Course for International Tourism in the Nineties, An Agenda for Managers and Executives*. US Department of Commerce, US Travel and Tourism Administration, Washington, DC.

Edgell, Sr, David L. (1999). *Tourism Policy: The Next Millennium*. Sagamore Publishing, Champaign, IL.

Fayos-Solá, Eduardo. (1996). Tourism Policy: A Midsummer Night's Dream? *Tourism Management*, **17**(6), 405–412.

Frechtling, Douglas. (1994). Assessing the Impacts of Travel and Tourism – Measuring Economic Costs. *Travel, Tourism, and Hospitality Research: A Handbook for Managers and Researchers* (2nd ed.), Eds J.R. Brent Ritchie and Charles R. Goeldner. Wiley, New York, p.401.

Goeldner, Charles A. and J.R. Brent Ritchie. (2006). *Tourism: Principles, Practices, Philosophies* (10th ed.). Wiley, Hoboken, NJ.

Klinkenborg, Verlyn. (2007). Splendor of the Grass. *National Geographic*, **211**(4), 120–141.

Klein, Yehuda L., Jeffrey P. Osleeb, and Manano R. Viola. (2004). Tourism-Generated Earnings in the Coastal Zone: A Regional Analysis. *Journal of Coastal Research*, **20**(4), 1080–1088.

Merriam-Webster Online Dictionary. (n.d.). Retrieved 19 December 2006, from http://www.m-w.com/dictionary/policy.

Porter, Michael E. (2004). *Competitiveness in Rural U.S. Regions: Learning and Research Agenda*. Institute for Strategy and Competitiveness, Harvard Business School.

Ruf Strategic Solutions. (2004). Inquirer Profiles Analysis. Ruf Strategic Solutions, Olathe, KS.

Travel Industry Association of America. (2004). *Travelers' Use of the Internet, 2004 Edition*. Travel Industry Association of America, Washington, DC.

Travel Industry Association of America. (2005). Travel Part Composition. *Domestic Travel Market Report, 2005 Edition*. Travel Industry Association of America, Washington, DC, 103–105.

Travel Industry Association of America and Smithsonian Magazine. (2003). The Historic/Cultural Traveler. Travel Industry Association of America, Washington, DC.

Tourtellot, Jonathan B. (2005). Destination Scorecard: How Do 55 National Park Regions Rate? *National Geographic Traveler*, **22**(5), 80–92.

United Nations World Tourism Organization. (2007). *Another Record Year for World Tourism* (News release). Retrieved 31 January 2007 from http://www.world-tourism.org/newsroom/Releases/2007/january/recordyear.htm.

US Travel and Tourism Advisory Board. (2006). *Restoring America's Travel Brand. National Strategy to Compete for International Visitors.* US Travel and Tourism Advisory Board, Washington, DC.

Williams, Wayne and Kevin Riley. (2003) Economic Impact Studies to Gain Support for Youth Sports from Local Businesses. *The Journal of Physical Education, Recreation & Dance,* **74**(6), 49, 3p, 1 chart, 1bw.

World Travel and Tourism Council. (2006). *Travel and Tourism – Climbing to New Heights, The 2006 Travel & Tourism Economic Research.* London, England, 1, 6, 7.

2

Tourism policy issues of yesterday

Travelling is almost like talking with men of other centuries.
René Descartes, French philosopher (1596–1650),
from *Le discourse de la Méthode*

Historic perspectives

There is no single moment in the history of tourism to pinpoint as the sole foundation for tourism policy development. Humans always have travelled for one purpose or another. Primitive man travelled place to place as he searched for food, shelter from the weather and safety from wild beasts and hostile tribes. Records of early travel are limited, at best, to cave drawings, folk tales and songs, hieroglyphics and epic sagas. Certainly, in relation to prehistory, it is difficult to imagine how decisions related to travel developed.

Religious pilgrimages played an important role in travel. Planning such pilgrimages added new dimensions to the ways and means of travel as well as the necessary preparations to

Figure 2.1   Visitors from Australia and Holland respectfully visit the Sacred Rock in Machu Picchu, Peru (Photo: Matt Schuttloffel)

receive guests at the final destination. Planning emanated from the religious organizations' involvement rather than being designed specifically for the leisure traveller (Figure 2.1).

Down through the ages, various historic civilizations have made major contributions to travel. The Sumerians (Babylonians, approximately 4000 BC) were early traders, bringing goods from Egypt and India into the Fertile Crescent and have been credited with major contributions to civilization (writing, the working wheel, money and the concept of a travel guide), all of which were useful to early tourism development. (Note: While the travel guide is a useful tool for planning, it does not necessarily connote tourism policy, and there are no records suggesting that the Sumerians had a tourism policy as we think of policy today.)

By 2000 BC, the Phoenicians, with their impressive sea-going vessels and mapping of trade routes, increased the knowledge of waterways and coastlines throughout the Mediterranean region. They also established trading centres along the coasts of North Africa, Sicily and Spain, spreading their culture and knowledge among less-advanced peoples. There are even theories that the Phoenicians were the first to travel to America, and accounts written by the Greek historian Herodotus imply that they circumnavigated Africa. Certainly their travels added information to existing accounts of identified destinations. As with the Sumerians, there are no known records suggesting the Phoenicians wrote any tourism policy guidelines (Casson, 1974).

The Egyptians travelled mainly for trade and military purposes, but their pleasure cruises along the Nile River and into the sea influenced tourism in general and coastal visitations in particular. They travelled on the Nile to participate in religious festivals and cultural events. The walls of the temple of Deir el-Bahri in Luxor hold bas-reliefs and text describing Queen Hatshepsut's journey to the land of Punt, circa 1480 BC, and the building of the great pyramids and the Sphinx led to travel for pleasurable pursuits. While we know the Egyptians enjoyed tourism related activities, their tourism policy and planning was mainly confined to the identification of festivals and planning the organization of such events.

The Greeks were one of the first societies to understand and write about tourism as we think of it today. Homer, writing in *The Odyssey* in the ninth century, BC, said: 'A guest never forgets the host who had treated him kindly'. This quotation is a precursor to the modern definition of 'quality tourism'. In Plato's *Phaedo*, Socrates has this to say, 'A great many different countries go to make up our world . . . It is an enormous place, and we, whose civilization spreads from the river Phasis to the Pillars of Hercules, occupy only a small part of it. In other places, there are other men living in countries similar to ours'. Herodotus (about 480–421 BC), the Greek historian, geographer, traveller and writer, provided early descriptions of travel (inclusive of previous travellers), with an emphasis on scenic beauty, history, unique structures, festivals and culture. While his journals on travel are fascinating reading, they did not suggest policy issues in tourism.

There is interesting information (*History of Tourism*, 1966) on tourism as described by the Roman Sidonius Apollinarius (AD 430–489). The Romans did have a 'policy' that facilitated travel by means of the building of good roads (many of which were paved), rest stops and recreation centres throughout their empire. There are earlier accounts of roadways, such as the well-developed roads in India as early as 326 BC, and in Persia, between 500 and 400 BC. History tells us that the Romans built their roadways mainly to facilitate their war efforts; however, their methods were similar to those used today. Their principal contribution to modern tourism policy was an emphasis on security: keeping the roads safe from terrorists, bandits and marauding enemies and the seas clear of pirates. The Romans' efforts to meet travellers' demands for accommodations and tourist services were certainly a prelude to tourism policy and planning.

As civilizations advanced in different parts of the world, travel became more commonplace. The Mongol empires and the reign of the Khans added a completely new dimension to land travel. We tend to forget that the empire of Genghis Khan was more than twice the size of the Roman

Figure 2.2   The ancient buildings of Machu Picchu, Peru (Photo: Jane M. Allen)

Empire at its zenith. Even with the enormity of travel taking place, much of it was disorganized, and we would be hard put to suggest that tourism policies were involved (Figure 2.2).

Travel by boat was advancing at different stages and for differing reasons throughout the world. The travel by the Vikings, even though much of it had to do with their ruthless marauding along the coastlines, nevertheless added to the travel lore. Records of their travel and explorations were by word of mouth and therefore not always easy to follow. However, it is clear they made many new discoveries but certainly left no tourism guidelines or planning documents.

We have to wait for Marco Polo (1254–1324), one of the early Europeans known to have crossed the continent of Asia, recording what he saw and heard, to give us some (possible) 'policy' direction in tourism. His vivid accounts of travel, written in his book *The Travels of Marco Polo* (also referred to as *Marco Polo's Description of the World*), allow us to begin to understand the early, broad ramifications of tourism development and some possible policies governing tourism at that time. We do know that travel in the world of 700 years ago represented anything but rational order. For example, a foreign traveller was beset with strange customs, chaotic travel conditions, and dependent on the chosen destination and culture for varying degrees of hospitality. To pursue the wonders of the world at that particular moment in time, Marco Polo was willing to travel by foot, horseback, camel, carriage and boat under some of the most difficult circumstances imaginable. This famous traveller endured enormous hardships in his quest to arrive at his destinations. However, Marco Polo brought back with him copious amounts of information revealing new inventions, different customs, interesting products and nuances of other cultures. His interactions with the great ruler Kublai Khan of China and his ability to learn and to transfer knowledge are aptly chronicled in his writings.

Educated Europeans read Marco Polo's book, which further stimulated Europe's interest to obtain spices, silks and other products from the East. Indirectly it was Polo's book, read many times and in detail by Christopher Columbus that stimulated Columbus' interest in travel and explorations. This was also true of another explorer, Ferdinand Magellan, who (reportedly) read Marco Polo's book before and during his circumnavigation of the globe.

Marco Polo, then, is the best early 'cornerstone' person to provide information which made rational sense out of travel, gave it some direction and helped us to understand how travel impacts world culture. He identified socio-cultural aspects of travel, environmental conditions at a number of locations, and the complications of travelling in sparsely populated areas. His writings aroused curiosity in others, thus stimulating world travel, which continues to grow to this day. He most likely deserves partial recognition as the 'father of early tourism policy'.

Many great travellers followed Marco Polo, including Ibn Battuta (1304–1374), the great Muslim traveller of the Middle Ages. Often referred to as the 'Muslim Marco Polo', he was a man of enormous curiosity and energy, but his writings were confined to matters mainly of interest to Muslims. Battuta's travels changed the outlook for Muslim travel and, while he added greatly to the knowledge of important destinations of that time, tourism policy was beyond his scope.

Another great traveller following Marco Polo and Ibn Battuta was Cheng Ho (1405–1433) of China. Emperor Yung Lo chose Cheng Ho to organize the largest armada of boats to announce to the world his great accomplishments in China, sparing no costs. Cheng Ho had more than 300 vessels with approximately 37,000 men in the crew. At that time, the world had never seen such an extravagant expedition nor ships as large (the largest was 444-feet long). Cheng Ho visited nearly every inhabited land bordering the China Sea and the Indian Ocean. His travel set the stage for future travel and explorations. While highly organized and exceedingly well planned, the 'policy' was to let the world know of the great Chinese empire and not necessarily to increase tourism.

While others would follow these great travellers and explorers, tourism policy as we know it today did not become a reality until the twentieth and twenty-first centuries. In searching for a place to begin the discussion of tourism policy, the authors focus on the history of the most important global tourism policy body, the United Nations World Tourism Organization (UNWTO).

The beginnings of modern tourism policy

If Marco Polo is the father of early tourism policy, we have to wait almost another 700 years to reach a place in history where we can identify the beginnings of modern tourism policy. It has taken place at different stages in different parts of the world. Reviewing tourism policies from individual countries with limited exceptions is beyond the scope, research and interest of this book. However, one way to trace world tourism policy is a partial review of the history of the UNWTO.

The UNWTO had its beginnings as the International Congress of Official Tourist Traffic Associations, organized in 1925. In 1934, it became the International Union of Official Tourist Propaganda Organizations, and by 1947, another conversion took place resulting in a new name: the International Union of Official Travel Organizations. After numerous discussions and meetings throughout the early 1970s, the UNWTO was born in 1975 and its headquarters established in Madrid, Spain, in 1976.

The UNWTO became a United Nations specialized agency in 2003; it is the leading international organization in most every aspect of tourism, including tourism policy. It serves as a global forum for tourism policy issues, definitions, directives, data, research, education, facilitation, crisis guidelines, sustainability, development and worldwide economic cooperation. UNWTO's membership is comprised of about 150 member states, 7 associate members and 300 affiliate members representing the private sector, educational institutions and others (http://www.world-tourism.org/aboutwto/eng/menu.html 18 December 2006). UNWTO has sponsored many tourism policy forums that have discussed tourism's capacity to generate income, its impact on society and to consolidate cultural and environmental assets. (More about UNWTO appears later in this book.)

International tourism policy for the United States

As an example of the development of a country's tourism policy, the authors have chosen the United States. The development of a tourism policy for the United States came very late in comparison with most major countries of the world. In a convoluted way, initial US tourism policy was linked to economic conditions in Europe shortly after World War II. Europe was in economic shambles resulting from the devastation and destruction caused by the war. US efforts sought ways and means to help rebuild Europe's economy, and tourism became a prime tool for economic development and a potential source for quickly earning badly needed foreign currency exchange. Despite widespread destruction, most of Europe's ancient historic treasures, beautiful architecture and unique structures survived the war. As part of the effort toward the restructuring of Europe's economy, the US Government encouraged American citizens to visit Europe, which resulted in a large infusion of US currency at a critical point in time. In brief, the United States' development of an ad hoc international tourism policy was, at first, principally aimed toward Europe's economic recovery (Figure 2.3).

Figure 2.3 Buildings of the Louvre Museum in Paris, France and other parts of the city were largely spared the destruction caused in many urban centres in Europe during World War II (Photo: J.R. Gast)

It is true that in 1940 the US Domestic Travel Act was passed, but this legislation was a minor domestic tourism policy designed to direct the US National Park Service to encourage travel to the parks. World War II overtook this legislation and all potential tourism directives. As mentioned earlier, following the conclusion of this conflict, the United States began encouraging its citizens, as part of its European recovery policy, to travel to Europe to help stimulate the economies of Europe during the post-war reconstruction period. Americans had the economic means to travel, and Europe was in a position to rekindle its tourism industry much faster than its industrial production base.

Probably the best place to begin a study of US tourism policy is with the 'white paper' titled: *Tourism in the European Recovery Program,* June 1950, developed jointly by the US Economic Cooperation Administration and the US Department of Commerce. These two administrative units of the US Government worked with various European groups largely through the Organisation for European Economic Cooperation (a predecessor of the Organisation for Economic Cooperation and Development) to alleviate travel restrictions and barriers and to promote American travel to Europe. Much of the effort in this regard came about in 1948–1949 as part of 'Travel in the Marshall Plan'. The US Government worked to lift visas and other restrictions, while the US private travel sector was encouraged to provide reasonable travel costs and to help promote the program. Based on the statistics available during the early 1950s American travel to Europe increased dramatically.

By 1954, it became clear that a tourism policy, which was beneficial to the United States, needed to be developed. US Government agencies needed guidelines to follow when engaged in foreign economic policy discussions with other nations regarding tourism. On 27 May 1954, recognizing the need for a tourism policy, US President Dwight D. Eisenhower sent a memorandum to the Secretary of Commerce giving general guidelines for such a policy. This memorandum is reproduced here in its entirety:

> In my message to the Congress on the subject of foreign economic policy I emphasized the importance of international travel both for its cultural and social advantages of the free world and for its great economic significance. In my message I stated that I would instruct the appropriate agencies and departments, at home and abroad, to consider how they can facilitate international travel. I made specific note that these agencies would be requested to simplify procedures where practicable relating to customs, visas, passports, exchange or monetary restrictions, and other regulations that sometimes harass the traveler. I request that you take appropriate steps on these and related matters, consistent with your responsibilities in this field, to encourage international travel consonant with the national interest.

I am sending similar requests to the Departments of Justice, State and Treasury.

(D. Edgell, *personal papers*, 21 May 2007)

Finally, under the Mutual Security Act of 1957, President Eisenhower directed that a study of the barriers to international travel and ways of promoting such travel be undertaken. A very small Office of International Travel was then created within the US Department of Commerce to assist with this process. This study was completed on 17 April 1958 and submitted as a 'Report to the President of the United States' by Clarence B. Randall, Special Assistant to President Eisenhower (D. Edgell, Sr, personal papers, 21 May 2007.) In his transmittal letter to the president, Randall identified some of the policy implications of international tourism and stated:

I hold the strong conviction that tourism has deep significance for the peoples of the modern world, and that the benefits of travel can contribute to the cause of peace through improvement not only in terms of economic advancement but also with respect to our political, cultural, and social relationships as well . . .

The freedom to travel is a dramatic freedom. It is a unique instrument of the friendly, peaceful communication among the nations and the peoples of the earth . . . The United States could exercise no more powerful influence in behalf of peace than to display strong leadership in promoting through travel the interchange of friendly visits among the people of the world.

Randall's report, *International Travel*, stimulated the Eisenhower Administration and the US Congress to action in developing legislation that resulted in the International Travel Act. By the time this legislation passed in Congress, John F. Kennedy had been elected President of the US, and he signed the International Travel Act into law in 1961. Kennedy, too, served in World War II and wished to promote international travel as an economic development tool and as a means to lead toward a more peaceful world. This Act established the United States Travel Service (USTS) and mandated that USTS seek to 'stimulate and encourage travel to the United States by residents of foreign countries for the purpose of study, culture, recreation, business, and other activities as a means of promoting friendly understanding and good will among people of foreign countries and the United States'. (For a clearer understanding of the issues discussed and the details of the comprehensive research undertaken, see the individual reports of the National Tourism Policy Study.)

This Act was an effort to promote travel from abroad to the US, collect statistics and reduce barriers to international travel. In 1970, a modification of the Act took place to create the National Tourism Resources Review Commission to study tourism. The Commission published an impressive report on the importance of tourism but it received very little attention by the then US President Richard M. Nixon and the US Congress.

In a side note to this discussion on tourism policy, during World War II General Dwight D. Eisenhower witnessed and fought a horrific war against genocide. According to *People to People International 2001 Annual Report*, the memories of the devastation and suffering that took place literally haunted him for the remainder of his life. In that respect, President Eisenhower founded People to People International in 1957 with the idea that the people of the world, if given the opportunity to communicate and directly discuss issues with one another, might be enabled then to resolve their differences and find a way to live in peace. He also recognized this as a form of international tourism that would have some of the same positive benefits. Today, People to People International is a vital enterprise following its original purpose.

Possibly the most important contribution to domestic tourism in the United States was also conceived by President Eisenhower, emanating from his strong interest in establishing the US system of interstate highways. His initial interest came from his military background. Eisenhower realized early on the need for a high-quality system of roadways throughout the United States for the movement of military personnel and equipment, should the need ever arise. Eisenhower also envisioned the importance and benefits of uniting US communications and transportation systems that a strong interstate highway system would provide. On 29 June 1956, President Eisenhower signed the Federal Aid Highway Act of 1956, which provided the funding for the building of interstate highways throughout the nation. The actions mandated by this Act forever changed domestic tourism (and to a lesser extent international tourism) in the United States. Initially the interstate highway system was called the 'National Highway Defense System' but later was renamed the 'Dwight David Eisenhower National System of Interstate and Defense Highways' (Snyder, 2006).

President Eisenhower's contributions to international tourism policy are now fully recognized. As recent as just a few years ago, The J. Willard and Alice S. Marriott Foundation gave The George Washington University a gift that was used to establish the 'Eisenhower Professor of Tourism Policy' currently occupied by the distinguished professor Dr Donald E. Hawkins in the Department of Tourism and Hospitality Management in the School of Business.

The importance of the National Tourism Policy Act of 1981

The next step in the focus on tourism policy in the United States began to evolve in 1974. Senate Resolution 347, co-sponsored by seventy-one Senators and unanimously agreed to by the Senate on 24 June 1974, authorized the Senate Commerce Committee to undertake a National Tourism Policy Study. (The US Department of Commerce was a major resource and contributor to several of the studies taking place.) The purposes of the study were 'to develop legislation and other recommendations to make the Federal role in tourism more effective and responsive to the national interests in tourism, and the needs of the public and private sectors of the industry'.

In October 1976, the Committee issued the study's first interim report, *A Conceptual Basis for the National Tourism Policy Study*. This report gave an overview of legislation that affects tourism, tentatively identified the national interests in tourism and listed some of the problems associated with the federal role in tourism policy at that time.

In June 1977, a second interim report was issued, the *National Tourism Policy Study Ascertainment Phase*. This report detailed and analyzed input from the tourism and travel industry on the issues, problems and needs of the state and local, public and private sectors of the industry, both in general terms and in terms of their specific relationships to federal agencies and programmes. The last phase, the *National Tourism Policy Study Final Report*, saw completion in April 1978. It incorporated findings from the earlier reports and made recommendations for a national tourism policy for the United States.

On 27 March 1978, author David L. Edgell, Sr discussed the need for a US Government Tourism Policy when he addressed the 'Eighth Annual Conference of the Society of Government Economists' in Washington, DC. He suggested that 'The success of the tourism sector as an economic development tool will depend heavily on the United States pragmatically exercising its responsibility in planning public policy initiatives, coordinating policy with the public and private sectors, and explaining to the public the important role tourism plays in international (and domestic) economic policies'. He was advocating at that time that international trade in tourism policy would bolster the US balance of trade and add to the overall economic policies of the country.

After considerable discussion of the results of this study, debates in Congress and within the executive branch as well as consultations with states, cities and the private sector, a compromise piece of legislation – S. 1097 – the National Tourism Policy Act – received passage by Congress. However, then President Jimmy Carter surprisingly vetoed the legislation on 24 December 1980. In January 1981, Ronald Reagan became President of the United States and charged his Secretary of Commerce, Malcolm Baldrige, to review S. 1097. The legislation was reintroduced early in 1981. After more Congressional discussions, the National Tourism Policy Act of 1981 was passed by Congress and signed into law by President Ronald Reagan on 16 October 1981 (retroactive to 1 October 1981). This Act (see case study at end of this chapter) redefined the national interest in tourism and created the United States Travel and Tourism Administration (USTTA), which replaced the USTS as the nation's government tourism office.

The principal mission of USTTA under the Act was to implement broad tourism policy initiatives, to develop travel to the United States from abroad as a stimulus to economic stability and the growth of the US travel industry, to reduce the nation's travel deficit and to promote friendly understanding and appreciation of the United States abroad. Through the passage and implementation of the Act, the importance of tourism policy within the United States, through the US Department of Commerce, was elevated. The appointment of an Under Secretary of Commerce for Travel and Tourism was a major step. (Up until then the highest-level tourism position in the US Government was an 'Assistant Secretary' while most other countries hosted Cabinet-level 'Ministers of Tourism'.) It is important simply to recognize that this Act was the most comprehensive identification of tourism policy within the United States and allowed the United States to be a major player in the UNWTO. Under President William Clinton's administration in 1996, the US Congress abolished USTTA placing the burden of governmental tourism policy on the backs of the states and the private sector. While a very small Office of Travel and Tourism Industries is maintained in the US Department of Commerce, essentially the US Government abandoned tourism policy for the US by this action. In addition, the United States resigned its membership in the prestigious UNWTO.

Following the 11 September 2001 terrorism tragedies in the United States and the consequential decline in international travel to the US, the US Government began again to recognize the importance of tourism policy. It has tried (most unsuccessfully) to use the government-led Tourism Policy Council (a holdover from the National Tourism Policy Act) as a mechanism for a partial tourism policy. There are many in the travel and tourism industry today who would like to see a renewed effort in tourism policy by the US Government but nothing of any consequence has yet happened. As a result, the US is in the worst-case global scenario in regards to tourism policy from a governmental perspective.

While the National Tourism Policy Act was a major breakthrough in gaining recognition of tourism policy in the United States, its eventual demise has led to a lack of awareness and understanding about the significance of international tourism to the United States and, more importantly, to the US's meager influence in tourism policy across the globe. This isolation in global tourism policy continues to this day; however, there are groups both within and without the tourism industry in the United States that are beginning to push for a national tourism policy, most especially as a component of an overall globalization tourism policy initiative. With some changes, the authors of this book believe that the National Tourism Policy Act of 1981 has enough creditable features to mark it as a foundation document for US tourism policy in today's world.

Some reasons for a US tourism policy

In recent years and certainly since the tragedy of 11 September 2001, the US Government has been floundering in its understanding of the magnitude tourism exerts in relation to economic, environmental and social policies. A number of the state tourism offices yearn to have some influence on US Government tourism policy but their contributions are fragmented and weak. One organization that has influenced US Government tourism policy is the eleven-state Southeast Tourism Society's 'Tourism Policy Council'.

The private sector, for many of the right business reasons, has often pursued tourism with a very narrow focus that only helps their own economic pursuits whether or not this is necessarily in the best interests of tourism policy decisions for the country. The US is one of the few major countries that do not belong to the UNWTO, thus isolating itself from world tourism policies and discussions. In terms of tourism policy, the US is like the 'ostrich with his head in the sand'. Finally, the US currently has the worse world image it has had in recent history. A good tourism policy could help alleviate this negative image.

In the August 2005 issue of *Travel Insights* (a publication of the Travel Industry Association of America), the cover page is titled 'The Challenge to Brand America: The Travel Industry Is the Answer to Reversing America's Deteriorating Image Abroad'. The publication states, 'The image of the US in the international community is poor and has been slow to improve. While inbound international travel grew 12 per cent from 2003 to 2004, it is still more than 5 million visitors behind 2000 levels. Travel Industry Association of America analysis shows the US market share of worldwide international travel has declined 36 per cent since 1992. In this day and age of a global economy and the global village that is shrinking as more and more people have easy access to travel quickly and easily, the US is being marginalized in the new global travel market'. The article further cites many additional problems and the fact that the US Government has no firm budget for promoting international tourism while the rest of the world's governments, for the most part, are actively promoting tourism to their respective countries. This is just one more example of why the US needs a tourism policy. The time to act is now. Tourism policy can help prevent the US becoming even more isolated, continuing to have a bad international image and lacking tourism directives regarding economic and foreign policy. A viable US tourism policy could generate billions of dollars for the US economy and promote a more favourable international image.

On 4 November 2005, former Secretary of State Colin Powell delivered the keynote address during dedication events for Rubenstein Hall, the second building of the Terry Sanford Institute of Public Policy in North Carolina. In that speech, he said that after the 11 September 2001 terrorist attacks, people got the impression that America was not as friendly, due in part to tighter immigration measures. He said the US had to take such steps, but after a few years, he saw that America was paying a price for it. Further, he said that America needed to show the world that it had not changed, that it is still generous and open. 'If we convey to the rest of the world you're not welcome, we don't want you here, then the terrorists are winning', Powell said.

Former Secretary of State Colin Powell's successor, Secretary Condoleezza Rice recently acknowledged some of the difficulties the United States is having with its image abroad. During a 12 April 2006 address at the 'Global Travel and Tourism Summit Breakfast', Secretary Rice set the stage for her remarks about the US image with several statements. She observed, 'Since the attacks of September 11th, (2001), our nation's commitment to openness has been tested by new and unprecedented threats from global terrorism'. These remarks followed, 'We recognize, though, that striking a balance is important. And we certainly do not want to make things more difficult for legitimate travelers. I know that some of our initial security measures after September 11th have caused delays in getting visas and even led some foreign citizens to believe that the United States is no longer welcoming to them. We've heard these legitimate concerns and we are doing everything that we can to improve our visa policy while also maintaining our security'.

These remarks by Colin Powell and Condoleezza Rice suggest that the US needs to do something about its image. A US Government tourism policy that promotes a positive image of the US would be an important first step. Also from a tourism policy perspective, if the US were a member of the United Nations' sanctioned World Tourism Organization, the US could pursue foreign policy, economic policy and tourism policy more favourable to the United States.

In *The Power of Travel 2006*, the Travel Industry Association of America has a special section titled 'America's Image Abroad'. It said:

> In recent years, the US travel and tourism industry has suffered from America's declining image abroad. Some of our policies, our economic power and aspects of our culture have obscured our positive attributes like freedom, opportunity and openness.... The image issue is most pressing when you consider worldwide market share. The US share of international tourism declined 36 percent between 1992 and 2004 while world tourism was growing by 52 percent.... Reversing this trend is vital to the economic health and prosperity of our nation and industry. If the US increased its market share by just 1 percent it would equal 8 million more visitors, $12 billion more in expenditures, 151,000 new jobs, $3 billion increase in payroll and $2 billion more in federal, state and local tax revenues....Reversing America's declining image abroad is a big job but not an impossible one. A recent Pew Institute study showed that when travelers come to America and experience the culture, the history and most of all the people, their impression of America improves. And the more they visit, the more positive their opinion becomes.

The most popular textbook for tourism, *Tourism Principles, Practices, Philosophies* (Goeldner, 2006), used by thousands of US and global students had this to say about US tourism policy, 'The United States is an example of how not to develop tourism. In April 1996 the United States Travel and Tourism Administration (USTTA), which served as the nation's official government tourist office charged with developing tourism policy, promoting inbound tourism from abroad, and stimulating travel within the United States, was eliminated.' This is truly a sad commentary on US policy toward tourism and the US image.

One of the authors of this book, Dr Edgell, has noted a decided downturn in US international tourism interests precipitated, in general, by the United States' negative image abroad and the difficulties of operating without a US Government tourism policy since 1996. Through his travels and those of the other authors, it is the consensus that it is plainly unacceptable for a nation as powerful as the United States and capable of leadership in many dimensions of tourism policy, planning and practices to lack its own tourism policy. In addition, the UNWTO, which has been so active in global economic, environmental and social policies especially during international catastrophes, could be greatly strengthened by US involvement.

As an example of suggested ingredients for a national tourism policy, the (US) *National Tourism Policy Act of 1981* is presented in its entirety as Case study 2. It is a classic illustration of a national tourism policy from 'yesterday'. While some of the pieces of the Act would be helpful in designing a tourism policy for 'today' and 'tomorrow', many changes would be necessary, as tourism is a highly dynamic industry that requires a tourism policy that can adjust to the new and changing needs of the tourism industry.

Case study 2

National Tourism Policy Act of 1981

Begun and held at the City of Washington on Monday, the fifth day of January, one thousand nine hundred and eighty-one

AN ACT

To amend the International Travel Act of 1961 to establish a national tourism policy, and for other purposes.

Be it enacted by the Senate and House of Representatives of the United States of America in Congress assembled.

SHORT TITLE

"SECTION 1. This Act may be cited as the "National Tourism Policy Act."

NATIONAL TOURISM POLICY

Sec. 2. (a) The International Travel Act of 1961 (hereinafter in this Act referred to as the "Act") is amended by striking out the first section and inserting in lieu thereof the following: "That this Act may be cited as the 'International Travel Act of 1961'."

"TITLE I – NATIONAL TOURISM POLICY"

"Sec. 101. (a) The Congress finds that

"(1) the tourism and recreation industries are important to the United States, not only because of the numbers of people they serve and the vast human, financial and physical resources they employ, but because of the great benefits tourism, recreation and related activities confer on individuals and on society as a whole;

"(2) the Federal Government for many years has encouraged tourism and recreation implicitly in its statutory commitments to the shorter work year and to the national passenger transportation system, and explicitly in a number of legislative enactments to promote tourism and support development of outdoor recreation, cultural attractions and historic and natural heritage resources;

"(3) as incomes and leisure time continue to increase, and as our economic and political systems develop more complex global relationships, tourism and recreation will become ever more important aspects of our daily lives; and

"(4) the existing extensive Federal Government involvement in tourism recreation, and other related activities, needs to be better coordinated to effectively respond to the national interest in tourism and recreation and, where appropriate, to meet the needs of State and local governments and the private sector.

"(b) There is established a national tourism policy to

"(1) optimize the contribution of the tourism and recreation industries to economic prosperity, full employment, and the international balance of payments of the United States;

"(2) make the opportunity for and benefits of tourism and recreation in the United States universally accessible to residents of the United States and foreign countries and insure that present and future generations are afforded adequate tourism and recreation resources;

"(3) contribute to personal growth, health, education and intercultural appreciation of the geography, history and ethnicity of the United States;

"(4) encourage the free and welcome entry of individuals travelling to the United States, in order to enhance international understanding and goodwill, consistent with immigration laws, the laws protecting the public health, and laws governing the importation of goods into the United States;

"(5) eliminate unnecessary trade barriers to the United States tourism industry operating throughout the world;

"(6) encourage competition in the tourism industry and maximum consumer choice through the continued viability of the retail travel agent industry and the independent tour operator industry;

"(7) promote the continued development and availability of alternative personal payment mechanisms which facilitate national and international travel;

"(8) promote quality, integrity and reliability in all tourism and tourism related services offered to visitors to the United States;

"(9) preserve the historical and cultural foundations of the Nation as a living part of community life and development, and insure future generations an opportunity to appreciate and enjoy the rich heritage of the Nation;

"(10) insure the compatibility of tourism and recreation with other national interests in energy development and conservation, environmental protection and the judicious use of natural resources;

"(11) assist in the collection, analysis and dissemination of data which accurately measure the economic and social impact of tourism to and within the United States, in order to facilitate planning in the public and private sectors; and

"(12) harmonize, to the maximum extent possible, all Federal activities in support of tourism and recreation with the needs of the general public and the states, territories, local governments, and the tourism and recreation industry, and to give leadership to all concerned with tourism, recreation and national heritage preservation in the United States."

Duties

Sec. 3. (a) The following heading is inserted before section 2 of the Act:

"TITLE II – DUTIES"

(b) Section 2 of the Act (22 U.S.C. 2122) is amended by striking out "purpose of the Act" and inserting in lieu thereof "the national tourism policy established by section 101 (b)."

(c) Section 3(a) of the Act (22 U.S.C. 2123(a)) is amended by striking out "section 2" and inserting in lieu thereof "section 201", by striking out "and" at the end of paragraph (6), by striking out the period at the end of paragraph (7) and inserting in lieu thereof a semicolon, and by adding after paragraph (7) the following new paragraphs:

"(8) shall establish facilitation services at major ports-of-entry of the United States;

"(9) shall consult with foreign governments on travel and tourism matters and, in accordance with applicable law, represent United States travel and tourism interests before international and intergovernmental meetings;

"(10) shall develop and administer a comprehensive program relating to travel industry information, data service, training and education and technical assistance;

"(11) shall develop a program to seek and to receive information on a continuing basis from the tourism industry, including consumer and travel trade associations, regarding needs and interests which should be met by a Federal agency or program and to direct that information to the appropriate agency or program;

"(12) shall encourage to the maximum extent feasible travel to and from the United States on United States carriers;

"(13) shall assure coordination within the Department of Commerce so that to the extent practicable, all the resources of the Department are used to effectively and efficiently carry out the national tourism policy;

"(14) may only promulgate, issue, rescind and amend such interpretive rules, general statements of policy, and rules of agency organization, procedure and practice as may be necessary to carry out this Act; and

"(15) shall develop and submit annually to the Congress, within six weeks of transmittal to the Congress of the President's recommended budget for implementing this Act, a detailed marketing plan to stimulate and encourage travel to the United States during the fiscal year for which such budget is submitted and include in the plan the estimated funding and personnel levels required to implement the plan and alternate means of funding activities under this Act."

(d) (1) Paragraph (5) of section 3(a) of the Act is amended (A) by striking out "foreign countries;". and inserting in lieu thereof "foreign countries.", (B) by striking out "this clause;" and inserting in lieu thereof "this paragraph.", (C) by inserting the last two sentences before the first sentence of subsection (c) and (D) by striking out "this clause" in such sentences and inserting in lieu thereof "paragraph (5) of subsection (a)".

(2) Paragraph (7) of section 3(a) of the Act is amended by striking out "countries. The Secretary is authorized to" and inserting in lieu thereof "countries; and the Secretary may" and by striking out "this clause" and inserting in lieu thereof "this paragraph."

(3) Section 3 of the Act is amended by striking out "clause (5)" each place it appears and inserting in lieu thereof "paragraph (5)."

(e) (l) Sections 2 and 3 of the Act are redesignated as sections 201 and 202, respectively, and section 5 is inserted after section 202 (as so redesignated) and redesignated as section 203.

(2) Section 203 of the Act (as so redesignated) is amended by striking out "semi-annually" and inserting in lieu thereof "annually".

(f) The following section is inserted after section 203 of the Act (as so redesignated):

"Sec. 204. (a) The Secretary is authorized to provide, in accordance with subsections (b) and (c), financial assistance to a region of not less than two States or portions of two States to assist in the implementation of a regional tourism promotional and marketing program. Such assistance shall include

"(1) technical assistance for advancing the promotion of travel to such region by foreign visitors;

"(2) expert consultants; and

"(3) marketing and promotional assistance.

"(b) Any program carried out with assistance under subsection (a) shall serve as a demonstration project for future program development for regional tourism promotion.

"(c) The Secretary may provide assistance under subsection (a) for a region if the applicant for the assistance demonstrates to the satisfaction of the Secretary that

"(1) such region has in the past been an area that has attracted foreign visitors, but such visits have significantly decreased;

"(2) facilities are being developed or improved to reattract such foreign visitors;

"(3) a joint venture in such region will increase the travel to such region by foreign visitors;

"(4) such regional programs will contribute to the economic well-being of the region;

"(5) such region is developing or has developed a regional transportation system that will enhance travel to the facilities and attractions within such region; and

"(6) a correlation exists between increased tourism to such region and the lowering of the unemployment rate in such region."

Administration

Sec. 4. (a) (1) The first sentence of section 4 of the Act (22 U.S.C. 2124) is amended to read as follows: "There is established in the Department of Commerce a United States Travel and Tourism Administration which shall be headed by an Under Secretary of Commerce for Travel and Tourism who shall be appointed by the President, by and with the advice and consent of the Senate, and who shall report directly to the Secretary."

(2) The second sentence of section 4 of the Act is amended by striking out "Assistant Secretary of Commerce for Tourism" and inserting in lieu thereof "Under Secretary of Commerce for Travel and Tourism."

(3) Section 4 of the Act is amended by striking out the last sentence and inserting in lieu thereof the following: "The Secretary shall designate an Assistant Secretary of Commerce for Tourism Marketing who shall be

under the supervision of the Under Secretary of Commerce for Travel and Tourism. The Secretary shall delegate to the Assistant Secretary responsibility for the development and submission of the marketing plan required by section 202(a)(15)."

(4) Section 5314 of title 5, United States Code, is amended by striking out "Under Secretary of Commerce" and inserting in lieu thereof "Under Secretary of Commerce and Under Secretary of Commerce for Travel and Tourism."

(b) Section 4 of the Act is amended by inserting "(a)" after "Sec. 4.", and by adding at the end the following:

"(b) (1) The Secretary may not reduce the total number of employees of the United States Travel and Tourism Administration assigned to the offices of the Administration in foreign countries to a number which is less than the total number of employees of the United States Travel Service assigned to offices of the Service in foreign countries in fiscal year 1979.

"(2) In any fiscal year the amount of funds which shall be made available from appropriations under this Act for obligation for the activities of the offices of the United States Travel and Tourism Administration in foreign countries shall not be less than the amount obligated in fiscal year 1980 for the activities of the offices of the United States Travel Service in foreign countries."

(c) (l) The following heading is inserted before section 4 of the Act:

"TITLE III – ADMINISTRATION"

(2) Section 4 of the Act is redesignated as section 301 and the following new sections are inserted after that section:

"Sec. 302. (a) In order to assure that the national interest in tourism is fully considered in Federal decision-making, there is established an inter-agency coordinating council to be known as the Tourism Policy Council (hereinafter in this section referred to as the 'Council').

"(b) (1) The Council shall consist of

"(A) the Secretary of Commerce who shall serve as Chairman of the Council;

"(B) the Under Secretary for Travel and Tourism who shall serve as the Vice Chairman of the Council and who shall act as Chairman of the Council in the absence of the Chairman;

"(C) the Director of the Office of Management and Budget or the individual designated by the Director from the Office;

"(D) an individual designated by the Secretary of Commerce from the International Trade Administration of the Department of Commerce;

"(E) the Secretary of Energy or the individual designated by such Secretary from the Department of Energy;

"(F) the Secretary of State or the individual designated by such Secretary from the Department of State;

"(G) the Secretary of the Interior or the individual designated by such Secretary of the National Park Service or the Heritage Conservation and Recreation Service of the Department of the Interior;

"(H) the Secretary of Labor or the individual designated by such Secretary from the Department of Labor; and

"(I) the Secretary of Transportation or the individual designated by such Secretary from the Department of Transportation.

"(2) Members of the Council shall serve without additional compensation but shall be reimbursed for actual and necessary expenses, including travel expenses, incurred by them in carrying out the duties of the Council.

"(3) Each member of the Council, other than the Vice Chairman, may designate an alternate, who shall serve as a member of the Council whenever the regular member is unable to attend a meeting of the Council or any committee of the Council. The designation by a member of the Council of an alternate under the preceding sentence shall be made for the duration of the member's term on the Council. Any such designated alternate shall be selected from individuals who exercise significant decision-making authority in the Federal agency involved and shall be authorized to make decisions on behalf of the member for whom he or she is serving.

"(c) (1) Whenever the Council, or a committee of the Council, considers matters that affect the interests of Federal agencies that are not represented on the Council or the committee, the Chairman may invite the heads of such agencies, or their alternates, to participate in the deliberations of the Council or committee.

"(2) The Council shall conduct its first meeting not later than ninety days after the date of enactment of this section. Thereafter the Council shall meet not less than four times each year.

"(d) (1) The Council shall coordinate policies, programs and issues relating to tourism, recreation, or national heritage resources involving Federal departments, agencies, or other entities. Among other things, the Council shall

"(A) coordinate the policies and programs of member agencies that have a significant effect on tourism, recreation and national heritage preservation;

"(B) develop areas of cooperative program activity;

"(C) assist in resolving interagency program and policy conflicts; and

"(D) seek and receive concerns and views of State and local governments and the Travel and Tourism Advisory Board with respect to Federal programs and policies deemed to conflict with the orderly growth and development of tourism.

"(2) To enable the Council to carry out its functions

"(A) the Council may request directly from any Federal department or agency such personnel, information, services, or facilities, on a compensated or uncompensated basis, as he determines necessary to carry out the functions of the Council;

"(B) each Federal department or agency shall furnish the Council with such information, services, and facilities as it may request to the extent permitted by law and within the limits of available funds; and

"(C) Federal agencies and departments may, in their discretion, detail to temporary duty with the Council, such personnel as the Council may request of for carrying out the functions of the Council, each such detail to be without loss of seniority, pay, or other employee status.

"(3) The Administrator of the General Services Administration shall provide administrative support services for the Council on a reimbursable basis.

"(e) The Council shall establish such policy committees as it considers necessary and appropriate, each of which shall be comprised of any or all of the members of the Council and representatives from Federal departments, agencies, and instrumentalities not represented on the Council. Each such Policy committee shall be designed

"(1) to monitor a specific area of Federal Government activity, such as transportation, energy and natural resources, economic development, or other such activities related to tourism; and

"(2) to review and evaluate the relation of the policies and activities of the Federal Government in that specific area to tourism, recreation, and national heritage conservation in the United States.

"(f) The Council shall submit an annual report for the preceding fiscal year to the President for transmittal to Congress on or before the thirty-first day of December of each year. The report shall include

"(1) a comprehensive and detailed report of the activities and accomplishments of the Council and its policy committees;

"(2) the results of Council efforts to coordinate the policies and programs of member agencies that have a significant effect on tourism, recreation, and national heritage preservation, resolve interagency conflicts, and develop areas of cooperative program activity;

"(3) an analysis of problems referred to the Council by State and local governments, the tourism industry, the Secretary of Commerce, or any of the Council's policy committees along with a detailed statement of any actions taken or anticipated to be taken to resolve such problems; and

"(4) such recommendations as the Council deems appropriate.

"Sec. 303. (a) There is established the Travel and Tourism Advisory Board (hereinafter in this section referred to as the 'Board') to be composed of fifteen members appointed by the Secretary. The members of the Board shall be appointed as follows:

"(1) Not more than eight members of the Board shall be appointed from the same political party.

"(2) The members of the Board shall be appointed from among citizens of the United States who are not regular full-time employees of the United States and shall be selected for appointment so as to provide as nearly as practicable a broad representation of different geographical regions within the United States and of the diverse and varied segments of the tourism industry.

"(3) Twelve of the members shall be appointed from senior executive officers of organizations engaged in the travel and tourism industry. Of such members

"(A) at least one shall be a senior representative from a labour organization representing employees of the tourism industry; and

"(B) at least one shall be a representative of the States who is knowledgeable of tourism promotion.

"(4) Of the remaining three members of the Board

"(A) one member shall be a consumer advocate or ombudsman from the Organized public interest community;

"(B) one member shall be an economist, statistician, or accountant; and

"(C) one member shall be an individual from the academic community who is knowledgeable in tourism, recreation, or national heritage conservation.

"The Secretary shall serve as an ex-officio member of the Board. The duration of the Board shall not be subject to the Federal Advisory Committee Act. A list of the members appointed to the Board shall be forwarded by the Secretary to the Senate Committee on Commerce, Science, and Transportation and the House Committee on Energy and Commerce.

"(b) The members of the Board shall be appointed for a term of office of 3 years, except that of the members first appointed

"(1) Four members shall be appointed for terms of 1 year, and (2) four members shall be appointed for terms of 2 years, as designated by the Secretary at the time of appointment. Any member appointed to fill a vacancy occurring before the expiration of the term for which the member's predecessor was appointed shall be appointed only for the remainder of such term. A member may serve after the expiration of his term until his successor has taken office. Vacancies on the Board shall be filled in the same manner in which the original appointments were made.

No member of the Board shall be eligible to serve in excess of two consecutive terms of 3 years each.

"(c) The Chairman and Vice Chairman and other appropriate officers of the Board shall be elected by and from members of the Board other than the Secretary.

"(d) The members of the Board shall receive no compensation for their services as such, but shall be allowed such necessary travel expenses and per diem as are authorized by section 5703 of title 5, United States Code. The Secretary shall pay the reasonable and necessary expenses incurred by the Board in connection with the coordination of Board activities, announcement and reporting of meetings, and preparation of such reports as are required by subsection (f).

"(e) The Board shall meet at least semi-annually and shall hold such other meetings at the call of the Chairman, the Vice Chairman, or a majority of its members.

"(f) The Board shall advise the Secretary with respect to the implementation of this Act and shall advise the Assistant Secretary for Tourism Marketing with respect to the preparation of the marketing plan under section 202(a)(15). The Board shall prepare an annual report concerning its activities and include therein such recommendations as it deems appropriate with respect to the performance of the Secretary under this Act and the operation and effectiveness of programs under this Act. Each annual report shall cover a fiscal year and shall be submitted on or before the thirty-first day of December following the close of the fiscal year."

Authorizations

Sec. 5 (a) Section 6 of the Act (22 U.S.C. 2126) is redesignated as section 304 and the first sentence is amended to read as follows: "For the purpose of carrying out this Act there is authorized to be appropriated an amount not to exceed $8,600,000 for the fiscal year ending September 30, 1982."

(b) Section 7 of the Act (22 U.S.C. 2127) is redesignated as section 305 and sections 8 and 9 of the Act (22 U.S.C. 2128) are repealed.

Effective Date

Sec. 6. The amendments made by this Act shall take effect October 1, 1981.

References

Cassion, Lionel (1974). *Travel in the Ancient World*. Hakkert, Toronto, Canada.

Edgell, Sr, David L. (1990). *Charting a Course for International Tourism in the Nineties, An Agenda for Managers and Executives*. US Department of Commerce, US. Travel and Tourism Administration, Washington, DC.

Edgell, Sr, David L. and Stephen A. Wandner. (1978). 'Role of Tourism in the International Economic Policy of the United States'. Paper presented at the Western Economic Association Annual Meeting, Honolulu, Hawaii, 22 June 1978.

Goeldner, Charles A. and J.R. Brent Ritchie. (2006). *Tourism: Principles, Practices, Philosophies (10th ed.)*. Wiley, Hoboken, NJ.

History of Tourism. (1966). From the Leisure Arts Ltd Series, 'Discovery of Sciences,' London, 9–13.

Horsley, Laura (ed.). (2006). 'America's Image Abroad'. *The Power of Travel 2006*. Travel Industry Association of America, Washington, DC, 8.

International Travel Act of 1961, Chapter 31, Section 2122, 158.

People to People International, 2001 Annual Report: 1.

Snyder, L.T. (2006). Broader Ribbons Across the Land. *American History*, 32–39.

United Nations World Tourism Organization. (2006). About the World Tourism Organization (UNWTO-OMT). Retrieved 9 March 2006, from http://www.world-tourism.org/aboutwto/eng/menu.html.

United States Committee on Commerce. (1976). *A Conceptual Basis for the National Tourism Policy Study*. US Government Printing Office, Washington, DC.

United States Committee on Commerce. (1977). *National Tourism Policy Study Ascertainment Phase*. US Government Printing Office, Washington, DC.

United States Committee on Commerce. (1978). *National Tourism Policy Study Final Report*. US Government Printing Office, Washington, DC.

United States Department of State Travel Warnings. (2006). *Remarks by Secretary Condoleezza Rice* at the Global Travel and Tourism Summit Breakfast on 12 April 2006. Washington, DC.

US Government. (1950). *Tourism in the European Recovery Program*, June 1950, Washington, DC.

3

Tourism policy issues for today

The world is becoming a global village in which people from different continents are made to feel like next-door neighbours. In facilitating more authentic social relationships between individuals, tourism can help overcome many real prejudices and foster new bonds of fraternity. In this sense tourism has become a real force for world peace.

Pope John Paul II,
papacy 1978–2005 (1920–2005)

Introduction and overview

Tourism in the twenty-first century is a major vehicle for fulfilling people's aspirations for a higher quality of life. Whether this happens at the local, state/provincial, regional, national or international level, the basic tenets remain consistent. One aim is to facilitate tourism interactions between individuals and, it is hoped, lay the groundwork for peace through authentic social relationships. Tourism is part of the growing international trade-in-service, travel-sector industries. As such, it has the potential to be an important stimulant for future improvement in the economic, political, sociocultural and ecological dimensions of people's lives. Combining the elements of creating economic income with the potential to foster greater international understanding and goodwill, tourism holds promise for serving as a vehicle for peace throughout the world. This supports the lofty view that the highest purpose of tourism policy can be to balance its benefits and costs for communities as tourism destinations and to improve the quality and sustainability of life for local citizens. Tourism as a policy for peace is presented in Chapter 5.

Today's key tourism policy issues include tourism regulation and public policy, areas facilitating tourism such as information technologies, financial organizations and organizations related to tourists themselves as consumers of travel. This chapter provides an overview of such important issue areas with examples of their effects on tourism policy formation. In this context, tourism policy first is described in an ethical framework, its core components identified, and an issues-focused working definition proposed in order to provide an adequate framework for analysing and understanding the complex issues confronting the production and distribution of international tourism products and services in today's world.

Business ethics in a tourism policy issues framework

The Global Code of Ethics for Tourism adopted 21 December 2001, by the 13th session of the General Assembly of the United Nations World Tourism Organization (UNWTO) outlines principles to guide tourism development. It also serves as a powerful frame of reference for the different stakeholders in the tourism sector 'with the objective of minimizing the negative impact of tourism on the environment and on cultural heritage while maximizing the benefits of tourism in promoting sustainable development and poverty alleviation as well as understanding among nations' (UNWTO, 2001, A/RES/56/212, p. 1). The Code further states that 'provided a number of principles and a certain number of rules are observed' it should be possible to reconcile tourism in its increasingly prominent role in the services industry with contending issues in international trade such that all stakeholders in tourism development – 'with different albeit interdependent responsibilities . . . rights and duties' – will contribute collectively to this aim. This is envisioned through 'genuine' partnership and cooperation between public and private stakeholders in tourism development in an 'open and balanced way'.

In sum, the UNWTO calls upon all individuals involved in tourism-related organizations – from local destinations to tourism generating and receiving economies and their negotiations in global trade organizations – to develop and adhere to 'a set of interdependent principles for the interpretation and application' of the Code of Ethics for Tourism. This provides a business ethics framework for examining the effect of international tourism policy issues as they apply to contemporary local, state/provincial, regional, national and international affairs.

In this light, following is a set of core tourism policy component issues (identified in spring 2005 by Master of Tourism Administration candidates in The George Washington University Tourism Policy Analysis course – TSTD 262.10 – taught by Dr Ginger Smith, co-author, and Juan Luna-Kelser):

- Guidelines/set of rules/regulation for the common good/influence behaviour/education;
- Framework – participatory process;
- Codes of conduct;
- Philosophy – vision to make tourism 'the sector';
- Dynamic change;
- Collaboration/converging views = effective policy;
- Consensus among key stakeholders;
- Based on research – measurable.

In consideration of these elements, the co-authors developed their tourism policy definition as first framed in Chapter 1 to say tourism policy is 'a progressive course of actions, guidelines, directives, principles, and procedures set in an ethical framework that is issues-focused and best represents the intent of a community (or nation) to effectively meet its planning, development, product, service, marketing, and sustainability goals and objectives for the future growth of tourism'.

Types of tourism policy evaluation stages

To understand key tourism policy issues in the largest possible context, it is especially important for students to identify in what stage of tourism policy development a particular project or case resides. Aligning the tourism policy analysis with the proper developmental phase of tourism is a critical first step in establishing a robust research design that is both supported by adequate and accessible data and able to be completed on funding deadlines or a timeline viable to the client (which includes semester-based course professors). In this regard, a brief overview of three tourism policy development segments is offered here, with greater emphasis on the third – the summative stage – as the most useful for contemporary tourism policy analysis and destination management research.

Stage 1. Formative phase tourism policy evaluation

The formative phase in tourism policy development means exactly this – that tourism-related issues have arisen requiring new tourism policy formulation. This can occur at any level of stakeholders in the desired outcome – from local citizens to relations between and among nations. A rapid rise in tourist visits to popular 'gateway' or entry communities, whether the US National Forests in Colorado or Arizona or to cultural heritage sites such as Machu Picchu, Peru (shown in Figure 3.1), have fostered unplanned tourism development. This has led to unexpected needs for formative tourism policies to cope with increased road congestion and pollution, potable water over-consumption, public utility resources depletion and real estate price escalation resulting in a scarcity of affordable housing for local citizens employed in the new hotels, car rental agencies and other travel-related businesses. As a result, tourism development revenues are not equally distributed. Furthermore, these overly popular

Figure 3.1 Machu Picchu, sometimes called the Lost City of the Incas, has been restored to near its pre-Columbian appearance after being rediscovered in 1911 (Photo: Matt Schuttloffel)

original destinations then become degraded, putting at risk their inherent environmental, sociocultural and heritage values important to both tourism and local level quality of life. Thus, a well-known, mature tourism destination such as Machu Picchu must, for the sake of its own future success as a world heritage destination, reformulate its tourism policies regarding the sustainability of its infrastructure and provision of quality tourism products and services.

Other drivers for tourism policy analysis at the formative phase can be to evaluate a decision on the part of a tourism organization, destination or entire industry sector to participate in new technology. A powerful example of this at the tourism organization and destination management levels is provided by the 11 September 2001, terrorist airplane attacks in the United States on the New York City World Trade Center towers and the US Pentagon outside Washington, DC. Bill Hanbury, president of the Washington DC Convention and Visitors Corporation, was confronted by a 'new' and historic event in the United States that, at large, severely affected travel to and within the United States and the District of Columbia (DC). The US east coast suffered region-wide telephone outages on September 11 preventing President Hanbury's communication with his own employees as well as with DC public officials. Within days after September 11, he developed an unplanned, unanticipated formative tourism policy methodology for the creation of a reliable, networked alternative emergency information communication system encompassing the DC convention centre and US national capital region as a whole. The true value of this formative phase tourism policy for heightened communication preparedness fortunately to date has not been measurable in a comparable emergency situation (Hanbury, 2002). This underscores the challenge in data collection in conducting formative phase tourism policy research.

Stage 2. Development phase tourism policy evaluation

Similarly, development phase tourism policy analysis is extremely important in many instances as it enables evaluation of policy implementation midstream. In 1999, for example, the Government of Belize established a new tourism policy placing high priority on tourism as a preferential development option with a focus on the cruise ship sector. In addition to international tourism promotion to Belize, the results also included a development phase tourism policy plan for environmental compliance for live-aboard passenger vessels, including cruise ships visiting Belize Harbour. It was premised on reassurances to Belize local tourism industry stakeholders that efforts would be made by the Department of the Environment in conjunction with the Fisheries Department and Belize Tourism Board to ensure the sustainability of the Belize tourism industry as a whole. New tourism policy rules and regulations were developed covering such issues as anchoring of cruise ships, waste disposal and passenger recreational activities onboard, such as requiring the purchase of seasonal fish and locally grown produce versus imported food. Onshore, tourism policy rules included requirements for the preservation of coral reefs during tourist diving and snorkeling activities, among others. As the cruise industry to Belize progresses, a monitoring system put in place now assists in a review and ongoing assessment of the effectiveness of the tourism development intentions of the tourism policy plan (Toy, 2004).

Stage 3. Summative phase tourism policy evaluation

Many examples exist of summative phase tourism policy analysis which evaluates long-standing policy issues and accepted norms and doctrines for continued validity. This phase often provides the most available opportunities for semester-long student tourism policy case studies and/or research projects. For example, when the citizens of the US State of Colorado in 1994 voted to oppose the continuation of an existing state tax for state tourism marketing, Colorado fell in three years from the top five to 17th place in US state travel destinations (Sommars, 1997, pp. 16–21). Only a short duration was required for summative evaluation of the adverse results of the tax policy eliminating funding for tourism marketing and promotion to Colorado. Summative phase tourism policy research requires that evaluation questions be matched with appropriate information gathering techniques, the data collected and analysed, and tourism policy information and advice provided to public and private sector officials and other interested parties.

Another example of summative phase tourism policy analysis would be to study tourism issues serving as indicators of improved relations among neighbouring economies. With an overarching goal to improve relations between Pakistan and India, the objective is to create international tourism between the two countries to gain greater mutual understanding among citizens and increased currency exchange. Tourism facilitation includes air rights policy to create air routes between the two countries and border crossing policy to speed visa approvals. Measurable tourism policy issues in the summative evaluation might include the number of flown routes and visa inquiries and permits issued (Figure 3.2).

In conclusion of this section, one word about methodological approaches for the study of tourism policy, whatever the evaluations phase. Tourism policy provides a lively domain for contemporary quantitative and qualitative research – or a mixture of both. Comparative case study research, used in support of a larger tourism policy critical analysis framework, provides an especially rich laboratory.

Figure 3.2   The Palacio de Justicia is a popular sight to see in Lima, Peru (Photo: Matt Schuttloffel)

Importance of tourism policy issues

Why are ongoing evaluations of tourism policy issues in all contexts important? It is because of tourism's integrative role in triggering growth – for better or worse in some cases – across multiple sectors of local, state/provincial, regional, national and international business commerce and services industries worldwide. Tourism's performance as an optimal growth multiplier in economic development for a large majority of modern economies matches up well against current given and future perceived needs. Not always, but often, tourism is viewed as fungible across the spectrum of economic, sociocultural and environmental aspects of development – a premier standing as well as a tall order for tourism policy issues.

Tourism, regulation and public policy

Sustainable tourism, sex tourism, traveller safety and security and health and medical tourism, among others are examples of sub-factors involving regulation, planning and public policy related to tourism. As significant in the future as they are today, such issues are covered in greater depth in Chapter 10 'Tourism Policy Issues for Tomorrow'.

Even within one tourism industry segment, multiple issues exist that require tourism policy and planning. For example, international airline industries carry cargo and passengers making air rights and safety issues consummate. Cargo is rarely checked for bombs whereas domestic travellers' luggage is thoroughly checked. Effecting change to include cargo inspection could lead to a $3.6 billion dollar cost to the industry (Frank, 2005, p. 01a). With aviation air rights, it is a function, in a sense, of who owns the air and what means are used to protect the citizens while allowing air traffic. Tourism policy in this arena collides with privacy rights and business profits versus traveller safety and security issues, as acutely experienced by both international leisure and business travellers since September 11.

Furthermore, airlines often are seen as a major catalyst in conducting business. City managers for smaller cities see airlines as an integral part of attracting business (De Lollis and Hansen, 2002). Colleges also see airlines as a key component to recruiting students (Brush and Straut, 2005, p.1p, 1c). Hence, city managers must address both business and college needs as well as tourists.

Sex tourism

Policy as created by elected officials can demonstrate which path to take on ethical issues in tourism. Currently, countries such as Thailand are experiencing an increase in tourism demand due to sex tourism (tourism activities which lead to sexual activity, particularly involving children). 'In 1998, the International Labour Organization reported its calculations that 2–14 per cent of the gross domestic product of Indonesia, Malaysia, the Philippines and Thailand derives from sex tourism. In addition, while Asian countries, including Thailand, India and the Philippines, have long been prime destinations for child sex tourists, in recent years, tourists have increasingly travelled to Mexico and Central America for their sexual exploits as well' (Nair, 2006). Countries which are starved for hard foreign currency often look the other way as the cash flows in (Nair). Western governments, including the United States, are now enacting laws which allow prosecution for sex tourism and the tourists despite the crimes taking place in foreign soil. Existing laws make it illegal to travel with the intent to have sex with a minor. Proposals for new laws that would make it illegal to have sex with a child in another country are now being pursued. Policy creation and implementation is complex and difficult to implement as the activities are international in scope, with victims and perpetuators coming from different countries. Further complicating this situation is the fact that each country, in many cases, has jurisdiction over only part of the criminal activity. To give more force to existing laws, a bill was introduced in the US Government on 28 April 2005, entitled the 'End Demand for Sex Trafficking Act of 2005.' The bill included a provision that would amend the language specifically to state that individuals engaging in sexual activity can be charged with a criminal offense as 'a purchaser of commercial sexual activities'. Passage of this amendment would clarify for federal prosecutors that enforcement of the law can and should be used to prosecute US-based sex tour operators (Equality Now, 2006). Further efforts to eliminate child sex tourism are being pursued by the tourism industry itself.

European airlines are showing videos on their long-haul flights, which inform travellers of the laws against child sex tourism. The Untied Nations World Tourism Organization (UNWTO) established a Child Prostitution and Tourism Watch Task Force, whose goals are to 'prevent, uncover, isolate and eradicate' the exploitation of children in the sex trade. The International Federation of Women's Travel Organizations (IFWTO) holds seminars across the United States and globally to educate their members about the problems of child sex tourism and what they can do to help.

In 1994, the Universal Federation of Travel Agents' Association (UFTAA) was the first tourism industry organization to adopt the Child and Travel Agents' Charter. In 1996, the members of the International Air Transport Association (IATA) unanimously passed a resolution condemning the commercial sexual exploitation of children.

- A 'No Child Sex Tourism' logo has been adopted worldwide by industry organizations that are actively working to prevent and eliminate child prostitution. These sticker-logos can be obtained from the IFWTO.
- In 1996, the International Hotel and Restaurant Association passed a resolution against the sexual exploitation of children and published a leaflet urging its members to help stop child sex tourism.
- In Europe, tour operators have adopted codes of conduct for agents to combat sex tourism (ECPAT, 2006).

In other words, various approaches to implementing tourism policy goals are being used to fight sex tourism. While these efforts do not use the force of law, the approaches do include moral persuasion for both the industry and the consumer. The question remains whether voluntary tourism policy compliance is enough in the face of this tragic human activity.

Tourism and health related issues

As the recent Severe Acute Respiratory Syndrome (SARS) epidemic demonstrated, health concerns are now a major factor in tourism. In some cases, the concerns for health are positive for the industry. For example, the rapid growth in the health spa industry has created an upscale niche in the travel-for-health market; however, other health concerns have a negative impact on the industry such as SARS, AIDS and other contagious diseases that are spread much more rapidly in part because of tourism and its related activities. Should one country be able to prohibit or strongly discourage travel to another nation and effectively cripple another country's economy? Policy decisions on limiting travel to countries with an epidemic may result in a significant downturn in travel overall and, in turn, affect the supporting travel and tourism infrastructure worldwide. The SARS epidemic affected travel to Asian nations with a ripple effect that resulted in lower Visa credit card use. The Asian market 'was significantly affected by the downturn in tourism prompted by the outbreak of SARS, but volume has been returning to normal there in recent weeks', Visa said (Lee, 2003, p. 20).

Often medical travel offers another set of competing policy needs. As medical practices improve worldwide, many countries offer tourism combined with plastic surgery. 'The Confederation of Indian Industries estimates that 150,000 foreign patients came to India for treatment in 2004. And McKinsey & Co., an international consulting firm, estimates that outsourced medical care could bring India $2.2 billion a year by 2012' (Landers, 2005).

Issues centre on insurance, monitoring medical practices and malpractice – both insurance for the doctors and prosecution for poor medical services provided during medical tourism. At what level should citizens who are used to high levels of government intervention in medical practices expect the same protections when travelling in other countries? And, to what level should the governments of these countries of origin for medical tourism intervene to protect its citizens while abroad? This concern for citizens' medical safety is not limited to exposure to germs and viruses from other countries; the continued growth of adventure travel has resulted in more mishaps needing attention. Rescue missions, field emergency medicine – the appropriateness of government resources being used to aid people who undertake risky travel behaviour – have all come to the forefront as tourists increasingly explore multiple environments and seek new travel experiences worldwide.

Tourism and safety/security

As a result of September 11 and the spate of terrorist bombings throughout the world, safety for groups is a leading policy issue for tourism and safety officials. Policy clashes between privacy and safety abound. There are personal privacy issues such as luggage checks, personal scans and body checks versus the need to ensure that the person and their belongings are weapon free. Information conflicts are common – access to tourism data routinely collected (name, address, credit card information, personal preferences) and who is allowed to access such information.

To what extent should governments be allowed to view and use the information gathered by various tourism entities (particularly airline computerized reservation and Personal Information Number/PIN data)? Ongoing debate centres on the legality of expanded use of the US Department of Homeland Security data-mining program called Automated Targeting System. Its expansion and redesign from cargo screening to create a vast database of terrorism risk assessments including name, date of birth, flight itineraries, credit card information and customs inspector's interview notes for every traveller who enters or leaves the country has triggered an information ownership and security contest between the government and airlines. Outcries from the US American Civil Liberties Union regarding privacy issues also include concerns regarding the unauthorized sale of such information for marketing purposes. How can this traveller information be used and by whom; and at what point should there be tourism policy interventions by private sectors and governments on controlling access to such information? Tourism brings clashing values to the forefront. Privacy versus security, freedom to move around versus safety are two such examples, and both issues then conflict with a locality or travel company's right to economic freedom. Policy formulation helps guide government officials attempting to weigh these factors in decision-making and planning.

Space travel

Space tourism is one of hottest new tourism activities today. Issues arising from this present new, creative requirements in tourism policy and planning. One of the contending issues, logically, is overall investment costs of which the launch itself is a large part. It is believed that the only potential means for significant reduction of the recurrent launch cost, which results in a stimulation of human space colonization, is to make the launcher reusable, to increase its reliability and to make it suitable for new markets such as mass space tourism. Space projects that have long-range aspects are very difficult to finance as all interested parties, even politicians, expect to see a reasonable benefit during their period of involvement or term in office. They want to be able to explain this investment to the investing companies or to the taxpayers. Planners are then forced to use benefit models instead of intuitive judgment to convince skeptical decision makers to support new investments in space. Benefit models provide insights into complex relationships and compel a better definition of goals and expected benefits to be gained from a new space venture.

One main objective as to why humans should explore space is to 'improve the quality of life'; and this is important to different interest groups – the operator of a space transportation system, the passenger and the government for various reasons. For example, the operator is strongly interested in profit, the passenger's interest is in amusement, while the government is primarily interested in self-esteem, prestige and increased national security. Each perspective leads to different individual satisfaction levels. For example, on April 22, 2007, US billionaire Charles Simonyi, 58, a native of Hungary who helped design Microsoft Word and Excel, landed in the Kazakh steppe in a Russian space capsule after completing a two-week, $25 million, voyage of his childhood dreams to the international space station (Washington Post, April 22, 2007, A21). And Simonyi is not the first and far from the last space tourist, following 'in the footsteps of Dennis Tito, Mark Shuttleworth, Gregory Olsen and Anousheh Ansari – all of whom have also traveled to the international space station aboard Russian rockets in trips brokered by US-based Space Adventures Ltd.' (A21). Combined, these interests contribute to optimization in the development process for reusable launch vehicles (American Institute of Physics in Goehlich, 2003). Further discussion of this topic occurs in Chapter 10.

Agritourism

The significance of agriculture in social terms stems largely from a community's desire to retain agriculture's aesthetic and heritage values and their contribution to sense of place and charm. Consistent with the findings from US studies that indicate resident attitudes are influenced by 'amenity value' rather than production value, perceptions about agriculture find many individuals consider agriculture very important or of higher importance but they have little understanding regarding the actual situation of agriculture in terms of economic contribution, benefits to the region, land uses and the implications of changes in agricultural production in the future. The direct aims are to generate jobs and increase returns to farmers while the indirect aims are landscape conservation through retention of agriculture, attitudinal changes in the farming community to farming practices, marketing and diversification and sustainable development that links the farming community to other sectors of the economy (Figure 3.3).

What does a destination need to do to become an agritourism attraction? Guidelines vary from country to country, and regimes can be highly bureaucratic. In the Veneto region of Italy, farmers providing holidays are limited to hosting 30 overnight guests per night for a maximum of 160 days per year and must sell over 50 per cent of the food they produce to tourists. In Britain, Germany and elsewhere, there are stringent health and safety controls, including fire regulations and rules governing contact with farm animals (Gumbel, 2004). All in all, agritourism is blooming worldwide and cultivating the need for tourism policy and planning in this emerging tourism sector.

Figure 3.3 The Crook Farm in Bradford, Pennsylvania has been turned into a community asset that is important to both visitors and residents alike (Photo: Jason Swanson)

Complexity of tourism policy issues

Why are tourism issues more complex when introduced into the tourism policy domain? Understanding the interrelated nature of tourism industry sectors requires monitoring and evaluation when tourism policy issues are involved. Measurement and monitoring are essential to transportation systems that move people, products and services, which, in turn, make up a major component of the international tourism industry. Similarly, restaurants and entertainment organizations serve local residents and tourists alike and are involved in business activities (such as special events, conferences and meeting planning) that are demanded by both populations. This duality adds additional complexities to the planning process for simultaneous usage in areas accommodating both tourist and host community needs. Seasonal activities with peak period use, as in ski or beach resort locations, greatly benefit from tourism policy, planning, development and evaluation in understanding 'best use' growth and sustainability measures.

Policy uses tools such as zoning to aid tourism development while mitigating the potentially negative impacts of growth and development. Minas Gerais State in Brazil, for example, currently is experiencing minimal water contamination. This situation is expected to destabilize as water demands rise due to increases in tourism-related activities (increased influx of visitors accompanied by a growing residential workforce supporting the industry). Zoning to protect the natural resources, which in turn protects water quality, is being recommended. In Colorado, USA, zoning has been used in an effort to mediate the competing needs of the tourists and the local community. 'Over the past decade, county and city officials, tourism leaders and local ranchers in Routt County, Colorado, have worked together to preserve the remaining agricultural open space' (Parizzi et al., 2001, p. 57). With a change in zoning laws, one county adopted regulations that encouraged clustering homes to preserve open space. Housing lot size requirements were reduced allowing developers to build more units using a smaller footprint overall. In exchange, the developers must set aside undeveloped land as open space. In other words, zoning concerns involve allocation of scarce land, public and private utility, and public support services and resources – what to put where and who to best undertake and accommodate tourism policy goals and objectives are important agenda items.

Tourism technologies and information communication

A great majority of travel and tourism companies worldwide are small-to-medium-sized enterprises. Via the World Wide Web, strategically managed smaller companies now can compete with larger companies for international visibility and positioning. This combination of attributes places the tourism industry in an excellent position to achieve world leadership in the movement and management of capital and information embodied in global trade in service industries. For this reason, tourism services industries dominate supply and demand for travel-related reservation systems. The case study developed by Zachary Rozga included at the end of this chapter illustrates this synergy and access to power in terms of information distribution on the Websites of small family-run tourism hotel businesses throughout South Africa, now linked with the rest of the world via simply designed Web pages in a communication telecommunications network called the World Hotel Link.

Since the late 1970s, growth of airline and car rental computerized reservations systems has occurred rapidly. The hotel industry lagged behind, starting later in the 1980s with the advent of THISCO (the hotel information system coalition), a hotel reservation system opening first-time Internet access to tourist hotel bookings online with later links to online airline reservations systems. The tremendous expansion and diversification over the last two decades of online tourism products and services (ticketing, car rentals, hotels rooms, transportation, tour operators, etc.) beyond basic travel services formerly provided by airline computer reservation systems, such as American Airlines' Sabre CRS, typify the high value now placed on the collection and (re)distribution of tourism consumer information and financial expenditures (much of it via credit cards).

Tax legislation

Tourism and taxes have brought the industry to the forefront of travellers' concern. While seeking the benefits of the industry, travellers often do not want to support the infrastructure. As noted earlier, Colorado experienced a large decrease in tourism when the travel-marketing budget was reduced. Taxing residents to support the tourism industry is as unpopular as other taxes; therefore, city officials often tax the visitors. Councilor Bob Finsland from Superior, Wisconsin, USA, has gone on record as saying the extra revenue could go toward tourism facilities and events, such as hockey tournaments, thereby attracting organizations to host similar events in the city. 'I think there are a lot of ways to use that money wisely as far as tourism development goes', Finsland said. 'We don't want to raise the taxes on individual citizens of Superior. We don't want to raise the taxes to the individual motel owners. We want to raise the taxes for the people who stay at these hotels and pass through our city' (Reinke, 2006).

Another example of this thought process emanates from the USA Commonwealth of Virginia – '... the additional tax shall be designated and spent for the development and improvement of the Virginia Performing Arts Foundation's facilities in Richmond, for promoting the use of the Richmond Centre, and for promoting tourism, travel or business that generates tourism and travel in the Richmond metropolitan area' (Virginia Tax Code, §58.1-3823). Other Virginian localities, such as Williamsburg, levy a flat $2.00 fee per occupied room night in lodging establishments for marketing the historic triangle of Williamsburg, James City County and Yorktown, which is shown in Figure 3.4.

Internationally, European finance ministers are leaning toward legislation taxing airline passengers to finance development aid for foreign countries. The EU airline industry is fighting this new tax saying it threatens jobs and tourism (Tardy, 2005, p. 3). Tax issues are divisive – on the one hand, they are necessary for generating revenue to finance the tourism industry. On the other hand, travellers are growing weary of the added expense to the trip. In some places, auto rental taxes can be as much as 40 per cent of the bill.

International development aid

Finance for tourism development often requires an international commitment. The World Bank is heavily involved with committing monetary resources to sustainable tourism projects. Through the International

Figure 3.4 The historic waterfront district in Yorktown, Virginia adds to the Historical Triangle experience (Photo: Jason Swanson)

Development Association (IDA), the World Bank grants long-term interest free loans and grants for the purpose of supporting economic growth, reducing poverty and improving living conditions. 'IDA's long-term no-interest loans pay for programs that build the policies, institutions, infrastructure and human capital needed for equitable and environmentally sustainable development. IDA's grants go to poor countries already vulnerable to debt or confronting the ravages of HIV/AIDS or natural disasters' (WorldBank.org).

Three factors determine eligibility for assistance:

- Relative poverty, defined as Gross National Product (income) per person below an established threshold, currently US $965 per year.
- Lack of credit worthiness to borrow on market terms and therefore a need for concessional resources to finance the country's development program.
- Good policy performance, defined as the implementation of economic and social policies that promote growth and poverty reduction (WorldBank.org).

The top 10 borrower countries in fiscal year 2005, according to the US World Bank, are shown in Table 3.1. Two examples of World Bank/IDA supported projects are Mozambique's initiatives in conservation and tourism development. The first initiative resulted in support with an 'IDA credit of US $20 million to support the conservation of biodiversity and natural ecosystems as well as promote economic growth and development

Table 3.1 FY05 top 10 IDA borrowers

Borrowers	US $ million
India	1, 138
Vietnam	699
Bangladesh	600
Pakistan	500
Ethiopia	450
Ghana	364
Tanzania	356
Nigeria	330
Uganda	328
Afghanistan	285

Source: The World Bank.

based on the sustainable use of natural resources by local communities in Mozambique' (M2 Presswire, 2005). This demonstrates the interconnectedness of tourism and other municipal functions – and, therefore, requires policies that cross departmental boundaries. IDA has also supported a project emphasizing ecological and commercially sustainable solid waste collection and disposal services in Montenegro coastal municipalities, which are needed to maintain a clean, environmentally attractive coastal area for tourism development. It is hoped that the project also will help develop the sector's institutional policy and regulatory framework and benefit tourism prospects by eliminating solid waste collection and disposal problems negatively affecting coastal tourist areas.

Banking loans and bonds

Alternative sources for financing include bank loans and bonds. Often poor nations turn to these sources when they have exhausted the IDA backing. Developing nations often turn to wealthy countries for support through direct loans – where the bank backs the money and bonds are floated, then used as collateral for the loans. The Japan Bank for International Cooperation has agreed on an IDA loan totalling 5.732bn yen (US $52.874m) with Egypt, for the Borg El Arab International Airport Modernization Project. The development consists of the construction of an air terminal with a capacity of one million passengers and 4000 tons of cargo annually, as well as improvements in related facilities at the airport, 40 km southwest of Alexandria (JBIC 2005).

Guam, a US territory in the Pacific Ocean, can issue bonds that are exempt from federal, state and local income taxes. The island's growing tourism industry and a planned increase in US military personnel point to economic developments necessitating more spending on infrastructure. Infrastructure improvements, however, financed by military construction funds will not address all of Guam's critical infrastructure, essential services and economic development needs.

Proceeds from bonds sales would be reissued in the form of loans to finance reconstruction projects. Like the bond banks that already serve 12 US states, a US territory bond bank would use federal grant money as collateral to guarantee the loans. The concept of a bond bank was discussed in 19 April, 2006, at a meeting of the Interagency Group on Insular Areas, which coordinates federal policy toward Guam, American Samoa, the US Virgin Islands and the Northern Mariana Islands (McConnell, 2006).

Grants

Grants are a preferred method of obtaining money for tourism development because no repayment is required; however, one condition often set forth is that matching amounts of money must be raised to receive the grants. Other stipulations may include partnerships or other support mechanisms. A project in Mozambique, which received IDA money, also received grants. The Global Environment Facility (GEF) Board, which approved the credit was also financed by a US $10 million grant in accordance with the work program approved by the GEF Council in October 2005 as well as a US $3.7 million grant from the Japanese Policy and Human Resources Development (PHRD) Fund (M2 Presswire, 2005).

Tourism policy issues, destination management and the future – an open-ended conclusion

Weimer and Vining (2005) state that in its simplest definition 'policy analysis is client-oriented advice relevant to public decisions and informed by social values' (p. 24) and offer their conclusion that, '[t]he professions of planning and public administration have moved much closer to the policy analysis paradigm in recent years' (p. 25). In other words, anytime an action or activity related to tourism may have an effect on a group or location is what, when, and where tourism policy issues matter the most at the destination management level.

Tourism policy at its best provides direction for the management of destination organizations around a unified strategic plan without which people may inadvertently or intentionally enact conflicting laws or rules negating tourism policy planning attributes. Preservation of status quo versus environmental sustainability for tourism purposes will continue as a debate worldwide in the areas of tourist access to world monuments and cultural heritage sites. National park year-round recreational access via snowmobiles and other off-road vehicles versus limited off-season use in support of nature and wildlife preservation are permanent issues in tourism policy evaluation in most regions of the world. State-controlled forest fires versus unregulated wild fires also challenge tourism policy formation in management of recreation with preservation goals.

Other significant issues related to zoning are exemplified in efforts by the Italian hotel industry working with municipal government to manage uncontrolled growth in hotel construction resulting in unsafe hotels built too close together marring historic views. Gettysburg, Pennsylvania, USA, for example, a major US battlefield, also provides both a long history and interesting future for tourism policy and planning regarding the impact of controlled growth as it relates to marketing and demand. Gettysburg deconstructed a privately built and owned look-out tower to 're-authenticate' the original battlefield landscape. Beach communities such as Ocean City, Maryland on the US Atlantic coast, too, must grapple with high tourist numbers during 'spring flings' or college fun tourism. The effect on local residents experiencing seasonally related tourism's 'bombardment' from the outside world requires coordination of tourism policy and planning efforts.

Summary and conclusion

Through all the stages of tourism policy formation, development and implementation, one sees the conflicting needs that call for effective actions and evaluation. Tourism policy provides direction on what action is appropriate. In the formative stage, policy addresses new concerns such as disease or terrorism. At the development phase, policy addresses on-going issues. This is particularly relevant for developing countries and other regions of the world addressing economic, sociocultural and environmental sustainability issues, such as air and water pollution, crowding, degradation and depletion of tourism resources. Lastly, there is the summative stage where existing tourism policy results are reviewed for continued relevancy and efficacy. Tourism policy and planning evolve as the industry itself grows generating new requirements for areas such as commerce activity, telecommunications, sustainability and land use.

Why tourism policy issues point to – and will matter so dramatically in – the future is the way this chapter ends while ongoing evaluation of *how* contending issues central to today's tourism policy development and implementation affect future populations just begins. Adoption of tourism policy issues sustaining all of tourism's environments – natural and physical, human and man-made – would seem the greatest contribution still possible for tourism to make.

Case report 3

WORLD HOTEL LINK – AN ICT (INFORMATION AND COMMUNICATION TECHNOLOGY) DRIVEN APPROACH TO EQUITABLE AND SUSTAINABLE TOURISM

April 2006
Zachary Rozga, The George Washington University Master of Tourism Administration Graduate, President of GeoSavvy Development, Cape Town, South Africa, www.geosavvydev.com, zachary.rozga@gmail.com. To access this and other GW web-based tourism policy case studies, please go to the following link to the GW/American University Trade and Environment (TED) Database (www.american.edu/ted).

Identification

The issue

The question this case study attempts to answer is, how have governments and nongovernmental organizations (NGOs) used information and communication technology (ICT) to improve development of small-to-medium-sized tourism enterprises (SMTEs)?

SMTEs have been targeted in a number of countries as a sector to be focused on for overall economic development of traditionally impoverished and undeveloped lands and peoples. Tourism has been one sector deemed most appropriate for rural developing nations because the point of sale in the commerce is generally in the rural area and provides an alternative form of income generation to traditional agrarian methods.

This case study focuses on a new online booking agent that was created specifically to attend to the needs of the developing world and support SMTEs – The World Hotel Link (WHL).

The Pro-Poor Tourism Partnership says, "One of the critical issues for poor producers is often access to the market – access to the established industry and to tourists". Most small hotels and guesthouses and local NGOs have little or no opportunity to market to tourists via the Internet, thus they gain little share of the dollars tourists spend. Most tourism dollars end up offshore. Typically, only US $10–20 of every US $100 spent by the tourist in developing countries remains in the country. According to United Nations Environment Program, of each US $100 spent on a package tour, only around US $5 actually stays in a developing country's economy.

The George Washington University's International Institute of Tourism Studies (GWU/IITS) commissioned a survey of worldwide tourism development practitioners, academics and stakeholders to assess what issues were concerned with donor-funded tourism development and what they perceived to be the most important issues facing tourism. The number one response from the survey in the "poorest perfor-mance" category was market access for tourism development projects (GWU/IITS, 2004).

Description

In the developed world, some innovative nations have grasped the importance of effective clustering and the use of networks to spread the eco-nomic impact of tourism through proper ICT usage. The Australian Federal Government has realized the impact that the Internet has on promotion of the tourism product, and they also understand the need to have a consistent tourism product. Tourism is a highly fragmented industry that is made up of numerous SMTE (95–98 per cent of all tourism companies fall into this cate-gory), and the success of the industry is based on the sum of the parts. The Department of Industry, Science and Resources created the policy of *Australia dotcom* to aid each and every SMTE to utilize the Internet.

In line with that thinking a small team of tourism, sustainability and technology specialists set out to find an ICT-driven solution to market access for developing world SMTE accommodation providers. The out-come, the World Hotel Link (WHL), offers a unique online platform to help small and mid-sized accommodation providers market sustainable tourism to the independent traveller. Launched as an IFC technical assis-tance project for hotels and guesthouses in Vietnam, Cambodia and Laos in 2004, it is now a private company whose various sites in an ever-increasing number of countries (30 plus in May 2006) attract about 5000 visitors a day.

Although parallels to the WHL (www.worldhotel-link.com) model can be drawn with Expedia, Orbitz and Hostelworld, it is different in that it has been designed specifically for the developing world, seeking to:

- bridge the digital divide
- deliver pro-poor outcomes and
- drive the uptake of sustainable tourism practices.

Each destination is served by a *local* e-marketplace operator (MPO) who is responsible for collecting and managing content for the Websites, responding promptly to travellers on the booking system and interfacing with accommodation providers. The local MPO serves as an ICT intermediary for product owners who may not communicate in English, possess technical skills or have access to ICT facilities. Meanwhile, the global WHL acts as an intermediary for the local MPOs by undertaking central coordination; improving technology development/support; and undertaking Web marketing, data hosting and online payment gateways, and so on. WHL has been built from the ground up with technology specifically designed to make the franchise MPO model work even for accommodation providers who do not have ICTs including telephones, computers or other easy avenues of communication.

The following model is a representation of how WHL's initiatives are implemented into less developed areas and the how the "Tourism Cluster" by-product is created (Figure 3.5).

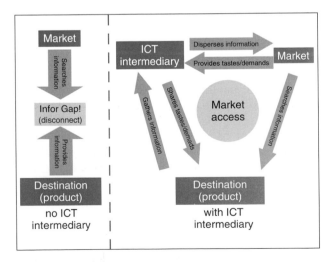

Figure 3.5   Information communication technology (ICT) intermediation [*Source:* Zachary Rozga (copyright 2004)]

The model on the left shows the relationship in an environment without an ICT intermediary. The product and market have a major disconnection, and information flow between them is stopped. In the model on the right, the product is accessible to the market through the intermediary plus the market can provide tastes and demands to the product. As the cycle continues, the process should enhance the product, increasing adherence to the demand of the market, thus providing a better and more sustainable product responsive to market demand.

In addition to bringing SMTEs into the global marketplace, WHL is working with mainstream operators who are trying to make a difference in their destination. To demonstrate the power of ICT networks, WHL is pioneering a new "Sustainable Tourism Ranking" into the booking engine. WHL is leveraging the network of sites and clients – independent travellers booking via the sites – to apply an eBay-style supplier–buyer ratings system to get sustainable tourism on the radar screen.

To date, sustainable tourism has always remained a fringe niche market and not had the profound impact that experts say it does. Under the WHL approach, accommodation providers display their product in a way that helps travellers understand what they are doing whether from an environmental, social or cultural standpoint to care for the local destination. Displayed visually as a "Caring for the Destination" rating, there is an opportunity for travellers to provide feedback and inform other travellers about this product or activity. As demand grows, more suppliers will want to be listed with this rating.

WHL approach as ICT intermediary

WHL sets up and supports local Internet portals that enable smaller hotels and guesthouses to be marketed on the Internet. WHL works as a franchise. Local partners with local knowledge own and operate the local WHL portals while being connected seamlessly to WHL's global network. WHL provides the technical platform, the web marketing and management support.

More stable jobs

The hotels on WHL are usually three-star or less and often depend on walk-in guests, which means their income is unstable. This also means their employees face seasonal unemployment. Increased market access through the WHL allows these SMTEs to become less dependent on walk-ins and have a more regular income, which in turn benefits everyone – hotels have lower employee turnover and provide more stable jobs. It also means more secure income for people in the associated businesses that offer products and services linked to the tourism sector.

WHL makes it easier for independent travellers to find small hoteliers

Independent travel is the fastest growing segment of the travel industry. A 2004 International Finance Corporation study on Eco-Lodges put the global independent traveller market at 50 per cent. Many travellers use guidebooks and the Internet to select destinations and accommodation and rarely use tour packages. Thus they spend and leave more money locally. By serving smaller accommodation providers, WHL is making it easier for independent travellers to find interesting travel experiences, which in turn translates into more bookings for local SMTEs.

Commissions and booking jobs stay local

WHL operates as a global franchise network with local ownership of the booking service in each destination. This means the commissions and booking jobs remain in the country. While WHL charges a monthly service fee to franchise owners, it represents only a small portion of their revenue.

More local accommodation providers

Small local accommodation providers have problems reaching the market. There are large numbers of interesting and unique places to stay in guidebooks, but few are online. Some do not even have a phone number. Thus tourists book only with the hotels they can find on the Web. Because WHL franchisees are local people on the ground with local knowledge, they can actively coach and support the smallest guesthouses who otherwise would not be online or able to receive advance bookings. WHL provides access – a major obstacle for SMTEs – where others cannot.

"Caring for the destination"

Through its sustainability ratings and traveller feedback, WHL encourages local SMTEs to develop and manage interesting traveller experiences through connections with local NGOs and community groups that operate orphanages, schools or hospitals and eco- or cultural projects. Typically, these initiatives benefit the poorest and most vulnerable in the local community, as well as preserving the local culture and environment for future generations.

Providing a global market for sustainability

The approach taken in most regions of the world in driving the uptake of sustainable tourism practices has been driven largely by industry experts and government. It has involved a top-down approach with little effort to engage travellers and has resulted in the production of numerous codes, standards and certification or labelling schemes. The fact is, however, that despite significant expense in developing and promoting these approaches over the past 15 years, industry has largely ignored them, and the travelling public has almost no idea what they are. Even the jargon used extensively by industry players to describe the sector (e.g., terms such as sustainable tourism, responsible travel, eco-travel, geo-savvy, interactive travellers, etc.) remains unfamiliar to the majority of travellers.

Despite this, there is growing evidence that travellers are sensitive to issues of environmental, social and cultural degradation and would prefer, all things being equal, to support those industry players who are doing a good job – economically, environmentally, socially and culturally. This is particularly true of independent travellers. Further, there is a shift occurring from "things to see" type of travel to "things to experience" as travellers seek to connect more closely with the local destination. These travellers are seeking a more genuine travel experience deriving from a closer interaction with the local communities and the natural environment. Recognizing the failure of the certification approach trying to encourage the industry to meet minimum "standards", Worldhotel-link.com Limited (WHL – an accommodation booking company) has developed a new approach with a strong bias toward engaging SMTE accommodation providers and travellers. In this model, SMTE accommodation providers undertaking any activities which preserve a sense of place or are in some way caring for or preserving the destination, socially and/or environmentally, are provided a free branding opportunity on the web (a chance to differentiate themselves), intended to appeal to the growing body of interested (i.e., geo-savvy, responsible, interactive) travellers. These travellers are then encouraged to provide feedback, which is published online, informing other travellers about the initiative (e.g., whether it is real or simply a "green wash"; whether the initiative "moved" them;

whether the accommodation management/staff "walk the talk", etc.). The traveller feedback, if positive, should encourage more like-minded travellers to select the accommodation provider, improving occupancy and returns. By showing SMTE accommodation providers that doing good is good business, this should over time encourage more SMTE accommodation providers to start incorporating initiatives which care for the destination.

In doing the work of collecting information about SMTE accommodation providers to put online, WHL identified many small SMTEs actively engaged in projects, which, in their own way, were positive steps toward improving sustainable outcomes for the destination. None of the initiatives were of themselves "certifiable", but they all were valid. They were meaningful to the SMTE involved and addressed specific local needs. Examples included employing and training orphan children, supporting local schools, running a turtle hatchery, restoring a damaged coral reef, teaching traditional building skills, supporting volunteer workers and restoring historical buildings.

WHL then started to write up some of these initiatives as "brand differentiators" for the respective accommodation providers, highlighting for travellers what the accommodation providers were doing. Some initiatives were small, some large, but many offered the guests either a unique experience or, at least, an opportunity to feel that by staying with this accommodation provider they were doing some good. As a small SMTE, trying to differentiate yourself only on price, location and facilities is a slippery slope. Good service is a given, so what you have left as an option is really related to selling a unique experience, and it is this WHL is tapping. This then led to the idea of an "eBay style" bottom-up sustainable tourism marketing model. The SMTE accommodation provider (the supplier) markets their initiative(s) now a core part of their product, and the traveller (the buyer) after staying at the property gives them a rating and provides feedback online for other travellers to read and evaluate in making their buying decision.

Why is this approach likely to work where others have failed?

First, it is free for the SMTE accommodation provider to participate.

Second, it is up to the accommodation provider what they undertake. This means that programs are more likely to be addressing perceived local needs either at the enterprise level or the community level. This increases ownership. Third, WHL is providing a direct link to a commercial benefit. If travellers like what the accommodation provider is doing and provide positive feedback, more business results. Doing good becomes good business. Fourth, travellers are engaged. They can now feel good about where they are staying and provide positive feedback for others. A virtuous circle has been built.

Regular traveller feedback on the authenticity of the initiatives and the commitment of the SMTEs will play a powerful role in keeping the checks and balances and in driving improvement. This approach also ensures that costs are kept low. Most of the traditional certification systems currently rely on external funding, and Font (2005) says they would not survive without it. According to Font, "Blue Flag has relied on European funds for nearly 15 years, struggling to survive when these finished. The International Network on Fair Trade in Tourism (operating mainly in African countries with support from Tourism Concern from the UK) folded as soon as the donor grant ran out".

Toward a sustainable future

The scheme is inclusive of all stakeholders. It does not detract from traditional top-down expert certification rather it complements it with a truly bottom-up traveller and industry driven component. The WHL vision is to get enough SMTEs involved in this approach at the destination level to start to shape the destination.

Scope

The developing world

Tourism is a major economic sector worldwide and especially in developing countries. According to the World Bank's *World Development Indicators Report 2002*, more than 70 per cent of the world's poorest countries rely on tourism as a key engine of economic growth. Poorer countries have the most to gain from pro-poor tourism initiatives. But they are also the most vulnerable to the negative effects of mass tourism, in terms of social, environmental and cultural degradation.

Geographical framework

International – In the developing world, many individual private sector players, government employees and NGOs have come to understand the importance of the Internet and its effect in the tourism industry. However, many of these players have not understood the expanse and change of the Internet toward commercial ventures as opposed to purely informational. In tourism jargon, this has become known as "booking versus looking". Even when actors have grasped this concept, they have not understood the breadth of sites that exist on the web. Even subregional sites get lost in the myriad of tourism Websites that now exist.

On the other hand, the large well-established international booking agents (Expedia, Travelocity, Opodo, etc.) have not been able to figure out how to sell the developing world to its clientele, mainly due to the fact that there is a greater proliferation of individually owned SMTEs in the developing world that is not on any mainframe booking systems.

WHL is the first booking agent that has understood both the importance of local presence (the MPO) and international branding and marketing.

National – In the developing world, at the national level, there is a real misunderstanding of tourism as a private sector activity. Many times the decision makers at this level have no real tourism experience and do not understand how to market or sell at the enterprise level. Therefore, it is much easier to ignore the situation and focus on the nation as destination and allow the private sector to sort itself out. This attitude has a tendency to isolate nations and allow large private sector (and typically foreign-owned) operators to dominate the value chain. This is the exact behaviour that leads to offshore booking agents dominating the sales and not taking place in the nation. Also, with this attitude, very little information about the destination is maintained locally, increasing reliance on a foreign operator to manage the trip for the traveller out of fear.

Regional – Regions within nations not only do not cooperate to sell the product but battle for individual travellers. Many times adversarial campaigns are undertaken with little understanding of growing the whole market. WHL helps to mitigate concerns by forcing an identity of destination and then by not discriminating who can and who cannot be listed in the destination. WHL will work to ensure that appropriate products are given equal status and add value to the destination.

Local – This is where WHL is at its strongest. As described in the ICT intermediation, many operators have no voice at all in the global tourism value chain. These single "mom and pop" SMTEs are completely ostracized from the mainstream tourism economy, even though they provide the most authentic experience. WHL has specifically engineered the franchise system to allow for adequate coverage to support these SMTEs (Figure 3.6).

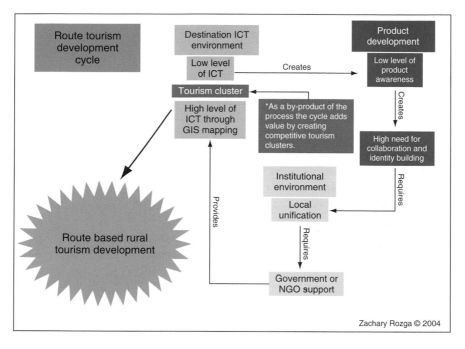

Figure 3.6 Value chain perspective

Conclusion

Policy implications

For nations that are attempting to use tourism as a means of economic stimulus for their country, they must consider the means at which the intended audience will receive this information. The Internet is a powerful tool and must be looked at as a means to broadcast the message about product. Instituting computers, e-mail, software and the Internet to populations of people who do not even have clean running water is a daunting task, yet it is necessary. The governments of countries need to look for innovative means to implement ICT into the rural areas that they are promoting for tourism.

In order to understand the importance of these policy implications, one must consider the sustainability of these projects. At this point, the largest barrier to sustainability is market access. The model depicted in Figure 3.6 is a visual representation of information flow in rural destinations. In areas where most of the inhabitants have never used a telephone, the likelihood of Internet implementation is quite low.

Recommendations

The World Hotel Link concept currently looks at the accommodation portion of a trip. Tours encompass a much wider span of activities and products. The WHL concept should be broadened to capture the spectrum of products such as transportation, handicrafts, eco-activities, adventure sports, safaris, festivals, artistry, and so on.

Governments can learn a great deal about how to manage their destination by looking at the holistic approach that WHL employs from the private sector and find their role in the development process and focus on those activities. Too often government tries to play too large a role in tourism development and disconnects with the market and in the end the traveller.

As a model, the WHL platform could quite nicely work in other industries that affect the economies of the developing world.

Social

The idea behind the policy of community-based tourism promotion is to protect the cultural heritage and value of the local population that some culture focused routes take place in. Some examples of where this has been extremely successful in the developed world are *The Camino de Santiago* in Northern Spain and Southern France and *Hadrian's Wall* in Northern England. Both of these destinations were driven by government policies to enhance rural livelihood through the promotion of cultural preservation and tourism.

In both cases, on macro-level planning, importance was placed on creating defined strings of clusters that were displayed and defined geographically using GIS and Internet technologies. Without the economies of scale for multiplying the budgets and efforts of local municipalities, they would never have been able to raise the amount of private sector or donor support. As well, the necessary infrastructural demands would not have been met to create an effective globally competitive destination.

Environmental

Tourism historically has been criticized as a major detriment to the environment. The World Hotel Link ICT model attempts to engage the traveler as well as the host destination in tourism development that is environmentally sustainable.

Economic

The hope is that these routes will provide economic stimulus to the developing areas. The goal is to provide jobs, income and basic infrastructure to impoverished regions through tourism.

Other

One other impact is a positive one as well. The hope is through showing the rural populations the benefits of ICT they will gain in interest in the various technologies. This will ease the eventual facilitation of training and hardware into the rural areas.

Bibliography for case report 3

Aniskovich, J. and M. Donohue. (2006). Culture and Tourism Partnership, Grants Available, *US Fed News Service*, Including US State News, Washington, DC, January 20.

Brush, S. and E. Strout. (2005). Cutbacks at Small Airports Threaten to Leave Some Colleges Stranded, *Chronicle of Higher Education*; **52**(6), September 30, p. A33–A33, 1p, 1c.

Ceballos-Lascurain, H. (1996). *Tourism, Ecotourism and Protected Areas*. Gland, Switzerland: IUCN. Based on papers presented at the tourism workshops held during the IV World Congress on National Parks and Protected Areas, Caracas, Venezuela, 10–21 February 1992, and additional material and research.

Corser, S. and R. Knack. (2003). From Ranchland to Conservation Community. *Planning*. Chicago, **69**(8), August/September, 26.

Coulton, A. (1997). Affinity Card Targets Visitors to Branson, Mo. Series: 18 *American Banker*, New York, NY, **162**(144), July 29, 28.

De Lollis B. and B. Hansen. (2002). Airlines Abandon Small Cities, *USA Today*, November 23.

Dickerson, M., (2006). *Buoyant Belize Cruise Trade May Sink Paradise. Los Angeles Time*, March 13.

Economist. (2005). *In Terminal Decline?*, 00130613, Vol. 374, January 18.

ECPAT (04/10/2006) Child Sex Tourism, http://www.ecpatusa.org/travel_tourism.asp.

Edgell, D., Sr. (1999). *Tourism Policy: The Next Millennium*. Sagamore, Champaign, IL.

Equality Now, (10/2006) Women's Action 27.1, http://www.equalitynow.org/english/actions/action_2701_en.html.

Fennell, D., and R. Dowling (Eds). (2003). *Ecotourism Policy and Planning*. Cabi, NY.

Frank, T. (2005). Report: Most Airline Cargo Isn't Checked for Explosives, USA Today Section: News, November 16, 01a.

Garrett, R. (2006). City Needs $8 Million Match: $40 Million Riverfront Grant Requires Local Contribution, *Knight Ridder Tribune Business News*, Washington, DC, February 3, 1.

Gmelch, G. (2003). *Behind the Smile: The Working Lives of Caribbean Tourism*. Indiana University, IN.

Goehlich, R. (2003). Benefit Estimation Model for Tourist Spaceflights, *AIP Conference Proceedings*; 2003, **654**(1), p. 1049, p. 8.

Gumbel, P. (2004). Making A Living Off the Land Vacationers Are Increasingly Turning to the Pastoral Pleasures of Rural Holidays – and Europe's Farmers Are Reaping the Benefits, *Time International* (Atlantic ed.), New York, **164**(6), August 16, Olympic Preview, 70.

Hall, M. and J. Jenkins (1995). *Tourism and Public Policy*. Routledge, NY.

Hanbury, W. (2002). Personal interview, DC Convention and Visitors Corporation, Washington, DC.

Hatziolos, M., A. Hooten and M. Fodor (Eds). (1998). *Coral Reefs: Challenges and Opportunities for Sustainable Management*. World Bank, Washington, DC.

Howe, J., E. McMahon and L. Propst. (1997). *Balancing Nature and Commerce in Gateway Communities*. Island Press, Washington, DC.

JBIC Supports Airport Modernisation in Egypt. (2005). *Anonymous*. Middle East. London, May, no. 356, 49.

Landers, J. (2005). 'Medical Tourism' on Rise, *Advertising Age*. (Midwest region edition). Chicago, **76**(47), p. 14, p. 1, November 21.

Laws, E., B. Faulkner and G. Moscardo (Eds). (1998). *Embracing and Managing Change in Tourism: International Case Studies*. Routledge, NY.

Lee, W. (2003). In Brief: Visa Card Volume Climbs 10.8%, *American Banker*, New York, NY, **168**(142), July 25, 20.

M2 Presswire. (2005). World Bank: Mozambique receives assistance for conservation and tourism development project, December 2 (accessed 12 April 2006).

McConnell, A., M2 Communications Ltd. (2006). Guam Representative Urges Pooled Bond Bank for Territories. *Bond Buyer*, New York March 3, **355**(32331), 6.

McCool, S. and R. Moisey. Monitoring Resident Attitudes Toward Tourism– http://www.forestry.umt.edu/personnel/faculty/smccool/personal%20website/ Recent%20Publications_files/monitoringresidentatittudes.pdf.

Nair, S. (2006). Child Sex Tourism. http://www.usdoj.gov/criminal/ceos/sextour. html (accessed 10 March 2006).

Parizzi, M., L. Velasquez, A. Uhlein, P. Aranha and J. Goncalves. (2001). Environment, Tourism and Land Use Planning – Riachinho Basin, Brazil. *Environmental Management and Health*. Bradford, **12**(1), 57.

Pizam, A. and G. Smith. (2000). Tourism and Terrorism: A Quantitative Analysis of Major Terrorist Acts and Their Impact on Tourism Destinations, *Tourism Economics*, **6**(2), 123–128.

Reinke, M. (2000). *Tourism and Heritage Relationships: Global, National and Local Perspectives*. Centre for Travel and Tourism and Business Education, UK.

Reinke, M. (2006). *Superior, Wis., City Council Votes Against 2 Percent Hotel-Tax Hike* .Knight Ridder Tribune Business News, Washington, DC, March 22, 1.

Robinson, M., J. Swarbrooke, N. Evans, P. Long, and R. Sharpley (Eds). (2000). *Environmental Management and Pathways to Sustainable Tourism*. Centre for Travel and Tourism and Business Education, UK.

Smith, G., and H. Mowlana. (1993). Tourism in a Global Context: The Case of Frequent Traveler Programs. *Journal of Travel Research*, **31**(3), 20–28.

Smith, G. (1999). Towards a US Policy on Traveler Safety and Security, 1980–2000. *Journal of Travel Research*, August, 62–65.

Sommars, J. (1997). Why Is Colorado Tourism Dropping? *Colorado Business Magazine*, Littleton, **24**(5), 16–21.

Tardy, M. (2005). French Parliament Vote to Tack Development Tax on Airline Tix. *Aviation Daily*, Washington, **362**(48), June 12, 3.

Timothy, D. (2001). *Tourism and Political Boundaries.* Routledge, NY.

Toy, M. (2004). http://destinationsbelize.com/cruise_s.htm.

Veverka, J. (1998). Interpretive Master Planning: The Essential Planning Guide for Interpretive Centers, Parks, Self-guided Trails, Historic Sites, Zoos, Exhibits and Programs. Acorn Naturalists, Tustin, CA.

Virginia Tax Laws. (2006). Accessed Feb 12, §*58.1-3823. Additional Transient Occupancy Tax for Certain Counties.* http://leg1.state.va.us/cgi-bin/legp504.exe? 000+cod+58.1-3823.

United Nations World Tourism Organization. (2001a). Enzo Paci Papers on Measuring the Economic Significance of Tourism, UNWTO, Madrid, Spain, Vol. 1.

United Nations World Tourism Organization. (2001b). Global Code of Ethics for Tourism. UNWTO, Madrid, Spain, A/RES/56/212, www.world-tourism.org, UNWTOGlobalEthicsCode.pdf.

United Nations World Tourism Organization. (1998). Guide for Local Authorities on Developing Sustainable Tourism. UNWTO, Madrid, Spain.

United Nations World Tourism Organization (1992). *An Integrated Approach to Resort Development*, UNWTO, Madrid, Spain.

Washington Post (2007). US Billionaire Back After Ride Into Space, April 22, p. A21.

Weimer, D. and A. Vining. (2005). *Policy Analysis: Concepts and Practice.* 4th ed., New Jersey: Prentice Hall.

Wolfensohn, J., L. Dini, G. Bonetti, I. Johnson and J. Martin-Brown (Eds). (1999). Culture Counts: Financing, Resources, and the Economics of Culture in Sustainable Development. DC: IADB/WB.

4

Tourism as a commercial and economic activity

> Every morning in Africa, a gazelle wakes up.
> It knows it must run faster than the fastest lion
> or it will be killed. Every morning in Africa, a
> lion wakes up. It knows it must run faster than
> the slowest gazelle or starve to death. It doesn't
> matter if you are a lion or a gazelle, when the
> sun comes up, you had better be running.
>
> Maurice Greene, American athlete (1974–)

The above quote is apropos to the economics of tourism today. Working within one of the largest and most competitive industries today, industry members must be cognizant of the dynamic world of tourism. When strategically well-planned and executed, tourism provides an economic stream both into and throughout a country or state/province and is an incentive to preserve the best things the destination has to offer – from its scenic coastlines, its wildlife habitats, its historic districts, its local culture, folklore or heritage. For example, components of the National Park Service

Figure 4.1   A historical warning sign of the impending coastline, the Cape Lookout Lighthouse in North Carolina now also signals the opportunity for heritage tourism adventures (Photo: Jason Swanson)

in the United States, such as the Cape Lookout National Seashore in North Carolina (shown in Figure 4.1), combine together outdoor recreation and heritage tourism assets. Properly integrated as part of an overall local economic strategy, tourism can provide a local community economic development, environmental sustainability and social benefits.

The pursuit of tourism's potential economic benefits needs balancing with the potential conflicts or negative externalities that tourism may also bring. This is particularly true in communities transitioning from industries that are more traditional to tourism. Development in Lanai, Hawaii provides a quick case study. Lanai was, up until the early 1990s, the world's largest pineapple plantation and one of Hawaii's most inaccessible islands for nearly 70 years. After a shift in the cost structure associated with pineapple production, the majority of the island was sold and transformed into a high-end, exclusive destination resort. This influx of development and transformation from an agriculture-based economy to a tourism-based economy has been an economic success, but was, in many ways, a social disaster. A study by the National Institute of Mental Health (Kakesako, 1997) concluded that the transition led to family instability and conflict, absentee parents, increased suicide attempts among teenagers and increased unemployment for long-term residents as most new jobs went to newcomers to the island.

However, with a balanced approach to tourism development appropriately addressed by the destination's tourism leaders, governments, businesses, communities, educational institutions and/or non-profit entities, individual destinations can garner a small percentage of the larger sustainable tourism market that fuels this economic engine. Through collective promotion, coordination and marketing of a variety of attractions, the local communities will have the opportunity to increase economic development, realize increased revenues, create new jobs, benefit from a diverse economy, add new products, generate additional income, spawn new businesses and contribute to overall economic integration while enriching the public and private sector partnerships and improving the quality of life of the local citizenry. Figure 4.2 illustrates the schema of tourism as a commercial and economic activity.

Indications herald that tourism will grow steadily over the next 20 years as we see a worldwide increase in leisure time and disposable income for millions of people in both the developed and developing countries of the world. Historical information provided by the United Nations World Tourism Organization (2005) tells us: '[s]ince 1950, when international travel started to become accessible to the general public, tourist activity has risen from 25 million to around 800 million arrivals (or more) in 2005. International tourism receipts have risen from US $2.1 billion to US $623 billion in 2005'. Indeed, for the most part, shorter working hours, greater individual prosperity, faster and less expensive travel, the impact of advanced technology and the consumers' use of the Internet have all helped make the travel and tourism industry the fastest-growing industry in the world. Impact of business and international education travellers further affect this growth.

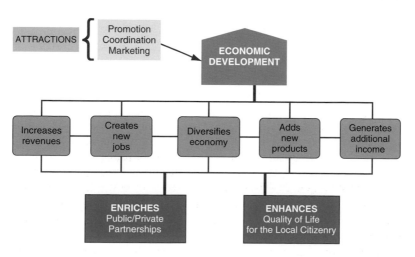

Figure 4.2 Schema of tourism as a commercial and economic activity

Global importance

As an economic factor, tourism is growing faster than the rest of the world economy in terms of visitor expenditures, export output, capital investment, income and employment. The UNWTO has displayed the impact that international tourism has worldwide in 'Tourism Highlights 2006 edition' by summarizing International Tourist Arrivals (Table 4.1) and International Tourism Receipts (Table 4.2).

Tourism is an important export product in both industrialized and less-developed countries. However, the extent to which tourism contributes to a country's foreign exchange earnings varies considerably. Case in point, the appreciation of several of the world's currencies (i.e., the euro and Japanese yen) since 2004 in comparison to the depreciation of the US dollar attribute to this phenomenon, although overall receipts rose by 9 per cent when expressed in terms of local currencies at constant prices. As evidenced from Table 4.2, the world's economy is rebounding from the setbacks of previous years, most recently from the SARS epidemic of 2003 and the terrorists' attacks of 11 September 2001.

Tourism as an economic development tool

Today, tourism is indeed an activity of considerable economic importance throughout the world. Studies conducted in 2005 by the United Nations World Tourism Organization support the hypothesis that as the world economy expands, so does tourism; conversely, the growing significance of tourism as a source of income and employment and as a major factor in the balance of payments for many countries is attracting increasing attention from governments, regional and local authorities and others with an interest in economic development and planning.

As true today as first noted in 1990, co-author D. Edgell, Sr (1990) wrote:

The tourism industry plays an important role in the economic and technological development of nations. Tourism:

a. stimulates the development of basic infrastructure (such as airports, harbours, roads, sewers and electrical power);
b. contributes to the growth of domestic industries that supply the tourism industry (e.g., transportation, agriculture, food processing, commercial fishing, lumbering construction);
c. attracts foreign investment (especially in hotels); and
d. facilitates the transfer of technology and technical know-how. (p. 29–30)

Table 4.1 International tourist arrivals

	International tourist arrivals (million)						Market share (%)	Change (%)		Average annual growth (%)
	1990	1995	2000	2003	2004	2005*	2005*	04/03	05*/04	00/05*
World	439	540	687	694	764	806	100	10.1	5.5	3.3
Europe	265.6	315.0	395.8	407.1	424.4	441.5	54.8	4.3	4.0	2.2
Northern Europe	31.6	40.1	45.8	45.8	49.6	52.9	6.6	8.4	6.5	2.9
Western Europe	108.6	112.2	139.7	136.1	139.0	142.7	17.7	2.2	2.6	0.4
Central/Eastern Europe	31.5	60.0	69.6	78.5	86.3	87.9	10.9	10.0	1.9	4.8
Southern/Mediter. Eu.	93.9	102.7	140.8	146.8	149.5	158.0	19.6	1.9	5.7	2.3
Asia and the Pacific	56.2	82.4	110.5	113.3	144.2	155.4	19.3	27.3	7.8	7.1
North-East Asia	26.4	41.3	58.3	61.7	79.4	87.6	10.9	28.6	10.3	8.5
South-East Asia	21.5	28.8	36.9	36.1	47.1	49.3	6.1	30.4	4.8	6.0
Oceania	5.2	8.1	9.2	9.0	10.1	10.5	1.3	12.1	3.8	2.6
South Asia	3.2	4.2	6.1	6.4	7.6	8.0	1.0	18.5	5.5	5.7
Americas	92.8	109.0	128.1	113.1	125.7	133.5	16.6	11.1	6.2	0.8
North America	71.7	80.7	91.4	77.3	85.7	89.9	11.2	10.9	4.9	-0.3
Caribbean	11.4	14.0	17.1	17.1	18.1	18.9	2.3	5.9	4.3	2.0
Central America	1.9	2.6	4.3	4.9	5.7	6.5	0.8	15.6	15.7	8.5
South America	7.7	11.7	15.3	13.8	16.2	18.2	2.3	17.2	12.2	3.6
Africa	15.2	20.3	28.2	31.0	33.8	36.7	4.6	9.1	8.5	5.4
North Africa	8.4	7.3	10.2	11.1	12.8	13.7	1.7	15.1	7.5	6.0
Subsaharan Africa	6.8	13.0	17.9	19.9	21.1	23.0	2.9	5.8	9.1	5.1
Middle East	9.6	13.7	24.2	29.5	36.3	39.1	4.8	22.8	7.7	10.1

Source: World Tourism Organization (UNWTO) ©

(Data collected by UNWTO 2006)

Table 4.2 International tourism receipts

	Change local currencies, constant prices (%)			Share (%)	US$			Euro		
					Billion		Receipts per arrival	Billion		Receipts per arrival
	03/02	04/03	05*/04	2005*	2004	2005*	2005	2004	2005*	2005
World	-1.7	9.3	3.3	100	633	680	840	509	547	680
Europe	-1.5	3.2	2.4	51.2	328.5	348.2	790	264.1	279.9	630
Northern Europe	-2.2	5.8	8.4	7.9	48.9	53.8	1,020	39.3	43.3	820
Western Europe	-3.3	1.8	1.5	17.9	117.6	121.9	850	94.6	98.0	690
Central/Eastern Europe	-2.6	5.5	0.3	4.7	29.0	32.3	370	23.3	26.0	300
Southern/Mediter. Europe	0.8	2.9	1.5	20.6	133.0	140.2	890	106.9	112.7	710
Asia and the Pacific	-9.3	24.4	4.3	20.4	127.8	138.6	890	102.7	111.4	720
North-East Asia	-11.1	30.4	7.7	10.4	64.0	70.8	810	51.5	56.9	650
South-East Asia	-16.7	26.1	0.0	4.9	32.2	33.4	680	25.9	26.8	540
Oceania	0.6	8.3	0.5	3.6	22.9	24.5	2,330	18.4	19.7	1,880
South Asia	17.9	20.6	5.7	1.4	8.7	9.8	1,220	7.0	7.9	980
Americas	-2.1	11.5	3.8	21.2	132.0	144.6	1,080	106.1	116.2	870
North America	-4.7	12.9	4.2	15.7	98.2	107.1	1,190	79.0	86.1	960
Caribbean	5.8	3.9	1.9	3.0	19.2	20.4	1,080	15.4	16.4	870
Central America	13.0	13.0	8.9	0.7	4.0	4.6	700	3.2	3.7	560
South America	5.0	13.6	2.3	1.8	10.6	12.5	690	8.5	10.1	550
Africa	24.2	6.9	8.5	3.2	19.2	21.5	590	15.4	17.3	470
North Africa	-0.3	13.4	14.5	1.0	6.1	7.0	510	4.9	5.6	410
Subsaharan Africa	38.0	4.0	5.7	2.1	13.1	14.5	630	10.5	11.7	510
Middle East	20.6	11.3	1.5	4.0	25.5	27.6	710	20.5	22.1	570

Source: World Tourism Organization (UNWTO) ©

(Data collected by UNWTO 2006)

Developing and less-developed countries are recognizing the need and the benefits of committing resources to these four segments. One example, technological improvements in the building of airports has been necessitated by the new technology of today's larger body aircraft. This results in raising the economic base of areas requiring skilled construction workers, the use of specialized materials in building facilities (construction as well as décor) and better-trained personnel (to attend to the aircraft, handle the control tower operations and service providers within the terminal). The further addition of foreign currency (in infrastructure development investments and revenues from travellers) and the transfer of communication technologies (facility and airline systems operations) have positive impacts on the local economy.

Worldwide, developing countries are also recognizing the growth potential afforded by the tourism industry. Because tourism can promote economic development, it can attract much-needed financial capital, increase awareness of a country, improve infrastructure and provide new job opportunities. The country, overall, can benefit from increased tourism through the multiplier effect, creating ripples throughout local, provincial and/or regional economic development. Almost every country in the world has some resource, attraction, activity, event or adventure opportunity that can motivate a traveller. Collaboration, whether among destinations or within governmental agencies and referred to as 'coopetition' (discussed later in this chapter) can serve to enhance the economic impact of the tourism industry. The point to remember is that there is hardly a place in the world that is not conducive to tourism. Even if the locale is not a destination in and of itself, it still may have tourism potential. It may provide overnight lodging, food, fuel or other services to the traveller. Alternatively, changes in travellers' demand may enhance its development by diversifying the employment base, escalating income and increasing visibility and desirability of place.

Another derived benefit is from an increase in the economic base and tax revenues, such as sales and use tax on tourist expenditures. It is important to note that travellers expend more and bring 'fresh' rather than 'recycled' money to the economy. Historically, small businesses dominate the travel and tourism industry. These benefits are also felt in the traditional industries and services of the locale, whether from an increase in agriculture, commercial fishing, food production, employment or the many sectors contributing to the hospitality providers. In some communities, the beneficiaries are often micro-enterprises such as those pictured in Figure 4.3. (Note: just as developing countries gain from these factors, so do all local, state/provincial, regional and national entities.)

This increased awareness has historically been slow in coming; yet today, it is beginning to gain major recognition by economic policymakers who are looking towards the spreading horizon of positive growth in revenues

Figure 4.3 Farm products are sold in various ways by local business owners in Bangalore, India (Photo: J.R. Gast)

derived from tourism. Educational facilities are expanding their research and community engagement activities to sharpen their focus on the economic benefits of tourism. A study completed by the Institute for Tourism at East Carolina University looked at the impact sustainable tourism has had on economic development along the coastlines. (See case study at the end of this chapter.) One conclusion of this study is that sustainable tourism, and by default, tourism itself, has a strong impact on all the areas that tourism affects.

Table 4.3, which was developed by Travel Industry Association of America, provides a quick overview of the economic impact that travel has in the United States.

Consideration of the significance of tourism as an economic development tool to the state/province, region or country should not be overlooked. Of note – the considerable impact tourism receipts have in the regions

Table 4.3 Economic impact of travel in the US, 2005p (including both US resident and international travel)

Travel expenditures[‡]	$653.8 billion
Travel-generated payroll	$171.4 billion
Travel-generated employment	7.5 million jobs
Travel-generated tax revenue	$104.9 billion
Travel trade surplus	$7.4 billion

[‡]Includes spending by domestic and international travellers in the US on travel-related expenses (i.e., transportation, lodging, meals, entertainment and recreation and incidental items); p = preliminary.
Source: Travel Industry Association of America, Bureau of Economic Analysis/US Department of Commerce.

Figure 4.4   An outdoor market in South America collects money from tourists visiting from around the globe (Photo: Matt Schuttloffel)

that contain developing countries. Visitors generate a cash flow into the economy, which in turn fuels the economic engine. Not only does the business community gain benefits from the traveller – i.e. shopping, dining in restaurants, utilizing on-site services – but also the local citizenry gains, too, in terms of jobs/wages, improved infrastructure and facilities, and tax revenue. To repeat from the beginning of this chapter, tourism receipts allow local communities the opportunity to increase economic development, realize increased revenues, create new jobs, benefit from a diverse economy, add new products, generate additional income, spawn new businesses and contribute to overall economic integration while enriching the public and private sector partnerships and improving the quality of life of the local citizenry (Figure 4.4).

Demand side of tourism

The demand side of the tourism industry is important in today's global marketplace. The demand side includes the potential interests and motivation of tourists. Added to this in the demand analysis are the elements of location and identification of the markets, marketing and promotion, and pricing techniques. Unlike many industries, though, is the impact that demand has on the corresponding commercial activities of travel. For example, a hotel accommodates the traveller and provides additional services, which complement the tourist's stay – the rent of the room, the in-house restaurant and supplemental items supplied by the local industries: such as the nearby book store or souvenir shop. Also influencing demand in the tourism industry is the fluctuation caused by seasonality (preferred times of the year when more travellers converge on any given destination) and the resulting effects often referred to as 'peaks and valleys' of demand. It is important that proper planning is accomplished to respond to the difficulties experienced by providers in the tourism industry. One way a destination can mitigate seasonality is to develop a themed festival in the shoulder or off-seasons (Figure 4.5).

Due in large part to the availability of pre-travel information, travellers are savvier today than ever before, and this is reflected in the services expected at the destination. One explanation for this is their use of the Internet and the ease in which information is distributed. Industries may share links to their respective Websites, and it is easy to search the Internet to review comments on one's destination of choice to see what 'ranking' it received from previous tourists. It is no longer enough for a hotel to offer a 'restful haven' to the traveller; the destination hotel must now also provide access to amenities such as exercise facilities, spas, wireless Internet connectivity, high-quality restaurants and entertainment. Today and into the future, the total experience is what matters, and it must be provided well.

Figure 4.5 Crowds gather for a festival held in the fall shoulder season in a beach destination in the United States (Photo: Jason Swanson)

The airline industry has attempted to adapt to increased consumer demand by offering links to more than just the transportation to the destination, such as the availability of car rentals, special accommodation rates and travellers' insurance. To some degree, airlines still offer some of these services; however, the greatest complaints voiced by travellers today are when poor service is provided by airlines, their lack of flexibility in dealing with customers and their seeming disregard for the special needs of tourists. This plethora of service demands has increasingly collided with the need for improved governmental policies for airline transportation and traveller safety and security.

Travellers are seeking a variety of new experiences in new places. The Internet has led to an 'eye opening' effect; in other words, the ability to surf the Internet has introduced people to destinations and related activities that are new and attractive to them. There are few unknown destinations because of the ease of use of e-commerce tools. Coupled with this is an increase in disposable income and the changing demographics of today's traveller towards an aging, more educated population. Competitive pricing is the norm in today's global market, and the traveller's demands mandate adherence to this economic factor.

Special concerns that need to be addressed focus on two main topics. The first topic is money – whether it's the fluctuation in spending ability as experienced by the traveller or a reduction in discretionary income. The exchange rate between two countries is perhaps the most influential factor when considering fluctuation in spending ability. If the exchange rate is disadvantageous, international travellers will exercise caution in their spending or downsize their activities. With regard to business travel, business professionals may find that the company has initiated restrictions on flight, hotel accommodations and budget for daily expenses. Discretionary income, the amount 'left over' from disposable income, can also have a negative effect on demand. A reduction in the discretionary income of the traveller has effects on demand and this, in turn, negatively affects use of tourism supplier products and services at the destination.

The second topic – the Internet – affords the traveller more power of choice through access to information and can adversely influence the traveller's decision to visit a given destination. Fairly instant information can advise the traveller of the political situation within a given country, the risks of contracting an illness or the cost of basic needs. It also allows the potential traveller to preview the destination and the local amenities. If the destination does not offer desired facilities or services or is weak in its presentation, this can lead to a decline in visitor satisfaction of place, and the destination may not attract the number of visitors needed to ensure success.

Supply side of tourism

Basic to the tourism product are several supply factors. Natural resources such as scenic land, mountains, good climatic conditions, flora, fauna, water and beaches are basic to tourism development. The availability of water supply systems, sewage disposal plants, transportation facilities and related kinds of infrastructure is fundamental to meeting the needs of tourists. At times, infrastructure and attractions can be combined, as shown in Figure 4.6. Also needed are hotels, restaurants, shopping centres and public transportation – an almost endless list of supply components that tourists have come to expect. Less easily defined are some of the 'hospitality' services, such as friendliness of the host community, availability of the arts, entertainment and other attributes and activities that enhance the tourist product and add value and quality.

Detractions from tourism supply may exist when travellers evidence restrictions to destinations due to

A. Pricing
    • the affordability of destination
    • an unfavourable exchange rate
    • a drop in traveller's discretionary income

Figure 4.6 A trail developed along the levee system near Wilkes-Barre, Pennsylvania provides both protection and recreation for members of the host community and for visitors (Photo: Jason Swanson)

B. Quality
- adequate accommodations
- substitution of activities
- local environment
C. Knowledge of location
- good transportation
- security/safety of place
- visitor information

Another important factor to consider when addressing tourism supply detractions is leakage. Leakage occurs when tourism revenue generated in one destination is spent in other communities who produce goods or services not purchased in the original destination. For example, a visitor orders fish for lunch at a local seafood restaurant in coastal Spain. If the fish was not caught and processed locally, then the money the restaurateur pays to a non-local purveyor is an example of tourism revenue leakage. On a larger scale, leakage can also occur if a hotel's ownership group is not from the local community. In this case, the profits from hotel operations are taken outside the local economy. Leakages also arise when tourism businesses hire employees who reside outside the destination.

Travellers want to experience the flavour of a new environment but often expect foreign/imported goods to be available at any given destination. In many cases, today's travellers still desire what they are used to and what makes them comfortable, expecting the destination to provide 'all the comforts of home'. This limited scope can adversely affect the economy and resources of the local area. However, comparative advantage, as described later in this chapter, may justify some leakage.

Coopetition

First introduced in 1995, coopetition is emerging as an important means to facilitate economic growth through tourism. The definition of this word (Edgell and Haenisch, 1995) is the need for *coope*ration among tourism destinations in order to better market the tourism product effectively and meet the com*petition* at the regional or global level. In effect, this means that local communities that might otherwise compete against each other need to form partnerships or alliances to better market their tourism products and to increase the number of visitors from further distances. Figure 4.7 and Figure 4.8 juxtaposes two differing entities combining their resources through coopetition. The first diagrams larger entities' intertwinement while the second shows its adaptability for smaller units, such as two destinations. This model can be adapted for use by any number of entities

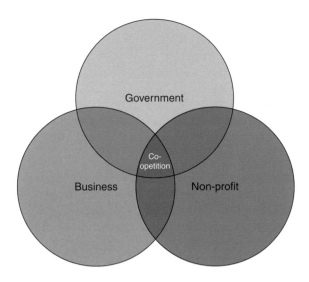

Figure 4.7   Venn diagram of government, business and non-profit coopetition

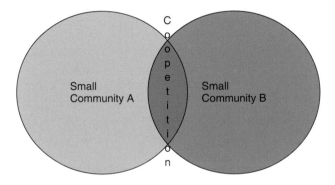

Figure 4.8   Venn diagram of two small communities practicing coopetition

and/or by any combination, and that in the case of smaller communities, even by two or more sites within one area seeking to boost their economy.

The formation of partnerships is perhaps the more important factor in the idea of coopetition. For example, we are all familiar with the airline reservation system practice, when booking a flight, or asking if they can assist in the reservation of a rental car and/or a hotel room. This practice also is showing up on Websites, particularly when travellers schedule their own itineraries and reservations. The opportunity of a complete package, whether at one location or spread among several locations, is a compelling reason for the utilization of coopetition and can augment travel organizations' quest to improve overall economic capability.

Collaborative multi-stakeholder processes can lead to an agreement on priority issues in setting tourism policy goals. In addition, tourism enterprises, destinations and communities working cohesively can bring about improved policies that will lead to enhancement and enrichment of the traveller's experience while advancing the economic vitality of the combined destinations. Coopetition has proven to be an effective tool for increasing tourism to areas that are not often represented in the tourism mainstream. Partnership formations assist in the transition of competition into a healthy, profitable environment of cooperation.

Comparative advantage

The idea of comparative advantage in tourism is not new. More new, however, may be viewing tourism as a comparative advantage from the supply side rather than demand side. When formally introduced in 1817 by David Ricardo, the economic theory of comparative advantage in its basic interpretation stated that countries will specialize in producing and exporting those goods and services in which they have an advantage in terms of land, labour, capital, technology or other factors of production. In summation, according to Ricardo (as cited in Samuelson, 1969),

> . . . the gains from trade follow from allowing an economy to specialize. If a country is *relatively* better at making wine than wool, it makes sense to put more resources into wine, and to export some of the wine to pay for imports of wool. This is even true if that country is the world's best wool producer, since the country will have more of both wool and wine than it would have without trade. A country does not have to be best at anything to gain from trade. The gains follow from specializing in those activities, which, at world prices, the country is *relatively* better at, even though it may not have an absolute advantage in them. Because it is relative advantage that matters, it is meaningless to say a country has a comparative advantage in nothing . . . .

In other words, a country that has petroleum, iron ore, fishing waters or similar resources would concentrate on the development, production, investment and management of these supply side resources to produce and export in those areas. In the past, this was based on the demand for the product or good.

The same is true in the supply of tourism resources, services and facilities. Good beaches, beautiful mountains, historic monuments, progressive transportation systems and other supply side attractions having potential as tourism 'products' are as important to a country as the production and export of more tangible products such as oil and steel. Figure 4.9 depicts

Figure 4.9   Unique scenes such as this of the Rio Petrohué and Vulcan Osorno in Chile cannot be replicated and must be protected (Photo: Matt Schuttloffel)

one of the most important exports of a community – beautiful vistas and pristine natural resources.

In fact, in some respects, tourism is a superior export product because much of the 'productive capacity' is less exhaustible and causes less disruption and pollution of the environment. Particular to the introduction of the Internet, today we see the savvy traveller looking at what is supplied at the destination – whether it is from an affinity to experiencing a specific type of tourism (i.e. cultural, heritage, sports) or from dedication to a multinational corporation (i.e. global hotel, based on reputation).

Tourism can express a comparative advantage where the environment is not conducive to industrial businesses. Often, the destination has the natural beauty and the basic provisions to facilitate tourism development but not necessarily the ingredients necessary for industry needs. It can be said that this current trend has greatly aided developing nations in improving their economy through tourism. Today's traveller is better educated, more sophisticated and travels more often; therefore, the need for a destination to not only recognize what the traveller wants (demands) but also to provide (supply) it in order to increase the economic benefits to the country is essential. The comparative advantage helps developing nations earn foreign exchange more rapidly and with less difficulty than they might with other products. Table 4.4 suggests the comparative advantage

Table 4.4 Comparative advantage of the top 10 countries 2006, both in international tourist arrivals and international toursim receipts)

International tourist arrivals (million)

Rank	Series[1]	Million		Change (%)	
		2004	2005*	04/03	05*/04
1 France	TF	75.1	76.0	0.1	1.2
2 Spain	TF	52.4	55.6	3.1	6.0
3 United States	TF	46.1	49.4	11.8	7.2
4 China	TF	41.8	46.8	26.7	12.1
5 Italy	TF	37.1	36.5	-6.4	-1.5
6 United Kingdom	VF	27.8	30.0	12.3	8.0
7 Mexico	TF	20.6	21.9	10.5	6.3
8 Germany	TCE	20.1	21.5	9.4	6.8
9 Turkey	TF	16.8	20.3	26.1	20.5
10 Austria	TCE	19.4	20.0	1.5	3.0

International tourism receipts (US$ billion)

Rank	US$				Local currencies	
	Billion		Change (%)		Change (%)	
	2004	2005*	04/03	05*/04	04/03	05*/04
1 United States	74.5	81.7	15.8	9.6	15.8	9.6
2 Spain	45.2	47.9	14.1	5.8	3.8	5.8
3 France	40.8	42.3	11.6	3.5	1.5	3.5
4 Italy	35.7	35.4	14.1	-0.7	3.8	-0.7
5 United Kingdom	28.2	30.7	24.6	8.7	11.1	9.5
6 China	25.7	29.3	47.9	13.8	47.9	12.7
7 Germany	27.7	29.2	19.7	5.6	8.9	5.5
8 Turkey	15.9	18.2	20.3	14.2	14.7	7.8
9 Austria	15.3	15.5	9.9	0.9	-0.1	0.9
10 Australia	13.6	15.0	21.7	9.6	7.7	5.8

Source: World Tourism Organization (UNWTO) ©

(Data collected by UNWTO 2006)

of the top 10 countries today, both in International Tourist Arrivals and International Tourism Receipts.

Like several other major destinations, Australia has a comparative advantage in tourism. Australia is particularly blessed with an abundance of natural resources with tremendous tourism potential: wondrous woodlands, beautiful beaches, lovely islands, spectacular forests, colourful deserts, impressive savannahs, striking bodies of water (oceans, lakes, rivers and streams) and immense isolated land masses. While Australia lacks some of the great edifices, especially ancient historical buildings and artifacts, it does have great cities and interesting small towns and villages. Other attractions abound, and there are a never-ending number of events, festivals and local celebrations of interest to visitors. Participatory activities, such as swimming, scuba diving, sailing, surfing, boating, river rafting, camping, spelunking, hiking, hunting, bird watching, tennis, and golf are limited only by the imagination. In addition, there are a multiplicity of personal services and amenities that are particularly advantageous and conducive to business travel. In brief, the opportunities for participation in all aspects of tourism are greater in Australia than in most countries of the world, thus giving Australia a comparative advantage in tourism.

Employment

One of the reasons tourism is so important economically is that it is labour intensive. Tourism employment is concentrated mainly in the services sector rather than in the goods-producing sector, and the services sector tends to be less automated. Thus, much labour is used with relatively little capital. In the United States, tourism is one of the largest employers with over $171.1 billion travel-generated payroll, generating 7.5 million direct jobs according to Travel Industry Association of America's 2006 *Travel Industry Fun Facts*. Travel services directly generated more jobs than any other industry except health services.

Travel and tourism plays a key role in providing employment opportunities for minorities, women and immigrants who often encounter the greatest difficulty in finding jobs. It also is beneficial in developing countries. Tourism is a particularly good potential source of jobs because it is both labour intensive and growing; this means that for each additional dollar expended on the growing tourism sector, more jobs will be created than in most other areas of the economy. In several national economies, many new tourism jobs are absorbing available workers into the labour force, particularly those displaced by the decline in manufacturing and textile industries.

While it demands large numbers of highly skilled workers and well-trained and educated managers, tourism has the further advantage of also providing employment in the hard-to-employ, lower-skilled occupations. Oftentimes, it is these occupations that have the highest unemployment rates and that are the most resistant to broad fiscal and monetary policy aimed at lower unemployment. For example, the travel industry in the United States provides a disproportionate number of jobs for traditionally disadvantaged African Americans, Hispanic Americans and women. Thus, 'microeconomic' efforts concentrated on stimulating the growth of the tourist sector are more likely to create jobs for all levels and representative groups of the labour force than the 'macroeconomic' measure of tax reduction, government expenditures or increasing the rate of growth of the money supply.

Income

While creating jobs, international tourism is an important generator of national income as well. Foreign visitors make large expenditures on a wide variety of goods and services, and these yield a substantial increase in income. They are interested in shopping for high-quality goods, good dining, general sightseeing and cultural activities, which in turn represent a significant source of foreign exchange receipts (Figure 4.10).

In its broadest sense, tourism encompasses all expenditures for goods and services by travellers. It may include purchase of travellers' checks/cards, transportation, lodging, attractions, meals, beverages, entertainment, souvenirs, car rentals, travel agency and sightseeing tour services, and

Figure 4.10   American tourists appreciate works of art in Europe (Photo: Elke Bielecki)

personal grooming services; and therefore, covers the output produced in various segments of many industries. In addition, tourist activities make use of the services of other industries – insurance, banking services, credit cards, auto clubs, parks, taxi services, cameras and film, reservation systems, computers, televisions and telephones. The primary advantage of attracting the international tourist over the domestic tourist is that international visitors spend much more on tourism services. The influx of foreign exchange into a country's economy as new revenue, particularly into a developing country, also has a quicker impact on improving its economic environment. Tourism has a rippling effect on an area's economy through the importance of the 'multiplier effect', which happens when the overall impact on the economy is even greater than the actual expenditures for goods and services. Most of the former socialist countries and less-developed nations need tourist revenues, especially 'hard' financially stable Western currencies, for economic growth. These governments are continually seeking avenues to entice the traveller to their destinations and are effecting policy changes – not necessarily tourism-related policies – to accommodate inbound travel.

Multiplier effect

Investorwords.com provides this definition of a multiplier, 'A number which indicates the magnitude of a particular macroeconomic policy measure. In other words, the multiplier attempts to quantify the additional effects of a policy beyond those that are immediately measurable. For example, a decrease in taxation will have more of an effect than just the value of the reduced taxes. It will lead to greater disposable income, which might cause an increase in consumption, which in turn might increase employment in industries, which enjoy greater demand and so on. So the total effect of the implemented policy equals the effect of the policy measure, times the multiplier. This is true of most macroeconomic policy measures, because the actual effect of the measure cannot be quantified by the effect of the measure itself'.

An important point to bear in mind is that a nation's economic well-being is usually measured in terms of national income, which is the sum total of the flow of all incomes. Economists have long realized that an increase in public or private investment in an economy increases national income by an amount greater than the amount invested. Economists use the term 'multiplied amount' because, as it changes hands, the initial investment is re-spent and generates new rounds of spending whether through direct, indirect or induced expenditures. Export earnings have the same multiplier effects on national income as does an increase in domestic investment. International tourism receipts represent an infusion of fresh money from outside the economy and have the same impact as any other export in improving a nation's overall economy. International tourism is subjected to the 'given moment' exchange rate of one country to another, which can fluctuate dramatically. The international traveller planning a pleasure trip may be influenced by the exchange rate, and tour operators must 'hedge' on purchasing fares. For example, the recent continued strengthening of the euro is making destinations in the European Union more expensive for travellers from non-European Union nations while impacting domestic travellers less.

Angelo and Vladimir (2001) tell us 'While the [income] multiplier effect is highly variable among cities and countries around the world, many industry analysts use a figure of 1.6 as a reasonable multiplier on a general basis'. In other words, for every dollar, yen, euro, peso, the multiplier effect generated in the economy is 1.6 times. The economy of an area may be stronger or weaker and thus effect the analysis' measurement, but rarely will the multiplier move more than 0.2 points either way. In categorizing the multiplier, Lickorish and Jenkins (2002) related that there are five main types of multipliers, which are generally accepted:

1. Transactions *or sales multipliers*. An increase in tourist expenditure will generate additional business revenue. This multiplier measures the ratio between the two changes.
2. *Output multiplier*. This relates the amount of additional output generated in the economy as a consequence of an increase in tourist expenditure. The main difference with the transactions or sales multiplier is that the output multiplier is concerned with changes in the actual levels of production and not with the volume and value of sales.
3. *Income multiplier*. This measures the additional income created in the economy as a consequence of the increased tourist expenditure.
4. *Government revenue multiplier*. This measures the impact on government revenue as a consequence of an increase in tourist expenditure.
5. *Employment multiplier*. This measures the total amount of employment created by an additional unit of tourism expenditure.

Taken together, these five divisions provide an excellent example of the importance of the tourism multiplier and its effects on the economy.

What economists also tell us, however, is that the multiplier is a double-edged sword. A sudden drop in investment, export earnings or tourism receipts reduces national income by a multiplied amount. A decline of $1 million in a nation's tourism earnings can result in a decline of more than $1 million in that nation's national income. That decline affects not only sales, profits and employment in the tourism industry but also the fortunes of feeder industries that supply the tourism industry – agriculture, fishing, food processing and packing, floriculture, brewing and distilling, transportation, handicrafts and many others. Another detriment to full utilization of the multiplier is that it often takes time to gather the information and figures necessary to determine the methodology, thereby rendering the results as outdated. Regardless of this, it is critical for planners to include the multipliers in their processes as generated dollars have a 'cause-and-effect' philosophy on the local economy.

Exporting tourism

The tourism sector is highly diverse: part public, part private and composed of many industries and many firms. It can be estimated that more than one million enterprises in the United States are involved in travel-related businesses. These small firms, examples of which are presented in Figure 4.11, include family-owned or 'mom and pop' operations such as family-owned motels, restaurants, amusement areas, and souvenir, gift and other retail establishments.

The tourism sector also includes large corporations that own hotel chains, airlines, cruise ship lines, rental car agencies, theme parks and airport catering operations. These individual firms collectively produce a

Figure 4.11 Small businesses in storefronts along Main Street in Mt Airy, North Carolina cater to visitors interested in experiencing small-town America (Photo: Jason Swanson)

travel product that is sometimes thought to be a 'lesser' product than a 'manufactured' product. Yet in terms of the balance of trade, tourism as a service export is equal to, for example, a 'merchandise product'.

Tourism is sometimes referred to as an 'invisible' product. Tourism is invisible in the sense that, as an export product, it is not produced, packaged, shipped or received like 'hard' goods. In tourism, consumers bring themselves to the point of sale, pay for the product (services), and at some point in the future or almost immediately, receive the services. Furthermore, even though tourism may be sold abroad, it is consumed within the selling country, thus generating additional opportunities for selling other goods and services.

Another aspect of tourism that is contrary to the export of goods is the way it is marketed. For example, at an export trade show most manufactured products will be available for display and to touch, whereas the tourism product being sold is not tangible nor visible. A respectable agent who represents the product through visual aids, such as brochures, posters, Internet, PowerPoint presentations, Websites or videotapes, markets it. The basic point is that while tourism and other related service items may have a number of special characteristics, others may not be as well understood in discussions of exports. Trade in tourism services is an important export and does have an impact on the trade balance.

Economic development

Technology transfer has been particularly evident in the hotel industry as hotels in developing countries have acquired computer-based reservations systems and have contracted with North American and Western European hotel corporations for management and manpower-development services. Many countries place strong emphasis on the demand and supply of tourism services as part of their overall economic development. As mentioned earlier in this chapter, the demand side of the coin has historically been the direction countries took in planning their tourism destinations. This flowed from the (then proven) process which mandated stakeholders to first research the potential interests and motivations of tourists; then acknowledge location and identification of the markets, marketing and promotion, and pricing techniques, which became the main elements of demand analysis.

Today, it can be said that the supply side is exerting a more powerful affect on tourism; however, it is these very factors that are coming to the forefront for stakeholders in present-day planning and development, as well as policymakers. The host of travel and tourism organizations are highlighting the importance travellers, particularly international travellers are exerting on these hospitality services. A reading of current matter shows travellers often decide on their destination due to loyalty, whether to a hotel or cruise-line; a desire to engage in a specific experience; or resultant of an affinity to a type of tourism. A quality tourism product requires careful planning on the part of the travel organization or destination to ensure that the demand and supply components are equally available. If tourists like a tourism product, the receiving state or country can reap the benefits. But without a clear strategic plan for tourism development (see Chapter 9), the economic benefits may be unsustainable and short-lived.

Rural tourism in the United States

The problems of rural areas are well documented. Many locations around the globe have experienced the losses of manufacturing industries, agricultural production and out-migration of better educated youth and skilled workers. Residents of rural communities sometimes face the economic obstacles of poor highway systems, a lack of technological training and limited educational opportunities necessary for effective marketing of destinations and products. Historically, the economic competitiveness of rural areas has been declining, but progress is occurring as local destinations form partnerships and communities strengthen their efforts in tourism promotions. Figure 4.12 shows a community fundraiser held at one of the more popular tourism attractions on rural Ocracoke Island, North Carolina – the Fish House, which is a non-profit cooperative run by local fishermen. Through the effective use of 'coopetition', many rural areas are realizing their marketability thereby improving the economic vitality of the area. Also, a desire of increasing numbers of tourists to experience 'rural living' is prompting the rise of agritourism, heritage tourism, adventure tourism and, in some instances, ecotourism.

Economic planners state that new industries must be developed in rural areas to replace those that are waning economically and are no longer competitive, that undeveloped rural resources must be utilized and that rural residents be offered new marketing skills. According to Edgell (2002), rural environments worldwide have vast expanses of land and water and widely diverse topographies (forests, mountains, plains, riverfronts, grasslands and deserts) that provide outstanding settings for tourism and recreation. Economists also point out those non-metropolitan, pastoral locales that are dependent on tourism, retirement income and specialized government spending exhibit much greater stability than those that are dependent

Figure 4.12 The Fish House on Ocracoke Island, North Carolina hosts an oyster roast in late December to raise funds for the operations of the working waterfront (Photo: Jason Swanson)

on rural manufacturing or farming. Rural communities are recognizing and acknowledging the need to seek economic development alternatives to once dominant industries such as farming, ranching and mining. The popularity of agritourism, tourism to farms and agricultural settings, is gaining in popularity as a major form of tourism. In North Carolina (NC), one of the first states in the United States to recognize this travel trend, there is a state office devoted to this activity – NC Agritourism, in the NC Department of Agriculture and Consumer Services – as well as a cooperative agreement between NC State University, NC Agriculture and Technical University and the NC Cooperative Extension. New research in rural areas by Harvard University, Cambridge, Massachusetts (cluster tourism) and East Carolina University, Greenville, North Carolina (history, heritage and cultural tourism) is proving the economic impact generated by rural areas through their unique opportunity to develop rural tourism. Many look to their own attractiveness, often based upon the area's cultural, historic, ethnic and geographic uniqueness, as potential for tourism development (see Chapter 6). Such changes are progressively viewed as opportunities for keeping rural communities economically viable.

Economics of tourism information

It is generally accepted in the business world that access to and control over information generates power. In addition, in today's world, through our various communications networks and information technology, tourists and businesses diffuse information almost instantaneously. For business travel particularly, this has resulted in a change in the methods used to secure reservations for airlines, hotels and other necessities. Websites are changing our systems of offering information about destinations. Tourists are now able to research and plan every moment of their travel thoroughly with the help of the information highway. While this eliminates unplanned 'moments of surprises' (which, when one does occur, can lead to a pleasurable experience as the traveller is more knowledgeable of their chosen destination), it also causes tourism providers to rely heavily on the use of e-commerce tools to promote tourism. The ease with which pertinent and timely information can be accessed and forwarded to the traveller becomes paramount.

Just as important as the information flow by electronic means is the informal communications system of human beings travelling from one place to another. This informal human information system is of great economic and social value. The interaction of travellers with others, whether met on various travels or with someone from home, leads to effective communication. This sharing of information can occur locally or globally and serves as an effective marketing tool. When tourists have quality experiences, they will then tell many others about that experience and encourage travel to the same destination.

The growth in credit card use has facilitated the international flow of money for tourism transactions easing the currency exchange issues, which confronted people in the past, and this industry now fuels many high-priced purchases such as vacation packages. The convenience of plastic money has had a significant impact worldwide. Credit cards have also aided in the acceleration of buying services and products online where transactions are instantaneous. Furthermore, the airline industry has come to rely on the credit card business, not for reservation transaction processing alone. The credit card companies also provide a wealth of data for the airlines regarding traveller personal information and travel and buying habits.

Conclusion

As stated throughout this book, tourism is an important economic development strategy. It is important not only at the local level, but it is also a viable tool in developing national economies. This is particularly true as traditional industries such as mining, manufacturing and agriculture decline in many parts of the world. Tourism is also beneficial for transitional economies, providing much-needed foreign exchange, jobs and induced benefits through tourism multipliers. While not without risks and potential negative externalities, tourism can serve as a catalyst for revitalization in large and small economies throughout the planet. Acknowledging the potential risks and mitigating them through sound planning and policy will assist local, regional, state/provincial and national communities create sustainable tourism destinations and enjoy the benefits tourism can provide.

Case study 4

SUSTAINABLE TOURISM AS AN ECONOMIC DEVELOPMENT STRATEGY ALONG COASTLINES (EDITED FOR THIS PUBLICATION)

Researched and Written by: David L. Edgell, Sr, PhD and
Maria DelMastro Allen
Institute for Tourism
College of Human Ecology
East Carolina University
Greenville, North Carolina, USA

Introduction

Sustainable tourism as an economic development strategy along coastlines (Study) charts a course of action that navigates the nebulous territory where sustainable tourism precepts and economic development strategies converge. Coastal sustainable tourism development is a connatural composite topic that is sometimes controversial and often misunderstood. The key to balancing the equation of conserving the natural, built and social environments on the one hand and adding economic value on the other is a well-planned and well-managed sustainable tourism programme. Good sustainable tourism planning and management techniques promote the effective and efficient use of resources, enrich the economy of the local community and improve the quality of life for the local citizens.

To ensure that sustainable tourism as an economic development strategy along coastlines flourishes in the future, there must be efforts to inspire businesses and people to accept good practices, whether they choose to enhance the natural scenic beauty as it intermingles with flora and fauna or enrich the built environment. In that respect, a major challenge of this Study is to provide best practices to help guide the management process and provide future generations the opportunity to enjoy and benefit from sustainable tourism. The premise for review in this Study is based on "sustainable tourism as an economic development strategy". As this report progresses, the correlation between sound sustainable tourism practices and economic development will emerge.

Measures of sustainable tourism

Several important elements make the sustainable tourism experience unique along the world's coastlines. For example, the shorelines of the coasts may offer scenic natural beauty, flora and fauna, and/or rich cultural and heritage resources. The surrounding land and water resources may provide visitors with activities such as swimming, sunbathing, surfing, fishing, scuba diving, snorkelling, boating, whale and dolphin watching, bird viewing, climbing, painting, photography, visiting historic communities and numerous other recreational opportunities. Accordingly, it is critical for sustainable tourism development along the coastlines to include

- Good coastal management practices;
- Clean air and water; healthy ecosystems;
- Maintenance of a safe and secure recreational environment;
- Beach restoration, including beach re-nourishment;
- Sound policies for wildlife and habitat conservation;
- Protection of the built environment: history, heritage and culture;
- Educational/awareness programmes that promote good sustainable tourism practices.

While discussions and controversy may arise over how these attributes can best be accomplished, the businesses, developers, tourists, local communities, not-for-profit entities and educational institutions all have a stake in working towards a healthy, clean, safe and well-managed coastal environment. If it is not protected now, the stakeholders will lose in the future. It is imperative that strategies be developed to sustain productivity, the economy and social values of coastal areas and communities. These seven standards, as noted above, can serve as complementary measures for appraising *sustainable tourism as an economic development strategy along coastlines*.

Supplementary to the above general standards for "sustainability" (or stewardship) are some relatively new measurement norms developed by the *National Geographic Society*'s Center for Sustainable Destinations (established in 2001). In the March 2004 edition of *National Geographic Traveler*,

115 global destinations, many of them along coastlines, were rated on tourism sustainability using the following criteria:

- Environmental conditions
- Social/cultural integrity
- Condition of historic structures
- Aesthetics
- Tourism management
- Outlook

This March 2004 article raised eyebrows in the world tourism community, bringing unwanted attention to specific coastline destinations in some cases. Almost overnight "sustainable tourism" was highlighted via the Internet, on Websites, and discussed in emails as people, community leaders and tourism officials reviewed these ratings and their potential impact on each respective site/destination. In brief, it was a "call to action" and stimulation for greater research in the field of sustainable tourism management.

Using the criteria cited above, a global panel of over 200 experts in a variety of fields ranging from ecology, sustainable tourism, geography, urban and regional planning, travel writing and photography, historic preservation, cultural anthropology, archaeology – all seasoned travellers who had a good basis for comparing destinations – evaluated the 115 global destinations (each expert only rated those destinations that he/she had visited in the last 5 years; and incidentally, one of the authors of this report participated in the evaluations). These ratings, then, were a compilation of informed judgements and perceptions by the experts. It is worth noting that the highest score and rank was awarded to the Norwegian fjords (score of 82, ranked 1st) and the lowest score and rank was Costa del Sol, Spain (score of 41, ranked 115th), respectively. This analysis heralded a tangible wake-up call, particularly for the criterion of "tourism management", for many destinations located along marine areas.

This Study identifies an additional dimension, predicated on more recent research. Referred to as "Sustainable Tourism Prescriptions for Success",[1] these general "prescriptions" are gentle reminders of ". . . the opportunity that tourism offers towards positive economic, environmental, and social benefits for tomorrow that depend on the decisions being made today. We can plan well for the development of tourism by adhering to important principles, policies, and philosophies of sustainable tourism or let it happen haphazardly and hope for the best. If we do not define clear-cut directions for sustainable tourism at this juncture in the growth of tourism, there may never be another chance".[2]

The goal is to promote orderly economic growth as part of the management of sustainable tourism. The need is to balance the numbers of visitors with the capacities of the given environments, both natural and built, in a way that allows for the greatest interaction with the least destruction and disruption. There are many differences of opinion on how this can best be accomplished; however, there is some agreement that establishing a workable sustainable tourism policy and management philosophy is a beginning point.

Tourism: past and present

Early settlers often sought out the coastlines and nearby waterways as fertile areas for development since they frequently offered the optimum opportunities for food supply, safety and security. As time progressed, many of the travel experiences that were simply necessary to ensure survival later led to the development of destinations for leisure travellers. Today's sustainable tourism practices, particularly in marine areas, offer immeasurable new advantages for developing quality destinations. Expanding interest in wildlife viewing has given rise to a sizable range of wildlife tourism products from whale and dolphin watching in the oceans to a vast array of wildlife viewing of birds, bears, otters, wolves, deer, wild horses and other fauna along the waterways and coastlines. Beautiful scenery, unique geological structures, vibrant flora, endless beaches and historic sites have inspired outdoor activity, especially with the use of new photography technology and digital cameras. Such natural area tourism opportunities have grown immensely in the past few years.[3] When recreational activities are added to this mix, such as surfing, canoeing, fishing, diving and boating, it is easy to see why water-related tourism is so popular. The increase in cultural awareness is rising, also, as many travellers seek to experience firsthand the "flavour" of the locale. As stated earlier in this study, the composition of sustainable tourism incorporates the natural environment and the built environment – the history, heritage, culture, arts and structure of place.

Coastal tourism is an important area for the application of the principles and practices of sustainable tourism. Research (Miller et al., 2002) shows that tourism along coastlines is a fast-growing segment of the travel industry and offers numerous opportunities to discuss some of the issues of sustainable tourism. "... Some coastal tourism is organized for a special purpose such as ecotourism, adventure tourism, scientific tourism, and dive tourism. As with other human endeavors in the coastal zone associated with development, tourism is viewed positively by some for the opportunities it creates, while others condemn coastal tourism for its unacceptable consequences".[4]

Today, tourism is recognized as one of the fastest growing industries in the world. This rapid growth and its concurrent development practices put particular pressure on coastal sustainable tourism management, planning and policy. The concern with respect to sustainable tourism is to acknowledge that tourism experiences may be positive, or in some circumstances negative, and to perceive the need for policy guidance to ensure that the continued growth of tourism will allow for a balanced tourism experience. The coastlines are excellent laboratories to study "sustainable tourism as an economic development strategy" and to convince those engaged in activities related thereto to better understand the major role sustainable tourism management plays in the overall strategies to maintain these important resources for the future.

Sustainable tourism

United Nations World Tourism Organization

Sustainable tourism has become the most prominent new millennium trend in tourism. Much leadership in sustainable tourism has come from the newest addition to the United Nations, the United Nations World Tourism Organization (UNWTO), headquartered in Madrid, Spain, that promotes effective management of sustainable tourism as a positive contributor to economic development.[5] According to UNWTO

Sustainable development of tourism:

Sustainable tourism development guidelines and management practices are applicable to **all forms of tourism in all types of destinations**, including mass tourism and the various niche tourism segments. Sustainability principles refer to the **environmental, economic and socio-cultural** aspects of tourism development, and a **suitable balance must be established** between these three dimensions to guarantee its long-term sustainability. Thus, sustainable tourism should:

1. **Make optimal use of environmental resources** that constitute a key element in tourism development, maintaining essential ecological processes and helping to conserve natural heritage and biodiversity.
2. **Respect the socio-cultural authenticity of host communities,** conserve their built and living cultural heritage and traditional values, and contribute to inter-cultural understanding and tolerance.
3. Ensure viable, long-term economic operations, **providing socio-economic benefits to all stakeholders** that are fairly distributed, including stable employment and income-earning opportunities and social services to host communities, and contributing to poverty alleviation.

Sustainable tourism development requires the **informed participation of all relevant stakeholders, as well as strong political leadership** to ensure wide participation and consensus building. Achieving sustainable tourism is a **continuous process** and it requires **constant monitoring of impacts**, introducing the necessary preventive and/or corrective measures whenever necessary. Sustainable tourism should also maintain a **high level of tourist satisfaction** and ensure a meaningful experience to the tourists, raising their awareness about sustainability issues and promoting sustainable tourism practices amongst them.

(UNWTO Conceptual Definition, 2004)

World Travel and Tourism Council

Another important global organization that recognizes the significance of sustainable tourism is the World Travel and Tourism Council (WTTC), headquartered in London, England, that is comprised of 100 private sector enterprises. In July 2003, WTTC announced its *Blueprint for New Tourism*.[6] One section of this report focuses on the need for tourism-related businesses to balance economics with the environment, its local citizens and the culture of place.

Many of New Tourism's key tasks for the private sector are very concrete:

- Expanding markets while promoting and protecting natural resources and local heritage and lifestyles.
- Developing careers, education, employee relations, promoting smaller firms, raising environmental awareness, and helping in its own way to narrow the gap between the "haves" and the "have-nots".
- Sensitive provision of traditional tourism products and imaginative product diversification that reduce seasonality and increase yields.
- Improving the quality of tourism products and services, and adding value for money while increasing consumer choice.
- Agreeing and implementing quality standards at all levels and in all areas, including staff training.
- Transfer of industry skills and best practice that spreads the benefits widely and efficiently.
- Increasingly sophisticated and more precise measurement of the sector's own activity, to feed into strategic business decisions.
- Communicating more effectively with the world in which it operates – including energetic input from Travel & Tourism umbrella organization to government, at strategic and local levels.

The cumulative effect will be a shift towards Travel & Tourism that continues to serve the private sector's own needs, while embracing the wider interests of the countries and communities in which it operates.

(Blueprint for New Tourism, p. 6)

Economics of tourism

Tourism is perhaps the largest industry on earth. When strategically well-planned and executed, tourism provides an economic stream both into and throughout a country or province and is an incentive to preserve the best things the destination has to offer – from its scenic coastlines, its wildlife habitats, its historic districts, its local culture, folklore or heritage. Properly integrated as part of an overall local economic strategy, tourism can provide a local community economic development, environmental sustainability and social benefits. When appropriately addressed by the country's tourism leaders, governments, businesses, communities, educational institutions and/or not-for-profit entities, individual destinations can garner a small percentage of the larger sustainable tourism market that fuels this economic engine. Through collective promotion, coordination and marketing of a variety of attractions, the local communities will have the opportunity to increase economic development, realize increased revenues, create new jobs, benefit from a diverse economy, add new products, generate additional income, spawn new businesses and contribute to overall economic integration while enriching the public and private sector partnerships and improving the quality of life of the local citizenry.

Coopetition

A "buzzword du jour" is "coopetition".[7] Introduced in 1995, "coopetition" is emerging as an important means to facilitate economic growth through tourism. The need for *coop*eration among tourism destinations in order to better market the tourism product to effectively meet the com*petition* at the regional or global level defines coopetition.[8] In effect, this means that local communities that might otherwise compete against each other need to form partnerships or alliances to better market their tourism products and to increase the number of visitors from further distances. In effect, collaborative multi-stakeholder processes can lead to agreement on priority issues in setting sustainable tourism policy goals for the destinations. In addition, tourism enterprises, destinations and communities working cohesively can bring about improved policies that will lead to enhancement and enrichment of the traveller's experience while adhering to the principles of sustainable tourism along the coastlines. "Coopetition" has proven to be an effective tool for increasing tourism to areas that are not often represented in the tourism mainstream.

Tourism's impact

From an economic perspective, it is important to understand why people travel and what activities they enjoy during their trip. While economic concerns drive much of the tourism that has taken place over the last several years along the coastlines, there is now a greater incentive to provide visitors a clean and healthy environment as part of a quality sustainable tourism product.

Increased visitation without good planning leads to complications, particularly on the highways and at tourism sites along the coastlines. As a result of inadequate planning, tourists as well as the local citizens face increased traffic, and its subsequent congestion and pollution. It is important that any negative element be recognized early so that policies and plans regarding tourism development can seek to minimize its harmful impact on natural resources and the economy of the community.

Beach preservation is also a vital issue for beach communities and stakeholders as a result of the economic value visitors generate. Demand is increasing dramatically for property with coastal/shore frontages, and along the more secluded waterways, and are scarce resources today. It is, therefore, inevitable that conflicts for the best uses of such resources are on the rise. It also suggests the need for heightened attention to the aforementioned sustainable tourism measures.

Cultural tourism overview

Cultural tourism defined

When sustainable tourism along coastlines is discussed, often the culture of the area as a visitor attraction is ignored. The tendency is to emphasize all the water-related recreational activities; thereby placing very little emphases on the cultural resources of the area.

Recognized as a distinct subset within sustainable tourism, cultural tourism is one of the most important and fastest growing tourism trends. Also known as "cultural heritage" tourism, it is highlighted in this chapter because its impact is often overlooked in research on coastal destinations. This type of tourism has been ascribed a variety of definitions. Culture tourism may be defined by its destination – such as museums, theatres, art galleries, historical sites, architectural treasures and heritage or ethnic events. Alternatively, cultural tourism may be defined by the motivation of cultural tourists to seek an authentic experience with a unique heritage, social fabric or place. Nonetheless, the foundation for cultural tourism is a community's cultural and heritage assets, which include built environments (e.g. museums, theatres and art galleries), historical sites, natural environments, as well as cultural practices and collections.

All of these options for cultural tourism exist along coastlines throughout almost every country of the world. Unlimited numbers of communities along coastlines have multiple opportunities to enhance cultural tourism products or develop new ones. The predominance of festivals, heritage gatherings, historical re-enactments and plays, the variety of museums and local events indigenous to the destination are a common denominator in many of the communities of the world. Visitors can partake in a vast array of experiences that afford them the opportunity to embrace the cultural ethnicity of a locale. Many destinations have made significant progress in this respect, but much more needs to be accomplished and implemented to ensure successful economic development through sustainable tourism along the coastlines.

The cultural traveller

Travel Industry Association of America and *Smithsonian Magazine* produced a major study, *The Historic/Cultural Traveler 2003 Edition*,[9] which explored the impact of cultural tourism and will be the basis for discussion of this point. Although this study only researched the United States, the results and other research suggest a worldwide trend. According to this publication, 56 per cent of the United States' adult population is considered to be historic/cultural travellers (118 million travellers). Travellers surveyed for this study reported that during 2002, they participated in at least 1 of 15 cultural events – such as arts, museums, humanities, historic or heritage activities – while travelling. Furthermore, cultural travellers spend more ($623 vs. $457 – in 2002 dollars) and travel longer (5.2 nights vs. 3.4 nights) than other tourists. As compared to those surveyed in 1996, the demographic profile of today's cultural traveller has shifted; these travellers are wealthier, younger (49 years of age), better educated and more technologically savvy.

Benefits of cultural tourism

Many global economies have been transitioning from their traditional economic means to a more creative economy as international tourism is on the rise. Sustainable tourism factors well into this movement and the recognition of cultural tourism as a means of diversifying urban and rural economies alike are acting upon this trend. In addition to the economic opportunities, cultural tourism can produce social and community development benefits. These include conveying a sense of local pride and identity, enhancing connections across a country, encouraging an entrepreneurial spirit, creating a sense of place, preserving cultural assets and providing educational benefits. "Process" benefits of cultural tourism include improved partnerships and collaborations across sectors and regions as well as the development of new marketing and communication tools that promote a cultural tourism initiative.

Coastline cultural tourism

While the trend towards more interest in cultural tourism is general in its application, certainly it is applicable to the world's coastlines. The tourist today is very active both with respect to recreational activities along the coasts and interests in the cultural heritage of the area. Every indication is that this phenomenon will continue into the future and will offer coastal communities many new alternatives beyond those traditional amenities along the coasts.

Tourism congestion

Physical congestion, or "crowding", occurs when too many people or vehicles, or both, are present in an area that is not designed to accommodate such large numbers. This actuality is often referred to as "over capacity" or lack of "carrying capacity". There are certain circumstances in which tourism congestion is expected, as for example, at sporting events, concerts, festivals, high season or major events. In other cases, it may be attributable to evacuations due to storms, hurricanes, tsunamis, earthquakes or other natural disasters. Whatever the situation, congested areas detract from a quality tourism experience.

The UNWTO states that "Tourism congestion at destinations and particularly at natural and cultural sites can suffer from an accumulation of impacts, resulting in

- A major reduction in the visitor's enjoyment and appreciation;
- Damage the flora, fauna, scenic values, physical fabric or special or special values of the place;
- Adverse impact on conservation or presentation programs;
- Reduce opportunities for visitors to spend money locally;
- Generate considerable stress on the local community through competition for local services;
- Increase litter and pollution;
- Strain the capacity of local infrastructure; and/or
- Reduce the efficiency of tourism services".[10]

This situation is particularly acute along many of the world's coastlines. If the destination is not careful, it can destroy the very attractions that brought visitors to the area in the first place.

Tourism areas receiving large numbers of visitors need to constantly monitor the impact of intense demand on the natural and built environment and on the social and cultural values. Some warning signals to watch for along the coastlines include

- Erosion of the natural environment due to over-development or intensive use;
- Pollution of ocean fronts with litter and other pollutants;
- Visual, noise and air pollution from too much tourism traffic;
- Lack of the availability of utilities because of an over capacity of visitors;
- Traffic congestion at airports, roadways and tourist sites during the high season;
- Lack of public facilities, i.e., restrooms, trash disposal and parking places;
- Inadequate attention to the safety and security needs of visitors;
- Friction and resentment between the host community and tourists;
- Social problems including general crime, drug abuse and prostitution;
- Damage to national shrines, monuments and historical structures (Edgell and Allen, 2005).

Coping with these issues in a positive manner is a major concern of sustainable tourism. In the following section of this *Study*, Best Practices Recommendations, judicious attempts to alleviate these problems will be mentioned.

At the very least, the business plan for a destination along the coastline should identify, from the beginning, a set of guidelines or standards that determine the "carrying capacity" of the project. When the visitor and host population are both experiencing exceptionally crowded conditions, then the upper limits of the carrying capacity has been surpassed and negative effects of tourism begin to manifest. Many parts of Europe suffer from overuse of facilities during the popular travel month of August. Some destinations are seeking to spread out the effects of such over-visitation. Many are encouraging visitation to other areas, while others are expanding and promoting tourism products that are not as seasonal. For example, "The [popular] Spanish island of Mallorca is expanding its tourism image away from the traditional summer holiday mass market towards the development of additional market niches through promoting the cultural attraction of numerous art galleries and museums and off-season walking and hiking tours in the mountains".[11] These efforts point to a major marketing campaign that increases visitors' awareness of the many tourism resources available, beside just the beaches. Such a move will add quality to the overall visit for tourists while increasing the economic activity in other areas of the island.

Best practices recommendations

In a Study such as this, the author would be remiss without outlining some best practices recommendations for sustainable tourism along the coastlines of the world. This Study recognizes the possibilities of variances from the criteria discussed in this chapter due to the environmental, geographical, economic, physical, political and social development make-up of coastlines in the different countries. The intent here is to show the relational importance of sound sustainable tourism practices to positive economic activity and growth; thus, the recommendations within this *Study* are guided by this goal. Also, this researcher, based on numerous years of field experience and tourism research, exercises expansive discretion in his application of the sustainable tourism "prescriptions" to best fit the circumstances and interests of the local area.

The following are a few best practices recommendations and courses of action as helpful guidelines in the policy, planning and management of sustainable tourism along the coastal areas. They emanate from a variety of different sources and are general in description but reflect considerable knowledge and research in the field of sustainable tourism. They should be applicable to most coastlines the world over. No attempt has been made to prioritize these recommendations.

RECOMMENDATION No. 1
The UNWTO has identified local involvement as a major factor in sustainable tourism project development. This element is certainly applicable to development along coastlines.

- Early contact with local groups, active individuals, and those most likely to be affected by any changes.
- Provision of forums, meetings, discussion opportunities where all interested stakeholders can identify their interests and concerns.
- Provision of feedback in a clear form – showing participants that their input has been taken into consideration.
- Ongoing involvement of key players throughout the process (openness and transparency are essential).

RECOMMENDATION No. 2
In the book *Managing Sustainable Tourism: A Legacy for the Future*, David L. Edgell, Sr includes in his planning strategy some of the following warning signals to watch for in sustainable tourism. They are as follows:

- Erosion of the natural environment due to over-development or over-intensive uses.
- Pollution of ocean and waterway environments through boating, littering, or other tourism-related activities.
- Visual, noise, and air pollution resulting from too much tourist traffic in congested areas.
- Traffic congestion along roadways and within tourist sites in coastal zones during the high season.
- Lack of public facilities, i.e., restrooms, trash disposal, and parking when tourism exists beyond the capacity of the area.
- Friction and resentment between host communities and tourists because of misunderstandings, increases in crime, and violation of local social mores.

These are just a few of the problem areas to watch for in sustainable tourism development. Many of the coastline areas of the world are currently facing these challenges.

RECOMMENDATION No. 3
In the book *Tourism: Principles, Practices, Philosophies, Tenth Edition*, Charles R. Goeldner and J.R. Brent Ritchie mention that the Canadian tourism industry has developed and adopted a "Code of Ethics and Practices" that, while not specifically designed for "coastlines", nevertheless has many applications to coastal environs:

- Enjoy our diverse natural and cultural heritage and help us to protect and preserve it.
- Assist us in our conservation efforts through the efficient use of resources, including energy and water.
- Experience the friendliness of our people and the welcoming spirit of our communities. Help us to preserve these attributes by respecting our traditions, customs, and local regulations.
- Avoid activities that threaten wildlife or plant populations or that may be potentially damaging to our natural environment.
- Select tourism products and services that demonstrate social, cultural, and environmental sensitivity.

Adopting such good advice as detailed in the above "Code of Ethics and Practices" will lead to a high quality tourism experience.

RECOMMENDATION No. 4

When all is said and done, *sustainable tourism as an economic development strategy along coastlines* is predicated on sound policies, good management practices, careful and well-designed planning, education/awareness programmes and strategic marketing efforts, all of which take account of the well-being of the local community. The following list catalogues some important characteristics:

- A sound sustainable tourism policy should aim towards achieving economic prosperity while maintaining social, cultural and environmental integrity.
- Careful strategic planning in developing good sustainable tourism projects must involve all the interested parties at the local level.
- Responsibly managed tourism enhances, enriches and embraces the need to preserve nature, heritage and cultural values so that the community and visitor have a quality tourism experience now and in the future.
- All stakeholders, whether they are governments, tourists or businesses need to be educated and informed about best practices in sustainable tourism.
- Once the sustainable tourism attributes are intact at the destination, marketing personnel need to develop creative and innovative marketing programmes and promotion campaigns.
- A major goal of sustainable tourism development should include protecting and conserving the unique natural and cultural resources of the site, on which the tourism industry in most destinations is based.
- Ensure that natural and cultural resources protection is seen as a collaborative activity between all partners, for example, the public and private sectors as well as non-governmental groups and communities.
- Foster a positive awareness for the general public of the contribution sustainable tourism makes to the destination's prosperity and overall improvement of the quality of life of the people.
- Conduct an active policy dialogue that links sustainable tourism to local, provincial, regional, national and international plans and priorities.

Sustainable tourism as an economic development strategy along coastlines should have as part of its mission to recognize

> Responsibly managed tourism enhances, enriches, and embraces the need to preserve nature, heritage, and cultural values so that the community and visitor have a quality tourism experience.
>
> *(Edgell and Allen, 2005)*

Notes

1. The 'Sustainable Tourism Prescriptions for Success' emanated from research conducted by David L. Edgell, Sr, first introduced in a study conducted for a North Carolina Sea Grant programme, under the auspices of the National Oceanic and Atmospheric Administration, 2005.

2. David L. Edgell, Sr (2006). *Managing Sustainable Tourism: A Legacy for the Future.* Haworth Press, Inc.

3. It should be noted that word associations vary internationally and should be used carefully. One example is 'wilderness' as it can project differing connotations.

4. Marc L. Miller, Jan Auyong and Nina P. Hadley. (2002). *Sustainable Coastal Tourism: Challenges for Management, Planning, and Education.* Retrieved 16 September 2005 from http://gso.uri.edu/washu/washuw99003/1-Introduction_Miller.pdf.

5. World Tourism Organization. (2004). *Indicators of Sustainable Development for Tourism Destinations*, Madrid, Spain, 7.

6. The report can be seen in its entirety at http://www.wttc.org/blueprint/WTTCBlueprintFinal.pdf.

7. Note: from newspaper article, ' "Coopetition" is needed in eastern N.C.', *The Daily Reflector*, Greenville, North Carolina, 04 November 2004.

8. David L. Edgell, Sr and R. Todd Haenisch. (1995). *Coopetition: Global Tourism Beyond the Millennium*, 2.

9. Information draws from Travel Industry Association of America and Smithsonian Magazine (2003). *The Historic/Cultural Traveler.* TIA, Washington, DC, 3.

10. *Tourism Congestion Management at Natural and Cultural Sites*, 9.

11. *Tourism Congestion Management at Natural and Cultural Sites*, 61.

References for case study

APEC Tourism Working Group, Asia-Pacific Economic Cooperation. (1996). *Environmentally Sustainable Tourism in APEC Member Economies*, published by the APEC Secretariat, Singapore.

Edgell, Sr, David L. (2006). *Managing Sustainable Tourism: A Legacy for the Future*, The Haworth Hospitality Press, Binghamton, NY.

Edgell, Sr, David L. and R. Todd Haenisch. (1995). *Coopetition: Global Tourism Beyond the Millennium.* International Policy Publishing, Kansas City, Missouri.

Goeldner, Charles A. and J.R. Brent Ritchie. (2005). *Tourism: Principles, Practices, Philosophies* (10th ed.). Wiley, Hoboken, NJ.

Miller, Marc L., Jan Auyong and Nina P. Hadley. (2002). *Sustainable Coastal Tourism: Challenges for Management, Planning, and Education.* Available on UW library digital reserves or at http://nsgl.gso.uri.edu/washu/washuw99003/1-Introduction_Miller.pdf.

Tourtellot, Jonathan B. (2004, March). *National Geographic Traveler.* Destination Scorecard: 115 Places Rated, 60–67.

Travel Industry Association of America and Smithsonian Magazine. (2003). *The Historic/Cultural Traveler*, Washington, DC.

World Travel and Tourism Council. (2003, July). *Blueprint for New Tourism*, London, England.

References

Angelo, Rocco M. and Andrew N Vladimir. (2001). *Hospitality Today: An Introduction* (2nd ed.). Educational Institute of the American Hotel & Lodging Association, Lansing, MI.

Edgell, Sr, David L. (1990). *International Toursim Policy.* VNR Toursim and Commercial Recreation Series, Van Nostrand Reinhold, New York.

Edgell, Sr, David L. and Maria DelMastro Allen. (2005, September). *Sustainable Tourism as an Economic Development Strategy for the Waterways and Coastline of North Carolina.*

Edgell, Sr, David L. and R. Todd Haenisch. (1995). *Coopetition: Global Tourism Beyond the Millennium.* International Policy Publishing, Kansas City, MO.

Goeldner, Charles A. and J.R. Brent Ritchie. (2006). *Tourism: Principles, Practices, Philosophies* (10th ed.). Wiley, Hoboken, NJ.

investorwords.com. Retrieved December 20, 2006, from http://www.investor words.com/5669/multiplier.html.

Kakesako, G.K. (1997, March). 'Lanai folk suffer from loss of rural lifestyle'. *Honolulu Star-Bulletin.* Honolulu: March.

Lickorish, Leonard J. and Carson L. Jenkins. (2002). *An Introduction to Tourism.* Butterworth-Heinemann (Elsevier), Oxford, England.

Travel Industry Association of America. *Travel Industry Fun Facts*, Washington, DC. Retrieved April 25, 2007 from http://www.tia.org/pressmedia/fun_facts.html.

Travel Industry Association of America. *Economic Research – Economic Impact of Travel & Tourism Summary*, Washington, DC. Retrieved April 25, 2007, from http://www.tia.org/researchpubs/economic_research_impact_tourism.html.

United Nations World Tourism Organization. *Tourism and the World Economy*, Madrid, Spain. Retrieved November 29, 2005, from http://www.world-tourism.org/facts/eng/economy.htm.

United Nations World Trade Organization. *Comparative Advantage*, Geneva, Switzerland. Retrieved 12/02/2005 from http://www.wto.org/english/res_e/reser_e/cadv_e.htm.

United Nations World Tourism Organization. (2005, October). *WTO World Tourism Barometer* 3(3).

United Nations World Tourism Organization. (2006). *Tourism Highlights, 2006 Edition*, Madrid, Spain.

5

Political and foreign policy implications of tourism

> Tourism is a simple continuation of politics by
> other means.
>
> Jean-Maurice Thurot, *Economia*, May 1975

The political aspects of tourism are interwoven
with its economic consequences. As a 'continuation of politics' and an integral part of the
world's political economy, tourism is a useful
tool for achieving both economic and political goals. For obvious economic reasons, most
countries seek to generate a large volume of
inbound tourism, and examples of the political and foreign policy implications of tourism
abound. The history of travel contains numerous
references to tourism with political overtones,
ranging from Marco Polo's vivid descriptions
of political events in the Orient to the lack of
knowledge, and myths associated with the 'dark
continent' prior to the exploration of Africa by
Europeans.

As we learned in Chapter 4, expenditures
by foreign visitors add to national income and
employment and are a valuable source of foreign

exchange earnings. This chapter describes tourism agreements among nations, intergovernmental organizations and regional industry associations, as well as international tourism facilitation and tourism as a policy for peace.

Tourism agreements

While the reason for tourism agreements is the promotion of trade through tourism, these agreements also serve additional national policy objectives, such as encouraging international understanding, friendly relations and goodwill. In the past 30 years, the United States has negotiated tourism agreements with many countries. Using those made by the United States with other nations as an example, tourism agreements generally focus on the following specific criteria:

- increasing two-way tourism,
- supporting efforts by the National Tourism Organization travel promotion office(s),
- improving tourism facilitation,
- encouraging reciprocal investments in the two nations' tourism industries,
- promoting the sharing of research, statistics and information,
- recognizing the importance of the safety and security of tourists,
- suggesting mutual cooperation on policy issues in international tourism,
- providing for regular consultations on tourism matters,
- acknowledging benefits from education and training in tourism,
- enhancing mutual understanding and goodwill.

Two prominent examples of international tourism agreements involving the United States and its trading partners are those with the United Mexican States and with the Republic of Venezuela. Both agreements accredit tourism officials as members of a diplomatic or consular post and facilitate the exchange of tourism statistics and information between the two nations involved in the agreement. Interestingly, these and other agreements state that the United States will participate in the United Nations World Tourism Organization (UNWTO), although, as stated in the following section, the United States is not a member of that august organization.

The tourism agreement entered into by the United States and Mexico in October 1989, which superseded an April 1983 agreement, assists in facilitating motor carrier and other ground transport across the international border and calls for the nations to share information about automobile liability with one another. Understanding policies involving ground transportation is critical for visitors, as many cross the border in private vehicles. The agreement includes provisions for developing bi-national cultural events to strengthen ties and promote tourism, waiving applicable visa fees for teachers and experts in the field of tourism, promoting travel to regions and developing and improving tourist facilities and attractions in regions which contain examples of native culture in each country, and conducting joint marketing activities in third countries.

The US–Mexican agreement explicitly states that the nations 'will endeavour to facilitate travel of tourists into both countries by simplifying and eliminating, as appropriate, procedural and documentary requirements'. This will conflict with the border crossing policy outlined in the Western Hemisphere Travel Initiative (WHTI), which will require all citizens to provide a secured passport when entering the United States or Mexico. This is, of course, in response to acts of terrorism in the United States. This situation is a good example of the need for fluidity in tourism strategy and policy, so that it is not only reactive but also proactive as market conditions and foreign policy change.

An interesting aspect of the tourism agreement entered into by Venezuela and the United States on 7 September 1989 is that it calls for complementary agencies in the two countries to enter into their own agreements with each other. For example, the US National Park Service and Venezuela's Instituto Nacional de Parques are encouraged to pursue cooperative policies related to tourism development and facilitation. The agreement is specific about exchanges and mutual assistance, including efforts to identify tourism experts for short-term exchange assignments and identifying volunteer private-sector executives and professors of tourism who are eligible for sabbatical leave. This arrangement promotes cross-cultural understanding and has increased the body of knowledge in the field of international tourism development.

Intergovernmental organizations and regional industry associations

Organized associations of governments and tourism organizations comprised of groups at the national, regional and local levels can have a particular influence on the politics and foreign policy implications of tourism. There are a number of such intergovernmental organizations designed specifically to handle International Tourism Policy issues. Two organizations at the world level are the UNWTO and the World Travel and Tourism Council (WTTC). Regional organizations include the Organisation for Economic Cooperation and Development (OECD), the Organization of American States (OAS), the Asia-Pacific Economic Cooperation (APEC) and the Caribbean Tourism Organization (CTO). An important regional organization within the United States is the Southeast Tourism Society (STS), which consists of twelve member states. While there are many other organizations that cannot be described here due to space limitations, these seven groups are examples of proactive organizations working to advance tourism in their jurisdictions.

United Nations World Tourism Organization

The UNWTO, as part of the United Nations, is the leading international organization in the field of travel and tourism and is headquartered in Madrid, Spain. Originally established as the International Congress of Official Tourist Traffic Associations in 1925, it was renamed the International Union of Official Travel Organizations after the Second World War, before restructuring occurred in 1967. In 1974, in Lusaka, Zambia, a UNWTO budget formula and statutes were adopted allowing for the UNWTO to become an official organization the following year. Its first General Assembly was held in Madrid in May 1975, and the intervening years have seen its emergence as the key world organization for tourism.

In 2003, the UNWTO achieved status as a UN-specialized agency. Its current mission statement summarizes its primary responsibility as '... (providing) a central and decisive role in promoting the development of responsible, sustainable and universally accessible tourism, with the aim of contributing to economic development, international understanding, peace, prosperity and universal respect for, and observance of, human rights and fundamental freedoms'. UNWTO offers national tourism administrations and organizations the machinery as a clearing house for the collection, analysis and dissemination of technical tourism information, developing partnerships between the private and public sectors, and supports the Global Code of Ethics for Tourism. Activities include facilitating international dialogue and implementation of worldwide conferences, seminars and other means for focusing on important tourism development issues and policies. The official languages of the UNWTO are English, Spanish, French, Russian and Arabic.

Membership includes roughly 145 member countries, 7 associate members and about 300 affiliate members composed of private sector companies, educational institutions, tourism associations and local tourism organizations and authorities. One country that is not a member of UNWTO is the United States. As part of the downgrading of the US national tourism office in 1996, its membership in UNWTO was cancelled; however, there is new political momentum to have the United States rejoin UNWTO.

The structure of UNWTO is multipartite. At its core is the General Assembly, which meets every two years to discuss its budget, programme and policy. The Executive Council, the governing board for the UNWTO, is composed of 27 members as elected by the General Assembly and meets biannually. The Secretariat, located in Madrid, is made up of officials who are entrusted with implementing UNWTO's programmes and responding to members' needs. There are six regional commissions (Africa, the Americas, East Asia and the Pacific, Europe, the Middle East and South Asia) who meet annually. Nine committees of UNWTO members advise on management and programme content. These are the Programme Committee, the Committee on Budget and Finance, the Committee on Statistics and Macroeconomic Analysis of Tourism, the Committee on Market Intelligence and Promotion, the Sustainable Development of Tourism Committee, the Quality Support Committee, the UNWTO Education Council, the UNWTO Business Council and the World Committee on Tourism Ethics. (Part of the reference for this section was obtained from www.world-tourism.org/aboutwto.)

World Travel and Tourism Council

The World Travel and Tourism Council (WTTC) is unique in its structure as it is the only organization representing the private sector in the global context of the travel and tourism industry. It is comprised of business leaders from around the world who are presidents, chairs and CEOs of 100 of the world's foremost travel and tourism companies representing almost all sectors of the industry. According to WTTC, their mission 'is to raise the awareness of the full economic impact of the world's largest generator of wealth and jobs – travel and tourism'. WTTC was established in 1991 by a group of chief executives from major companies within the industry to convince governments concerning travel and tourism's strategic importance. Over the past decade and a half, WTTC has worked with governments to increase understanding of the industry's economic benefits and to persuade them to re-evaluate the role of travel and tourism in their overall policy priorities. An Executive Committee resides in WTTC's headquarters in London, England, and hosts the administration of its programmes.

In July 2003, WTTC revealed its *Blueprint for New Tourism* that proffered the statement 'which issues a call to action for both government and the industry to make several long-term commitments to ensure the prosperity of travel and tourism – one of the world's largest industries, responsible for over 200 million jobs and over 10 per cent of global GDP (Gross Domestic Product)'. The reasoning for this action stems from recovery measures necessitated by recent set backs experienced in the industry as a result of terrorism, war, economic slowdown and SARS. The president of WTTC, speaking at the 2003 Global Travel and Tourism Summit, stated,

'There is now a new consciousness amongst governments that they cannot leave the growth of travel and tourism to chance. What is needed is a new vision and strategy involving a partnership between all stakeholders – public and private to turn future challenges into opportunities. The *Blueprint for New Tourism* spells out how that can be achieved'. The guiding principles of 'New Tourism' recognize global consciousness of the importance of tourism, takes a fresh look at the opportunities and partnerships it produces and the delivery of commercially successful products that provide benefits for everyone – not just the traveller but also the local people and communities with respect to their natural, social and cultural environments.

In response to recent acts of terrorism and to prepare for the possibility of future attacks, the WTTC formed a Crisis Committee. The Crisis Committee has been charged with producing an immediate forecast of the impact of such events on travel and tourism so that the industry and government leaders can make informed planning decisions. A model was developed based on the real effects of catastrophic events including the Gulf War (1991), Croatia Peace (1996), Luxor Attack (1997), Hurricane George (1998), September 11th USA (2001), September 11th World (2001), Bali Bombing (2002) and Hong Kong SARS (2003). The London Underground bombing on 7 July 2005, allowed the global tourism industry to showcase its new proactive preparedness. The WTTC Crisis Committee was convened within 24 hours to forecast impact and propose strategies. In this case, historical non-peace has made the tourism industry more proactive. (Part of the reference for this section was obtained from www.wttc.org.)

Organisation for Economic Cooperation and Development

The Organisation for Economic Cooperation and Development (OECD), located in Paris, France, is bipartite in its structure. It serves as a forum in which governments work together to focus effectively on the challenges of interdependence and globalization through economic, social and environmental segments. In its efforts to 'underpin multilateral cooperation', OECD produces global research data, analyses and forecasts to enable economic growth and stability, strengthen trading systems, expand financial services and cross-border investments and promote best practices on the international forefront. It was started after the Second World War as the Organisation for European Economic Cooperation to coordinate the Marshall Plan, and in 1961, adopted its current name in order to address trans-Atlantic and, ultimately, its global reach. There are 30 member countries and more than 70 developing and transition economies working in partnership with OECD who share a 'commitment to democratic government and the market economy'.

The mission of OECD is as follows:

- To achieve sustainable economic growth and employment and rising standards of living in member countries while maintaining financial stability, hence contributing to the development of the world economy.
- To assist sound economic expansion in member countries and other countries in the process of economic development.
- To contribute to growth in world trade on a multilateral, non-discriminatory basis.

The OECD's Tourism Committee, headed by an executive-level Bureau, has taken a leadership role in identifying and working towards the reduction of barriers to travel in its member countries. In view of the major importance of tourism among the principal service industries, the OECD Trade Committee in 1979, 1981 and again in 1983 addressed updating and revising the Code of Liberalization of Current Invisible Operations by carrying out a survey of obstacles to international tourism and reporting its findings in a comprehensive report to the OECD Council.

In 1985, a milestone was achieved in efforts to reduce impediments to travel with the approval of a new instrument on International Tourism Policy, which reaffirmed the importance of tourism to the political, social and economic wellbeing of the member countries and agreed to set up formal procedures to identify travel impediments and to take cooperative steps to eliminate them. The OECD tourism instrument recommended minimum amounts for the import and export of national currency, for travel allowances, and for duty-free allowances for returning residents and for non-residents. It also made recommendations concerning travel documents and other formalities that strive towards facilitation of tourism. A finding then was that the most numerous and highly rated concerns among the countries responding were those impediments related to market access and the right of establishment. This reflects the importance of reaching customers in the country of residence in order to attract tourist and travel business. Without a local branch or subsidiary, travel agents, tour operators, airlines and other tourist companies are unable to market their services adequately, placing them at a competitive disadvantage. Today, the OECD is involving itself with emerging issues dealing with sustainable tourism and new directions in rural tourism. (Part of the reference for this section was obtained from www.oecd.org.)

Organization of American States

The Organization of American States (OAS), headquartered in Washington, DC, is currently composed of the following countries: Antigua and Barbuda, Argentina, the Bahamas, Barbados, Belize, Bolivia, Brazil, Canada, Chile, Colombia, Costa Rica, Cuba (by resolution in 1962, the current Government of Cuba is excluded from participation in the OAS), Dominica, The Dominican Republic, Ecuador, El Salvador, Grenada, Guatemala, Guyana, Haiti, Honduras, Jamaica, Mexico, Nicaragua, Panama, Paraguay, Peru, Saint Kitts and Nevis, Saint Lucia, Saint Vincent and The Grenadines, Suriname, Trinidad and Tobago, The United States of America, Uruguay and Venezuela (Figure 5.1).

This organization actually had its beginnings in the 1820s, stemming from Simón Bolivar's vision of a region 'united in heart'. In 1890, the nations of the inter-American region formed the Commercial Bureau of American Republics, which later evolved into the Pan American Union, and finally became the OAS. In 1948 it expanded into the English-speaking nations of the Caribbean and Canada, encompassing the hemisphere.

The OAS is committed to democracy for the people (all people have a right to democracy) and governments (government has an obligation to promote and defend democracy) in the member countries of the Western Hemisphere. 'Building on this foundation, the OAS works to promote good governance, strengthen human rights, foster peace and security, expand trade and address the complex problems caused by poverty, drugs and corruption. Through decisions made by its political bodies and programmes carried out by its General Secretariat, the OAS promotes greater inter-American cooperation and understanding' (www.oas.org).

Figure 5.1   Cusco is a popular heritage destination in Peru, a member of the Organization of American States (Photo: Matt Schuttloffel)

The OAS promotes 'Peace, Justice, and Solidarity in the Americas' as titled in their organizational heading. Sustainable tourism is of major concern to the OAS.

The Inter-American Travel Congress (IATC) was established in 1939 to develop travel and tourism in the Americas by conducting studies that maintain dialogue between governments and the private-sector. The organization also provides technical and research support for tourism development initiatives. Today, this focus still prevails. The purposes and functions of the IATC are:

- to aid and promote, by all means at their disposal, the development and progress of tourist travel in the Americas;
- to organize and encourage regular meetings of technicians and experts for the study of special problems related to tourist travel;
- to foster the harmonization of laws and regulations concerning tourist travel;
- to take advantage of the cooperation offered by private enterprise through world and regional organizations concerned with tourist travel which hold consultative status with the United Nations or maintain relations of cooperation with the OAS;
- to promote cooperative relations with similar world or regional organizations, either governmental or private, and to invite them to participate as observers at the meetings of the Congresses;
- to serve as advisory body of the organization and its organs in all matters related to tourism in the hemisphere.

Within this organization is the Inter-Sectoral Unit for Tourism. This branch promotes sustainable tourism practices and the importance of tourism as an economic development tool, in recognition of tourism's role as the world's number one growth industry. Recent activities have 'focused on tourism development programmes and projects aimed at encouraging cooperative and operational ties at the internal, regional and international levels'. It utilizes the Internet and Websites to promote its findings. (Part of the reference for this section was obtained from http://www.oas.org/main/english/.)

Asia-Pacific Economic Cooperation

Convening its activities in 1989, the Asia-Pacific Economic Cooperation (APEC), headquartered in Singapore, was formed as the 'premier forum for facilitating economic growth, trade and investment in the Asia-Pacific region'. The general philosophy is that strong, vital economies cannot be supported by government alone, thus the need for melding government and the key stakeholders in the business sector, academia, industry, policy and research institutions and interest groups within the community. APEC is consistent in its approach to ensure open dialogue and equal respect among its 21 Member Economies, which are Australia; Brunei Darussalam; Canada; Chile; People's Republic of China; Hong Kong, China; Indonesia; Japan; Republic of Korea; Malaysia; Mexico; New Zealand; Papua New Guinea; Peru; The Republic of the Philippines; The Russian Federation; Singapore; Chinese Taipei; Thailand; United States of America and Vietnam (Figure 5.2).

These Member Economies account for more than 2.5 billion people and 46 per cent of world trade. Its uniqueness is that it is 'the only multilateral grouping in the world committed to reducing trade barriers and increasing investment without requiring its members to enter into legally binding obligations'.

Under this umbrella, there are eleven working groups focusing on agricultural technical cooperation, energy, fisheries, human resources development, industrial science and technology, marine resources conservation, small and medium enterprises, telecommunications and information, tourism, trade promotions and transportation. The Tourism Working Group (TWG) has set four policy goals to support its function of creating

Figure 5.2 Coastal areas in Chile, such as this scene on Lake Llanquihue add to the vibrancy of the nation, which is a member of APEC (Photo: Matt Schuttloffel)

jobs, promoting investment and development, and improving the tourism industry across the region. These policy goals are

1. removal of impediments to tourism business and investment;
2. increase mobility of visitors and demand for tourism goods and services;
3. sustainable management of tourism outcomes and impacts;
4. enhance recognition and understanding of tourism as a vehicle for economic and social development.

The focus for the APEC TWG is on public and private partnership for facilitating tourism investments in the APEC Member Economies and exploring best practices of e-commerce application to the small and medium tourism enterprises in the APEC region. (Part of the reference for this section was obtained from www.apec.org/about.)

Caribbean Tourism Organization

In 1989, the Caribbean Tourism Organization (CTO) emerged from its predecessors, the Caribbean Tourism Association founded in 1951 and the Caribbean Tourism Research and Development Centre founded in 1974. The CTO, headquartered in Barbados, is an international development agency and the official body for promoting and developing tourism throughout the Caribbean. This organization provides information and assistance to its member countries and non-governmental members in order to achieve sustainable development. According to the CTO, the organization and its members work together to encourage sustainable tourism that 'is sensitive to the economic, social and cultural interests of the Caribbean people, preserves the natural environment of the Caribbean people, and provides the highest quality of service to Caribbean visitors' (Figure 5.3).

CTO also has offices in the United States, Canada, the United Kingdom, with smaller chapters in France, Germany, Holland, across the United States and in the Caribbean. Its composition is not only destination countries, but also private companies including airlines, hotels, cruise operators and travel agencies. Membership is open to all Caribbean countries and currently consists of English, French, Spanish and Dutch speaking nations and territories including the following member countries: Anguilla, Antigua and Barbuda, Aruba, Bahamas, Barbados, Belize, Bermuda, Bonaire, British Virgin Islands, Cayman Islands, Cuba, Curaçao, Dominica, Grenada, Guadeloupe/St Barts/St Martin, Guyana, Haiti, Jamaica, Martinique, Montserrat, Puerto Rico, St Eustatius, St Kitts & Nevis, St Lucia, St Maarten, St Vincent & the Grenadines, Suriname, Trinidad & Tobago, Turks & Caicos Islands and the US Virgin Islands.

Figure 5.3   A variety of creative accomodations are offered throughout the Caribbean (Photo: J.R. Gast)

The central thrust of the CTO is to promote the Caribbean as a 'vacation destination'. Over time, the CTO has produced high-quality Websites, which, in turn, address travellers' quests to make better decisions regarding destination choices. The CTO has successfully and efficiently utilized database marketing as a promotion tool. The organization supports sustainable tourism practices, development of tourism education and awareness programmes, financial guidelines and technical assistance to its members. (Part of the reference for this section was obtained from www.onecaribbean.org.)

Southeast Tourism Society

The Southeast Tourism Society (STS), headquartered in Atlanta, Georgia, is just one example of a regionally based tourism organization found in the United States as well as in other countries. STS is a non-profit membership organization, which started in 1983 and represents the interests of tourism industry members in twelve states: Alabama, Arkansas, Florida, Georgia, Kentucky, Louisiana, Mississippi, North Carolina, South Carolina, Tennessee, Virginia and West Virginia (Figure 5.4).

Membership includes state travel offices, convention and visitor's bureaus, destination marketing organizations, accommodations, attractions, advertising, media, educational institutions, product suppliers, travel writers and other related industry segments. STS goals are

(a)   to develop, market and promote domestic and international travel to the member states;
(b)   to have a governmental relations programme to serve as advocate of the Tourism Industry;

Figure 5.4   Beaches such as this at Key Biscayne, Florida characterize many of the destinations in the territory covered by the Southeast Tourism Society (Photo: J.R. Gast)

(c)   to develop tourism accreditation criteria to certify professionals in the tourism management field who want to dedicate their careers to the tourism industry;

(d)   to provide for an annual Tourism Marketing College with a curriculum that will further the education in marketing expertise of the members and others;

(e)   to provide programmes and services to the membership as identified by the Board of Directors.

STS continues its dedication to promoting and developing tourism and travel by leading regional and national organizations in innovative programmes and research. In 2002 STS formed the Southeast Tourism Policy Council (STPC), which interfaces with United States federal agencies and members of Congress. The STPC is featured as a case study of this chapter. (Part of the reference for this section was obtained from www.southeasttourism.org.)

Tourism facilitation

A number of political, economic, and social factors influence the government actions and regulations affecting tourism facilitation. Travel bans are imposed from time to time for political reasons. It is not unusual, for example, for a government to prohibit travel of its citizens to war zones or to territories of hostile nations where it has no means of protecting their lives and property. The US Department of State through the auspices of the Bureau of Consular Affairs, American Citizens Services, issues travel warning and consular information sheets, which are travel advisories to warn Americans about adverse conditions in specific countries or territories. Following the terrorism attacks of 11 September 2001, the US Department of Homeland Security was established to serve this purpose and to provide other safeguards for US citizens and international visitors.

In the past, visas were issued freely for travellers and other entry requirements were held to a minimum to avoid discouraging potential visitors. In the aftermath of worldwide terrorist attacks and actions in recent years, safety and security have become high priorities, and governments are re-addressing their regulations. As this book goes to print, new policies are being formulated, as discussed below, which will have a major impact on tourism facilitation.

In the United States, as well as other countries, the biometric chip (integrated chip) is being considered as a way of ensuring the proper identification of travellers. The biometric identifiers most commonly used for identification are face imagery or electronic fingerprint impressions. The accuracy of identification registers above 90 per cent when both are used. This technology is now being applied to travellers from nations who previously enjoyed easier access to the United States through the Visa Waiver Programme (VWP).

Residents from 27 countries participating in the US VWP are allowed to travel to the United States for stays of less than 90 days without obtaining a visa. Participating nations, include Andorra, Australia, Austria, Belgium, Brunei, Denmark, Finland, France, Germany, Iceland, Ireland, Japan, Luxembourg, The Netherlands, New Zealand, Norway, Portugal, San Marino, Singapore, Slovenia, Spain, Sweden, Switzerland and The United Kingdom.

This programme began in 1986 to facilitate travel and promote better relations between the United States and the participating countries. Despite the previous ease of travel, as of 26 October 2006, all new or renewed passports of travellers from these countries attempting to enter the

United States are required to have a machine-readable passport with an integrated chip (the United States is mandating two index-finger scans). At the same time, transportation carriers will be fined up to $3300 per violation for transporting any visitor travelling under the Visa Waiver Programme to the United States who does not meet these requirements.

Another screening process utilized by the United States began in 2004 aimed at securing our borders, facilitating entry/exit processes, enhancing the integrity of our immigration system, and protecting the privacy of visitors. The US Visitor and Immigrant Status Indicator Technology (US-VISIT) programme implemented by the Department of Homeland Security also employs biometric chip technology. Its purpose is to facilitate legal trade and travel across the borders of the US and is in place throughout selected airports, seaports and land ports of entry. This programme is administered by the Departments of Homeland Security and State. New technology is being introduced using radio frequency identification (RFID) technology for land ports in conjunction with heavy reliance on the machine-readable passport and the biometric chip for other ports of entry; but implementation has not been well thought-out, timely or efficient.

In a similar measure to facilitate travel while maintaining homeland security, the Department of Homeland Security also experimented with a Registered Traveler Program (RTP). The RTP allowed selected frequent airline travellers to have priority in airport security lines in exchange for providing more personal information. The programme operated with several thousand frequent travellers hand picked by the airline companies, and was implemented at six airports. Although the Transportation Security Administration (TSA) suspended the programme while evaluating its success, it is expected to be fully implemented and expanded because of strong support from the travel industry and major airports.

Currently, there is considerable discussion arising about the determination of security measures. Uppermost in the tourism industry's debate is determining the most effective and efficient methods of security inspections without overly disrupting travel. As shown by the examples of the VWP, RTP and US-VISIT programmes, careful consideration and cooperation with all participatory countries must occur to bring about desired policy outcomes. Added to this, governments are also seeking ways to stimulate the construction of needed tourist infrastructure, access roads, communications, airport facilities and the many other supply-side requirements for supporting tourism. Efforts are being devoted to conserving areas of natural beauty and developing and maintaining resort areas and sightseeing attractions. Local and national governments often encourage special festivals, sports-related events, entertainment and cultural activities to entice tourists to the area. As a result of increased visitation, other government services, such as police protection and crime control, maintenance of proper health and sanitary conditions and good communications are also necessary to support tourism. Together, the tourism industry and government must work to ensure that the best practice is used in providing these services for the traveller.

Special precautions in facilitating travel must also be taken when episodes of contagious diseases occur, as evidenced by the outbreaks of SARS (Severe Acute Respiratory Syndrome) and West Nile Virus or potential outbreaks such as Avian Influenza A, also denoted as 'H5N1'. On 3 April 2006, the World Health Organization reported an outbreak of H5N1 affecting humans in Egypt, which was the ninth country to report laboratory-confirmed human cases after the first case in Vietnam in December 2003.

Food handling and preparation require special precautions to reduce intestinal illnesses and/or exposure to life-threatening epidemics. Information can be found on the Websites of international travel organizations addressing warnings and advisories. While these measures may result in discouraging or inconveniencing travellers, they are necessary to not only ensure enjoyable tourism experiences at the destination but also to decrease the chance of global epidemics.

As the model for travel safety and security, the airline industry has introduced the most noticeably burdensome practices (exhaustive inspections of luggage and restrictions on items in carry-on bags and one's person). Many travellers may perceive these measures as a hardship which they choose not to endure. They may alter their destination choice and stay closer to home, which allows the selection of alternative modes of travel, such as trains, buses or private cars. Others may see it as part of the travel adventure and will not be deterred. The outcome depends, of course, on the motivations of individual travellers.

A continuing concern of many governments is immigration control. Nearly all countries strictly control the entrance of immigrants and enforce laws against illegal entry. Of particular concern are social pressures created by the need to care for jobless immigrants, and opposition expressed by the local labour force when jobs are scarce. Governments, entrusted with safeguarding their homelands must address the veracity of immigrants' paperwork. To admit foreign visitors and to facilitate their travel within a nation's borders is a political action. Therefore, the method by which a nation's international tourism is regulated becomes an aspect of its foreign policy, as well as its economic and commercial policy, and requires careful planning.

In the fall of 2005, the United States Bureau of Customs and Border Protection issued an Advance Notice of Proposed Rulemaking for the implementation of the WHTI. The WHTI would require passports as identification for travellers to the United States from Mexico and Canada. An encumbered entrance is likely to have a negative impact upon these two important feeder markets for the United States. Tourism industry leaders have expressed concerns over the reliance on passports as the only acceptable form of identification and have encouraged the government to develop a robust and focused public communications campaign to keep domestic and international travellers informed.

Many countries sponsor extensive exchanges, cultural programs, lecture services and other events to make people of the world aware of their customs and standards of living. The knowledge gained from contact between persons of different cultures can lead to increased understanding and a relaxation of tensions between nations. The adage mentioned in Chapter 2, 'When peace prevails, tourism flourishes', bears repeating here. (We examine this concept in depth later in this chapter.) International organizations, such as People to People and Rotary International, recognize this truth and support the exchange of people and culture. The implementation of *Glasnost* in the 1980s led to the doors being opened in Russia in the 1990s, thereby increasing travel into the country, and the dramatic 1989 demise of the Berlin Wall had a profound effect upon East–West travel and continues to do so.

The result is a deeper understanding among people of the world, increased commerce, and a greater step towards international cooperation. Today, a different climate prevails in which Russian relations with the rest of the world are shifting back to more centrist governmental functions. One positive effect of this change may be seen in the field of education. East Carolina University in Greenville, North Carolina, USA, for example, has recognized the contributions of Russian scholars and has supported hiring faculty and promoting visits by its faculty members to Russia as well as hosting Russian visitation on its campus.

Tourism and foreign policy

Jean-Maurice Thurot, noted for his research in tourism advertising, suggests that tourists create an economic dependence by the host country on tourist-generating countries. This dependence can influence the foreign policy of the host country towards that generating country. This is especially true in nations needing foreign exchange, or hard currency, for economic development. Nations in the process of economic development need to buy key items, especially capital equipment and technology, from the industrial nations in order to speed their own growth. They, in turn, can sell these tourism products to the developed nations.

Tourism as a policy for peace

A country must be made safe for residents and visitors. Civil strife and disorder, such as that occurring in Northern Ireland and England, have had a detrimental impact on tourism. The 1999 military discord in the former Republic of Yugoslavia, a country that used to welcome over 10 million visitors a year, has brought tourism to a virtual standstill. The current political problems in Venezuela and other parts of the world discourage tourism. Using Sri Lanka and the 2006 Israeli/Lebanese conflict as examples, the effects of war on tourism are described in detail later in this section.

In addition to war, the constant threat of terrorism weighs heavily on international tourism in the United States. The impact of terrorism in New York, Pennsylvania and Washington, DC in 2001 has significantly affected international arrivals to the United States, as evidenced by declines in international tourism in 2002 and 2003. Fortunately, since 2004 the trends have shown increasing numbers of international tourists to the United States. If present trends continue, the United States should be at or above pre-11 September 2001 levels by 2008.

Travelling contributes to '... interchange between citizens which helps to achieve understanding and cooperation', according to Ronald Reagan, a leading historical international peacemaker (Reagan, 1985). Can tourism be a generator of peace in today's society or is tourism simply a beneficiary of peace? Using democratic peace theory as a foundation in light of recent world conflicts and non-peace events, the answer to both queries could be yes.

The democratic peace theory is founded upon the premise that democracies rarely enter into war or militarized disputes with one another because of their common values. Although there are several examples of disputed cases, the claim that democracies do not engage each other is generally accepted as empirical fact by democratic peace theorists (Rosato, 2003). However, debate continues on the legitimacy of the theory. The American Revolution, the Second World War (in which Great Britain and the United States were pitted against, among other nations, the democratic nation of Finland) and the Border War in 1995 (in which Peru fought Ecuador) are three examples of nearly two dozen commonly debatable democratic wars. The list of disputable battles dates back to the Greek Wars of the fifth and fourth centuries BC (White, 2000).

Since democracies do not generally engage each other, then democratic states are motivated to spread global democracy because it will enhance national security and promote world peace – true even though it may involve engaging in war to create sustainable peace. This is a distinguishing characteristic of the democratic peace theory.

The democratic peace theory is based on the principles Immanuel Kant laid out in his essay entitled *Project for Perpetual Peace* in 1795 (Kant, 1795). In the essay, he proposed that the three definitive articles for perpetual peace are

1. The civil constitution of every state should be republican.
2. The law of nations shall be founded on a federation of free states.
3. The law of world citizenship shall be limited to conditions of universal hospitality.

A republican civil constitution ensures representation and requires citizen consent for the declaration of war. As citizens are the bearers of the financial and human burdens of war, they are less likely to support the declaration of unnecessary wars. Democratic leaders will typically not engage in a conflict that is unpopular among constituents for fear of being removed from office. Through a federation of free states, nations would be under a set of parameters that would transcend the laws of any one nation. If that set of laws ruled out war, then countries would be legally bound to settle disputes in peaceful ways. As the federation is extended, so too would be the principles of peace. Universal hospitality implies the right of a visitor in a foreign land to be treated hospitably – not as an enemy. Because of the finite size of the earth, its inhabitants must peacefully coexist for humanity to be sustainable.

As the theory has evolved since Kant's original work more than two centuries ago, the following are the three generally acceptable reasons that could lead democracies to engage in war: (1) self-defence in protection of the homeland; (2) prevention of blatant human rights violations in other states and (3) to bring about conditions in which democratic values can take root abroad (Rosato, 2003). The theory also provides at least two reasons why democracies do not compromise peace with other democratic states. They are norm externalization and mutual trust and respect. This foundation of democratic peace is illustrated in Figure 5.5.

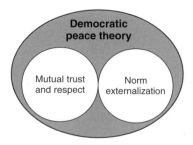

Figure 5.5 Components of the democratic peace theory

Under the assumption that peace can be achieved through the spreading of democratic ideals, and if two countries share similar democratic norms and values, then there are no norms that must be externalized upon other nations. Therefore nations with similar values will not fight with each other. Mutual trust and respect connotes that when conflict arises between democracies they will be inclined to accommodate each other or refrain from engaging in hard-line policies. Democracies trust the judgment of nations that believe similarly.

The expansion of democracy in the former Soviet states lent credence to Kant's theory of democratic states seeking pacific relations with one another. In other words, once democratic, the Soviet Union (or its remnants) was no longer the enemy of the United States.

A reason to maintain peace

International tourism is the world's largest export earner, making it vital to global trade. Tourism growth is also positively correlated to growth in global GDP. As global economies grow, disposable income typically also rises. The growth of international tourism arrivals generally outpaces GDP. However, because of the elasticity of demand for travel, if the economic situation tightens, spending on tourism will also typically decline (WTTC, 2005).

The absence of peace disrupts global trade and investment. And when global trade is disrupted, travel declines, which compounds the decline in global GDP. Therefore, tourism benefits from peace and the global economy benefits from tourism development.

Political stability, safety and tourism

When safety and security is endangered by expansionist policies of others, it is an occasion for democracies to jeopardize peace (Rawls, 1999). The democratic peace theory implies that democracy will bring about political stability. Political stability leads to safety and security in democratic nations. When safety and security is threatened, war will be engaged to ensure future safety and security.

Kant explicitly states that the visitor to a foreign land has the right 'not to be treated as an enemy when he arrives in the land of another'. In principle, the visitor must not be treated with hostility, as long as the visitor acts peacefully within the destination, but visitors to foreign countries today, and in the future, may not find this to be the case as a growing number of countries experience terrorist attacks. Heightened suspicion towards outsiders can lead to less than hospitable conditions where such attacks have occurred.

Travellers rank safety and security as key factors in planning a vacation or convention. Sixty-three per cent of international travellers to the United States report a destination's safety and security as extremely important. Without safety and security in the destination, both business and leisure travel will be negatively affected. In a study conducted by one of the authors of this book, 'Safety and Security' occupies the number one position in *The Ten Important World Tourism Issues for 2007* (Edgell, 2007). Once again, tourism benefits from peace.

An excellent example of the effects of war on a nation's tourism industry is Sri Lanka, which was involved in civil war from 1983 to 2003. The conflict stemmed from the desire of the Liberation Tigers of Tamil Eelam to create an independent state in the northeast region of the island, and resulted in fatalities estimated at 60,000 people. While the clash officially ended in 2003, the August 2005 assassination of the Lankan foreign minister has threatened to revive it (Figure 5.6).

During the years leading up to the war, the island nation had played host to a steadily increasing number of international visitors. As shown in Figure 5.7, international visitor arrivals decreased by 17.1 per cent in 1983,

Figure 5.6   The Elephant Orphanage at Pinnewela in Sri Lanka is a popular attraction during peaceful times (Photo: Jason Swanson)

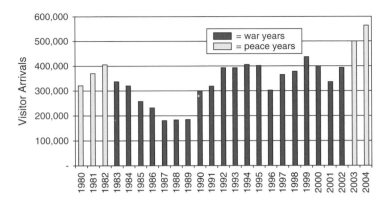

Figure 5.7   International Visitor Arrivals to Sri Lanka (*Source*: Sri Lanka Tourist Board)

the first year of the conflict. During the 20-year war, international visitation averaged 326,064 persons, ranging from 182,620 in 1987 to 436,440 in 1999. Only once in 20 years did visitation surpass pre-war numbers. After the end of the war, international visitation made significant gains, increasing 27.3 per cent in 2003 and 13.1 per cent in 2004 (Sri Lanka Tourist Board, 2004). Civil war in Sri Lanka stifled tourism for 20 years.

Similar effects were felt by tourism businesses in Israel and Lebanon during the month-long conflict that occurred in July and August of 2006. Known in Israel as the Second Lebanon War and in Lebanon as the July War, most of the action took place in Northern Israel and Southern Lebanon, killing over 1500 people and displacing 900,000 Lebanese and 300,000 Israelis.

Tovah Pinto, Director General of the Israel Hotel Association, reported after the conflict that crisis was looming, as the war had stifled 39 months of growth in Israel's tourism sector. The organization expected demand to fall by 50 per cent in the year following the conflict. Inbound international tourism to Israel is expected to decline by $1.1 billion, and its contribution to the GDP is expected to drop by $1.5 billion, according to the Israel Hotel Association. The Israeli government contributed to recovery efforts by compensating northern Israeli hotels for 60 per cent of their losses during the conflict.

In Lebanon, as the Israeli army entered, tourists naturally fled. Despite tourism development plans put in place before the conflict, the Lebanese Minister of Tourism stated the conflict will negatively affect tourism in Lebanon for 3 years afterward. Upon certainty of a cease-fire, the Lebanese tourism ministry planned a US $2.6 million marketing campaign to revitalize the image of the war-torn nation.

Mutual trust and respect created by tourism

Tourism is often promoted by industry organizations as a vehicle for cultural understanding. The UNWTO, states its position on the matter as, 'Intercultural awareness and personal friendships fostered through tourism are a powerful force for improving international understanding and contributing to peace among all the nations of the world'. Indeed, an entire subset of tourism has developed around the concept of promoting peace through travel. The International Institute for Peace Through Tourism was founded in 2000 to foster and facilitate tourism initiatives that create a peaceful and sustainable world through travel.

In addition to tourism industry organizations endorsing tourism's awareness-creating abilities, world leaders throughout modern history have also realized the benefits of tourism. Mahatma Gandhi said, 'I have watched the cultures of all lands blow around my house and other winds have blown the seeds of peace, for travel is the language of peace' (cited in Theobald, 1994). In 1963, John F. Kennedy stated, 'Travel has become one of the greatest forces for peace and understanding in our time.... we are building a level of international understanding which can sharply improve the atmosphere for world peace' (Kennedy, 1963).

US Secretary of State Condoleezza Rice, addressing the Global Travel and Tourism Summit Breakfast in April, 2006, celebrated the power of tourism by stating, 'Travel fosters understanding. It builds respect. The knowledge and experience that citizens gain in their private travels is vital to the cause of diplomacy and international understanding in the twenty first Century'.

Tourism cannot flourish without political stability and safety, which are restricted when peace is absent. Without peace, tourism is diminished; therefore, tourism is a beneficiary of peace. Through creating cultural awareness, tourism can be a stimulus for peace (assuming peace can be incremental). Unfortunately, tourism through intercultural awareness can also be used to impart violence or any other ideal closely held by either the traveller or host.

As indicated in Figure 5.8, peace can lead to political stability, which can lead to safety and security in the destination, which facilitates tourism. Depending upon the motivation of the traveller and the structure of the destination, tourism can create cultural understanding. Understanding of the people of other nations is a key ingredient leading to norm externalization and mutual trust and respect – critical components that lead to peace among nations, according to the democratic peace theory, as previously discussed in this chapter.

Tourism development – demand creation through marketing and supply expansion through investment – can be part of a strategy for geopolitical stability that includes the promotion of peace, economic development and

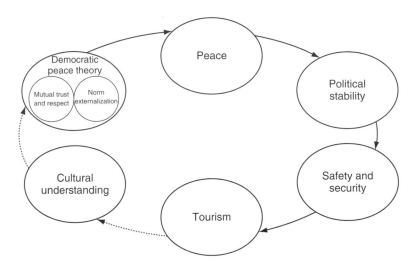

Figure 5.8 The relationship of tourism and peace

cultural awareness. However, a sound governmental strategy for peace must be based on more than just tourism.

Conclusion

The prospective economic benefits of tourism frequently influence the internal and foreign policies of governments. In some corners of our globe, inbound tourism is used to showcase the accomplishments of the government or party in power and to increase understanding abroad of the government's policies. Sometimes this approach is successful; sometimes it is not.

In terms of foreign policy, the response by governments to the impact of terrorism on tourism surpasses any prior attentions to security. The global tourism industry has been generally unprepared to deal with increasingly sophisticated acts of violence that use elements of the industry as weapons or targets, such as attacks against passenger trains in Madrid in March 2004, the October 2002 night-club bombings in Bali and the use of commercial airliners as missiles in the US in September 2001. As security becomes more important, organizations such as the WTTC have measures in place to proactively handle crises as they happen.

Private sector groups have conducted training sessions to deal with potential terrorism in light of recent attacks. The aftermath of such devastation has raised the awareness of service organizations, the medical community and the individual. Such efforts help, but for many pleasure travellers the worry, strain and inconvenience exact too much of a toll. It will take a strongly concerted effort of global cooperation, through policy, if the terrorism of the past three decades and its effects on travel and tourism are to be avoided in the future. This will facilitate international trade and development and contribute to efforts to foster peace and understanding. One means to facilitate this cooperation is through the work of intergovernmental tourism organizations such as those described, and many other proactive and productive groups throughout the world.

Case study 5

SOUTHEAST TOURISM POLICY COUNCIL: AN EMERGING MODEL FOR FEDERAL TOURISM ADVOCACY

Researched and Written by: Jason R. Swanson
Member of Southeast Tourism Policy Council

The Southeast Tourism Policy Council (STPC) is the government advocacy arm of the STS, a tourism industry trade association representing the interests of twelve states in the southeastern United States. While STS was established in 1983 and has long been active in governmental affairs, the STPC was formalized after the first-ever State-Federal Tourism Summit, organized by STS in 2002. Within two years after the Summit, the STPC established formal relationships with several federal agencies including the Departments of Interior, Agriculture, Commerce, Army and Transportation, the Environmental Protection Agency, the Advisory Council on Historic Preservation and the National Oceanic and Atmospheric Administration.

Many of these relationships were formalized on February 24, 2004 at a signing ceremony held at the Department of the Interior where a Memorandum of Understanding (MOU) was signed between the STPC and various federal agencies. Secretary of the Interior Gale Norton observed that all of the signatories were "strong advocates with common goals in support of public lands and the economic viability of tourism". Below is a list of signatory organizations on the MOU.

1. Department of the Interior
    a. Bureau of Indian Affairs
    b. Bureau of Land Management
    c. Bureau of Reclamation
    d. Fish and Wildlife Service
    e. National Park Service

2. Department of Agriculture
    a. Forest Service
    b. Natural Resource Conservation Service
3. Department of Commerce – Office of Travel and Tourism Industries
4. Department of the Army – Corps of Engineers
5. Department of Transportation – Federal Highway Administration
6. Environmental Protection Agency
7. Advisory Council on Historic Preservation
8. Southeast Tourism Society – Southeast Tourism Policy Council

The MOU led to the creation of the Federal Interagency Team on Public Lands Tourism, which consists of representatives of each agency. These representatives regularly attend STPC meetings and serve as liaisons between their agencies and the STPC.

The signing of the MOU gave the STPC significant credibility in Washington, DC and leverage when working on issues with the Federal Interagency Team and other federal agencies. In an effort to maintain visibility in Washington, DC the STPC arranges the STS/STPC Congressional Summit on Travel and Tourism each spring. The conference is an opportunity for any STS member who chooses to participate to hear about current policy issues from members of the Federal Interagency Team and members of the STPC. Attendees are also able to schedule appointments with members of Congress and their staff. This is an excellent opportunity for STS members to push STPC issues as well as other policy issues that are important at the local level.

Tourism policy issues

Listed below are the issues the STPC was actively involved with in December 2005. Following the list is a description of each issue, as supplied by Bill Hardman, Jr, President and Chief Executive Officer of the STS.

*   Proposal to sell forest and BLM lands;
*   Recreation fee program;
*   Impact of Katrina and Rita;
*   Reauthorization of the Federal Highway Program;
*   Public lands appropriations;
*   Facilitation of international travel;
*   Gateways bill;
*   National Outdoor Recreation Policy Act;
*   New Forest service estimate of recreation economic impact;
*   National Parks management policies;
*   Celebrating the interstate and new partnerships;
*   National Scenic Byways Program.

Proposal to sell forest and BLM Lands

The House adopted a proposal by Resources Committee Chairman Richard Pombo (R-CA) and Energy and Mineral Resources Subcommittee Chairman Jim Gibbons (R-NV) that would permit the sale of national forests and Bureau of Land Management (BLM) and Corps of Engineers lands that contain minerals. This would not apply to the National Parks, refuges, wild and scenic rivers, national trails or conservation and recreation areas. The provision was included in H.R. 4241, the Deficit Reduction Act of 2005. Although the provision refers explicitly only to "Mineral Development Lands Available for Purchase", it would apparently not preclude the purchased land to be used for straightforward development purposes, including residential and commercial development. Environmental organizations have strongly objected to it, and at this time, it has not received much support in the Senate, where it was not included in the Senate Deficit Reduction Act.

Recreation fee program

In subsequent discussions with Members of the Senate and key staff following the 26 October Senate Hearing described below, STS has been told that no further Congressional legislation regarding the recreation fee program is likely until next year at the earliest and probably not until 2007. At this point, Congress seems willing to wait for the agencies to complete their protracted implementation process.

On 26 October 2005, STS testified before the US Senate Subcommittee on Public Lands and Forests regarding the new recreation fee program. In this testimony, STS supported the recreation fee program and the work done by the Federal land agencies to implement it, although it was urged that implementation be expedited. STS urged that the new fee program be viewed as much more than another source of revenue, and should instead be regarded as part of a new, more innovative, flexible, visitor-focused way of managing the Federal lands and as encouraging closer partnerships between the Federal land agencies, State park and tourism agencies, the private sector and gateway communities.

STS continues to work with the Federal land agencies as they are developing guidelines for implementation of the 10-year new recreation fee authority passed by Congress in 2004 as the Federal Lands Recreation Enhancement Act (REA). Several interagency working groups have been formed to develop implementation guidelines for the new fee program. At a 11 February 2005 Department of Interior "Listening Session" with the interagency working group developing the newly authorized America the Beautiful Pass, STS urged the agencies to recognize the potential for this fee program as more than just a source of revenue, but also as a public information and marketing tool. STS also emphasized the importance of developing regional, intergovernmental passes and of working closely with state tourism offices and gateway communities in developing coordinated marketing campaigns combined with administration of the fee program. In a 21 March 2005 communication to Department of the Interior Director of External and Intergovernmental Affairs Kit Kimball, ARVC joined three other allied tourism and recreation organizations in urging that all interagency fee working groups meet with private and intergovernmental organizations to discuss the potential promise and ramifications of the new fee program.

At a 24 June 2005 "Listening Session" in DC on the Recreation Resource Advisory Committees (RRACs) mandated by the REA, STS recommended state-based RRACs instead of national or broad regional ones.

STS was assured in August by senior officials at the Department of Interior that a "state-centred" RRAC program will be established, and it has now been announced that existing state BLM Resource Advisory Committees would be relied upon to perform the RRAC role through special recreation subcommittees. STS questioned this approach in its 26 October 2005 Senate testimony because it is not clear whether the BLM RAC or the RRAC subcommittee would have greater authority. Senate Forests Subcommittee Chairman Larry Craig (R-WY) agreed with this STS concern.

The Forest Service has announced that it will discontinue entrance fees at 435 relatively undeveloped sites (while retaining fees at 4024 sites). The agency hopes this will mitigate continuing strong opposition to the fee program as evidenced by the passage by six state legislative chambers of resolutions condemning the program and demanding Congressional repeal. Congress is not expected to pass such repeal legislation but may hold further hearings on fee implementation by the agencies.

Gateway community businesses, outfitters and concessionaires are closely following reported plans to allow discounts to holders of America the Beautiful Passes for recreational activities such as camping. The concern is that such discounts will reduce net revenue for those private businesses.

Impact of Katrina and Rita

Hurricane Katrina and, to a lesser extent, Hurricane Rita have obviously inflicted severe human suffering and devastating property losses in the Gulf Coast. They are also having an enormous impact on Congress and the Federal government. Response and recovery to these two "storms of the century" have dominated debate and discussion on Capitol Hill. With overall projected costs in the $200 billion range, pressure is being exerted on every agency budget and general rescissions of 2–3 per cent are possible in already approved fiscal year 2006 budgets. The public lands agencies and international tourism marketing will not be exempted from such rescissions. Proposals have been made to cut back on the Federal Highway Program authorized by Congress just a few months ago, although this seems unlikely to happen.

The public lands agencies have also suffered considerable direct damage to their park and forest lands located in the Gulf Coast, with the cost of repair and replacement creating additional budget pressures. In November 2005, STS President Bill Hardman toured the coastal areas ravaged by Katrina to see the level of damage and how the travel and tourism industry is recovering in those areas.

Reauthorization of Federal Highway Program

Congress in July finally reauthorized the Federal Highway Program with the passage of SAFETEA-LU (H.R. 3), nearly 2 years and eight Congressional extensions after the 1 October 2003 expiration of TEA-21. SAFETEA-LU is a 3-year reauthorization that provides $286.4 billion.

The dollar amounts for the overall 6-year reauthorization and for specific programs are confusing because we are already 2 years into this reauthorization cycle, which will end 30 September 2009. Nonetheless, we can conclude that not only is the overall $286.4 billion nearly $50 billion more than TEA-21, but also, with one notable exception, that programs directly beneficial to tourism and recreation fared reasonably well compared with TEA-21, with the following amounts not subject to appropriations:

- Transportation Enhancements goes from $590 million annually to $686 million.
- Scenic Byways gradually increases from $26.5 million per year to $43.5 million in 2009.
- National Park Roads rises from $165 million annually to $225 million in 2009.
- Public Lands Highways, now $226 million, rises in steps to $300 million in 2009.
- Recreation Trails increases from $50 million to $85 million in 2009.

Supporters of recreational trails and sportfishing and boating were especially pleased with the outcome of SAFETEA-LU. Recreational trails will receive effectively a 62 per cent increase over TEA-21 and sportfishing and boating are rejoicing because the entire Federal tax of 18.3 cents per gallon collected on fuel used by motorboats and small engines will now go into the Wallop-Breaux fishing and boating trust fund. Previously, only 13.5 cents went into that fund. This means the allocation for sportfishing and boating should increase from $284 million per year to about $384 million. Unfortunately, attempts to establish a new categorical program of Recreational Roads with funding of $50 million, of which

68 per cent would have been allocated to Forest Highways and the balance to the BLM, Corps of Engineers and Bureau of Reclamation, was not included in SAFETEA-LU because of fiscal constraints. Very few new programs were authorized because there was not enough money to satisfy existing programs.

Controversy continues to rage over the wisdom of more than 5000 earmarked projects, or "set-asides", in SAFETEA-LU that absorb nearly 21 billion dollars in highway funds. It should be borne in mind, however, that many of these set-asides, including visitor centres, bridges, trails enhancements and restoration of historic sites, will directly benefit tourism and recreation, including many projects in western states.

Public lands appropriations

Both House and Senate have passed H.R. 2361, the fiscal year 2006 appropriations for the Federal land agencies. Following are the comparable amounts for key public land and recreation programs, showing the 2005 budget figures, President Bush's proposed budget for 2006, and the amounts approved by the House and the Senate. As the figures show, the public land agencies in general and their tourism and recreation programs in particular have not done badly in this time of very tight Federal budgets:

- NPS operations: 2006 appropriation, $1.744 billion. President Bush's Budget, $1.734 billion. Senate, $1.750 billion.
- NPS operations maintenance: 2006 appropriation, $594.7 million. President Bush's Budget, $595.6 million. 2005, $582.7 million.
- NPS construction: 2006 appropriation, $301 million. President Bush's Budget, $324.3 million. 2005, $353 million.
- NPS recreation and preservation: 2006 appropriation, $55 million. President Bush's Budget, $36.8 million. 2005, $61 million.
- Forest service recreation: 2006, $265.2 million. President Bush's Budget, $257.3 million. 2005, $257.3 million.
- Forest service trails: 2006, $72.5 million. President Bush's Budget, $63.8 million. 2005, $75.7 million.
- BLM recreation management: 2006, $66.1 million. President Bush's Budget, $664.6 million. 2005, $60.6 million.
- Fish and wildlife refuge management: 2006, $393 million. President Bush's Budget, $394 million. 2005, $381 million.
- Forest service fire fighting: 2006, $1.779 billion. President Bush's Budget, $1.735 billion. 2005, $2.099 billion.
- Interior department fire fighting: 2006, $762 million. President Bush's Budget, $756.6 million. 2005, $831 million.
- If there are agency wide rescissions because of Katrina/Rita recovery costs, the preceding figures will be lowered.

Facilitation of international travel

Western Hemisphere Travel Initiative (WHTI). On 31 October, STS President Bill Hardman submitted comments to the Bureau of Customs and Border Protection regarding the Advance Notice of Proposed Rule-making for the implementation of the WHTI. In his comments, he

- urged greater attention to the economic impact of any changes in border inspection and control procedures;
- expressed concern over reliance on passports as the only or de facto acceptable means of identification for travellers from Canada or Mexico;
- proposed that closer collaboration between the public and private sectors be institutionalized and made permanent;
- recommended that a robust and focused public communications campaign be developed to inform domestic and international travellers of any changes.

Biometric Passports for Visa Waiver Countries. On 15 June, DHS Secretary Chertoff announced that the United States will accept the production of digital photographs to satisfy the 26 October 2005, requirement of biometric identifications on passports for travellers from the 27 countries in the Visa Waiver Program. By 26 October 2006, the VWP countries will have to begin issuing passports with integrated circuit chips, or e-passports. (On 26 October 2005, VWP countries must present an acceptable plan to begin issuing e-passports by 26 October 2006.) There is concern that France and Italy will not be able to comply with this new digital photograph requirement.

Registered Traveller Program. After more than a year's experience, the Department of Homeland Security's Transportation Security Administration (TSA) on 26 September announced it would suspend a test program on 1 October that speeds airline travellers to the front of airport security checkpoints in exchange for providing more personal information. The "Registered Traveller" program operated at six airports and the participants were a few thousand frequent travellers hand-picked by the airlines. Because of strong support for the program from the travel industry and major airports, it appears now that the TSA will soon reinstate and expand the program following full assessment of the test program.

Gateways bill. H.R. 585 is expected to come up for a floor vote in the House of Representatives this fall. Representative George Radanovich (R-CA) reintroduced H.R. 585, the Gateway Communities Cooperation Act, in the first business week of the 109th Congress. The STS supports this legislation, while urging that state governors be given authority to designate communities as gateways.

In order to get H.R. 585 on the "Consent Calendar" in the House, which would mean prompt voice vote approval, revisions have been made in the legislation so that it will not be classified as creating a "new program" that would not qualify for the consent calendar. The main change has been to drop the small $10 million grant program from the bill.

National Outdoor Recreation Policy Act

There has been no further action with regard to the National Outdoor Recreation Policy Act. STS continues to work with the American Recreation Coalition and other recreation industry organizations to draft and advocate a National Recreation Policy Act. This would establish for the first time a national commitment to development of a recreation policy for the country. The bill itself would make no substantive changes in recreation policies or programs, but it could result in a sea change in the emphasis given to recreation on the Federal lands. It would accomplish three major goals:

(a)   It would "declare a national policy regarding the management and use of lands and waters administered by Federal agencies to provide the American public with abundant, high-quality and diverse recreational opportunities to enhance (1) public health and welfare, (2) appreciation of natural resources and the environment, and (3) economic benefits associated with outdoor recreation for gateway, rural and other communities";

(b)   It would direct the Secretary of the Interior to lead an interagency effort to prepare within 12 months "a national recreation strategy that identifies statutory and regulatory impediments to providing and facilitating a diversity of recreational opportunities on Federally-managed lands and waters, and appropriate means to increase the quantity and quality of recreation opportunities available to the public"; and

(c)   It would establish an ongoing Federal Recreation Inter-Agency Coordinating Council, with state and local government officials and others from the industry as advisors, to improve coordination of recreation programs and policies and implement the national recreation strategy.

STS joined other industry organizations in explaining this significant legislation to key staff on Capitol Hill. Resistance is expected from environmental organizations that will object to the emphasis given to recreation in this legislation and perhaps from some Federal land agencies that do not see recreation as a major part of their mission.

The draft bill is supported by at least 24 recreation trade associations although some have expressed concern that it would favour some modes of recreation over others. Most environmental and conservation organizations have not endorsed it. The Department of the Interior apparently has reservations about the need for national legislation and would prefer solving any problems through administrative actions.

New forest service estimate of recreation's economic impact

The Forest Service has drastically lowered its estimate of the economic impact of recreation on the national forests from $111 billion, which had been the figure for nearly a decade, to $11.2 billion. The agency maintains that this is a much more valid estimate because it is based on actual head counts of visitors and interviews of visitors to determine their spending patterns. Recreation industry organizations point out that this estimate only applies to visitor expenditures within 50 miles of National Parks and that it does not include billions of dollars in expenditures made farther away for recreation supplies and expensive "durables" such as boats, snowmobiles, skis and other durables, even though those purchases are made with the clear intent of using them on national forests. Concerns that the lower impact estimate will be used to justify a lower priority for recreation in the Forest Service budget are rejected by the agency, which points out that recreation is still the largest generator of revenue of all activities on the national forests.

The validity of the FS economic impact estimates has been supported by a new study of the economic impact of wildlife refuges by the US Fish and Wildlife Service. Although a much smaller impact of $1.4 billion is found for 2004, the economic assumptions and methodology are the same and the estimated impact is comparable to the FS when the smaller acreage of the National Wildlife Refuge System and fewer visitors to wildlife refuges are considered.

National Parks management policy

On 18 October 2005, the National Park Service proposed a new comprehensive policy for managing the National Parks, which is embroiled again in a conflict between those who see the agency's mission to be the unimpaired preservation of the natural resource and those who defend the right of the public to use and enjoy the parks.

In 2000, in the closing hours of the Clinton Administration, the last comprehensive parks policy was issued, over the opposition of recreation user groups who saw it as reducing access and use. Environmental groups are now concerned that the proposed plan will exalt use over protection of the parks. A draft proposal written last summer by Paul Hoffman, Deputy

Assistant Secretary of Interior for Fish and Wildlife and Parks especially stirred opposition from environmentalists.

The comment period for this new proposed management policy has been extended until 19 February 2006. The STS participated in a 16 November listening session at the Department of the Interior on the new policy on and is reviewing the proposed policy before deciding whether to submit comments.

Celebrating the Interstate and New Tourism-Transportation Partnerships

In 2006, the interstate highway system will be 50 years old. This 47,000-mile network is arguably the most significant public investment in the history of the nation, if not the world, and it has never cost the Federal treasury a dime since it has been entirely financed through the Federal motor fuel tax. Certainly, the tourism industry in America today has been dramatically shaped and boosted by the interstate system.

STS and the National Tourism and Recreation Coalition for Surface Transportation are joining with the American Association of State Highway and Transportation Officials (AASHTO) to plan an appropriate national celebration of the 50th anniversary of the interstate system in 2006. One project being considered is a reenactment of the 1919 military convoy across America led by then-Colonel Dwight D. Eisenhower, which left a lasting impression on the young colonel of the need for a modern national highway system, and resulted in President Eisenhower's signing into law the 1956 legislation and creating what became known as the Dwight Eisenhower National Defense Highway System. Although the 1919 coast-to-coast convoy spent 2 months traversing eleven states and the District of Columbia, next year's 2-week reenactment would feature participation from all fifty states. The travel and tourism industry and state transportation departments are being urged to work together to plan this celebration in every state.

At the same time, STS is working with the Transportation Research Board, AASHTO, and other travel and tourism and transportation organizations to develop a substantive strategy to promote better relationships between travel and tourism and state transportation departments in every state and to broaden support for future Federal highway policies.

National Scenic Byways Program

There is growing concern over the future of the national scenic byways program. Although the program fared modestly well in the TEA-LU highway reauthorization bill earlier this year, it is expected that it will come under increasing pressure in the next reauthorization bill in 2009, as fiscal resources diminish. STS participated in a 8 November meeting at the American Recreation Coalition to begin to develop strategies to strengthen political support for national scenic byways.

STS membership survey on policy issues

In the fall of 2005, the STPC surveyed members of STS, the people and organizations for whom the STPC serves as an advocate. The survey was conducted by Jason R. Swanson, a member of the STPC and one of the authors of this text. The survey had multiple purposes, including

- soliciting the input of STS members in developing the agenda for the STPC;
- creating a mechanism to periodically collect input from STS members;
- providing a guideline for prioritizing policy issues;
- proactively identifying emerging policy issues;
- generating information for policy makers regarding what is important to their tourism constituents.

The web-based survey was sent to all members of the STS, of which 149 tourism professionals responded. STS member organizations of all sizes and geographic locations were represented.

Respondents were asked to rank the importance of several policy issue categories, based on a five-point scale ranging from "1 Not important" to "5 Very important". The following list shows the average importance score for each of the policy issues.

Outdoor recreation (4.43)
Cultural preservation (4.21)
Environmental quality (4.13)
Transportation (4.09)
Federal highways (3.91)
Job creation (3.81)
Public lands (3.58)
Homeland security (3.54)
National tourism office (3.48)
National Parks (3.26)
International visitation (3.24)
Eminent domain (3.15)

This priority of importance can be considered when new issues are selected or when deciding on how to allocate resources for work with current issues. Accordingly, the priority can be applied to the December 2005 STPC issues, as shown below in Table 5.1.

Table 5.1 Priority for STPC issues based on membership survey

Possible priority for current STPC issues	Policy category numbered with priority of survey respondents		
1 Reauthorization of the federal highway program	1. Outdoor recreation	2. Cultural preservation	4. Transportation
2 National Parks management policies	1. Outdoor recreation	3. Environmental quality	7. Public lands
3 Proposal to sell forest and BLM lands	1. Outdoor recreation	3. Environmental quality	7. Public lands
4 National Outdoor Recreation Policy Act	1. Outdoor recreation	3. Environmental quality	7. Public lands
5 Recreation fee program	1. Outdoor recreation	7. Public lands	
6 Public lands appropriations	1. Outdoor recreation	7. Public lands	
7 New Forest Service estimate of rec. econ. impact	1. Outdoor recreation	7. Public lands	10. National Parks
8 National scenic byways program	2. Cultural preservation	4. Transportation	
9 National heritage areas legislation	2. Cultural preservation	10. National Parks	
10 Earth Island cases and categorical exclusions	3. Environmental quality	7. Public lands	
11 Celebrating the interstate and new partnerships	4. Transportation	5. Federal highways	
12 Gateways bill	7. Public lands	10. National Parks	
13 Facilitation of international travel	8. Homeland security	11. International visitation	

The survey validates the issues the STPC has chosen as being consistent with the needs or desires of the STS membership. However, several new categories of policy issues came out of the survey that should considered by the organization:

- Coastal land and sea issues: off-shore drilling, beach re-nourishment, coastal wetlands restoration;
- Federal per-diem rates for travel expenses;
- Third-party intermediaries (Expedia, Travelocity, etc.) and collection of occupancy taxes;
- Small business development;
- Cultural preservation, job creation, and environmental quality issues, which are important to mountain areas and cities could be expanded upon;
- Other "Other" responses from the survey (summarized):

  - Fuel prices;
  - Health insurance;
  - Motorcoach regulations;
  - Proposed Fair Tax law;
  - Federal flood insurance;
  - Improved federal system for tracking international visitation;
  - Eligibility for federal grants for tourism development projects;
  - Border crossing between Canada and US;
  - Government competing with private sector;
  - Federal money to promote niche tourism markets, such as agritourism;
  - Fair competition.

As previously stated, one of the purposes of the survey was to generate information for policy makers regarding various aspects of tourism. Specifically, the survey identified outdoor recreation as being extremely important to the tourism industry in the southeast as evidenced by the following:

1. Policy issues involving outdoor recreation are most important
2. Respondents think nature-based outdoor recreation attractions help motivate travellers to visit the area:
   - 49 per cent believe the majority of their visitors choose their destination because of its nature-based outdoor recreation attractions
   - 48 per cent report the majority of their visitors participate in nature-based outdoor recreation during their visit to the destination
   - 43 per cent indicate the majority of nature-based outdoor recreation attraction-use is attributable to visitors (as opposed to residents)
3. Nature-based outdoor recreation accounts for 15 per cent of total economic impact from tourism, according to survey respondents

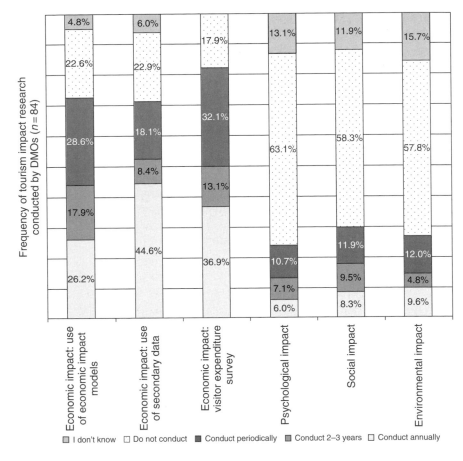

Figure 5.9 Tourism impact research conducted by DMOs

Many of the high-priority policy issues involve areas far beyond economic impact, such as outdoor recreation, cultural preservation, and environmental quality. However, not as much non-economic impact research is being done by DMOs, as shown in Figure 5.9. With a broader research spectrum, the tourism industry would be better able to provide information that is meaningful to a wider array of policy makers.

Opportunities for the future

A future hurdle for the STPC is conducting more rigorous policy analysis. Policy analysis is important for at least two reasons: (1) to decide on how STPC resources should be allocated based on those issues that may have the largest positive impact on the tourism industry and (2) to provide information that can be communicated in a meaningful way to the political decision makers, the media, and members of the tourism industry.

One way in which issues have been prioritized has been based on the likelihood that there will be success in achieving the objective of the particular policy stance. For example, if the political environment indicates the outcome on a particular issue is highly likely to be favourable to the STPC stance, then that issue is pursued. This approach does increase STPC's effectiveness, but the strategy may also take away consideration from other issues that may be more important to sustainable development.

Conducting valid policy analysis will help decide which side of an issue to be on when various members of the tourism industry may have competing agendas. Of course, it is often worthwhile in instances of conflicting views within the industry to pursue other issues that can serve to pull together, rather than polarize, the industry; or, alternatively, to come to a meaningful compromise.

One example of the tourism industry having conflicting views on an issue is funding for hurricane relief. Subsequent to the severe human suffering and devastating property losses sustained in the Gulf Coast region during the 2005 hurricane season, the US Congress proposed funding the expected $200 billion recovery by cutting the budgets of many of the programs that the STPC supports. The budgets of international marketing, federal highway reauthorization and public land agencies were among those programs targeted for budget cuts. On the one hand, STPC was interested in rebuilding an important tourism market; while at the same time, the organization did not want other programs it had supported to lose funding as a result. There was a significant federal appropriation towards the rebuilding of the Gulf Coast states and agency budgets were affected, however, a sort of compromise resulted. The Economic Development Administration within the Department of Commerce awarded STS a $625,000 grant program for a tourism marketing campaign focused on the Gulf Coast states of Louisiana and Mississippi, including the City of New Orleans. Undoubtedly, STS would have been far less likely to be awarded this grant had it not been for the relationships established through the STPC.

While it may not be in the current mission of the STPC, there could also be an opportunity for this organization, or similar organizations, to affect public policy at the state and local level. Through its policy analysis efforts on federal issues, the organization may also be able to offer policy analysis services, through dedicated policy professionals, to members of STS at the state and local levels.

In another means of affecting tourism at state and local levels, the STPC and its MOU could be a model for state tourism organizations to follow when trying to coordinate the efforts of various agencies in the state. The same can be true for tourism policy development at the local level.

Capitalizing on tourism's increasing economic and political importance, the STPC is now one of the most respected tourism advocacy groups in the United States and serves as a model for other regional policy advocacy organizations. More information on the STPC, including the organization's charter, can be found at http://www.southeasttourism.org/south_T_policy_council.html.

References

Edgell, Sr, David L. (2007). *The Ten Important World Tourism Issues for 2007.*

Kant, I. (1795). *Project for a Perpetual Peace.* Retrieved 22 November 2005 from http://www.mtholyoke.edu/acad/intrel/kant/kant1.htm.

Kennedy, J.F. (1963). *The Saturday Review,* January 5.

Rawls, J. (1999). A Theory of Justice. Oxford, England: Oxford University Press.

Reagan, R. (1985). Correspondence to 25th Session of the Executive Council of the World Tourism Organization. The White House, Washington, DC, 18 April.

Rosato, S. (2003). The Flawed Logic of Democratic Peace Theory. American Political Science Review, 97, 585–602.

Sri Lanka Tourist Board. (2004). Annual statistical report of Sri Lanka tourism.

Theobald, W. (Ed). (1994). *Global Tourism, the Next Generation.* Butterworth-Heinemann, Oxford, UK.

White, M. (2000). Democracies Do Not Make War on One Another . . . or Do They? Retrieved 14 October 2000 from http://users.erols.com/mwhite28/demowar.htm.

WTTC's World Travel & Tourism Economic Research. (2005). Retrieved 20 November 2005, from http://www.wttc.org/2005tsa/pdf/World.pdf.

6

Managing sustainable tourism

A guest never forgets the host who had treated him kindly.

Homer, *The Odyssey*, 9th century BC

As in times past, one of the strongest motivations for travel today is interest in the natural environment and in the heritage, arts, history, language, customs and cultures of people in other lands. The opportunity to observe how others live, think and interact with their environment exerts a powerful attraction. Travellers may seek to experience examples of a locale's arts, music, painting, sculpture, architecture, celebrations and festivals, or the cultural attraction may be food, drink, entertainment or some other special form of hospitality. The attraction might be an environment built with significant historical buildings or museums, or the natural environment with a beautiful landscape, a pleasant seashore, a magnificent mountain, a lovely forest, or the flora and fauna of the area. It simply may be the social interactions of human beings in their local surroundings. It is this quality of the environment – natural habitats, built structures, culture, heritage, history and social interactions – that will sustain tourism into the future and effect policy and management. It is essential to conserve and maintain these sustaining resources for future generations to enjoy as depicted in Figure 6.1.

Today, tourism is recognized as one of the fastest growing industries in the world. Such rapid growth and its concurrent development practices have put particular pressure on sustainable tourism planning and policy. Sustainability is uppermost among the concern of almost all industries at this time, so it is not unusual to see particular attention being paid to it. Significant new research on planning and policy concerns in sustainable tourism is contained in the book: *Managing Sustainable Tourism: A Legacy for the Future* (Edgell, 2006). The tenet with respect to sustainable tourism is to recognize that tourism experiences may be positive, or in some circumstances negative, and to recognize the need for planning and policy guidance to ensure that the continued growth of tourism will allow for a balanced tourism experience. Comprehensive planning decisions and implementation are prerequisite to policy decision-making. (The relationship of planning to policy will be more fully discussed in Chapter 9.)

Managing sustainable tourism depends on forward-looking policies and sound management philosophies that include a harmonious relationship among local communities, the private sector and governments regarding developmental practices to protect the natural, built and cultural environments while being compatible with economic growth. As stated earlier herein, sustainable tourism practices can be a viable means of providing a community or destination an improved quality of life and all that this encompasses.

Figure 6.1 Wildlife at Punta Arenas, Chile shares the land with visitors and members of the host community (Photo: Matt Schuttloffel)

A good example of this concept can be found in the services provided by the Kenya Wildlife Service (KWS) through its conservation programmes. KWS acknowledges responsibility for wildlife conservation and management practices, both within protected confines and in outlying, unprotected lands. Begun in 1992 with funding from the United States Agency for International Development, and continuing today, the Community Wildlife Services division collaborates with stakeholders on adjacent lands to lead conservation and land management efforts. The importance of successful management to sustainable tourism is summed up in the stated goal of KWS: 'To work with others to conserve, protect and sustainably manage wildlife resources outside protected areas for the benefit of the people. The community wildlife program of KWS in collaboration with others encourages biodiversity conservation by communities living on land essential to wildlife, such as wildlife corridors and dispersal lands outside parks and reserves. The premise is that "if people benefit from wildlife and other natural resources, then they will take care of these resources, using them sustainably".

Sustainable tourism – its essence

Pleasant climates, scenic wonders, beautiful coastlines and beaches, majestic mountains and valleys, rugged woods interspersed with rolling plains, magnificent skylines and the rhythmic sounds of the sea are all components of the natural environmental attractions that predicate large movements of travellers worldwide. Built structures, of which lodging, museums, attractions and art galleries are but a few, also form a major part of the tourism environment (Figure 6.2).

The common misperception of sustainable tourism is that it deals with the idea of being immediately 'renewable' or 'ongoing'. Simply put, sustainable tourism means achieving quality growth in a manner that does not deplete the natural and built environments and preserves the culture, history and heritage of the local community. Sustainable tourism references the natural surroundings plus the built environment, which consists of a montage of influences from history, heritage and culture.

In the context of this book, the co-authors define the word environment as the 'natural habitats, built structures, culture, heritage, history, and social interactions'. (This is meant not to diminish the importance of biota, but to emphasize the importance of cohabitation between it and the stakeholders.)

With orderly economic growth as part of the goal of sustainable tourism, the key is to balance the number of visitors with the capacity of the given environment, (whether natural or built) in a manner that allows the

Figure 6.2   Kauai, Hawaii, also recognized as 'The Garden Island', is representative of quality sustainable tourism and a popular destination for global visitors (Photo: Sarah J. Gust)

greatest interaction and enjoyment with least destruction. Another area to watch is the interdependency of the tourism industry with many other industries worldwide. There are many opinions on how this can be accomplished; however, there is general consensus that establishing a workable sustainable tourism policy is the beginning point. Such a policy must be comprehensive enough to include the concerns of the local population, but general enough to apply to tourists. As an example, carrying capacity is a major concern at the local level when discussing sustainable tourism. In its most straightforward definition, carrying capacity is the largest number of people a destination can efficiently manage within its given environ and management capabilities. When too many people convene at a location and the facility cannot handle this influx, the carrying capacity is compromised, which, in turn, harms the destination, its local citizenry and the economy. To meet this concern, effective planning steps must be taken in conjunction with overall policy guidelines. The case study that follows this chapter illustrates the balancing and compromising that must take place at the local level.

One might argue that no other industry shares a cause-and-effect relationship with so many different industries. It is this interdependency that sets the stage for the multidisciplinary nature of tourism. Current concerns in the petroleum industry (availability and pricing of gas) perhaps have the most impact, determining a traveller's decision to take an excursion, or how business travel is conducted. The airline industry is also affected by the petroleum industry, as well as by evolving safety and security procedures at any airport at any given time. The destination is influenced by the political environment of the locale, whether local or national, and health-related issues are important concerns influencing the tourism industry today. For a comprehensive discussion of the factors involved in the tourism mix, see Chapter 10. Since so many sectors of the economy have a bearing on sustainable tourism planning and policy, they should be 'part of the mix' when decisions are instituted.

A marketing trend has emerged in 2007 as the travelling public voices its concern about the impact on travel of the rising cost of fuels. New publications are developing, in print and on the Web, which make their pitch to the 'armchair' tourist, touting the adventure of travel without leaving your home and the 'zero cost' of the journey. With these advancements in telecommunications, the armchair tourist can visit an aquarium, tour an ancient castle, or trek the Great Wall of China. This phenomenon is also evidenced in the popularity of US television shows produced by The National Geographic Society, the Sundance Channel and the Travel Channel – all of which take the viewer to locations spanning the globe. Following on this concept, but involving some physical travel, is the publicity of destinations close to home. Articles advertise 'What's in Your Own Backyard' or 'Affordable Destinations Within a Day', that show the traveller economical ways to venture out on exciting journeys without spending much money on gas, hotels and so on. Another emerging item (albeit one that has been around for many years) focuses on 'environmentally friendly' destinations which, as the travelling populace has become more concerned and more expressive about sustainability issues, incline their efforts towards ecological methodology or 'green' awareness. More and more travellers are dedicated to the concept and support the growth of 'green' sustainable tourism destinations, such as those in St. John, US Virgin Islands, or in Homer, Alaska, as shown in Figure 6.3.

Figure 6.3 Small tourism businesses in Homer, Alaska, operate tours for those interested in the local environment (Photo: J.R. Gast)

Current trends in sustainable tourism

In 2002, Conservation International and *National Geographic Traveler* magazine created the 'World Legacy Awards' to recognize outstanding businesses, organizations and places that have made a significant contribution towards promoting the principles of sustainable tourism. National Geographic Society has developed a special unit, the Center for Sustainable Destinations, devoted to sustainable tourism initiatives. The March 2004 issue of *National Geographic Traveler* published criteria (described later in this chapter) to measure worldwide tourism destinations' adherence to best practices in sustainable tourism development. These criteria were first used to evaluate 115 world destinations as to their sustainability. In 2005, *National Geographic Traveler* released a special study on sustainable tourism practices in the National Parks of Canada and the United States, followed in 2006 by a survey of 94 world heritage destinations and a 2007 survey of island destinations, all using the same criteria. These four articles have provided much 'food for thought' throughout the sustainable tourism movement, as they have placed needed emphasis on the tourism industry's impact on our natural and built environments. (More of *National Geographic Traveler*'s findings can be found in the 'Global impact' section of this chapter.)

There is also increased awareness of sustainable tourism's place in the curriculum in higher education. This can be seen at such institutions as East Carolina University in Greenville, North Carolina, USA, where students in the College of Human Ecology can study undergraduate coursework on tourism, with an emphasis on sustainable tourism.

The concept of sustainability as a resource development and management philosophy is permeating all levels of policy and practice relating to tourism, from local to global. More than ever before, sustainable tourism management of the natural and physical environments must coexist with economic, socio-cultural, health, safety and security objectives of localities and nations. Finding a balance between economic growth and protecting the natural and built resources is challenging governments and businesses alike to cooperate in sustainable tourism development. The additional broad challenge of cooperation among the members of the tourism community to support sustaining tourism is also coming to the fore. The concept of utilizing sustainable tourism development as an economic stimulator to achieve growth while maintaining the natural and built environment is receiving greater attention and emerging simultaneously from industry, government and academia.

Environmental responsibility and land planning are two very important factors in adopting and managing sustainable tourism practices, and it is through such accomplishments that a 'sense and respect of place' can be achieved. One development that has proceeded in this vein is found at Bald Head Island, North Carolina, USA. Bald Head Island is actually a village, located off the coast of Brunswick County, with a land mass of 4.3 square miles and water mass of 1.5 square miles. Bald Head Woods Coastal Reserve, a maritime forest located in the centre of the island, Bald Head Island Natural Area, the estuarine waters next to Middle Island, and a significant parcel of land on the island's southeast point have been designated by the State of North Carolina as protected lands. Also overseeing the sustainability of the natural habitat of the barrier island are the Smith Island Land Trust and the Bald Head Island Conservancy, both originating locally. Four other areas are designated as Significant Natural Heritage Areas (SNHA), as defined by the North Carolina Division of Parks and Recreation.

Gleaned from the Bald Head Island Land Use Plan, Table 6.1 shows the total land area committed to the concept of sustainability in the Village of Bald Head Island. The Land Use Plan reports, 'Natural resource fragile areas are generally recognized to be of educational, scientific, or cultural value because of the natural features of the particular site. These areas include complex natural areas, areas that sustain remnant species, pocosins, wooded swamps, prime wildlife habitats, or registered natural landmarks. – The Bald Head Island Conservancy has ongoing efforts to acquire additional properties and conservation easements throughout the Village to further this cause'. Efforts such as those at Bald Head Island demonstrate that a harmonious coexistence between man and nature can occur.

Table 6.1 Village of Bald Head Island, Significant Natural Heritage Areas (SNHA) and protected lands

Area	Acres	% of total town acres
Bald Head Woods Coastal Reserve	191.1	6.1
Bald Head Island Natural Area	1143.3	36.5
Bald Head Island SNHA	1753.1	56.0
Bluff Island and East Beach SNHA	49.1	1.6
Lower Cape Fear River Aquatic Habitat SNHA	51.7	1.7
Middle Island SNHA	1026.3	32.8

Source: North Carolina Parks and Recreation Department and CGIA.

Apart from being inherently good for tourism, a clean, healthy and protected environment is also a key to its competitiveness. Increasing numbers of tourists are willing to pay more for a cleaner environment. An important survey by the Travel Industry Association of America found that 83 per cent of travellers would support companies that have good environmental practices. Moreover, the survey showed that travellers would spend 6.2 per cent more on average for travel services and products offered by environmentally friendly companies.

Tourists in New Zealand can have this experience. The country is proactively highlighting its Maori culture while preserving and promoting Maori traditions and the environment. According to Meriana Taputu, 'Whirinaki Escape Walk is proving popular with international visitors who want a 'genuine' cultural and environmental experience. People come because of the intimacy of the experience. It's more than eco-tourism; it's the connection my people have with the forest'. Numerous Maori tourism ventures operate in New Zealand, all focusing on the many contributions the Maori have made in the country's history. Another example is the Whale Watch Kaikoura which began when the elders of the Ngati Kuri iwi ('iwi' means tribe) wanted to improve relations between the iwi and the townspeople. Meriana Taputu continues, 'Whale Watch Kaikoura has won many awards including a gold award from the Pacific Asia Travel Association, the British Airways Award for best eco-tourism venture and the Green Globe Achievement Award in Berlin for distinction in tourism' (http://www.newzealand.com/travel/media/features/maori_maori-creativity_feature.cfm, 2006).

The bottom line is that the environment is the tourism industry's most important resource. The environment is the essence of most tourism products. Whatever the tourist's goal may be – lying on a beach, diving, whale watching, hiking, biking, kayaking as shown in Figure 6.4 or visiting sites

Figure 6.4   A group of young vacationers enjoy nature by kayaking, which has only a limited impact on the environment (Photo: J.R. Gast)

and attractions, it is the experience and enjoyment of the environment that the tourism industry markets.

In addition to cultural, historic, heritage and arts sites, ecosystems – reefs, forests, arctic tundra, rivers, coasts, islands, plains, lakes and mountains (with all their varied flora and fauna) – are powerful attractions to holidaying travellers. Almost no other industry is as dependent on the quality of the environment as tourism. In taking all necessary steps to ensure the protection and enhancement of the natural and built environments through sustainable tourism management, we increase the carrying capacity of such valuable sites.

Choosing a management approach or combination of approaches is a complex process, requiring the evaluation of economic, environmental, cultural, heritage and social factors. Whether working in the public or private arena, the objective must be to design the least intrusive form of intervention that results in efficient, effective and equitable decisions on tourism development and use of natural and built resources. Success depends on fostering practical, acceptable and profitable tourism enterprises while preventing damage to the local environment. These choices become critical in determining long-term tourism sustainability.

Stanley Selengut has been a pioneer in promoting good sustainable tourism management practices. His innovative approach to the precepts of sustainable tourism management is evident in his development of Maho Bay, Harmony, and Concordia Estate in St. John, US Virgin Islands, particularly upon notice that the lands of Maho Bay are greener and more beneficial to the ecosystem than the protected parklands surrounding this site (Edgell, 2006).

The natural environment

Most people conceptualize the word 'environment' as the natural world. *Webster's II New College Dictionary* (copyright 2001) defines environment simply as 'surrounding'. Tourist programmes designed around ecology, agriculture or adventure put the focus squarely on those surroundings.

History shows us that tourists and the natural environment are not always compatible. The natural environment deteriorates every time a tourist collects a piece of underwater coral or a special rock. Other tourists trample fragile tundra or otherwise alter natural flora and fauna. Some take indigenous artifacts or deface buildings as central to Western history as the Parthenon. Past experience paints a bleak picture for tourism's interaction with the environment, pointing to a need for educational programmes to help protect the world's natural and built environments. 'Only when it has been identified what it is about specific environments that make them attractive to tourists, can there be understanding about what may need to be done in order to keep them attractive to tourists' (Butler, 2000). Policy planners must examine tourists' needs and desires and weigh

Figure 6.5   Transportation infrastructure from the twenty first century co-exists with buildings from the sixteenth century in the area surrounding charminar in Hyderabad, India (Photo: J.R. Gast)

those considerations against factors such as environmental protection, overcrowding, traffic congestion (as shown in Figure 6.5) and an overload on the local infrastructure.

The built environment

There are representative expressions of people and places that provide powerful attractions for travel and it is this transculturation which fuels much of the tourism industry today. Given that a major force in tourism is the interest of people in language, customs, traditions, cultures and environments that are different from their own, it is clear that tourism has led to a closer association and mingling of people of different races, creeds, religions and cultures. Festivals celebrating Native American or other local cultures, or even particular fish or fruit, are commonplace in the United States, and many people are drawn to these events.

However, there is a growing concern about the detrimental impact that mass international tourism may have on local cultures and that an area's customs will become distorted if its festivals and ceremonies are staged as spectacles for the benefit of visitors. The business community must work closely with local citizens to garner their input into planned events and to ensure that any special needs or cultural preferences are considered.

Thus, tourism is viewed by some as contributing to the disappearance of traditional human environments and replacing them with towers of artificial concrete, ideas, ethics and morals and, in effect, threatening the whole fabric of tradition and nature. In addition, there is concern that as such distortions arise, the host and guest become a part of separate worlds leading to even greater prejudices and misunderstandings (Edgell, 2006).

Policy directives should address the social impact of tourism to the local citizenry if the destination is to be truly sustainable. Some questions follow:

- Are there sufficient key services to assist a local community's understanding of developing and marketing their product, and its subsequent delivery?
- Is there a plan in place to focus on stated provision of services?
- Is the community prepared for the influx of tourists?
- Does the product add to the 'quality of life' for the community's people?

Care should be taken in the planning stages to address these questions and others which may arise. Although a project may be economically viable or environmentally sound, it might not have the wherewithal to improve the quality of life of the host community. The overall plan should address the economic, environmental and social impacts of the project.

Global impact

Worldwide, the travellers' interest in sustainable tourism has grown enormously since the beginning of the twenty-first century, and it will likely continue to do so over the next several years as the international tourism community fully recognizes, endorses and promotes the concept. Sustainable tourism is part of an overall shift which recognizes the importance of orderly economic growth combined with concerns for the natural environment, cultural integrity and quality of life – social values that will be the driving force for long-term progress in sustainable tourism development plans and policies.

In 2004, the magazine *National Geographic Traveler* (March 2004) completed a survey, 'Index of Destination Stewardship'. The released rankings measured tourism sustainability in 115 world destinations. The magazine worked with members of the National Geographic Sustainable Tourism Initiative and a team from Leeds Metropolitan University in England to conduct this complex global survey. Over 200 experts in the sustainability of tourism and destination quality were asked to rate each destination they had recently visited personally. The rating of each destination was based on the following six criteria:

1. environmental and ecological quality;
2. social and cultural integrity;

3. condition of any historic buildings and archaeological sites;
4. aesthetic appeal;
5. quality of tourism management; and
6. overall outlook for the future.

The global 'Leeds' panel comprised of experts in a variety of fields – ecology, sustainable tourism, geography, urban and regional planning, travel writing and photography, historic preservation, cultural anthropology, archaeology and related disciplines. Most were seasoned travellers and generally had good evaluation skills. The results of the survey and subtitles of the published article (Tourtellot, 2004) were divided into three general categories: 'The Good', 'Not So Good' and 'Getting Ugly'. The pronouncement was revealing and surprising to many of the destination managers and to many in the travel world. It serves as a good measuring stick and an incentive for destinations to take stock and to seek improvements, where necessary, for the future of their areas. A 2005 article, also by Tourtellot, 'Destination Scorecard: How Do 55 National Park Regions Rate?' (*National Geographic Traveler* July/August 2005) focused on national parks in Canada and the United States and followed the same formula previously described. Tourtellot followed these two ratings with one in 2006 which questioned 'How Do 94 World Heritage Destination Stack Up?' He tells us 'Some are doing well; others suffer from pollution, poor management, overdevelopment – even, perhaps, from being added to the list.' (Tourtellot, 2006). (The island destination rating has not been published by press time of this book.)

Sustainable tourism policy in today's world is a positive approach that seeks to maintain quality tourism products over a sustained period of time in order to meet the growing domestic and international market for environmentally sound tourism experiences. Humans have the ability to manipulate and modify certain aspects of the environment for better or worse; therefore, unless careful policy prescriptions and management tools are utilized, tourism can lead to a degradation of the environment and otherwise diminish its attributes for use by future generations. It is notable that the visitor has an obligation to ethically support sustainable tourism, and destinations must responsibly educate their visitors towards meeting this goal. A good example of such is contained in a 'Code of Ethics for Tourists' as published in *Parks Canada Vacation Planner*. Its five mandates follow:

1. Enjoy our diverse natural and cultural heritage and help us to protect and preserve it.
2. Assist us in our conservation efforts through the efficient use of resources including energy and water.

3. Experience the friendliness of our people and the welcoming spirit of our communities. Help us to preserve these attributes by respecting our traditions, customs and local regulations.
4. Avoid activities which threaten wildlife or plant population, or which may be potentially damaging to our natural environment.
5. Select tourism products and services, which demonstrate social, cultural and environmental sensitivity.

The investment into sustainable tourism practices, whether made by international companies or the local community, has a great impact on the global tourism marketplace. Several international programmes have surfaced in response to the tourism industry's wishes to support sustainable tourism.

Planning first

The general concept of planning implies a relationship to the future based on an understanding of current trends and the environment's present condition. Also thrown into the process are the ever-changing factors of consumer demand, supply, the environment within the industry, health alerts, security threats and myriad other issues. Organization of the planning process to focus on all of the economic, environmental, social and cultural pulls of both the destination and the tourist that directly impact tourist visitation is a necessary first step towards creating successful tourism policy strategy.

The subject of planning is addressed here as it relates to the local level more than at the state/province, regional, national or international levels. It is at this level that the planners' concerns are maximized.

How will tourism development affect the local community? Will the area be able to continue its daily routine and services? Are the negative impacts on the community's resources too great? Exploration of all possible juxtapositions could go on indefinitely, but with the use of effective research techniques, good planning can take place.

Goeldner and Ritchie (2006) apply a 'systematic manner' for proper planning (summarized below) as follows:

1. Define the system.
    a. What is the scale, size, market, character and purpose?
    b. Formulate objectives.
2. Gather data.
    a. Fact finding, or research, provides basic data that are essential to develop the plan.

3. Analyse and interpret.
   a. Once collected, the many fragments of information must be inter-preted so the facts gathered will have meaning.
   b. This step leads to a set of conclusions and recommendations....
4. Create the preliminary plan.
   a. ...alternatives are considered and alternative physical solutions are drawn up and tested.
   b. Frequently, scale models are developed ...; sketches are prepared ... financial plans are drafted ...; and legal requirements are met.
5. Approve the plan.
   a. The parties involved can now look at plans, drawings, scale models, estimates of costs and estimates of profits and know what will be involved and what the chances for success or failure will be.
6. Create the final plan.
   a. ... typically includes a definition of land use; plans for infrastructure facilities ...; architectural standards; landscape plans; zoning and other land-use regulations; and economic analysis, market analysis and financial programming.
7. Implement the plan.
   a. ... carries out the plan and creates an operational tourism development.
   b. It also follows up and evaluates.
   c. ... provides mechanisms that give continuing feedback on the tourism project and the levels of consumer satisfaction achieved.

Policy and management strategy

The policy question often raised is: Can tourism be economically viable for private companies and local communities while also being sensitive to environmental, cultural and social needs? The short answer is yes (Edgell, 2006). Sustainable tourism policy should be dictated by the area's natural and built environments, incorporating preservation of sustainability of the locale. More than just economics, the development of tourism policy should focus on the principle of sustainable tourism. The intergovernmental United Nations World Tourism Organization stated in its conceptual definition of sustainable development of tourism (2004):

> **Sustainable tourism development guidelines and management practices are applicable to all forms of tourism in all types of destinations,** including mass tourism and the various niche tourism segments. Sustainability principles refer to the **environmental, economic and socio-cultural aspects** of tourism development, and a **suitable balance must be established** between these three dimensions to guarantee its long-term sustainability.

Thus, sustainable tourism should:

(1) **Make optimal use of environmental resources** that constitute a key element in tourism development, maintaining essential ecological processes and helping to conserve natural heritage and biodiversity.
(2) **Respect the socio-cultural authenticity of host communities**, conserve their built and living cultural heritage and traditional values, and contribute to inter-cultural understanding and tolerance.
(3) Ensure viable, long-term economic operations, **providing socio-economic benefits to all stakeholders** that are fairly distributed, including stable employment and income-earning opportunities and social services to host communities, and contributing to poverty alleviation.

Sustainable tourism development requires the **informed participation of all relevant stakeholders, as well as strong political leadership** to ensure wide participation and consensus building. Achieving sustainable tourism is a **continuous process** and it requires **constant monitoring of impacts**, introducing the necessary preventive and/or corrective measures whenever necessary.

Sustainable tourism should also maintain a **high level of tourist satisfaction** and ensure a meaningful experience to the tourists, raising their awareness about sustainability issues and promoting sustainable tourism practices amongst them.

Another aspect of tourism important to the host community is its anthropological and cultural heritage. Members of the host community are the best resources to create an authentic experience for visitors to the area. If anthropological experts are actively involved in tourism policy development, the destination stands a greater chance of building upon cultural transactions and the social consequences of tourism. Put simply, with successful collaboration between policy professionals and local officials, intricate relationships can be circumvented. This connection of both the resources and the values of a community aids in the development and planning practices implemented to balance demands and needs, and the cooperative effort benefits the community and the natural environment during the process.

In terms of natural resource utilization, there should be a careful balance between the needs of the host community and the needs of the tourism industry. Any negative environmental impact may, in turn, have considerable social impact if not properly managed through proactive policy. Upon successful consideration of the economic, environmental, social and cultural environs of a locale, a sound sustainable tourism policy can be adopted. An important document addressing the issue of sound policymaking and commitment to long-term sustainability has been published by the World Travel and Tourism Council (WTTC). In 2003, the

WTTC released its vision, *Blueprint for New Tourism*, calling for leaders in the travel and tourism industry to recognize the challenges the industry must take.

Benefits

Tourist attractions in both the natural and the built environments are tremendous engines for economic growth. Unspoiled natural ecosystems, well-maintained historic sites and cultural heritage events can produce economic gains and quality of life benefits. Satisfied visitors are likely to be repeat visitors and, in the long run, are keys to the overall economic growth of tourism to a local community. The more important question to consider is whether governments, private sector entities, local communities, non-profit organizations and tourists are ready to accept, plan for, participate in, lobby for and manage tourism programmes which are environmentally, socially, culturally and economically sensitive to support sustainable growth. The growth of the safari business in Kenya, for example, supports this ideal as well as the efforts of the KWS described earlier. Once again, education of the local and governing people and of the tourist is vital to accomplish this task.

The economic benefits of successful sustainable tourism management include developing new businesses, expanding job growth, increasing income, marketing new products, improving infrastructure, encouraging diversification, integration of the local economy and special opportunities to link with other services and products. When planners and policy makers consider these important segments in their development of a tourist destination, it can also promote community pride and yield a higher quality of life.

Sustainable tourism development may require changes in existing policies and practices depending on each locale. The problem that governments and the private sector often have with defining the economics of protecting the environment is attempting to assign values to the protected resource. Measures are being developed but, as of now, are not easily defined. However, 'Destination Scorecards', such as those produced by *National Geographic Traveler*, have succeeded in introducing the travelling population to these problems and providing a source of measurement for governments and the private sector enterprises engaged in this field. Also, some economic research is underway to produce environmental indicators along the same line as economic indicators. The key will be finding good management techniques to support sustainable tourism goals (Figure 6.6).

Figure 6.6 The balance between commercial development and environmental management is often a challenge (Photo: Jason Swanson)

Some of the needed strategy changes may be major and costly to a community, but the results will be worthwhile in the long run. Because local participation and/or control are important keys to success, progress depends on forging a partnership of stakeholders, both public and private, committed to implementing positive change. Recognizing the need for and importance of sound tourism initiatives, tourism organizations the world over are devoting their energies towards the development of sustainable tourism policy.

Important precepts

It is important to consider sustainable tourism strategies and guidelines as an area contemplates tourism development. Edgell (2006) stated certain basic precepts to keep in mind:

1. The first requisites are to inventory, assess and seek to develop as many visitor attractions as possible with roots in the local community or which complement local activities. If properly developed and maintained, local cultural and heritage initiatives can improve the overall ambiance of the area and add to the quality of community life. At the same time, local pride and cleanliness of the area may evolve with good leadership as tourism moves throughout the community.

2. Development within each local community should strive to keep the uniqueness of the environment preserved. If there are period historical buildings, special natural resources or sensitive culture traits available, a community should capitalize on such resources. This approach keeps the authenticity of the area intact which enriches its value to the visitors and local people alike.

3. Any realistic guidelines for sustainable tourism development must include community involvement. Not only is it good public relations to canvass the local population in the tourism development process but it also will result in the ultimate success of the endeavor. The community then becomes an effective force in assisting in the implementation of the program.

4. A local community should seek to measure tourism development in the light of environmental and social costs and benefits to the area. Sustainable tourism should be viewed in terms of both short-term and long-term values to the community. Intangible values such as 'quality of life' should be added or included in the overall quantification of sustainable tourism development.

5. Marketing of sustainable tourism must utilize e-commerce tools as well as taking advantage of 'coopetition' (partnerships, strategic alliances). Most sustainable tourism destinations will rely heavily on 'niche' marketing or other forms of database marketing. An effective, regularly updated Web site will be important in the marketing mix for the local tourism products.

The Credo

The key to sustainable tourism is to manage the destination within the given natural and/or built environment effectively to provide benefits to the local population, to enrich the visit of the tourist and to preserve the tourism products for future generations to enjoy. Natural areas must be preserved and flora and fauna protected. Customs and traditions must not be discarded, and privacy and dignity must be maintained. Ultimately, properly managed sustainable tourism will add far more than its cost in effort and planning to the quality of life of local communities, visitors and tourism employees alike. That is the reason for today's urgent call to develop strategies and guidelines to assure that this phenomenon happens.

When thinking about sustainable tourism, a good maxim is the proverb (original source unidentified), 'We have not inherited the Earth from our ancestors. We have only borrowed it from our children'.

Case study 6

SUSTAINABLE ECOTOURISM: BALANCING PRESERVATION AND ECONOMIC GROWTH (EDITED FOR THIS PUBLICATION)

Researched and Written by: Joseph P. Flood, PhD
Department of Recreation and Leisure Studies
East Carolina University.

Introduction

Sustainable Ecotourism: Balancing Preservation and Economic Growth creates a road map to address community challenges for balancing the preservation of both rural culture and ecology, while recognizing the reality of urban encroachment and development, and tourism impacts, such as traffic and pollution. Ecotourism is one of the fastest growing international industries but requires management, planning and policy for sustainable tourism programmes to succeed. Ecotourism embraces not only conservation of natural and built environments but includes agribusiness, geotourism, as well as the subset of heritage: museums, local historic sites, art, ethnic events and recreation in the form of canoeing, hiking, fishing and kayaking. Research suggests that each of these categories encourages enrichment of the local economies, the creation of jobs and the preservation of both cultural history and wildlife habitat.

Lascuráin's (1987) original definition of ecotourism was described as "traveling to relatively undisturbed or uncontaminated natural areas with the specific objective of studying, admiring, and enjoying the scenery and its wild plants and animals, as well as an existing cultural manifestations (both past and present) found in the areas". In 1991, the Ecotourism Society redefined ecotourism as "Responsible travel to natural areas which conserves the environment and improves the well-being of local people". Wight (1994) further suggested that it is critical that the principals fueling ecotourism must "promote understanding and involve partnerships between players, which could involve government, non-governmental organizations, industry, scientists, and locals (both before and during operations)". Honey (1999) offered a more refined definition stating that "Ecotourism is travel to fragile, pristine and usually protected areas that strive to be low impact and small scale; It helps the traveler, provides funds for conservation; directly benefits the economic development and political empowerment of local communities; and fosters respect for different cultures and for human rights" (p. 265).

While all these opinions and definitions shaped the foundation for future ecotourism developments, Drumm and Moore (2005) present the following elements as crucial to successful ecotourism efforts. They argue that a recipe for success must include initiatives that

- have a low impact on a protected area's natural resources;
- involve stakeholders (individuals, communities, ecotourists, tour operators and governmental institutions) in the planning, development, implementation and monitoring phases;
- respect local cultures and traditions;
- generate sustainable and equitable income for local communities, and for as many other stakeholders as possible, including private tour operators;
- generate income for protected area conservation; and
- educate all stakeholders about their role in conservation (p. 15).

Critical importance of stakeholder meetings

Gifford Pinchot (1910) believed that the best interest of the public, and their often conflicting interests, was most effectively served by the "greatest good of the greatest number [of people] in the long run". Today, it is still unclear who is best qualified to make choices on behalf of local communities. Recently, it has become common for community volunteers to work together as stakeholders to establish common goals and interests, satisfy disparate groups' opinions and create a collective success in protecting their local culture while generating the most responsible and cost-effective use of natural resources and protecting ecosystem function. While groups typically consist of a core group of residents with diverse backgrounds and agendas, they seek common ground on behalf of the community as a whole. Public interest in managing public lands for maximum community benefit, ecotourism revenues, preservation of culture, heritage and wildlife habitat involves predicating division and/or distrust with cooperation. Diversity of opinion among stakeholders can be as large as the issues themselves. An additional issue is that disparity may exist in terms of decision-making based on which members have the most time to invest in the process, or the deepest pockets. However, in addressing myriad challenges involved with policymaking and legal processes involving federal land managers, stakeholder meetings and forums are working together effectively to convey their interest in assisting the process.

The *Quincy Library Group*, located in northern California, and the Swan Valley ad hoc group from northwestern Montana were organized in the early 1990s for the purpose of settling a stalemate involving impacts of logging, use of public lands and forests, protection of endangered flora and fauna species and the actions of forest management practices on public lands. While historically these groups held strongly diverse and often antagonistic viewpoints, over a period of nearly 20 years, and myriad meetings, loggers and environmentalists began to see beyond polarized positions and started to work collaboratively to solve public land issues while creating innovative solutions that have demonstrated much promise.

Stakeholder groups often recognize quickly that a shift away from total dependency on natural resources to potential ecotourism opportunities and economic diversification enhances long-term community health. Ecotourism nationwide currently focuses on creating nature preserves, guided tours, educational centres, agritourism and museums, highlighting the unique richness of local culture, heritage and scenic beauty of a local area. Eastern North Carolina, in the counties of Tyrrell and Hyde, is a prime example of how ecotourism can generate revenue, create jobs and become an attractive tourist destination. Stakeholders, the public and businesses have bundled a tourism package featuring the reintroduction of the red wolf into the Inner Banks region, hiking opportunities, a red wolf centre and an abundance of local hotels/motels, shopping and restaurants. In doing so, benefits to the red wolf, economic sustainability to the communities, preservation of the environment and community solidarity promise not only a successful future for ecotourism but a flourishing and healthy interweaving of nature and the inevitable march of modern culture.

Critical to profitable, sustainable ecotourism is the inclusion of local stakeholders in planning processes to develop and implement management techniques promoting the effectiveness and efficiency of using natural resources, preserving local flora and fauna, while improving the quality of life for local citizens. The following case study highlights both the controversy and the coming together of two counties in Columbia, North Carolina. In the counties of Tyrrell and Hyde, stakeholders have developed innovative solutions to create a thriving ecotourism engine, while addressing the fears and concerns of community members: the reintroduction of the red wolf (*Canus rufus*).

Since the red wolf was designated as a threatened and endangered species in 1967, the community of Columbia has compromised, held meetings with US Fish and Wildlife Service and as a result cultivated both a cooperative consensus and an enthusiasm among local landowners, businesses and public stakeholders, and developed long-term strategic planning to establish compatibility between human and wildlife environments. This is often referred to as coopetition – a term meaning local communities do not compete against each other but rather band together to achieve and market a common goal (Edgell & Haenisch, 1995). Stakeholders create stewardship and through the use of e-mail, Web sites and mailings connect local community leaders and interested citizens. The red wolf has achieved significant success in re-establishing its population in eastern North Carolina. In 1970, the US Fish and Wildlife Service initiated a captive breeding programme and reintroduced a small pack of red wolves into the Alligator River Wildlife Refuge in 1987.

Stakeholder meeting: an executive summary

Public involvement invites local community members to participate in decision-making procedures that significantly influence and impact the long-term sustainability of their communities. The National Environmental Policy Act (1969) mandates the involvement of community members in both management and policy decisions involving federal lands with the potential to impact rural communities. However, the reality for community members is that both the level of commitment and the volunteer hours required to achieve viable change are often daunting for even the most active stakeholder groups. Regardless of public policies, real change occurs at a local level. In an effort to assist nascent efforts in two communities in rural eastern North Carolina, Tyrrell County and Hyde County, Defenders of Wildlife received a grant from The Alex C. Walker Foundation.

The purpose and inspiration of the Alex C. Walker Foundation grant were to stimulate community interest in developing common goals, organize a strong stakeholder group and provide those groups with skills to follow up preliminary investigations, recommendations and subsequent report generated by Dr Gail Lash (2005). In her report, she focused on community *Strengths, Weakness, Opportunities & Threats* (SWOT) in terms of ecotourism opportunities. She identified strategies to address rural community residents' concerns, as well as weaknesses and threats. She emphasized existing strengths and suggested investigating future opportunities for maintaining both the conservation and the integrity of the surrounding areas as red wolves are reintroduced into their traditional habitat. Dr Lash's report recommended that if red wolves are to become an economic engine for local economies, it is critical that a red wolf centre be built and that it be based on a strategically developed and locally supported ecotourism plan. Moreover, she emphasized that it was fundamental that rural residents and local regional tourism planners were given a voice in constructing a plan that includes ecotourism training opportunities.

In assisting Defenders of Wildlife with these issues, Dr Flood, an assistant professor at East Carolina University, facilitated a stakeholder meeting with 23 participants. Two goals were identified: (1) advancing equitable ecotourism opportunities within rural communities surrounding red wolf country and (2) developing a strategic plan for the implementation of rural ecotourism activities benefiting local residents while conserving red wolf habitat. Four speakers met with community members to discuss how to maximize ecotourism opportunities while maintaining the balance between ongoing threats to the ecology and culture of their local areas. The following issues were addressed: what is required to create prepared and productive ecotourism communities, what have we learned from previous studies, how does red wolf reintroduction influence local landowners' perspectives and what are the best practices for developing, marketing, packaging and generating ecotourism?

Prior to the stakeholder meeting, an ecotourism agenda committee was formed and identified the following four issues as being most critical: (1) marketing strategies for small businesses, (2) best methods for generating economic benefits, (3) strategies for addressing red wolf education and outreach and (4) creative incentives to keep tourist revenue in the communities. While six groups were initially formed to address these questions, groups 1 and 6 and groups 2 and 3 were combined to maximize information exchange.

Group 1 Marketing the Inner Banks
Group 2 Generating economic benefits
Group 3 Landowner incentives
Group 4 Red Wolf education
Group 5 Keeping money in the community
Group 6 Addressing liability issues for local and regional farmers and
  businesses

Groups 1 and 6 representing farmer and small business owner interests embraced a pragmatic approach to creating agritourism through the development and implementation of farm activities. Ideas to accomplish this included (1) inviting tourists and school children to spend a day on a farm assisting with farm work, (2) selling produce during seasonal pickings at farmers' markets, (3) creating seed planting tours and (4) aggressively marketing corn mazes. Collectively, this group felt that the creation of a farmers' market was the best choice because it could be implemented immediately. Group participants recommended that farmers and business owners work closely with county extension office personnel to better understand specific required regulations that will influence ecotourism efforts.

Groups 2 and 3 representing local business and landowners were interested in developing marketing strategies and landowner incentives. The group participants recommended establishing ongoing stakeholder meetings of invested individuals to address and plan red wolf ecotourism.

Additional suggestions included offering red wolf tours, building a red wolf centre and developing media packets for distribution to area businesses. Moreover, the participants expressed concern that any newly created opportunities for economic growth should not degrade existing businesses. Many members of this group were sensitive to what they believe is a lack of communication between government officials, landowners, farmers and businesses within the community. In an effort to improve communication, participants suggested publishing and circulating an ecotourism newsletter throughout the surrounding communities. Group participants recommended generating revenue through the sale of local products and training local guides as a way to offer tourists a quality experience, while reducing concerns that visitors will negatively impact farm lands.

Group 4 representing red wolf educators endorsed the continuation of red wolf education and outreach, felt that protecting the wolf was paramount and that red wolf habitat is critical to its survival. In order to accomplish these goals, the participants felt that the creation of a red wolf centre will assist with recovery efforts, as well as become a cornerstone for creating diverse economic and educational opportunities in the community.

Group 5 representing ecotourism businesses decided that they must complete a needs assessment of what ecotourism resources are available, such as number of available hotel/motel/bed and breakfast beds, restaurants and recreational opportunities. Group members agreed that positioning the town of Columbia as a red wolf ecotourism destination is critical and believe it is necessary to build an express hotel in the town to accommodate large tour groups. In addressing future ecotourism planning efforts, participants unanimously agreed that an effective strategy to attract tourists to Columbia as a destination spot would include bundling package deals to encourage visitors to spend more time in the area, spend more money and be able to experience and enjoy the uniqueness of the community. Moreover, the group felt that package deals have potential for uniting local businesses while generating word of mouth advertising. Their final recommendation was that community leaders need to identify what resources are available now and immediately begin developing ecotourism.

A significant number of goals at the stakeholder meeting were accomplished, and there was overall confidence that a more cohesive and clear vision for future ecotourism business opportunities was a viable and profitable option. Group participants were left to solve two major questions: (1) specifically define how sustainable ecotourism regarding the red wolf can be packaged with the support of local stakeholders and (2) how to recruit community members to actively step forward and become leaders of this important ecotourism effort.

Stakeholder meeting on red wolf ecotourism in North Carolina

A stakeholder meeting addressing red wolf ecotourism in eastern North Carolina was convened on 10 May 2006 at the Eastern 4-H Environmental Education Conference Center in Columbia, North Carolina. Dr Joseph Flood presided as the facilitator. In cooperation with the Ecotourism Agenda Planning Committee, Dr Flood developed and presented goals, as well as helped set the meeting agenda. Dr Gail Lash and Pamela Black's (2005) feasibility study *Red Wolves: Creating Economic Opportunity Through Ecotourism in Rural North Carolina* provided initial direction and established the focus of the meeting. Their study incorporated community research, tourist research and interviews to develop an analysis based on identified *Strengths, Weaknesses, Opportunities and Threats* (SWOT) of Tyrrell and Hyde counties.

As a result of the SWOT analysis, Dr Lash and Ms Black formulated strategies to initiate the next steps these two communities must initiate to make ecotourism a viable means of economic growth. The analysis also emphasized the importance of maintaining the conservation and integrity of the surrounding areas. Their report concluded that if red wolves are to serve as an economic engine for the local economy, a red wolf centre needs to be developed on a sound ecotourism plan. Furthermore, it is critical that the development of an ecotourism plan involve the active and committed participation of rural residents, local and regional tourism planners and include ecotourism training opportunities. Dr Flood, an expert in stakeholder meetings, helped organize and facilitate the meeting with the intention of both encouraging and passing on the leadership role to community stakeholders. The essential next step requires individuals from the community to step forward as leaders, ensuring that community decision makers are in control of steering their regional ecotourism efforts. For this to occur, it is critical that volunteers be recruited to organize meetings on a monthly basis.

Lash and Black's report on the red wolf highlighted several problems that currently prevent the implementation of a thriving ecotourism agenda in Tyrrell and Hyde counties. In the past, one major issue has been a lack of communication between the United States Fish and Wildlife Service (USFWS) managers and local residents and businesses. The report stated that "information has been unclear or unavailable" (Lash & Black, 2005, p. 41). This lack of communication has resulted in both confusion and hostility between locals and the USFWS with regard to economic partnerships on refuge lands.

An additional problem concerning tourism in the area arises from the fact that "Tyrrell County ranks 99th out of North Carolina's 100 counties on the amount of tourism revenue coming into the area" (Lash & Black, 2005, p. 14). Columbia is Tyrrell County's only incorporated town, and is located on Highway 64, only 35 miles from North Carolina's Outer Banks. This translates into millions of people driving past the town each year, unaware that they have no reason to stop, spend money and explore the local attractions. Currently, one of the only attractions for tourists is the Walter B. Jones Visitor Center Complex. In their report, Lash and Black suggested that improving roadside signage would be significant in attracting more potential visitors. They also highly recommended that a red wolf education centre would easily become a premier attraction for drawing visitors to the area.

The town of Columbia, North Carolina, is impaired aesthetically in having myriad abandoned buildings and rundown properties. In an effort to improve its economic viability, Columbia must pursue ongoing efforts to improve the town's visual appearance, coupled with a strategic eco-tourism marketing approach. Another major concern for the area is the possibility of outside development. Developers are hungry for land and could potentially and aggressively create a plan that will not include the input of local citizens, regional planners, state and federal land managers or incorporate the over-reaching goals of the red wolf recovery programme.

Stakeholder meeting goals

The two primary workshop goals for the stakeholder meeting included (1) advancing equitable ecotourism opportunities within rural communities surrounding red wolf country and (2) developing strategic plans to guide the implementation of rural ecotourism activity to benefit local residents and conserve red wolf habitat.

While the first goal primarily addressed advancing opportunities for increasing economic revenue for ecotourism development within the rural communities surrounding red wolf country, clearly defined short- and long-term goals are essential before these broader goals can be initiated. Joe Landino, a 45-year-old resident farmer, emphasized this point when he stated that "we actually have what we need here now, but it just needs to be put together and it won't happen in six months".

The second workshop goal focused on developing a strategic plan to guide the implementation of rural ecotourism activities to benefit local residents while conserving red wolf habitat. Local residents have the ability to create plans and maintain an appropriate infrastructure placing them in the driver's seat. However, they will require guidance to prevent ceding control of developing their economic markets for tourism to outside investors who may not take their wants or needs into consideration.

Goals for the stakeholder meeting on red wolf ecotourism

- Advance equitable ecotourism opportunities within the rural communities surrounding red wolf country
- Participants will develop a strategic plan to guide the implementation of rural ecotourism activity to benefit local residents and conserve red wolf habitat.

Presentation summaries

Four presentations took place during the red wolf stakeholders' meeting. Dr Joseph Flood was the first presenter. The focus of his presentation, *Stakeholder Meeting on Red Wolf Ecotourism in North Carolina* (Appendix A), provided an overview of ecotourism and strategic planning, while emphasizing the need for a group of local stakeholders to form an ecotourism action committee (Appendix B). His presentation laid the foundation and established ground rules setting the tone of the meeting. Dr Gail Lash followed with a *summary of findings from her feasibility study* (Lash & Black, 2005), which in turn became a catalyst for developing the stakeholder group by presenting empirical evidence strongly supporting the need for ecotourism in Tyrrell County. Joe Landino, a landowner and 45-year-old resident of Tyrrell County, presented the group with *an historical overview of red wolves in the county from a landowner's perspective*. His insights made stakeholders aware of the threats, fears and myths that red wolves have inspired in farmers and landowners for the past 20 years. Jill Simonetti, the final presenter, discussed *Successful Marketing Strategies in Ecotourism* (Appendix D). She emphasized that ecotourism is an exciting and evolving concept and provided an overview of marketing practices that have proved successful in other communities.

Presentations

Dr Joseph P. Flood, Assistant Professor, East Carolina University

Dr Flood's presentation highlighted the benefits of tourism for the community as well as its associated costs. Benefits included employment opportunities, additional income, economic diversification, tax revenues, visibility and cultural benefits. He emphasized that the cost of tourism included money needed for facilities and services, promotions, staff and employee training. As an associated cost, he pointed out that while tourism can be beneficial, it is also seasonal, and the resulting influx of more cars and

people coming into the area could lead to increased pollution and congestion on adjacent roadways. He further noted that strategic planning and
development will be a key factor in developing ecotourism in the area and
are vital to the area's futures.

Moreover, Dr Flood suggested that one focal point when considering
development are the concerns about ensuring that the benefits of tourism
are distributed equitably throughout the community and that proposed
development fits in with the surroundings. He feels it is equally important
to recognize that tourism has limitations, and plans should be made to
optimize potential growth without changing the rural nature and habitat
of the area. He stressed that planning for this kind of growth requires organizational evaluation, community involvement as well as clearly identified
product development and marketing. The overlying theme of his presentation was that local stakeholders have the ability to control development,
but must do so systematically, collectively and with a sense of urgency.

In order to develop ecotourism in Tyrrell County, Dr Flood highlighted
three steps that must first be attained: (1) a community vision must be
developed, (2) issues and concerns need to be identified and (3) clearly
articulated goals must be established. He emphasized that it is important
to develop goals that will help the community achieve their vision of the
future. An example used to identify goals and objectives was illustrated
using a SWOT analysis. The SWOT analysis is beneficial because it stimulates group participation, provides a framework for assessing capabilities
and community values and provides a base on which to develop a set of
goals that will take advantage of opportunities while building up weaknesses and warding off threats. Once the group had a general idea of how
ecotourism could work in their community, Dr Flood explained the small
group process and how prioritizing projects would benefit the group as
a whole. The presentation gave an overview of how to make ecotourism
work for the community.

Dr Gail Lash, Ecotourism Consultant

Dr Lash's presentation was a summary of the report *Red Wolves: Creating
Economic Opportunity Through Ecotourism in Rural North Carolina* (2005). She
addressed specific issues of concern for residents in Tyrrell County. These
issues included (1) lack of jobs in the area, forcing young people to leave
town to find work; (2) rising land costs; (3) lack of communication and
cooperation with federal agencies; and (4) fear of being overrun by tourists.
She went on to explain the benefits of red wolves in the area, the associated
costs, as well as residents' perceptions of marketing red wolves as a tourist
attraction. One hundred percent of the residents she interviewed during
her study agreed that if red wolves could be used as a marketing tool to

attract tourists and tourist dollars, they would feel both comfortable and confident about a red wolf reintroduction programme.

Dr Lash stressed that paying close attention to the type and pace of development in the region is crucial in order to maintain a desirable quality of life for residents. A major theme in her presentation underscored the fact that a red wolf education centre has the potential for becoming the keystone in the development process. Based on her report, she believes that a red wolf centre will generate revenue and tourists without overdeveloping the area. Furthermore, she stated that the centre will be important for creating a synergy between resident wants and tourists needs in order to generate optimal benefits from ecotourism. She also expressed the need for additional tourism facilities, such as hotels and restaurants, as well as packaging trips and tours. Dr Lash emphasized the importance of involving area youth and educating residents about what is changing and happening in their community. Finally, she accentuated the fact that in order to draw tourists to the area, marketing and advertising for the Inner Banks must be implemented. In closing, she again fervently recommended building the red wolf centre.

Joe Landino, local retired farmer

Joe Landino's presentation provided an overview of the landowners' perspective on red wolf reintroduction in Tyrrell County. Landino initially received a degree in forestry, and later became a farmer while working for a land development corporation. His breadth of experience in the region over the past 45 years offered insight into understanding the level of acceptance, and trepidation area farmers feel about red wolf reintroduction. While Landino shared his impassioned feelings regarding how farmers and landowners initially feared the release of the wolves on their lands, he emphasized that this was primarily based on a misunderstanding about wolves, their habits and the USFWS' unexplained plans to reintroduce wolves back into the region. The following quote by Landino represents the landowners' point of view: "the landowners felt like the public agencies were trying to grab control of our land without buying it".

He further stated that a major concern for area farmers was that USFWS personnel would be travelling on their land, anytime, without permission, while tracking the wolves. Landino emphasized that many landowners' concerns were about the potential expensive impact on the roads and fields and that farmers would be stuck footing the bill. Farmers and landowners felt they were being taken advantage of at the expense of the USFWS mandate that the red wolf had free reign throughout the region. Landino summed up past local concerns by saying, "if the red wolf shows up on your property you're going to have to cease everything you were doing and just let the red wolf have its way". These were real fears landowners and farmers once had regarding how wolves might potentially impact their livelihoods.

Landino went on to explain that over time his perspective has changed. However, there are still many who harbour doubts as to the red wolves' role in the environment. Some are worried about the sustainability of the red wolf. According to Landino, he and others have seen many wolves that look ragged and malnourished. He stated that because some wolves may be mating with coyotes and hunting dogs, it is hard for most locals to identify a true red wolf unless it has a collar. As the presentation drew to a close, Landino said, "I think that landowners would cooperate with something like this [reintroduction efforts] if they knew how to do it". In an effort to develop business plans for ecotourism opportunities, he stressed that guided tours led by respected locals would be more appreciated by local farmers: it would eliminate tourists roaming on their property and going into restricted areas. In closing, Landino recommended offering interpretive talks that incorporate both native flora and fauna within ecotourism programmes rather than completely focusing on the red wolf.

Jill Simonetti, Ecotourism Programme Coordinator, The Conservation Fund

In her presentation, Ms Simonetti offered specific information about marketing ecotourism in the region. She summarized the major steps which included (1) preparation, (2) execution and (3) evaluation. In the preparation stage, she noted that it is necessary to know "who you are" (the organization), understand customer wants and needs and know what media source to best utilize the organization's advertising needs. She emphasized that knowing who you are is best explained through knowledge of what your organization represents. This can be accomplished by evaluating sales, visitation numbers and trends. Ms Simonetti felt it is necessary to establish benchmarks and set realistic goals for the future. In order to understand the customer, it is first important to identify issues concerning general trends in tourism, ecotourism and specific customer trends in North Carolina tourism.

Simonetti stressed that a major challenge for effective ecotourism marketing lies in selecting the appropriate media source to portray the advertising image. Executing the marketing strategy can only follow the creation of the right image. While there are many pros and cons associated with specific media outlets, several were outlined in a handout: *North Carolina Visitor and Trip Profile 2004 & 2005 Fast Facts* http://www.nccommerce.com/tourism/econ/. The final step in the marketing process for ecotourism is evaluation. In order to determine if the organizations' goals are being attained, continual feedback must be collected, organized, analyzed and evaluated based on revisiting bench-marks and conducting surveys.

Following the presentations, participants took a lunch break and were asked to meet back in the conference room and be prepared to break into small groups. The small groups were organized by Dr Flood. Meeting participants had a choice to be involved in whichever group interested them the most.

Purpose

The goal of the small group exercise was to create interaction between participants, enabling them to exchange information in their specialty areas. Each meeting participant had the opportunity to read a brief definition of all the groups' concerns and interests and then chose which group to work with. While there were initially six working groups, groups 1 and 6 and groups 2 and 3 combined to maximize information exchange. The groups were given specific instructions by the facilitator, Dr Flood. Each of the groups met for approximately 2 h. Dr Flood assisted each group, answering questions and steering them in appropriate directions. A description of each group is listed below:

Group 1 Marketing The Inner Banks: marketing venues, Web-based marketing connections, best methods for reaching a broad audience, reaching the "right" audience.

Group 2 Generating Economic Benefits: what types of state or local fiscal mechanisms can be employed to distribute part of the revenues generated through ecotourism to local landowners who support red wolf populations on their agricultural lands? What are the economic benefits generated by red wolf conservation on public and private lands?

Group 3 Landowner incentives: incentives for landowners supporting red wolf recovery. How to successfully manage ecotourism communi-ties, assessing creative zoning, investigating conservation easements and other ways to benefit participating landowners. Determining lev-els of acceptable change.

Group 4 Red wolf education: existing curriculums, videos, *National Geographic* special, future publications "getting the word out". Partner-ships with whom? Best methods for reaching the "right" audience and implementing geotourism strategies.

Group 5 Keeping money in the community: completing a needs assess-ment of what ecotourism resources are available (number of avail-able beds/hotel, campsites, bed and breakfasts, restaurants, recreation

opportunities, walking trails, how to effectively bundle quality experiences, infrastructure for health and safety concerns) as well as what
shops, programmes or services that are missing. Identify ways current
business owners can prepare for and encourage ecotourism.

Group 6 Liability issues: assisting local farmers and business owners
in developing ecotourism businesses. How to go about establishing
shared insurance/umbrella policies for local and regional farmers and
businesses.

Small group summaries set stage for future direction

Based on the interests of the meeting participants, and due to the similarity
of several topic areas, groups 1 and 6 as well as groups 2 and 3 were
combined for participant convenience and group efficiency.

Groups 1 and 6

Because marketing is critical for local farmers and business owners, both
ecotourism-related groups were combined. These groups decided that they
needed to discuss ideas to create ecotourism before they could begin thinking about developing marketing strategies. Due to this obvious challenge
and the short time they had to meet, the group was unable to discuss
marketing strategies in depth, but did come up with a list of ideas to assist
local farmers and businesses in their attempts to create revenue through
ecotourism.

Group members first identified different products and projects already
available in the county and finished by developing ideas the county could
effectively utilize in the future. The most important factors for this group
related to preserving community culture and the environment. A primary
concern for the group focused on how the area will be developed in
the future. Collectively, the group decided on the following three areas
as being effective strategies for creating tourism: (1) heritage, (2) agritourism and (3) ecotourism. They identified three heritage sites in the area:
(1) Somerset Farm, (2) Davenport Homestead and (3) Columbia Theatre.
As a starting point, the group felt they needed to package heritage tourism
by directing tourists first to the Columbia Theatre, where they could then
receive additional information on red wolf reintroduction.

Agritourism was the next area of discussion and included creative ideas
generated by the group. Because much of the area is made up of farmland,
it seemed most appropriate to create agritourism through the development and implementation of farm activities. Ideas to accomplish this goal

included (1) spending a day on a farm (where tourists and school groups would assist with farm work), (2) selling produce through seasonal pickings and farmers' markets, (3) creating seed-planting tours and (4) finding ways to better market corn mazes.

Collectively, this group felt that the creation of a farmers' market was the most tangible project that could be implemented immediately. They recommended that farmers and business owners work with, and depend on, the county extension office to explain and implement the specific required regulations. The group decided that the following key questions needed to be answered before a farmers' market could move forward: what type of insurance is necessary, and what are the zoning requirements in the area? For farmers participating in agritourism, an additional concern was that of legal liability. Farmers within the group stated that they are apprehensive about letting people on their property for fear of potential lawsuits. The group recommended that landowners post warning signs, and both study and understand the implications of NC Statute HB 329 Session Law (2005).

Another innovative idea suggested by the ecotourism group was a project regarding the North Carolina Birding Trail. According to several participants, the organization is looking for a community to showcase potential birding opportunities in the area, and it is willing to train businesses and landowners. Site nominations can be submitted at http://www.ncbirdingtrail.org/site_nominations.asp. There may also be money available for bird-friendly businesses at http://www.goldenleaf.org/.

Additional suggestions and recommendations for creating ecotourism in the community included offering red wolf tours, building a red wolf centre and developing media packets for area businesses. While the group did not have time to discuss marketing in depth, they agreed that further research in marketing techniques is essential.

Groups 2 and 3

Participants from groups 2 and 3 were also combined because the participants felt that generating economic benefits for the community has direct impacts on local landowners. Participants agreed that economic benefits are a key incentive for farmers and landowners to cooperate with red wolf ecotourism. The main focus of this group was to create opportunities for economic growth without degrading existing businesses. One major problem discussed among members was the lack of communication between government officials, landowners, farmers and businesses within the community. They suggested that attempts to improve one-on-one communication among these varied groups would be a good place to start. They also endorsed the idea of creating incentives for landowners to support ecotourism efforts by sending newsletters to selected individuals to keep interested parties informed of red wolf locations, their mating seasons and mapping concentrated areas of red wolf habitat.

One member stated that there are roughly 80 farms in both Tyrrell and Hyde counties, which vary in size from several hundred acres to roughly 5000 acres. The group suggested that landowners should be compensated for the wildlife on their farms and that the decision should not be based on the size of the farm. Their opinion was based on the belief that a smaller farm could have a large proportion of red wolves, and a larger farm could have none at all depending on the geography of the area. Several group members indicated that Geographical Information Systems (GIS) could be used as a tool to overlay populations of wildlife to geographic features. One group member suggested that the entire area needs to be monitored because red wolves could easily be in at least five counties in the area.

The group identified two ways landowners could potentially benefit from red wolf ecotourism: (1) generating revenue or sales by offering products (e.g. t-shirts, mugs and paintings) and (2) creating trained local guide services which would bring tourists to the farms without impacting roads and habitats. Many farmers are reluctant to allow people on their property without supervision. However, they can benefit economically by having a locally paid guide disseminate information and feel secure that the guide will keep groups from disrupting the normal activities on their land.

The next benefit the group identified is not directly related to cash, but can potentially produce economic benefits. The idea of avoided costs or indirect benefits explains how many landowners are actually receiving unrealized benefits. Red wolves feed on nutria (*Myocastor coypus*) and raccoons (*Procyon lotor*). Both the nutria and the raccoon are considered pests by most farmers. Farmers in the group believe that red wolves are reducing both populations. Reducing raccoon numbers has resulted in improving quail hunting and reducing damage to cornfields. Another important impact red wolves are having on area farms is the reduction of nutria. Farmers indicated that they save money by not having to repair dikes and erosion created by these pests. An area biologist stated that he believes the US Department of Agriculture has money available for these types of conservation programmes. The group suggested that a pilot research project could provide science-based answers to prove that the red wolf is providing economic benefits to both hunters and farmers. The group felt it is important to bring this information to area landowners where the biggest benefits might be recognized. The group also concluded that the need to act is becoming urgent.

Group 4

Group four's task was to address issues related to red wolf education. The major theme of the group's discussion was that the basis for red wolf ecotourism is the wolves themselves. One participant stated that red wolves are shy and sensitive, and if anything interrupts their habitat, or way of life, ecotourism is not possible. They felt that it was important for the public to know that what is beneficial for farmers and landowners may not be good for the red wolf. Group member Kim Wheeler, executive director of The Red Wolf Coalition, stated that her 20-year programme is well guided and that we have to keep the wolves first. The group endorsed her comments and went on to further discuss potential red wolf projects and products.

One major activity already in operation for red wolf ecotourism is howling tours conducted by the Red Wolf Coalition. Nearly 1200 people participated in the tours last year and they are by far the biggest draw for tourists. Currently, there is no charge for the tours. The Red Wolf Coalition also educates the public through statewide education programmes which include school groups, community groups and presentations. Red Wolf Coalition educators use a discovery box containing a red wolf pelt, track cast and a radio collar to educate the public. Columbia, North Carolina, is home to the local office which disseminates printed materials, and further information can be obtained through the organization's Web site http://www.defenders.org/. The coalition has also developed an outreach list to help connect the community with information on red wolves. The coalition relies heavily on the USFWS for information and is in the process of developing a new programme where they would be able to use telemetry equipment, a spotting scope, and actually take people out to look for red wolves. The coalition's major project still in progress is the red wolf education centre. The group felt strongly that the centre will be a cornerstone to help create diverse economic and educational opportunities in the community.

Group 5

The goal for group 5 was to find ways to keep tourist revenue in the community. The participants decided that they need to complete a needs assessment of what ecotourism resources are available, such as number of available beds and recreational opportunities. Group members agreed that having Columbia as a red wolf ecotourism destination is critical and believe it would be helpful if there was an express hotel in the town to accommodate large tour groups. While the group believes there are nascent accommodations and opportunities already in place, they recommend that community members implement specific strategies to address these concerns. One member suggested utilizing existing visitor centres across the state as well as accessing Web-based information to disseminate more accurate and interesting red wolf facts to the public.

Participants agreed that canoe and kayak rentals can be a great way for communities to generate revenue while showcasing the natural beauty of the areas. Bicycle rentals were also recommended as a potential source for generating income. One member said that Pettigrew State Park is looking at possible campground space on the Scuppernong River which is a superb place to rent canoes and kayaks. These ideas dovetail with the group's suggestion that they work with government entities to develop other projects and entrepreneurial opportunities in the area, such as a visitor centre. Another consideration was the hiring and training of local guides for specific ecotourism education. Dr Lash suggested a guide co-op could utilize retired members from the community who would volunteer to lead tours, or employ high school or college students. This strategy would keep salaries low while still offering a credible guide service. She stated that "It looks like there is a good opportunity to start something soon".

Mapping the future: utilizing ecotourism as a guiding force

Stakeholders have developed best practices to guide management decisions in tandem with local agendas. Farmers and town stewards now agree that the reintroduction of the red wolf has the potential to generate economic steam benefiting both counties. Innovative suggestions about bundling package deals to visitors, which not only unite local businesses but create word of mouth free advertising, include the following: increasing the number of hotels/motels, restaurants and shopping venues in the areas to accommodate tourists, building a red wolf centre, advertising corn mazes, provide specialized marketing strategies and training for service providers and expand and support agribusiness by inviting tourists and school groups to visit and work on local farms.

Stakeholders recommended that community leaders evaluate what resources are available immediately to implement ecotourism and begin as quickly as possible to attract tourists and the revenue their visits will generate. A communal effort, vision, compromise and a can-do attitude between the communities of Tyrrell and Hyde demonstrates what can be achieved when group members come together, establish leadership and boundaries and work side by side for common goals. In their hands, they now collectively hold the potential for a prosperous future and long-enduring possibilities for both local ecotourism and the preservation of the red wolf.

Case study references

Agritourism Activity Liability, HB 329, NC. HR. §99E-30-32 (2005-236).

Ceballos-Lascurain, H. (1987). The future of ecotourism. *Mexico Journal*, January, 13–14.

Drumm, A. and A. Moore. (2005). *Ecotourism Development: A Manual for Conservation Planners and Mangers. Volume I: An Introduction to Ecotourism Planning.* The Nature Conservancy. Arlington, VA.

Edgell, D.L. and T.R. Haenisch. (1995). *Coopetition: Global Tourism Beyond Millennium.* International Policy Publishing, Kansas City, MO.

Honey, M. (1999). *Ecotourism and Sustainable Development: Who Owns Paradise?* Island Press, Washington, DC.

Lash, G.Y. and P. Black. (2005). *Red Wolves: Creating Economic Opportunity Through Ecotourism in Rural North Carolina.* Defenders of Wildlife, Washington, DC.

National Environmental Policy Act, 42 U.S.C. §4321-4347 (1969).

Pinchot, G. (1910). *The Fight for Conservation.* Doubleday Page and Company Press, New York, NY.

The Ecotourism Society. (1991a). *The Ecotourism Society Newsletter*, Number 1, Spring.

Wight, P.A. (1994). Environmental Responsible Marketing of Tourism. *Ecotourism: A Sustainable Option?*, Eds E. Cater and G. Lowman. John Wiley & Sons, Brisbane, 39–56.

References

Butler, Richard. (2000). Tourism and the Environment: A Geographical Perspective. *Tourism* Geographies, 2(3), 337–358.

CAMA Land Use Plan. (2006). Bald Head Island Land Use Plan. Fiscal Year 2004/2006.

Edgell, Sr, David L. (2006). *Managing Sustainable Tourism: A Legacy for the Future.* The Haworth Hospitality Press, Binghamton, NY.

Goeldner, Charles A. and J.R. Brent Ritchie. (2006). *Tourism: Principles, Practices, Philosophies* (10th ed.). John Wiley and Sons, Hoboken, NJ.

Kenya Wildlife Service. *Community Wildlife Service.* Retrieved 12 December 2006, from http://www.kws.org/community.html.

Maori Creativity. Retrieved 12 December 2006, from http://www.newzealand.com/travel/media/features/maori_maoricreativity_feature.cfm.

National Geographic Center for Sustainable Tourism. *About the CSD.* Retrieved 12 December 2006, from http://www.nationalgeographic.com/travel/sustainable/about_csd.html.

Tourtellot, Jonathan B. (2004, March). Destination Scorecard: 115 Places Rated. *National Geographic Traveler*, 21(2), 60–67.

Tourtellot, Jonathan B. (2005, July/August). Destination Scorecard: How Do 55 National Park Regions Rate? *National Geographic Traveler*, 22(5), 80–92.

Tourtellot, Jonathan B. (2006, November/December). Places Rated, How Do 94 World Heritage Destinations Stack Up? *National Geographic Traveler*, 23(8), 113.

United Nations World Tourism Organization. *About ST-EP*, Retrieved 19 December 2005, from http://www.world-tourism.org/step/step.htm.

United Nations World Tourism Organization. UNWTO-Sustainable Development of Tourism *e-bulletin, 3. Tourism and SIDS*. Retrieved 12 December 2006, from http://www.world-tourism.org/frameset/frame_sustainable.html.

World Travel and Tourism Council. (2003). *Blueprint for New Tourism*, 6.

7

Education and training in tourism

It seems to the traveler that he must have known these people forever.

Thomas Wolfe

Introduction and overview

The New Millennium brought a period of tumultuous events and stagnant growth to the tourism industry, but in 2004, international tourism experienced a spectacular rebound, with international tourist arrivals topping an all-time record of 766 million – an increase of 10 per cent over 2003 (UNWTO, 2005a, p. 7). The number of international tourist arrivals in 2005 is estimated at 808 million, up 5.5 per cent over 2004 and 1.5 per cent above the long-term annual growth rate of 4.1 per cent (UNWTONEWS, 2006, pp. 4–5).

In light of this growth, counterbalanced with the international industry's vulnerability in regard to safety and security issues, the success of the travel and tourism industry in the global environment will ultimately depend on the professionalism of its workforce. If a more professional workforce is to sur-face, tourism education and training programmes need to be strengthened from high school through graduate school and adult continuing educa-tion and training. While growing in recognition and support at the US high school level through the efforts of The National Academy Founda-tion (see www.naf.org), among others, the number of high school tourism programmes worldwide remain limited.

As the travelling population ages and becomes more sophisticated in its needs, desires and expectations, tourism suppliers must deal with more refined market demand. For example, to achieve more uniformity of branded products and services, the hotel industry has long focused strate-gically on staff training programmes in support of reliable quality service and customer satisfaction. The hospitality sector recognizes that quelling some of the fears and uncertainties that are inherent in travelling to an unknown place requires offering its guests the comfort of knowing that Hotel A offers certain amenities that are consistent and reliable throughout the branded chain.

Industry-wide improvements are being made in the areas of qual-ity service and customer satisfaction. Recognition of travel and tourism career patterns, and of the training and higher education policies and pro-grammes necessary to support them, has taken a longer time to evolve. Much more progress needs to be made in fostering policies to improve tourism education and training, but the prognosis now is better than ever.

This chapter examines a literature review of workplace supply and demand in the context of tourism education and training; provides def-initions of tourism and hospitality as they relate to education, training and human resource development; and examines the predominance of the hospitality sector. It concludes with an examination of key issues involved in human resource development for the tourism industry, highlighting leadership activities by the United Nations World Tourism Organization (UNWTO), and a small sample of higher education and training pro-grammes in tourism as examples of current activities. A detailed appendix is included at the end of the volume outlining a history of skills develop-ment, trends in higher education relevant to tourism including the role of government and issues for improvement. Co-author of this chapter and author of its appendix is Dr. Sheryl Elliott, Associate Professor, Depart-ment of Tourism and Hospitality Management, School of Business, The George Washington University, Washington, DC, USA. A case report on BEST EN (Business Enterprises for Sustainable Travel Education Net-work), involving higher education curriculum development and promo-tion of research in sustainable tourism, appears at the end of this chapter (Figure 7.1). The author of the BEST EN case report is Claudia Jurowski, School of Hotel and Restaurant Management, Northern Arizona Univer-sity, Flagstaff, Arizona, USA.

Figure 7.1   Musicians at a courtyard café in Old Havana, Cuba (2001)
(Photo: Sarah J. Gust)

Workforce supply and workplace demand: need for defining tourism

As early as 1982, Kelly (p. 22) suggested that the most critical undertaking for providers of tourism education and training is to have the right number of trained people, at the right time and place, with the right skills. This remains true today. Baum (1995a, p. 70) mentions many factors that influence or shift the workforce supply, including changing demographics, general economic conditions at local and national levels and structural shifts within economies.

There is a confusion of terms relating to the tourism sector, tourism and hospitality, and tourism education, training and human resource development. Defining the tourism sector in terms of education and training has been a subject of great interest to organizations such as the UNWTO, World Travel and Tourism Council (WTTC) and Organisation of Economic Development and Cooperation (OECD), for the obvious implication it has for their statistical research and analysis of travel expenditures and trip data. These organizations conclude that tourism is a service area spread over multiple sub-sector areas, with some exclusive to tourism and others inclusive of tourism (UNWTO, 1994; WTTC, 1995a; OECD, 1995). While this expanded notion of tourism is slowly achieving presence, the popular press and trade journals appear more interested in reinforcing single-sided aspects of the industry, with articles focused on the hospitality industry or the food and beverage, airline, campground and the bed and breakfast industries.

While there are many suggestions that tourism is an enormous economic phenomenon, there remains a lack of a uniform or universally accepted definition of this sector called tourism. To date, there is no universally accepted standard industrial classification (SIC) code or system for tourism. Compounding the problem is that the range of businesses and activities in the tourism industry has continued broadening to encompass expanding fields of interest such as meeting and special event management, sport management and trade show management. (Pavesic, 1993, p. 291ß).

If employers do not fully understand the overarching business to which they belong, and conversely, education and training providers do not understand the scope of the industry for which they are producing workers, there is little chance of matching the quantity and quality of workers demanded with the quality and quantity of workers supplied.

Several organizations, concluding that tourism is among the world's largest and fastest growing industries, have attempted to define tourism for measurement and analysis purposes. Of note is the work of the UNWTO, augmented by the WTTC, which developed a Standard International Classification of Tourism Activities (SICTA) to clearly delineate the supply side of tourism. SICTA was adopted by the United Nations Statistical Commission as a provisional classification in March 1993 (UNWTO, 1994). The activities included in SICTA are based on differentiating businesses whose sales are totally derived from tourists and those whose sales are partially derived from tourist spending. For example, cruise line sales are totally derived from tourist spending, whereas car rental revenues derive from both tourist and local spending. The business activities of tourism under 'Education' include adult education, driving schools, flying schools, boating instruction, hotel schools, tourism education programmes, recreation and park schools, and tourist instruction. For the purposes of this chapter, the adult education and tourism education programmes are the focus.

Discrepancies due to how tourism or the tourist activity is defined can also be observed between national organizations, such as the US Travel Industry Association (TIA) and the WTTC. TIA predicted employment growth for tourism in the United States during the years 1992–2005 to be 30 per cent, while the WTTC projected US employment growth for almost the same time period (1995–2005) to be 16.7 per cent, barely more than one half of the TIA prediction (TIA, 1994, 2; WTTC, 1995b, 22). Critics, such as Leiper (1991, pp. 157–167), argue that those who suggest that tourism is the largest industry in the world are making a superficial observation, 'utilizing defective notions about business and industry' (Leiper, p. 166). As a result, he contends, the number of jobs in tourism is grossly exaggerated, having important implications for education and training. Leiper contends that the futurist, Herman Khan, performed a disservice to the field 20 years ago when he predicted that tourism would be the largest industry in the world by the year 2000. Leiper argues this prediction was not based upon Khan's forecasting ability, but upon his ability in the art of public relations. Khan's projection, though, was quickly seized, adopted, and quoted widely at that time by a variety of interests it served, including academia (Leiper, p. 158).

Although this study, like many others, has characterized the tourism industry as highly fragmented, Leiper takes exception to this notion, suggesting this as a contradiction in terms. He contends that what defines an industry is its non-fragmentary nature. Not defining the tourism industry accurately, he believes, has led to tremendous miscalculations of its size and the true number of jobs it offers. He argues that misconception of the number of jobs available has resulted in a growth of courses and programmes in tourism at the higher education level, enticing students into an industry where jobs, in fact, may not be present or available.

Leiper's argument, if nothing else, suggests that an obstacle in analysing the human resource needs of tourism hinges on the ability to find identity and secure definitional footing for the sector. It is important to reconcile the differences between the UNWTO, WTTC and OECD in defining both the supply and demand sides of tourism in order to substantiate its true size and economic dimensions. This will provide the means to analyse the human resource component of tourism, with particular reference to identifying industry demand and how to meet this demand through appropriate education and training (Figure 7.2).

Defining tourism and hospitality education and training

Beyond the problem that exists in defining or conceptualizing the tourism industry is the equally challenging terminological confusion between tourism and hospitality. Are they one and the same? Is tourism a component of hospitality, or is hospitality a component of tourism? Baum (1995b) presents a comprehensive list of business activities, organizing them in the component areas of travel and transport; accommodations; catering; sports and recreation; history and heritage; natural scenic heritage attractions; built attractions; events; retail business; conferences and conventions; tourism and hospitality information and facilitation; and tourism hospitality support services. Baum's listing is more in compliance with the technical supply side definition of tourism advanced by the UNWTO and the WTTC. Thus, it would appear that in some instances the phrase tourism and hospitality (CHRIE; Baum, 1995b; Davidson, 1989) is interchangeable

Figure 7.2   Stairway exit atop La Pederera Apartment (Casa Mila) by architect Antoni Gaudi in Barcelona, Spain (Photo: Sarah J. Gust)

with the word tourism (UNWTO, WTTC, OECD) and in other instances it is used to imply hotel and catering or hospitality services (Stear and Griffin, 1993, p. 41).

Despite the perception of hospitality as the most significant component of tourism, travel and tourism programmes in higher education have grown in substantial numbers during the last three decades. UNWTO estimates the small handful of programmes at end of the Second World War had grown by 1992 to over 2000 worldwide (UNWTO, 1992). There are suggestions in the literature that the curricula for these programmes are highly varied and often developed on an ad hoc basis (Lavery, 1988, 168; Amoah and Baum, 1997). In many countries, institutional difficulties persist in knowing where to place tourism courses and programmes within academic structures. Rach (1992, p. 6) observed that tourism programmes and courses in higher education in the United States have been placed in a wide range of departments and disciplines, ranging from home economics to hotel school to business school programmes. In such instances, tourism education becomes compartmentalized and flavoured by the discipline of the department within which it is lodged; the development of skills and knowledge appropriate to the full breadth of the sector have thus been limited; however, whether these programmes are, as Stear and Griffin claim, usually hospitality programmes 'presented in the guise of tourism education' (1993, p. 50), can only be substantiated by an exhaustive worldwide study of all such programmes. The UNWTO, in fact, undertook a project to develop an accreditation programme for tourism at the higher education level, discussed later in this chapter, which is the concept TEDQUAL: to improve quality in tourism education and training.

Stear and Griffin raise a further issue, which appears to be a conspicuous omission in the literature at the time, having important consequence for tourism and hospitality education and the supply of workers. That is the question of whether tourism and hospitality education should by definition be the same for developing countries as it is for industrialized ones. Stear and Griffin suggest that in industrialized countries, such as Australia, domestic tourism far outweighs foreign or international tourism, and hospitality services are not as significant as they are in developing countries, where foreign tourism plays the dominant role. They contend that a great deal of tourism in industrialized countries does not require commercial hospitality (particularly lodging) services. As examples, they cite day trips to urban areas for museum visits, shopping, festivals or sporting events. In developing countries where foreign tourism is more likely to dominate economic revenues, commercial hospitality services would play a much larger role, and there hospitality may, indeed, be the most significant component in tourism education and training (Figure 7.3).

Defining education, training and human resource development

The subject of education and training, like the discussion on tourism, and the combined notion of tourism and hospitality, is taxonomic: what is the difference between education and training? Do workers in tourism and hospitality need more training or education? Cooper suggests that tourism education is more long term, whereas tourism training produces benefits that are 'relatively instantaneous' (Cooper, 1993, p. 66).

Baum (1995b, pp. 187–192), however, contends that the distinction is blurred. The historical precedent of training for craft skills through apprenticeships is quite different from the 'elitist' quest for self-fulfilment in

Figure 7.3   Kay Smith, Illinois (USA) Artist Laureate with Gregorio Fuentes (approx. 104 years old in 2001), former Captain of Ernest Hemingway's yacht, El Pilar, Old Havana, Cuba (Photo: Sarah J. Gust)

terms of knowledge gained through higher education. Training in this context implied a mastery of skills whereas education, an intellectual pursuit, resulted in broad-based knowledge. The distinction between training and education persisted well into the mid-twentieth century in the United States and other industrialized countries, with post-secondary education divided between those pursuing manual arts training (technical training) or liberal arts education. Liberal arts are recognizably a North American educational distinction. It is defined in standard dictionaries (Random House, 1987) as 'an academic course of instruction at a college intended to provide general knowledge comprising the arts, humanities, natural sciences, social sciences, as opposed to professional or technical subjects'.

It has been suggested that training is for skills and education for life, but Baum finds this distinction far too limiting and suggests that in a contemporary context both are integral in the human development process. Human development thus becomes a unifying phrase for combining the process of education and training appropriate to most levels of employment within tourism and perhaps to many other service sectors as well. The work environment itself can be expected to call for training and education beyond any credential, diploma or degree.

In 1993, Pavesic (p. 288) contended that the industrial economy will require not people who can do yesterday's jobs but those who can keep up with upcoming skills and knowledge requirements of the industry. Some of the training and education needed for tomorrow's jobs may come through experiential learning, and other learning may be required through more formal systems. Just as the Travel Industry Association continues to request research data on experiential travel, the essential idea is that one is never fully educated or fully trained. Rather, education and training are life-long experiences, a part of a life-long process (i.e., human resource development). In Pavesic's view, one-time education or one-time skill training is no longer sufficient for supporting the business environment.

The static notion of education, terminating in a degree, and training, terminating in the achievement of skills, is thus rendered passé. This argument was also presented by Sigala and Baum, who suggested that the commanding and changing business environment and working conditions in the tourism and hospitality field make 'lifelong learning, requiring both a willingness to continue to learn on the part of citizens and a commitment to provide opportunities for this lifelong learning' (2003, p. 367). Haywood and Maki concluded, in a study of employee/employer perceptions and expectations, 'Invariably people grow to a point where they are ready for responsibilities beyond their original assignment. When this happens, the organization can profit by helping them develop larger capabilities and realities' (1992, p. 246); this is the process of human resource development and one very apropos for education and training in tourism.

The strong continuing education and training programmes for hospitality management that have proliferated in the United States would confirm Baum's (1995b, pp. 187–192) forward-looking contention. Solomon noted, 'As businesses face globalization, rising costs, and leaner, meaner markets, many are turning to executive education to ensure that their employees are equipped with leading-edge strategies' (Solomon, 1992). In North America, the number of professional certification programmes in tourism grew from two in 1980 to over a dozen in a dozen years (Morrison et al., 1992). A sample of such programmes includes those offered by the American Hotel and Motel Association's Educational Institute, the Canadian Restaurant and Food Services Association's Food Service Manager Program, American Society of Travel Agents (ASTA) Travel Management Academy, Cornell University's Professional Development Program, the National

Tour Association Certified Tour Professional Program, the Executive Development Institute for Tourism and the Culinary Institute of America among many other reputable programmes established since this time.

Despite numerous delivery systems for education, training and human resource development, Pollock and Ritchie argued in 1990 that tourism/hospitality education still tends to be 'job training, rather than to a career development strategy', with the emphasis on getting an immediate job rather than a long-term career (p. 570). This prompted some governments, notably Canada, to develop more comprehensive human resource development strategies for the tourism industry by means of industry, government labour, and education councils which approach education and training within the context of long-term career development (Hawkins, 1996, p. 2). In terms of post-secondary education, the benefits to both individuals and economies are great. Higher education has been shown to help individuals improve their employability and earning power. In the United States, for example, among citizens aged 18–64, for example, adult learners, 'those who earn an associate's degree can expect on average an additional $7,200 in annual earnings . . . Attaining a bachelor's degree adds on average, $15,000 in annual income' (Tate, 2006). Tate continues, 'This increase in income levels also translates to increased state and federal tax revenues, and a higher skilled workforce that can staff positions of critical importance to the economy, national security, and public health'. Thus, the theory continues to be put forward that education and training need to be approached, as Baum suggested in 1995 (p. 192), not from the perspective that 'education is for professionals and training for the artisans and unskilled' but that these are continual, not terminal, elements in the development of human resources.

Factors contributing to the dominant role of the hospitality sector

A number of factors have contributed to the dominant roles played by the hospitality sector and vocational training and have an influence on tourism education and training. First and simply, a large proportion of jobs available in tourism are those in the hospitality sector. According to the OECD in 1995, in their member countries, hotel and catering represented over one-third of all tourism jobs (OECD, 1995, p. 36); over a decade later, this predominance holds true; however, beyond a substantial share of the jobs, the hospitality sector (primarily in hotels and food services) showed early awareness of the need to organize and address issues pertaining to education and training. Cooper et al. (1994, p. 25) suggested that this is largely due to the fact that these services experienced a steadier growth (when compared to tourism) stemming from a craft-based origin (inn-keeping, cleaning, cooking, bookkeeping, etc.).

Going back to the earliest of times, first services to be organized for the traveller were lodging, food and drink (for travellers and their modes of transport – the horse). There is considerable documentation on the historic development of this sector and its transformation into the broader context of hospitality. The need for overnight accommodations evolved from a 'cottage industry' of inns and alehouses to one of international stature somewhere around the beginning of the nineteenth century with the United States at the forefront. The City Hotel in New York City (1794), which was widely copied in the United States and around the world, made a radical departure from inns and inn-keeping of the past by adding refinements such as private baths, room locks, and room service (Lattin, 1985, pp. 39–40). Thus, the infant lodging industry gradually assumed a higher goal: hospitality, the art of receiving guests, of hosting, of making travellers feel at home while away from home (Hos). The adding of amenities to achieve this goal continues today: the chocolate on the pillow, fresh flowers in the room, morning paper at the door, tiny packs of ingredients for the hair, the skin, the shoes and so on.

After the end of the Second World War, with servicemen returning home and re-entering the US labour market, labour intensive service sectors such as hotels and food-service operations became viable employment options, particularly since hotels and food services were realizing healthy post-war expansion rates (Bosselman, 1996, p. 9). The returning GIs' re-entry was made easier by the federally assisted education and training provisions of the GI Bill. During this period, the US hospitality industry expanded rapidly; however, there was an expressed concern by industry that many workers were not sufficiently skilled and trained. At that time, there were very few 2- and 4-year hospitality programmes, and only one graduate programme in restaurant administration. There were, however, a large number of vocational programmes at the high school and trade school level (Bosselman, p. 9). The concern of industry led to an informal meeting in 1946 of hotel and restaurant professionals, as well as representatives from vocational and college programmes, to discuss mutual problems and find solutions to them. This meeting was the beginning of what became the Council on Hotel Restaurant and Institutional Education (CHRIE) (Bosselman, p. 9). Organizations such as CHRIE were instrumental in gaining support from such agencies as the US Office of Education and attention and research interest to the field of education and training in hotel and restaurant operation, that is, hospitality management (Bosselman, p. 13).

The development of the hospitality sector in the United States and its role in the development of the service economy is characteristic of other countries as well, particularly in Europe. In Germany, The Netherlands and

Switzerland, hospitality education and training began in the late nineteenth century (Parsons, 1991, pp. 197–198). In the United Kingdom, craft courses were first offered at Westminster College in London between 1900 and 1910. It should be noted that a surge in the hospitality sector, similar to that in the United States, occurred in Europe post-Second World War, in part due to a desire for tourism and hospitality to serve as a means to help war-torn regions to recover economically. To that end, tourism was included as a provision in the Marshall Plan of 1946 (Mill & Morrison 1985, p. 254). Today even greater emphasis is placed on tourism and hospitality services and management. The industry is at an important cross-roads whereby it can take a leading role in an increasing emphasis on hiring and retaining older workers. 'Employers need their expertise, experience, wisdom, reliability, and stability . . . Smart companies are already adjusting to be older worker-friendly' (The Herman Group, 2006, p. 1). Additionally, groups advocating for people with physical, mental and psychological disabilities are thrilled with new interest from employers anxiously seeking to expand their workforces (The Herman Group, p. 1.) (Figure 7.4).

Thus, the hospitality sector has commanded much attention in research and literature, owing to its early origins, its ability to become organized, its profitability, its breadth (involving all levels of workers, from the unskilled and semi-skilled to the skilled and highly skilled), and its ability to meet economic and political imperatives. [Appendix A offers a detailed

Figure 7.4 Mega-resorts, such as the New York–NewYork Hotel and Casino in Las Vegas, must rely on highly skilled managers and employees (Photo: J.R. Gast)

historical annotation of key illustrative studies focusing on (1) skill development in tourism education and training, including a focus on the role of government, (2) improving tourism education and training systems and (3) assessment of skill and training needs.]

Human resources issues for education and training in tourism

The ideas and recommendations articulated in conference forums, the opinion of educators such as Cooper, Ritchie, Messenger and others, the contents of UNWTO, WTTC and other studies on education and training and skills development, in addition to the conclusions of government reports and studies, are distilled into the following set of key issues considered critical for contemporary education and training in tourism. This is not an exhaustive list, but, nevertheless, one representing the most salient issues culled from literature and practice.

Need for understanding and reducing misperceptions

Tourism has historically been ill defined and often misunderstood. The lack of definition and the type of jobs offered have proved to be a barrier to those considering a career in tourism. During the Pacific Asia Travel Association's 41st Annual Conference, Jorge Rangle, in a presentation, 'Meeting the Supply Challenge' suggested that this problem should be addressed not only by government but by the industry itself in 'upgrading and enhancing the image of the profession' (Rangel, 1992).

Many studies have focused on the perception of jobs in tourism as constituting a disproportionate number of non-skilled or semi-skilled people at low wages (Choy, 1995, pp. 129–137). Choy and others argued that this has resulted in a low regard by the public for potential careers in the industry. Wood similarly argued that this is particularly evident in the hotel and catering sectors where 'both industry employees and wider society view hotel and catering labour as relatively low in status, mainly because of the personal service nature of the work involved' (Wood, 1993, p. 3). He further contended that tourism, particularly the hotel sector, while offering accessible stable entry-level positions has efficiently learned to take advantage of under-utilized parts of the labour force, particularly young people and women, in marginal employment (part-time or casual). Low wages persisted as a surplus supply condition, and the peculiarities of the industry enable it to incorporate this type of labour because of its need to continually adjust to varying consumer demand (Wood, 1992, p. 300).

Baum, however, argued that this is a Euro-centric or US-centric notion, and by no means an applicable model in developing countries where skill training for international service commands a substantial investment in human resources in order to produce services and goods that meet international visitor expectations. A porter who carries visitors' luggage in the United States may be considered an unskilled worker, but in a developing country, that person will need to communicate and interact with primarily foreign visitors, and the job escalates to one requiring a worker who may need to speak several languages and be multi-culturally skilled (Baum, 1996, pp. 1–2). Baum's point is even more significant today.

Although certain tourism sectors in industrialized countries, such as lodging and food services, may be driven by large numbers of low-skilled workers in industrialized countries, studies also indicate that even in those countries there is a proportionately large share of workers in supervisory, mid-level and high-level management positions.

In the United States, a 1995 study by the Travel Industry Awareness Council projected that growth in executive positions in the sub-sectors of food and beverage, air transport, hotels and resorts, and amusement and recreation would be faster than employment in the overall economy (TIA, 1994, p. 5). US Labour Department statistics project that 'employment in the food service industry increased 32 per cent between 1982 and 1995, compared to a 25 per cent increase for other occupations, and demand for managers in food service increased 47 per cent during the same period' (CHRIE 1995a, p. 5). A study by the WTTC indicates that while the 'labor force is varied in education and skill level', over 80 per cent of the workers are in management, supervisory, and semi-highly skilled positions (WTTC, 1994, p. i). Further supporting the economic value of travel and tourism careers, TIA (2006, p. 12) reports that in the United States alone there are 7.3 million direct travel-generated jobs – one out of eight working Americans is employed directly or indirectly by the industry providing a large range of jobs with varying levels of skill requirements and upward mobility.

Although the industry is often viewed for its most obvious segments, like airlines, hotels and travel agencies, it is actually far broader, encompassing accountants, architects, engineers, IT professionals, chefs, contractors, construction workers, entertainers, transportation workers and service personnel of all types. In contrast to the trend in other industries to outsource jobs to other countries, most travel and tourism jobs stay in America (TIA, 2006, p. 12). The same is true, not only in America, but also in every country that hosts visitors, such as the bus drivers, retail clerks, and tour guides in the South American tourist town shown in Figure 7.5.

Figure 7.5 The jobs of local service providers cannot be exported (Photo: Matt Schuttloffel)

Need for credibility of post-secondary education programmes

For many years, jobs in tourism have been filled by individuals with no specific expertise or education in either tourism or hospitality. Schulman and Greenberg (1992, p. 2) contended, 'Historically, individuals have entered the travel industry for a broad range of reasons, a great many of which have had little to do with a conscious decision to pursue a professional career in the tourism industry'. The cause of this is far less important than the effect it has on those currently planning for careers in the field. While students may be highly cognizant of the usefulness of specialization in post-secondary education which goes beyond a general degree, an uncertainty remains as to whether a specialization in tourism will be appreciated or even acknowledged. A 1995 study indicated that degrees in hospitality management had no significant effect on promotion rates (Sparrowe and Popielarz, 1995). Another study by Cargill (1995, p. 54) found that a non-hospitality master's degree, with a major in general business, was preferred by hospitality industry professionals in the United States over a hospitality master's degree. The growth in quality and quantity of tourism education and training programmes and their quality standards meeting industry needs, among other factors, are changing this career landscape.

For many graduates of tourism programmes, job placement historically has been a disheartening process. A study in England showed that job placement for tourism graduates over a decade ago could be as low as 30 per cent of a graduating class for any school year (Evans, 1993, p. 244). Many complain that recruiters are simply not aware that tourism education at the college level exists, and if they do, they discount it in favour of those with business degrees. The exception, of course, are hotel administration programmes which fare somewhat better in job placement over general tourism degree programmes, especially if the programme is nationally or internationally renowned, such as that at Cornell University's School of Hotel Administration or the Hague Institute of Hotel Management in the Netherlands. In the past, even with hotel programme graduates, entry pay has often been far below a comparative position in other employment sectors (Chreptyk, 1990, p. 2) and for women hospitality graduates, there has been even more of a gap (Diaz, 1994, pp. 10–11). While these data are improving over time as tourism gains in recognition and awareness as a global industry employer, tourism and hospitality graduates frequently shift away from their original career pursuits to those appearing more lucrative. This was also the finding in a sector-specific study of hotels, conducted by the International Hotel Association (1988, p. 26) which attributed high labour turnover, or the problem of worker retention, as clearly being a function of 'financial rewards available . . . and job satisfaction which is generally low'. Ross (1995) also concluded, from a study of job attributes and workplace evaluations that in addition to pay, negative employment perceptions of the industry regarding working conditions and what jobs would offer in terms of interest, achievement, and advancement, made it difficult for companies to recruit and retain workers. While much progress has been made over time, travel and tourism, to sustain its lead among services industries in quality service and customer satisfaction, will always require ongoing and high levels of education and training. Today, in fact, a 'full service' industry now means one that educates and trains its employees in personal service and style.

Need for investment in human resources in tourism

In the past, there has been much discussion regarding the industry's need to invest in human resources. This is made more pronounced by the number of small businesses that dominate the industry, and their inability either to support or recognize the importance of investing in human resources to improve overall professionalism and the quality of the tourism product (Cooper et al., 1994, p. 60). Too often in the past, managers view training as a cost rather than as an investment (Cooper, 1993, p. 66). Cooper stated that many in the industry are 'simply unconvinced of the benefits of tourism education and training' despite the obvious fact that tourism is a service business dependent on the quality of personal skills of those delivering the services (Cooper, p. 66).

In the context of organizational behaviour and the tourism industry, Wood (1994, p. 165) quoted Mary L. Tanke of Florida International University, who stated, 'When you think about it, it is really amazing that individuals that are willing to spend thousands and even millions of dollars building a new restaurant or renovating an old landmark hotel fail to allocate enough dollars for training'. Though the United States, as noted, has experienced significant growth in professional management development programmes (continuing education) and many of these are supported by large-scale hospitality firms, in other parts of the world this is the exception rather than rule. In 1995, Shepperd and Cooper (1995) stated that in the UK 'only a small minority of companies have developed or maintain links with education institutions'. Furthermore they contended, 'Many [companies] seem to distrust educational institutions, fearing it seems that these institutions are unable to offer the kind of relevant courses and skills that the tourism industry requires' (Shepperd and Cooper, p. 16).

Need for education and training performance standards and accreditation processes

Unlike other fields, such as medicine, teaching, law or accounting, until recently, there have been few generally accepted entry credentials for jobs at any occupation level within tourism. Thus, job recruitment and placement was made difficult for the recruiter and student alike. There have been attempts by several organizations, including the UNWTO, the European Union's CEDEFDP (the European Centre for the Development of Vocational Education) and CHRIE, to improve awareness and bring standards to tourism education. In 1990, for example, the UNWTO formed the Education and Training Network, a consortium of schools, to work with the UNWTO in developing a 'strategic plan to build an educational infrastructure for tourism education at the university level and improve the professionalism and quality of tourism education and training at every level' (UNWTO, 1992). CEDEFOP conducted a study across the European Community to determine the specific knowledge and skills needed for vocations in the tourism industry (Cooper, 1993, p. 70). As previously discussed, CHRIE is also to be commended for its long-term project for setting national skill standards for eight occupations within the tourism sector.

Worldwide, the number of tourism education providers of every type is vast and they differ widely in quality. Catalogues, indexes and databases abound, describing tourism and hospitality education programmes, among the first and most notable by the UNWTO (1992) and CHRIE (1995a). In the UNWTO catalogue, more than 1250 such educational institutions were identified (Figure 7.6).

With notable exceptions cited above, while the growth and number of post-secondary programmes in tourism and hospitality is impressive, accreditation systems, national standards and professional certification have been slower in the making. This is in sharp contrast to other

Figure 7.6   Hohenschwangau Castle (lit: *Castle of the High Swan*), childhood residence of King Ludwig II of Bavaria, Schwangau, Germany (Photo: Sarah J. Gust)

professional areas, such as business, medicine, law, nursing, optometry, engineering and theology, which all initiated accrediting activities in the 1920s and 1930s in the United States (Tanke, 1992, p. 287). In 1982, CHRIE charged its Committee on Accreditation with investigating the development of an accreditation process for 4-year bachelor's degree programmes, and implemented one in 1990. In North America, the tourism industry has dozens of certification programmes, whereas in 1980, it only had two (Morrison et al., 1992, pp. 32–40). In the mid-1980s, Canada began developing standards and implementing certification programmes through its Tourism Industry Standards and Certification Committee. Standards were developed for well over 40 occupations, great gains over 1992 when certification was available for only 6 (Swedlove & Dowler, 1992, pp. 283–286). Today fortunately education and training programs have became more rigorous and plentiful.

Leadership role of the United Nations World Tourism Organization

On 24 December 2003, the UN General Assembly adopted a resolution through which the World Tourism Organization (WTO) became a new, fully fledged specialized agency of the United Nations (UNWTO). This important status is well-earned, signifying long-standing acceptance by the international community of the multi-dimensional nature of tourism and the decades-long advocacy role in support of this recognition played by the UNWTO and other national and international tourism organizations mentioned in this volume. In response to the resolution, UNWTO Secretary General Francesco Frangialli stated that 'the impact of tourism on poverty alleviation, preservation of cultural heritage, environmental protection and promotion of peace and understanding among all nations has gained universal recognition' (UNWTO, 2004a,b, p. 1). The UNWTO Human Resources Development Programme and its THEMIS Foundation, the Business, Destination and Education Councils of the restructured Affiliate Members, among other UNWTO programmes and councils, played an important role in this UNWTO achievement.

UNWTO Education Council of the Affiliate Members. The Education Council of the UNWTO is the Education chapter of the UNWTO Affiliate (non-government) Members, numbering at present around 100 education, training and research institutions. It is an active policymaking body working in conjunction with the UNWTO Human Resources Development (HRD) department with periodic meetings to set policy issues in tourism education, training, and research at the global, regional and local levels. A critical focus for the Council is the important and integrative role that governments play in ensuring sufficient investment in knowledge and human resources to achieve the successful management of destinations. A 2003 Education Council conference included themes such as 'Quality Education for Quality Destinations' stressing the need for public officials to obtain higher understanding of the breadth and complexity of the tourism industry and 'Training for Excellence' focused on the role of training in achieving competitiveness and sustainability. An additional session concentrated on practicalities and how to use knowledge for tourism destination success (UNWTO, 2003, p. 5). The UNWTO HRD Department and UNWTO Education Council 2004 conference themes had expanded to include integrating education institutions into rural communities to fostering the transfer of knowledge. These conference themes as a total reflect core values for education and training for tourism worldwide.

UNWTO-Themis Foundation and TedQual Program. The Education Council's members are education, training and research institutions which have obtained the UNWTO TedQual Certification for one or more of their tourism education programmes and have joined the UNWTO Affiliate Members. These institutions participate actively with the UNWTO HRD department and its UNWTO-Themis Foundation to implement products and service such as the Graduate Tourism Achievement Test (GTAT). The mission of UNWTO-Themis Foundation is to promote quality and efficiency in tourism education and training and, in general, in the development of human resources in tourism. Located in Andorra la Vella, Principality of Andorra, UNWTO-Themis Foundation objectives include collection and dissemination of information databases covering different aspects of the demand and managerial know-how, design and management of quality standards in tourism education and training, strengthening training programmes and activities in support of national tourism administration human capital, and the provision of seminars and courses on education, training and development of tourism human resources of countries and regions (http://www.world-tourism.org, accessed 26 June 2005).

In January 2004, the UNWTO launched a 10,000-piece publication distribution programme and an updated UNWTO Education Web site to promote TedQual (tourism education quality) – certified institutions to governments, businesses and particularly to potential students around the world. TedQual is a voluntary quality assurance (fee-based) certification system offered to universities, technical institutions, vocational training centres and business schools. The goal is to establish a worldwide TedQual education system using mentor institutions to bring candidate institutions up to the TedQual Certification level. This will create a worldwide network in tourism education and training at the service of all UNWTO members States by more clearly defining the quality of tourism education systems using voluntary standards underpinned by a rigorous methodology. To date, 57 tourism and hospitality education and training programmes have achieved UNWTO TedQual certification. Benefits include international recognition, opportunity for UNWTO affiliate membership in the Education Council, use of the TedQual certification logo, and credibility of academic degrees obtained by graduates of the education institution.

In support of this goal, the UNWTO also has established a UNWTO Themis TedQual Practicum in tourism education, training and research for government officials of member States working in national tourism authorities, organizations, and promotion offices. This 10-day training programme enables government officials to gain an in-depth knowledge of the specialized tourism education and training products and services developed by the UNWTO in order to improve competitiveness of its members (http://world-tourism.org/education/tedqual.htm, accessed 27 June 2005) (Figure 7.7).

Figure 7.7 Tabacon Hot Springs and Spa located near the base of the Arenal Volcano, Costa Rica (photo: Sarah J. Gust)

Need for coordinated education and training infrastructure for tourism

The content of much formal education in tourism in the 1990s was characterized by its inability to find solid footing. Schulman and Green-berg (1992, p. 2) in their study argued that 'The educational infrastructure necessary to systematically attract and train tourism's fair percentage of the best minds and the most ambitious, most effective managers is just emerging'. Preoccupying much discussion and debate on tourism as an academic area of study is how to define it, place it, and defend it. A study by Partlow (1994) questioned the content of hospitality graduate education suggesting that graduates question whether their education was relevant to their professional employment. In a similar study, Burbridge (1994) contended that there is also a gap between the skills students consider are important and their perception of their own ability to perform those skills. Fortunately, this situation is rapidly changing.

The number of institutions and organizations involved with tourism education and training delivery today is immense. Businesses, themselves, often assume a significant proportion of training, in addition to professional associations, proprietary and vocational schools, high schools, community colleges and universities. The training modes for tourism education in the past were often based on guesswork, and since advancement in the industry is characterized by 'coming up through the ranks', or through in-house promotion, the value of a degree was and frequently still is questioned. Exacerbating the problem was the fact that the tourism industry lacks basic consensus on the need for education (Ritchie, 1993, p. 13). Shepperd and Cooper (1995, p. 15) suggest that there is even a 'distrust and a lack of understanding of the new range of tourism courses among large sections of the tourism industry'.

Over the last decade, a number of tourism academic and continuing education institutions have been dedicated to raising the standards for tourism education and training curricula not only to keep pace with the rapidly growing global tourism industry but also to take leadership roles in its quality and direction. A selected, but hardly exhaustive, list of these is provided below as diverse examples of the significant growth and development of education and training in tourism internationally over the last decade. There are many other outstanding schools and programmes which space does not permit including:

Higher education and training programmes in tourism

Hong Kong. Established in 1979, the Department of Institutional Management and Catering Studies was renamed as Department of Hotel and Tourism Management (DHTM) in 1992. The Department was designated a School in October 2001, which became an independent and autonomous academic unit within the University structure in July 2004. According to the Journal of Hospitality and Tourism Education in 2002, DHTM was the only one in Asia Pacific rated among the world's top 15 academic institutions in hospitality and tourism based on research and scholarly activities, exemplifying the School's motto of Leading Asia in Hospitality and Tourism Education. Supported by strong industry links, the programme has been developed from relevant research and consultancy activities. The applied and professionally oriented programmes are geared towards preparing students for a potential management or executive career in the hotel, catering and tourism sectors. DHTM recognizes that in the modern business environment, neither education nor work experience alone is sufficient as a foundation on which to build a career in the industry. To this end, some programmes incorporate work experience whereas others are aimed at upgrading skills and knowledge of those already in the industry. The International Academy for the Study of Tourism, which is incorporated as a non-profit corporation, has its official headquarters in the School of Hotel and Tourism Management, The Hong Kong Polytechnic University, and continues to address many of the critical issues in tourism policy.

United States. Several universities in the United States are addressing the needs of education and training in tourism, as evidenced by East Carolina University's (Greenville, North Carolina, USA) addition of the Centre for Sustainable Tourism. The Centre's primary goals are to develop and maintain vital curriculum for undergraduate and graduate level degrees, serve as a hub for tourism-related research throughout departments at East Carolina University, and engage in tourism-related community engagement. It is through this type of commitment that students, faculty, tourism industry representatives, community leaders and government officials can come together to share their thoughts, concerns, ideas, research and solutions.

The George Washington University ('GW'), Washington, DC, USA, Department of Tourism and Hospitality Management is located in the GW School of Business and offers a Master of Tourism Administration (MTA) degree with concentrations in sport, event and sustainable destination management and five-year bachelor in business administration in hospitality and tourism. The MTA provides students with a theoretical and practical understanding of the sport, event and hospitality industries. It prepares the students to work in the management and marketing of sport events, organizations, products and athletes as well as in special events, expositions, festivals and other entertainment properties. Those focused on hospitality will learn about the marketing, management and financing of both tourism destinations and those businesses that are related to tourism, with a focus on sustainability, including cities, attractions, hotels, restaurants and airlines. GW also offers its MTA degree fully online through its Accelerated Master of Tourism Administration (AMTA) program. Established over 30 years ago, the MTA was the first tourism and hospitality management curriculum at the master's level in North America. Additionally, the GW MTA programme was the first higher education programme in tourism and hospitality management in the United States to earn the TedQual (Tourism Education Quality) certificate designation by the UNWTO.

The Travel Industry Management School, University of Hawaii at Manoa, offers certificate, undergraduate and graduate programmes in tourism, transportation and hospitality. The School is accredited by the Accreditation Commission for Programmes in Hospitality Administration (ACPHA), and has also earned the TedQual (Tourism Education Quality) certificate designation by the UNWTO. The curriculum has an international perspective focusing on global issues.

Canada. The Hayscane School of Business, University of Calgary, offers tourism and tourism marketing concentrations in the Bachelor of Communications degree. Course work integrates general business curriculum with tourism-focused work. The University also offers a unique 2-year degree – Bachelor of Hotel and Resort Management – which is coupled with a 2-year technical degree.

Non-credit tourism training programmes

United States. Through its International Institute of Tourism Studies, The George Washington University's Department of Tourism and Hospitality

Management, School of Business, has for many years offered non-credit tourism certificates which are now fully online. Concentrations for degree and non-degree programmes include sustainable destination management, event and sports management, and international hotel management.

Need for vertical and horizontal coordination among key stakeholders

A study involving 200 educators from 25 countries ranked the most important issue facing tourism as the 'need to strengthen linkages between industry, government and educational institutions' (Ritchie, 1992, pp. 257–263). A 1993 study by Berger expanded the notion that a viable hospitality industry in the twenty-first century will need to create 'partnerships with employees, guests and universities'. A key point in the WTTC study (1994b) conducted by the University of Hawaii was that 'government and industry often carry out their human resource strategies in isolation from each other'. Achieving vertical linkages (government to industry to education) is made even more problematic by the fact that, at the national level, horizontal linkages in government, on human resource matters, that is, agency to agency, may be lacking or peripheral to national tourism policy (Baum, 1994a). Baum's survey of national tourism organizations further concluded that 'tourism policy statements and related documentation isolate the human resource area within virtually self-contained sections or clusters of objectives, without any attempt to integrate them with other areas of concern' (Baum, p. 191).

The absence of integration between industry and educational institutions is most detrimental to students in the development of experiential learning situations while they are in school. A common complaint of industry is the fact that job entrants 'lack experience'; yet developing work placements is often problematic, with companies often using student labour for menial clerical tasks instead of tasks which contribute to their overall education and career development (Shepperd & Cooper, 1995, p. 19). In some countries, notably the United States, Canada, France, Germany and the United Kingdom, experiential learning was a formal part of degree level programmes, and there were structured 'co-operative-Ed' programmes and internship contracts (Parsons, 1991, p. 204). In those situations, the experiential learning component is structured and monitored, with faculty closely supervising student placement and performance. It is not uncommon to find programmes at the higher education level which require participation a structured practicum, for which a student receives academic credit, and additional 400–800 h of required field experience, without academic credit.

The lack of integration between the tourism industry and education is illustrated also in recruitment criteria, which often do not include tourism knowledge. Examples of countries that embarked early on special initiatives to address this problem include Canada and Ireland. In Canada, a coordinating body designated as a Tourism Education Council was formed, representing industry, government, labour and education to meet human resource needs (Hawkins, 1996, p. 2). The formation of such a Council, as a separate entity or within an existing organization, helped members of the industry to work together and collaborate in raising professionalism, as well as eradicating negative perceptions associated with a career in tourism. In Ireland, the Council for Education, Recruitment and Training (CERT) was instrumental in developing programmes at all stages of the education cycle, including more cooperative work/education programmes, innovative forms of programme delivery, a transfer credit system for creating 'a balance between upgrading and pre-employment programs', and industry involvement with all programme development (Walsh, 1992, p. 130).

Observing the successful examples, such as CERT, where coordination and integration between tourism education, industry and the role of government have been achieved, Amoah and Baum (1997) were able to present a unifying conceptual model, Tourism Education Policy–Tourism Education Implementation (TEP–TEI) which outlines a structure for education and training flowing from coordinated policy but subject to the dynamic influences of exogenous environments (such as the economic and social climate).

Amoah and Baum, as early as 1997, contended that coordination between entities will not occur, and tourism and problems associated with the training of its manpower will continue to persist, unless destinations engage in long-term integrative thinking considering economic development (tourism environment) and educational policy together. It is difficult to argue with the underlying logic and simplicity of the model (Figure 7.8): this model, as a basic approach provides a platform upon which to build the complex realities of a market driven economy and the vastly different public policy towards education among countries. In some countries (notably in the Americas), higher education in tourism is a private sector initiative and any attempt to make it conform to public and state-wide education policy would be difficult or even impossible. The Travel Industry Association of America, for example, partners with academic and government agencies such as college and university tourism and hospitality management programmes and US Federal and State travel and tourism offices in the areas of applied research and education and training initiatives.

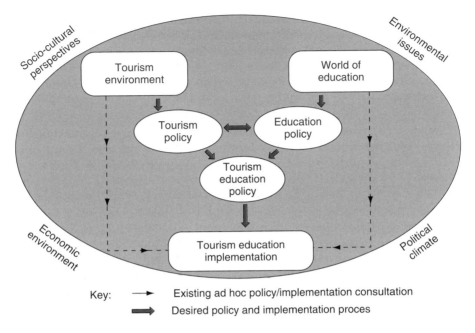

Figure 7.8   Tourism education policy–tourism education implementation model

Need to understand the dynamics of a rapidly changing world and the impact on workforce development

Rapidly changing technology and a competitive environment have contributed to an evolving workplace, which places new demands on the skills, knowledge and attributes workers will need to bring to their jobs. Additionally, the workforce itself is becoming much more diverse due to changing demographics, social structures, values and norms and the ease with which individuals migrate for work and leisure purposes (Christensen, 1993; Powers, 1994, p. 19).

In many countries there is a movement away from traditional job descriptions to a less formal work environment. The virtual office, or working from home, made possible by affordable communication technology, is a trend that may become commonplace in many countries by the end of the decade. As labour demands increases worldwide, so will opportunities for employment of traditionally under-represented groups in tourism, such as women, disabled workers and ethnic minorities.

Global competitiveness is resulting in the traditional workplace giving way to 'lean and mean' structures, but there will be greater emphasis on producing quality products and retaining quality workers. There is broad agreement about a shortage of professionals who are adequately qualified for working in tourism, particularly temporary workers. Conditions of flexibility, claimed to be key to face changes in demand, hinder the adequate qualification of staff, which at the same time is also considered necessary to be able to deal with those changes (Marhuenda et al., 2004). At the same time, there will be pressure on the workplace to adapt to changing attitudes among workers as they place higher value on their quality of life, and seek environments that contribute to mental wellness and fitness to provide them with greater job satisfaction. Cooper (1993) foresaw this trend in emphasizing that only those companies which develop worthwhile, satisfying and financially attractive long-term career potential will be able to retain workers and be viable.

In this light, 'encouraging students to consider a career in travel and tourism entails a greater effort on the part of the industry, universities, schools, and all types of training and research centers' (Tourism Works for America, 2004, p. 9). The Academy of Hospitality and Tourism, a high school-based tourism education programme of the National Academy Foundation based in New York, New York, reports that employment opportunities in hospitality, travel and tourism are expected to increase by 17.8 per cent through 2012, creating a critical need for dynamic employees with a strong background in both academic and industry-related work experience (Tourism Works for America, p. 9).

Importance of education and training in tourism

UNWTO Secretary General Francesco Frangialli stated, 'the tourism sector has gained substantially in resilience over the past years. In spite of the turbulent environment we live in nowadays, destinations worldwide added some 100 million international arrivals between 2002 and 2005' (UNWTO, 2006, p. 5). This outlines the enormous task of providing adequate education and training for the tourism workforce of today and the future. It reinforces the significant challenges posed in this chapter for employers, educators and researchers and suggests many opportunities that remain and that are being addressed by tourism higher education and training programmes today. These include the continuing need to: dispel misconceptions about the industry and the jobs it offers, increase credibility for education and training in tourism, improve coordination among education and training providers, achieve vertical and horizontal coordination among key stakeholders and meet the demands of a fast-changing workforce and workplace.

With few tourism education programmes equivalent to the executive MBA programmes flourishing at many universities worldwide, to create equity in higher education for tourism professionals, the tourism industry must seek partnerships with government and academia to utilize available technologies and methods, including distance learning, in support of the education and training of a first-class global workforce (Elliott and Smith, 2005, p. 1). What is needed now is knowledge management for tourism. Shikha and Deepika (2006, p. 45) state that 'relatively little knowledge transfer is taking place between the knowledge generators in the academic community on one side, and the managers and operators in the private and public sectors responsible for tourism and hospitality development on the other'. Shika and Deepika view tourism education as being sufficiently theoretical and able to move beyond vocational training to expose tourism students to a wider range of ideas, knowledge, and theory. 'One of the strengths of tourism is that it can offer 'extra-disciplinary' training oriented towards fulfilling the needs of the industry as well as orient students towards multi- and inter-disciplinary orientation for development of tourism as a whole' (Shika and Deepika, p. 41). An emerging emphasis in education and training on personal service and style gives new embodiment to the concept of full service in hospitality and tourism.

As we have seen in this chapter, historically, many studies have attempted to examine the problems and issues of tourism education and training and human resource development. Many have focused on skills needed for different tourism professions and describe one set of observations from a single survey of a population sample. What is needed are more studies researching quality issues in tourism education and employment by examining the multiple dimensions that differentiate tourism as an economic activity – geographic, occupational and sector. Needed are more studies attempting to examine quality issues in tourism education and employment by using a dynamic process which builds consensus on issues through feedback rather than a one-time observation of the problem at hand.

The UNWTO Tourism Enriches campaign, launched in early 2004, promotes the positive impacts of tourism thereby capturing what the authors of this volume believe to be both the spirit of and critically important work plan for the future of education and training in tourism. The aims of the Tourism Enriches campaign are to promote tourism as a basic human right and way of life, which enriches individuals, family, societies and nations, to stimulate communication about the benefits of tourism as the most prospective economic activity for local communities and countries, to enhance cooperation between destinations and the tourism industry with the local, regional and international media, and to link individual tourism entities to the larger community of international tourism.

It is hoped that this chapter and volume will contribute in this way to a specific detailing of the bridges underway leading to improving the future for quality tourism education and training – to increase economic benefits, international understanding, rural jobs and environmental protection through the benefits of world tourism development (UNWTO, 2004a, b, p. 1).

Case report 7

BEST EN
BUSINESS ENTERPRISES FOR SUSTAINABLE TOURISM EDUCATION NETWORK
CURRICULUM DEVELOPMENT THINK TANK PROCESS

As described by Dr. Abraham Pizam, founder with Dr. Ginger Smith of the BEST Education Committee in 2000 (originally under the auspices of The Conference Board in New York, New York), the educational modules prepared annually since that time by BEST EN represent the collective work of a group of volunteers composed of the leaders of BEST – academics and industry practitioners representing the various sectors of the tourism industry worldwide. These individuals have gathered annually for the last 7 years in various regions of the globe in think tank formats in order to develop a programme of study for the teaching of sustainable tourism and related research in the field. The organizers of the think tanks (a special meeting of experts on a particular subject matter) felt that in order to educate the future leaders of the worldwide tourism industry properly and to induce them to use sustainable practices in their daily operations, it would be necessary to treat sustainability as a *managerial philosophy* rather than an isolated subject matter taught in one comprehensive course. They were guided by a strong belief that sustainable tourism principles should be practiced in *all aspects of tourism operations* on a daily basis. Therefore, rather than prepare the curriculum and lesson plans for a comprehensive course on sustainable tourism, which may or may not be taken by all students of hospitality and tourism programmes nor be applicable to all the sectors of the industry, the leaders of BEST EN instead chose to adopt a modular approach and prepare a set of short learning units that are specifically relevant to each subject matter and each industry sector and that can be inserted into traditional tourism and hospitality course curricula. In this way, each student taking any course in tourism and hospitality management containing a BEST EN education module – be it in tourism marketing, food and beverage management, hotel engineering, hospitality operations, etc. – will get a "dose" of sustainable tourism practices during his or her studies that is specifically applicable to that subject matter.

BEST EN has held numerous think tanks and, as a result, has developed learning modules across the tourism and hospitality curriculum. The education think tank process allows 40 to 50 individuals in attendance at the conferences and think tank sessions to participate in several groups, each lead by a facilitator. Each day, the groups hold working sessions to discuss a given topic, using the Nominal Group Technique (NGT) format. Following this, all groups meet in an assembly format and report their results. On the last day of each think tank session, a comprehensive report is drafted. This report is then forwarded to a small sub-group of volunteers who produce the final sustainable tourism course outlines and lesson plans.

The outcome of the first two think tanks conducted in South Africa (2001) and Hawaii (2002) was a set of four modules on sustainable tourism that are meant to be infused into existing hospitality/tourism courses that cover the topics of tourism planning and development, hospitality/tourism marketing, hospitality/tourism human resources management, and hospitality operations. Through subsequent think tanks, BEST EN and its volunteer partners have continued the development of additional modules in other subject matters and/or for various sectors of the tourism/hospitality industry (i.e., hotels, restaurants, transportation and the travel trade, attractions, etc.) and have added a research conference component for paper presentations. Sustainable tourism modules developed in Costa Rica (2003) include food and beverage, energy, event management, and community tourism. Modules developed in Denmark (2004) include facilities management and triple bottom line, in Jamaica (2005), managing risk and crisis for sustainable tourism – research and innovation, and corporate social responsibility (2006). Think Tank VII in Flagstaff, Arizona, USA, focuses in 2007 on innovations in sustainable tourism, including drivers for innovation, barriers, social entrepreneurship and innovative technologies, among others.

It is the collective hope of all those who are involved in the process of creating the modules that hospitality/tourism educators and industry trainers will use them to advance the cause of sustainable tourism practices for generations to come.

As an example, following is a case report on BEST EN Think Tank V (prepared by Claudia Jurowski, School of Hotel and Restaurant Management, Northern Arizona University, Flagstaff, Arizona, USA), which focused on managing risk and crisis for sustainable tourism from both research and innovation perspectives.

BEST EN Think Tank V

The fifth Think Tank organized by Business Enterprises for Sustainable Travel Education Network (BEST EN) was held in conjunction with the University of the West Indies' Institute for Hospitality and Tourism in

Kingston Jamaica on 16–19 June 2005. The conference continued the organization's work in the development and dissemination of knowledge related to managing the tourism industry in a sustainable manner. BEST EN is an international consortium of educators committed to furthering the development and dissemination of knowledge in the field of sustainable tourism. During the annual Think Tank and Conference, academics and practitioners share and develop knowledge through two different forums. Refereed papers are presented to introduce cutting edge research and practices to participants, and think tank sessions are held to establish a research agenda and outline the contents of teaching modules on a specified topic. The teaching modules are distributed to instructors of undergraduate courses in hospitality and tourism and the research agenda is distributed through journal publications. This year's discussions focused on the timely subject of managing risk and crises for sustainable tourism. The 45 participants were educators, researchers, consultants, and practitioners from Australia, Canada, Denmark, Germany, the Netherlands, New Zealand, the United Kingdom, the United States and the West Indies.

Pauline Sheldon, Chair of BEST EN, Carolyn Hayle, Chair of Think Tank V and Marlene Hamilton, Pro Vice Chancellor of the University of the West Indies, welcomed the participants. The Jamaican Minister of Industry and Tourism, the Honourable Aloun Assamba, described how the Jamaican tourism industry put into practice the principles advocated by BEST EN. She explained that Jamaica's tourism strategy focused on greater harmony with the interests and culture of the local population, environmental responsibility, and wider distribution of the tourism benefits among the society. Her presentation acknowledged the importance of the conference noting that the Caribbean tourism industry was particularly at risk because of its vulnerability to hurricanes, earthquakes, floods, and landslides. Minister Assamba closed her remarks by stressing that education was the precondition for social transformation and crisis mitigation.

Three keynote addresses set the tone for the think tank. Security expert, Peter Tarlow, discussed the sociological and psychological relationship of leisure travel and tourism surety. He explained six areas of tourism protection: visitor protection, ecological management, site protection, protection of staff, economic protection and reputation protection. Risk management was identified as a pro-active strategy while crisis management was deemed a reactive strategy. Urging preparedness, he proposed that tourism risk could be reduced through planning and that the need for crisis management often occurred due to a lack of good risk management. Tarlow proposed self-assessment taxonomies to determine risk potential and to classify risk in relation to level of probability and consequences.

David Beirman, the director of the Israel Tourism Office in Australia, addressed post-event recovery strategies. He explained the difficulties in working with the media during the crisis and after a destination has recovered from a disaster. His presentation included a discussion of the importance of travel insurance, the role government travel advisories play in discouraging travel to destinations, a system for crisis ranking, the management of consumer perceptions, methods for rebuilding confidence for a destination along with recovery models and crisis related marketing. Beirman's presentation was largely based on international case studies. He emphasized that the most critical component of both the crisis and the recovery cycle was the public's reading and offered examples of how views could be influenced. Beirman concluded that a sustainable tourism industry needed good research and training that would take the interlocking roles of government, media and industry into account.

The final keynote speaker, Scott Cunliffe from Tourism Futures.Org, explained the importance of the awareness of the risk faced by small and medium sized business. He listed a series of proposals for sustainable tourism risk management and asked the delegates to identify efforts that would make these businesses autonomous and self-sufficient in dealing with risk and crisis.

Twenty-one other presentations organized in five distinct themed sessions addressed the issues of risk and crisis management from distinct perspectives. The first session, Management and Politics of Risk and Crisis in Tourism, began with a presentation by Sarah Ryu from Victoria University in Australia who discussed how tourism can be used as a tool for political and ideological goals, how the tourism industry can influence the reform of politically troubled nations, how tourism can be moulded by the political purpose, and the impact political instability has upon the healthy operation of tourism. In the same session, Marcella Daye of Coventry University in the United Kingdom presented "Framing Tourist Risk in UK Press Accounts of Hurricane Ivan". Her research, based on a case study of Hurricane Ivan, demonstrated that overseas reporting of Hurricane Ivan was more likely to emphasize tourist vulnerability and risk rather than the management strategies being implemented to ensure visitor safety. Daye advised monitoring media accounts and presented media management strategies that might repair damage to the image of a disaster stricken tourist destination. In their presentation, "Managing of Public Risks in Tourism: Towards Sustainability Management", Yoram Krozer and Else Redzepovic of the University Twente in the Netherlands used an industry-based model as an analytical tool for examining how to manage risks that endanger the sustainability of tourism. They advocated creating awareness about issues and possible solutions, assisting policy makers with directing sustainable tourism development and aiding companies with the implementation of cost-effective solutions.

The second session of the conference, Approaches to Mitigate Tourism Crises, included papers that described strategies for dealing with the effects of tourism crises. Bonalyn Nelson of St. Michael's College Vermont in the USA used examples from published case studies to illustrate six stigma management strategies that could be employed in image threatening predicaments. Knowledge management was addressed by Nina Mistilis of the University of New South Wales in Australia and Pauline Sheldon of the University of Hawaii in the USA. They presented a model of a knowledge management system for the public sector of a tourism destination that described the various types of knowledge and information needed and the specifics of the information system architecture. The final presentation in this conference segment by Yetta Gurtner of James Cool University in Australia used a case study approach to describe strategies related to institutional reform that could improve a destination's resistance and resilience when faced with a catastrophic event.

Communication issues in tourism crises and disasters were addressed in the next conference segment. Jack Carlsen of the Curtin University in Australia described how lessons learned from previous crises and disasters were useful in proposing tourism recovery strategies for the Maldives following the 2004 tsunami. Dr. Carlsen's paper, "Crisis Communication in the Maldives", won the Outstanding paper Award that was presented at the opening reception and dinner. The subsequent presentation by Kate Armstrong of University of Canberra in Australia examined the types of media used during and after the 2003 Bushfires in the Australian Capital Territory. Fellow Australian, Sue Beeton of La Trobe University, noted a shift in the reporting of disasters and other aversities by Fox News. She demonstrated selectivity in the reporting of events and the increase in encouraging visitors to return rather than discouraging tourism after an event.

The economics of tourism crises and disasters was explored from three different perspectives in another session. First, a team of researchers from three universities in Australia discussed two major crises – the Iraq War and SARS. Larry Dwyer of the University of New South Wales, Peter Forsyth from Monash University and Ray Spurr with the University of New South Wales reported that both inbound and outbound travel were affected by the crises. However, the net economic effects were less than that which was perceived by the stakeholders because the reduction in outbound travel resulted in an increase of domestic travel. Mondher Sahli from Victoria University of New Zealand and Jean-Jacque Nowak from the University of Lille in France presented a general equilibrium model that examines specific features of developing countries to determine the conditions under which an inbound tourism boom makes developing countries residents worse off. The final presentation by Tadayuki Hara of Cornell University in the USA proposed a quantitative model to forecast immediate short-term impacts of an unexpected event when multivariate/time series based modelling is not functional. Hara's deterministic model of an input–output social accounting matrix offered an alternative for achieving valid assessments.

One segment of the conference was devoted to general topics on sustainable tourism. Ercan Sirakayae of Texas A & M University in the USA presented the results of a resident attitude study conducted with his colleague Linda Ingram and Hwan Suk Chris Choi from the University of Guelph in Canada. SUS-TAS scales were used in a factor/cluster analysis to identify relatively homogeneous resident segments within the sustainability framework, and distinguish their similarities and differences regarding sustainable tourism development. Their work confirms the presumption that there are resident segments within the sustainability framework with varied levels of adherence to sustainability principles. Christian Schott from Victoria University of Wellington in New Zealand evaluated the role of eco-labels in making a meaningful difference in establishing sustainable tourism through the investigation of attitudes toward the labels as well as consumer awareness. The following presentation by Leo Jago of Victoria University in Australia elaborated on a study he conducted with his university colleague Liz Fredline and Margaret Deery of Australia's Griffith University. He described community perceptions of tourism and the potential risk to both the environment and the community well being based on the findings from community workshops and a survey of residents. The final presentation, "Tourism Education for Cambodia: A Case Study of its First University-level Course", by Ravi Ravinder of the University of Technology Sydney, Australia outlined the magnitude of tourism activity in Cambodia and described an approach to the development of a Masters course in Tourism Development.

In the last session titled Environmental Risk, Damian Morgan of Monash University in Australia analysed the risk of drowning at surf beaches by explaining the roles and relationships among risk factors, markers of risk and components of risk exposure for surf beach drowning. Nancy Scanlon from the University of Hawaii in the USA discussed response strategies to climate change impacts. She offered strategies to help tourism destinations respond to three major issues of climate change: the emergence of unpredictable weather patterns, the impact of severe weather and the challenge to deliver a consistent "experience" during changing weather patterns.

Local issues and initiatives were presented by Anthony Clayton, Alcan Professor of Caribbean Sustainable Development at the University of West Indies, Franklin McDonald, retired Director of the National Environment and Planning Agency and Hugh Cresser, Director of the Environmental Audits for Sustainable Tourism (EAST) Project. Clayton gave an overview of the challenges Jamaica faces while McDonald identified specific threats to the island noting that planning was necessary to reduce risks. The latter stressed the importance of risk reduction for the tourism industry and proposed the creation of what he termed a "disaster culture". Cresser informed the delegates about the EAST Project explaining that several major tourist facilities have already adopted environmental management systems.

Interspersed among the presentations were research and module development sessions during which delegates discussed risk and crisis management in relation to learning objectives and a research agenda. Since its inception, BEST EN has focused on the development of teaching modules that would fit into existing undergraduate hospitality and tourism management courses. Each module delineates the curriculum for six to eight teaching sessions. The goal of the module development discussions at Think Tank V was to identify learning objectives and recommend learning activities on the management of risk and crises for sustainable tourism. Claudia Jurowski of Northern Arizona University in the USA, the chair of the module development committee, led the discussions. The first session focused on setting objectives and identifying activities related to managing risk and preparing for crises while the second session focused on responses to adversities and crises and the third on recovery and restoration of destinations that had experienced a disaster or crisis. The objectives the group designed as well as the list of activities recommended for each objective were presented to the delegates in the final session. Damian Morgan and Scott Cunliffe volunteered to write the module that will be published on a compact disc and available for distribution through the BEST EN Secretariat at the University of Southern Denmark for US $20 or 15€ (plus shipping costs). Currently four modules developed at previous Think Tanks are available for purchase: Marketing for Sustainable Tourism, Sustainable Operations Management, Sustainable Tourism Planning and Sustainable Festivals, Meetings and Event Management. To procure one or more of the published teaching modules in CD format, contact Dr Janne J. Liburd, University of Southern Denmark (e-mail: liburd@sitkom.sdu.dk).

Larry Dwyer and Pauline Sheldon facilitated the research agenda sessions whose purpose was to identify critical research needs in the area of destination crisis management. Participants in the research discussion sessions were asked to identify knowledge gaps and highlight topics that deserve more attention from researchers. Issues addressed include crisis typologies, risk identification and assessment, managing the recovery and restoration, restoring confidence, marketing, recovery and rebuilding the tourist industry. A summary of the discussion was presented in the final session.

The final session included a visioning session where delegates were asked to express ideas and suggest innovations for future conferences and for the development of the organization. The need to develop training workshops for practitioners was offered by several delegates while others stressed the importance of developing partnerships with other organizations interested in sustainable travel. The delegates agreed to establish a membership structure to strengthen the organization. Janne Liburd of the University of Southern Denmark was inaugurated as the incoming Chair of BEST EN. She announced that the organization's home has been permanently established at the University of Southern Denmark where a Secretariat has been established. The theme for the 2006 Think Tank VI, "Corporate Social Responsibility for Sustainable Tourism" was announced. Details concerning the next Think Tank can be found on the BEST EN web site www.besteducationnetwork.org.

References

Amoah, V. and T. Baum (1997). Tourism Education and Training: Policy Versus Practice. *International Journal of Contemporary Hospitality Management*.

Baum, T. (1994a). The Development and Implementation of National Tourism Policies. *Tourism Management* 15(3), 185–192.

Baum, T. (1994b). National Tourism Policies: Implementing the Human Resource Dimension. *Tourism Management* 15(4), 259–266.

Baum, T. (1995a). *Managing Human Resources in the European Tourism and Hospitality Industry: A Strategic Approach*. Chapman and Hall, London.

Baum, T. (1995b). Introducing a Paradigm of Sustainable Human Development for the Hospitality and Tourism Industry, 1995 CHRIE Conference.

Baum, T. (1996). Unskilled Work and the Hospitality Industry: Myth or Reality? *International Journal of Hospitality Management* 15(3), 1–3.

Berger, F. (1993). Human Resources Management in the 21st Century: Predicting Partnerships for Profit. *Hospitality Research Journal* 17(1), 87–102.

Bosselman, R. (1996). Foundations of a Professional Organization: The Birth of CHRIE. *Hospitality and Tourism Educator* 8(2/3), 9–13.

Burbridge, D. (1994). Hotel in a Briefcase: A Simulation Model. *Hospitality Tourism Educator* 2(2), 53–57.

Cargill, C. (1995). The Master's Degree: Perceptions of Corporate Professionals from Three Segments of the Hospitality Industry. *Hospitality and Tourism Educator* 7(4), 51–54.

Choy, D. (1995). The Quality of Tourism Employment. *Tourism Management* 16(2), 129–137.

Chreptyk, D. (1990). Labor Crisis? What Labor Crisis? *Hotel Restaurant Journal* 69(2), 72.

Christensen, J. (1993). The Diversity Dynamic: Implications for Organisations in 2005. *Hospitality Research Journal*, 17(1), 69–86.

Cooper, C. (1993). An Analysis of the Relationship Between Industry and Education in Travel and Tourism. *Teros International*, 1(1).

Cooper, C., R. Shepperd and J. Westlake. (1994). *Tourism Hospitality and Education*. The University of Surrey, Guildford.

Council on Hotel. Restaurant and Institutional Education, Washington, DC. (1993). National Voluntary Skills Standards for the Hospitality and Tourism Industry.

Council on Hotel. Restaurant and Institutional Education, Washington, DC. (1994). Hospitality: A Look to the Future. Hosteur, *CHRIE*, 4(1), 15–20.

Council on Hotel. Restaurant and Institutional Education, Washington, DC. (1995a). A Guide to College Programmes in Hospitality and Tourism.

Council on Hotel. Restaurant and Institutional Education, Washington, DC. (1995b). Building Skills by Building Alliances.

Davidson, R. (1989). *Tourism.* Pitman, London.

Diaz, P. (1994). Sex Differences in Job and Salary Offers for Hospitality Graduates. World's Eye View on Hospitality Trends, *Arizona Hospitality Research and Resource Centre,* 8(3), 10–11.

Evans, J. (1993). *Tourism Graduates: A Case of Over-Production.* Tourism Management, August, 243–246.

Hawkins, D. (1994). Trends Report (unpublished paper), George Washington University, Washington, DC.

Hawkins, D. (1996). Investing in Human Resources: An Essential Sustainable Tourism Development Strategy for the Middle East and North Africa Region. Presentation, Seminar on Sustainable Tourism Development in the Middle East and North Africa, Amman, Jordan.

Haywood, M. and K. Maki. (1992). A Conceptual Model of the Education/Employment Interface for the Tourism Industry. World Travel and Tourism Review, Eds J.R. Ritchie, Donald Hawkins, et al. *CAB International* 2, 237–241.

International Hotel Association (1988). The World Hotel Industry in the 21st Century (Horawath & Horawath), *Travel and Tourism Analysis* 2, 19–30.

Kelly, T. (1992). Research into the Vocational Education and Training Requirements of the Hotel and Catering Industry in the UK. *Journal of Travel Research* 21(2), 22–26.

Lattin, G. (1985). *The Lodging and Food Service Industry.* The Educational Institute of the AHMA, East Lansing. MI.

Lavery, P. (1988). Careers in Tourism. *Tourism Management* 9(2), 167–171.

Leiper, N. (1981). Towards a Cohesive Curriculum in Tourism: The Case for a Distinct Discipline, *Annals of Tourism Research* 8(1), 69–84.

Leiper, N. (1991). Deflating Illusions of the Tourism Industry's Size: Implications for Education. New Horizons in Tourism and Hospitality Education, Training and Research (Conference Proceedings), World Tourism Education and Research Centre, The University of Calgary.

Marhuenda, F., M. Ignacio and A. Navas. (2004). *Career Development International* 9(3), 222.

Mill, R. and A. Morrison. (1985, 1992). *The Tourism System: An Introductory Text.* Prentice Hall, Englewood Cliffs, eds.

Morrison, A., S. Hsieh and C. Wang. (1992). Certification in the Travel and Tourism Industry: The North American Experience. *Journal of Tourism Studies* 3 (2), 32–40.

Organisation of Economic Cooperation and Development (OECD). (1995). Tourism Policy and International Tourism in OECD Countries 1992–1993: Special Feature: Tourism and Employment. Paris, France.

Parsons, D. (1991). The Making of Managers: Lessons from an International Review of Tourism Management Education Programmes. *Tourism Management* 12(3), 197–207.

Partlow, C. (1994). Is Graduate Hospitality Education Relevant? Ask Graduates. *Hospitality Tourism Educator* 6(3), 13–16.

Pavesic, D. (1993). Hospitality Education 2005: Curricular and Programmatic Trends. *Hospitality Research Journal* 17(1), 285–294.

Pollock, A. and J. Ritchie. (1990). Integrated Strategy for Tourism Education/Training. *Annals of Tourism Research* 17(4), 568–585.

Powers, T. (1994). Hospitality: A Look to the Future. *Hosteur. Council on Hotel, Restaurant and Institutional Education, Washington, DC* 4(1), 15–20.

Powers, T. (1995). Hospitality Management Development for the 1980's. *The Cornell H.R.A. Quarterly* 40–41.

Rach, E. (1992). A Study to Identify and Analyze Educational Competencies Relevant to Doctoral Studies in Tourism. Diss. The George Washington University, Washington, DC.

Rangel, J. (1992). Meeting the Supply Challenge. Monograph: PATA '92 Conference Record. Pacific Asia Travel Association, 131–135.

Ritchie, J. (1992). New Horizons, New Realities: Perspectives of the Tourism Educator, *World Travel and Tourism Review*, Eds J. Ritchie, D. Hawkins, et al. *CAB International* 2, 257–263.

Ritchie, J. (1993). Educating the Tourism Educators: Guidelines for Policy and Programme Development. *Teros International* 1(1), 9–24.

Ross, G. (1995). Tourism/Hospitality Management Employment Interest as Predicted by Job Attributes and Workplace Evaluations. *Tourism Recreation Research* 20(2), 63–71.

Schulman, S. and J. Greenberg. (1992). The Emergency of Travel and Tourism Education. Unpublished paper. January, 1–10.

Shepperd, R. and C. Cooper. (1995). Innovations in Tourism Education and Training. *Tourism Recreation Research* 20(2), 14–24

Sigala, M. and Baum, T. (2003). Trends and issues in tourism and hospitality higher education: Visioning the future. *Tourism and Hospitality Research* 4(4), July, 367.

Sikha, S., and Deepika, P. (2006). Knowledge Management for Tourism, Tourism: Theory and Practice, Tourism Resource Management Issue, Vol. 4., No. 1, January.

Solomon, P. (1992). Polishing the Brass: A Growing Number of Executives Taking Time to Hone Their Management Skills in University Classrooms. *The Globe and Mil*, B24.

Sparrowe, R. and P. Popielarz. (1995). Getting Ahead in the Hospitality Industry: An Event History Analysis of Promotions Among Hotel and Restaurant Employees. 1995 CHRIE Conference Abstracts, 26.

Stear, L. and T. Griffin. (1993). Demythologising the Nexus Between Tourism and Hospitality: Implication for Education. *Tourism Management*, February, 41–51.

Swedlove, W. and S. Dowler. (1992). Competency-Based Occupational Standards and Certification for the Tourism Industry. *World Travel and Tourism Review* 2, 283–291.

Tanke, M. (1992). Accreditations: Implications for Hospitality Management Education. *World Travel and Tourism Review* 2, 287–291.

Tourism Works for America. (2004). *Tourism Employment and Tourism Careers*, 13th Annual Edition, December, 8–9.

Travel Industry Association (TIA). (1994). *A Portrait of Travel Industry Employment in the US, Economy*. Travel Industry Association, Washington, DC.

United Nations World Tourism Organization (UNWTO), Madrid, Spain. (1992). World Directory of Tourism Education and Training Institutions.

United Nations World Tourism Organization (UNWTO), Madrid, Spain. (1994). Recommendations on Tourism Statistics.

United Nations World Tourism Organization (UNWTO). (2004a). WTO: A New Specialized Agency of the United Nations, *World Tourism Organization News*, Madrid, Spain, 4th Quarter Issue 4: 1.

United Nations World Tourism Organization (UNWTO). (2004b). WTO Launched the Tourism Enriches Campaign, *World Tourism Organization News*, Madrid, Spain, 1st Quarter Issue 1: 1, 14.

United Nations World Tourism Organization (UNWTO). (2005a). International Tourism Obtains Its Best Results in 20 years, *World Tourism Organization News*, Madrid, Spain, 1st Quarter Issue 1: 1, 7.

United Nations World Tourism Organization (UNWTO). (2005b). Retrieved 26 June 2006 from http://www.world-tourism.org.

United Nations World Tourism Organization (UNWTO). (2005c). Retrieved 27 June 27 2006 from http://world-tourism.org/education/tedqual.htm.

United Nations World Tourism Organization (UNWTO). (2006). The 'tourism paradox': Growth in the Midst of Changes. *UNWTONEWS,* 1, 4–5.

Wood, R. (1992). Hospitality Industry Labour Trends: British and International Experience. *Tourism Management*, September, 297–304.

Wood, R. (1993). Status and Hotel and Catering Work: Theoretical Dimensions and Practical Implications. *Hospitality Research Journal* 16(3), 3–15.

Wood, R. (1994). *Organisational Behaviour for Hospitality Management*. Butterworth-Heinemann Ltd, Oxford.

World Travel and Tourism Council (WTTC). (1993). Travel & Tourism: A New Economic Perspective. Brussels.

World Travel and Tourism Council (WTTC). (1994a). United Kingdom Travel and Tourism: A New Economic Perspective.

World Travel and Tourism Council (WTTC). (1994b). Gearing Up for Growth.

World Travel and Tourism Council (WTTC). (1995a). Travel and Tourism: Progress and Priorities 1995. Brussels.

World Travel and Tourism Council (WTTC). (1995b). Travel and Tourism's Economic Perspective. Brussels.

Supplemental readings

Gunn, C. (1994). A Perspective on the Purpose and Nature of Tourism Research Methods. *TTRA Research Handbook* 3–11.

Kerstetter, D., J. Confer and A. Graefe. (2001). An Exploration of the Specialization Concept within the Context of Heritage Tourism. *Journal of Travel Research* 39, 267–274.

Swanson, J. (2003). Does Policy Matter? Tourism Policy and Economic Input. Academic Monograph. Cornell University.

Williams, D. and C. Cartee. (1991). Measuring Travel and Tourism Impacts on a State's Economy: Policy Implications. *Journal of Economics and Finance* 15 (2), 161–170.

8

Affecting and influencing tourism policy

Certainly, travel is more than the seeing of sights; it is a change that goes on, deep and permanent, in the ideas of living.

Miriam Beard, US writer, 1901

Previous chapters of this book have clearly laid out various types of tourism policy, how tourism policy has developed, the importance of tourism and the foreign policy implications of the industry. This chapter presents practical approaches to affecting public policy and tourism legislation and how to choose between policy alternatives. Enhanced decision-making regarding policy, based on research and analysis instead of intuition and feeling, is currently a critical need in the global tourism industry. This chapter aligns well with the practical nature of Chapter 9, which describes the mechanics of strategic tourism planning.

Two things can be provided to elected officials to affect public policy decision-making –

money and information. This chapter provides an understanding of the political decision-making process, presents techniques for developing analytical information to be provided to political decision makers and analyzes the contributions made by members of tourism-related industries.

Loew's Hotel CEO and Chair of the Travel Business Roundtable, Jonathan Tisch has called for the hospitality industry to become more active players in shaping public policy. Tisch cited the importance of public policy issues involving immigration and international marketing. He stated, 'We need to have a free flow of commerce to help diminish the view of fortress America' (Barbara, 2006). This comment also speaks to the perception or image of the United States held by people around the globe.

Tisch also pointed out, as has been previously mentioned throughout this book, that the US government spends far less on tourism than does other countries. In fact, national tourism spending is a diminutive amount of the overall federal budget in the United States. The case study of this chapter, which is a cost–benefit analysis of coordinating international visitor information collection and distribution in the United States, addresses this issue in part.

Tisch noted that important government leaders are listening to the hospitality industry as progress has been made in recent years in getting the attention of political decision makers. Much of this progress has been the result of the tireless efforts of many of the industry trade associations that have governmental affairs arms, including those previously described in this text.

In recent years, the industry has become better organized, which is beginning to catch the attention of political decision makers. Another factor that has contributed to the increased attention is the decline of many traditional industries in most communities, such as mining, manufacturing and agriculture. In many areas, these traditional industries are being replaced with tourism, as civic leaders look for ways to sustain their communities. The increasing economic importance of tourism has given the industry more political power.

An applied study of tourism policy influences

Tourism policy is important because it provides a common, agreed-upon purpose for tourism and establishes the broad parameters for planning and coordinating the efforts of all tourism stakeholders. As tourism competes with more sophisticated and more respected industries such as health care, it is becoming increasingly important for tourism practitioners to be able to convince policymakers and political decision makers of the significance of sound tourism policy and strategic planning. In many cases, the most effective way to convince political leaders of its importance is to link policy with the economic success of tourism. This was among the findings presented in a Swanson (2003) monograph entitled, 'Does Policy Matter? The Connection Between Tourism Policy and Economic Input'.

The study compared US state-level tourism policy (qualitative) with economic impact (quantitative) in seven states: Alabama, Georgia, Louisiana, Mississippi, North Carolina, South Carolina and Virginia. This study investigated the link between the formulation and implementation of policy and economic impact. In addition to showing a relationship to support the connection between tourism policy and the economic impact of tourism, several interesting and important elements can be drawn after this careful investigation of tourism policy. These elements involve the politicization of the tourism office, the understanding of tourism policy and the perceived importance of the tourism industries.

Politicization of the tourism office

The less political the tourism office and its director's appointment are, the more effective the organization can be. In general, when the office is less politicized, an executive with experience in the tourism industry can be chosen who is then better able to implement effective tourism programmes. The directors of state tourism offices that are seemingly less politicized are three to four layers away from the governor, as, for example, Deputy Secretaries of Commerce, instead of cabinet members.

On the other hand, the advantage of being close to the governor is increased access to and attention from the governor and other senior administration officials. In Alabama, where the secretary of tourism is part of the governor's cabinet, the operation has been politicized to the point that the advertising agency handling state tourism often is the same agency that ran the advertising for the governor's election campaign. Therefore, the advertising message and marketing strategy is changed with each new administration. While the high-level position of the state tourism director in the administration may be a trade-off, it is better tourism leadership that makes a state tourism office more effective in promoting and developing tourism. It should be noted that changes in the gubernatorial administration always cause some disruption in the operation of the state tourism office and other agencies; however, those directors with a healthy mix of tourism experience and political savvy, who are able to present tourism concerns well to the press, the industry and the legislature, will operate the most effective state tourism offices.

Misunderstanding of tourism policy

Many tourism professionals lack an understanding of tourism policy in theory and in practice. Few of the state tourism directors interviewed in the Swanson study had a solid understanding of their state's tourism policy. This occurs because tourism policy is difficult to define and tourism executives are often more focused on marketing than on public policy issues, beyond funding for their tourism offices. This text serves as a partial alleviant to this problem by presenting tourism policy in an instructional context.

Generally, locales do not have *written* tourism policy and the question arises: do they have *written* policy for other industries? This situation emphasizes the need for the tourism industry, as a whole, to look upon itself in the same manner as other industries that contribute to the economic, political and sustainable well-being of their respective communities.

There needs to be a better practical understanding of tourism policy. Leaders need to be informed on what is important regarding tourism policy and how to influence it. States and provinces should initiate tourism policy acts so that there is effective integration with all appropriate agencies (i.e. transportation departments, commerce departments, parks and recreation departments and others) and all tourism stakeholders. The same is true at the national level in the United States. Until this is done, affecting other public policy will be more difficult.

Increasing importance of the tourism industry

Tourism professionals report the awareness of the importance of tourism among state legislators has increased over the past few years. As tourism satellite accounts become more widely implemented, the economic importance of tourism will be better understood by state legislatures and administrations. Tourism satellite accounting, based on the National System of Accounts, enables the economic impact of tourism to be compared to other industry groups and also between nations. As tourism becomes more prominent, supply management and tourism product development will also become more important.

Tourism should be dispersed throughout a given geographic area to all communities and districts. For example, if a tourism region contains 20 different political districts, some tourism product should be developed in each political district throughout the region. This will make tourism important to each governing legislator, as it constitutes looking after the best interest of their constituents. The wider geographical dispersion of tourism supply and demand will benefit a locale's economic and environmental circumstances and provide subsequent political advantages for the tourism industry.

To enhance the quality of life for members of host communities, tourism entities must consider the non-economic benefits as well as the economic and non-economic costs of tourism. Acknowledging these areas will help tourism leaders optimize tourism development and will help the tourism industry continue its rise in prominence. For example, as tourism becomes more important to a state, the state tourism office will be better funded. Tourism should also be less politicized to allow industry leaders and government decision makers to better understand the real importance of tourism policy. Understanding the issues will enable decision makers to formulate and implement more effective policy. Recognition of the connection between tourism policy and the results, as measured by economic impact, is important. Policy does affect the economic impact of tourism. Sound policy formulation and implementation does matter.

Understanding the public decision-making process

In order to influence those making political decisions, it is important to understand how political decisions are made. Public choice theory provides a framework for this understanding. While politicians may claim to represent the will of their constituency, in reality, the decisions they make are often in their own self-interests. This is a basis for public choice theory.

Although this concept might sound simple, this theory was first introduced by James Buchanan and Gordon Tullock in their seminal work published in 1962 entitled *The Calculus of Consent*. Public choice theory applies economic principles to the decision-making process of political leaders. Public choice takes a positivist look at how politics actually functions rather than how it should function, which is the normative viewpoint (Buchanan & Tullock, 1962). The theory developed over the following three decades resulted in a Nobel Prize in economics for Buchanan in 1984.

The thrust behind public choice shattered the common viewpoint that majority decisions are inherently fair. Under this assumption, it would be believed that a decision in the public interest would be unanimously supported by all voters. Instead, political decisions are made in the best interest of those making the decisions not in the interest of the voters because the interest of all voters cannot be served with a single decision. Moreover, the electorate masses do not have enough information about all of the issues to have a concerned opinion.

Among other areas, public choice observes and scrutinizes the activities of legislators. Although politicians might intend to spend taxpayer money efficiently, they are not necessarily inclined to do so because most of their decisions will not affect their own finances. In other words, a more efficient use of tax money will not result in any proportion of the public wealth saved being given to the politician.

The theory states that there are too many issues about which the voting public can be informed. Under this theory, when faced with the choice of deciding between powerful interest groups and an uninformed electorate, the group with the most influence will win. In almost every case, that is the special interest group. Therefore, the incentives are weak for sound management in the public interest. Interest groups, on the other hand, consist of individuals who stand to gain significantly from governmental action. In order to influence political decision makers, they donate money and volunteer time in exchange for increased access to the politician, with the aim of influencing the politician to support their issues (Shaw, 2002).

Logrolling, or vote trading, is a technique closely watched by public choice economists and is illustrated by the following example: Separate cost–benefit analyses are done on different issues for a state legislature. One study looks at providing free high-speed Internet access to parks in mountain communities, and another study reviews the net present value of beach re-nourishment along a 24-mile stretch of beach. Both projects are shown in the analysis to be inefficient and should not be supported by a rational decision maker. In order to gain support for the Internet access bill, a legislator from the mountain area agrees to vote for the beach re-nourishment legislation so that the representative from the beach will support the mountain Internet access programme. Through logrolling both legislators get what they want, and while both projects consume resources inefficiently according to the analysis, local uninformed voters see that their representative has done something for their area. They hold this view unaware that their tax money is supporting multiple inefficient projects because of logrolling.

When attempting to affect political decisions, the relationship of bureaucrats and special interest groups is also important to understand. As opposed to professionals operating in the private sector, bureaucrats do not have profit as a goal, but instead are motivated by achieving the mission of their agency. While relying on the legislature for agency funding, bureaucrats will informally rely on special interest groups to influence the legislature on their behalf so that they can accomplish their objectives. This leads to the potential for bureaucrats to be captured by special interest groups trying to advance their own agendas. This does not imply that the relationships between bureaucrats and special interest groups are negative. It is presented to give an understanding of how decisions can be made within bureaucracy. This is an opportunity for the tourism industry.

As principles of economics are basic tenets of public choice, competition is one way in which theorists propose to solve some of the conflicts that arise from government inefficiencies. An applied example of using competition to regulate tourism policy is for the Forest Service to charge hikers more than just a nominal fee so that the attention paid to hikers is more in line with the attention paid to those with a higher economic impact on the forest, such as timber harvesters. This should serve to increase the economic importance of hikers relative to other forest users and should reduce logging in popular recreation areas (O'Toole, 1988). It is unclear, however, what this might do to hiking demand. And undoubtedly, outdoor enthusiasts will cite the public benefits of nature-based outdoor recreation in their opposition to the fee. Conducting a cost–benefit analysis of this problem, a technique described in the following section, is a good application of public choice theory in a tourism setting.

This theory has yet to be widely applied to the practice of tourism, but new research will likely introduce this concept to political decisions in the tourism realm. For the purposes of this text, it is important to realize that politicians are unable to represent the will of the electorate as a whole. And it will be those interest groups who provide the most persuasive information and support for the decision maker that stand a higher chance of influencing public policy. Research-based policy analysis, the focus of the next section, is one way for the tourism industry to garner attention and influence policy.

Influencing political decisions with information

Cost–benefit analysis is a technique to aid in making decisions among public policy alternatives by analyzing a policy or programme's total expected costs versus its expected benefits. The technique has been used to determine the value of public expenditures ranging from education programmes to water resource projects and pollution control to health and nutrition policies. Cost–benefit analysis is used not only by government agencies but by those organizations wishing to persuade the opinions of public officials. Those groups who can provide information that is more meaningful to individual political decision makers stand higher chances of achieving their policy objectives.

Cost–benefit analysis was first adopted by the US Government during the 1930s and gained prominence in Great Britain and other Western countries in the 1960s, as a means to assess select public project expenditure decisions. Cost–benefit analysis began to be required for regulatory agencies at the federal, state and local levels of governments in the 1980s and 1990s.

Within the tourism industry in the United States, decisions influenced by cost–benefit analysis can be traced to the 1960s. During this time, the technique was used in transportation to establish methodology on valuing benefits such as the time savings to travelers. Other tourism-related areas that contributed to the advancement of monetizing techniques were environmental quality and natural resources.

Cost–benefit analysis has helped shape public policy in recent decades and assisted in the evolution of environmental management, which is critical to sustainable tourism. For example, the US Clean Air Act of 1970 and amendments to the Act in 1977 established air quality standards with no mention of benefits or costs; however, legislation passed in the late 1980s and 1990s included economic concerns enabling cost–benefit analysis. In the case of the 1990 US Clean Air Act Amendments, market incentives were introduced, through emission trading between polluting plants that encouraged cost-effective pollution reduction. This further encouraged research and development of pollution-reducing technologies.

In the next round of national tourism policy in the United States, as well as in other nations at the national and local levels, economic measures and cost–benefit analysis should be included so that the industry can provide more informative analysis relative to other industries in competition for scarce resources.

Environmental groups regularly employ economic analysis in support of their environmental policies. This is important for the environmental groups because to some political decision makers, economics are more meaningful than the environment. Those leaders may not appreciate the position from an environmental argument but may be fully persuadable with the right economic information. Providing the right kind of information to individual politicians increases the power of the environmental groups, which can result in a greater impact upon the decision-making process, as prescribed by public choice theory.

There has been a significant amount of attention paid to cost–benefit analysis by United States presidents since the mid-1970s. President Ford initiated the use of assessing benefits as part of federal regulations. President Carter set forth Executive Order (EO) 12,044 on 23 March 1978, which stipulated that agencies had 'to perform an economic analysis weighing the potential regulatory costs with the potential benefits for all proposed "major" regulations' (Fuguitt & Wilcox, 1999).

During the Clinton administration, several bills were introduced concerning cost–benefit requirements. The Risk Assessment and Cost–Benefit Analysis Act of 1995 (HR 1022) was perhaps the most prominent and controversial during this period. Although this bill passed the House, it did not garner the necessary votes in the Senate to become law. The merits of HR 1022 were widely contested with critics believing the measure would have increased bureaucracy as new staff members must be hired to perform analysis as well as the limitations of the technique and available data. One reason it failed was that there were significant questions about the reliability and validity of insufficiently developed techniques and because data are too difficult or costly to collect. A decade later, there is still opportunity for more effective measurements, particularly in tourism and related fields, for, as Fuguitt and Cox (1999) stated, 'Cost–benefit analysis offers the most comprehensive and informative systematic technique to assess decision choices inclining output or services not priced in markets'.

The field of health care frequently uses cost–benefit analysis to aid in decision-making when very tough choices are involved. For example, a particular policy choice may involve the saving or loss of a human life. As described in the next section, cost–benefit involves monetizing costs and benefits so that a net benefit can be calculated. In this example, human lives are valued in terms of the expected contributions the individual will make to national income through labour productivity.

Although tourism is serious business, tourism development rarely involves the end of human lives. This means two things: (1) public policies affecting tourism are often less controversial than many other types of public policies and (2) because other industries have to consider serious issues, such as the loss of human life, they are more inclined to provide thorough analysis of their policies and programmes. When trying to affect public decisions for the allocation of scarce resources, in the absence of politics, the case with the best information stands a better chance of prevailing. Because tourism may deal with less serious issues does not mean the analysis provided by the industry should be any less sophisticated.

Conflict and compromise

There are more than two sides to every issue and often members of the tourism industry are on opposing sides. Consider an analysis undertaken during the early 1970s regarding a third airport for the London area. Although it was approached from an environmental analysis perspective, the policy has a direct connection to tourism and travel. Recommendations made by the Roskill Commission regarding the location of the airport placed the new facility in a controversial inland site rather than on the coast, which was more politically acceptable. The recommendations were based on a cost–benefit analysis, which showed the noise and nuisance costs of the inland location near a significant resident base were far outweighed by the benefits of reduced travel time for those using the airport. While some may prefer less noise to less travel time, others may take the opposite stance. Although politics and other pressures of power sway opinion, cost–benefit analysis is one tool that should be part of the decision spectrum in important public policy cases.

Other examples of issues that might find members of the tourism industry on opposing sides include school start date, hurricane forecasting and

evacuation policy, economic development incentives and funding allocations. In reality, it is unlikely that any policy issue will gain the full support
of the various components of the tourism industry. How should industry
advocates decide between issues when they may pit industry members
against each other? In the absence of politics, cost–benefit analysis is the
most objective measure and may provide enough additional information
to achieve consensus.

Policy analysis also provides measures of accountability for programmes. In terms of aid, for example, the citizens of donor countries
want to know that the investments their government makes on their
behalf are producing positive returns. A pertinent example in the United
States is the careful attention that is being paid to monies provided
by federal agencies for hurricane relief following the devastating 2005
season along the Gulf Coast. Government accountability officers will
closely analyze the policies associated with funding relief efforts, particularly in light of fraudulent acts by some involved in handling recovery
payments.

With tourism's global reach, opportunities abound for professionals
possessing intimate knowledge of developing economies and capable of
analyzing national policies and international investments. However, monetizing costs and benefits is more complicated in developing nations than
in developed ones. As an example, market prices in developing economies
may be highly skewed for various reasons, making it difficult to determine
social value. Some of these difficulties have been mitigated by manuals
detailing cost–benefit techniques produced by Organisation for Economic
Cooperation and Development (OECD; Little & Mirrlees, 1974), the United
Nations Industrial Development Organisation (UNIDO, 1972) and the
World Bank (Squire & Van der Tak, 1975). Once again, tourism competes
with other industries for international investment, it is vital for decision
makers to be presented with persuasive information. These principles of
cost–benefit analysis need to be applied to tourism just as they are to other
economic and social sectors.

Cost–benefit analysis can also support the effort of the private sector.
During the 1970s, many private-sector businesses were grappling with
what they felt were burdensome federal regulations in the United States.
Using cost–benefit analysis, they persuaded legislators that curbing regulations would benefit business, government and society as a whole. Many
states require cost–benefit analysis when considering the offer of economic
incentive packages to entice new businesses to their state (Carlile, 1994).

In another private sector example, DuPont and other major corporations have analyzed the alternative environmental investments they might
pursue. This is in response to increased environmental regulation and the
need to monetize elements which typically are not weighed in economic
terms, such as air and water pollution (Epstein, 1994).

Cost–benefit analysis enables private firms to analyze not only the expected financial risks and rewards but also the social impacts on customers and the larger community. Smart companies can use this tool to identify long-term social issues that might outweigh short-term economic gain for the company. These principles could be utilized by land developers when considering tourism investment projects, such as condominiums, hotels or other attractions in areas that are environmentally sensitive, yet desirable and popular with consumers and travellers. In such cases, most developers faced with burgeoning consumer demand are unlikely to perform non-economic analysis; however, a responsible developer will do it and a good government will require it.

Cost–benefit analysis has developed reactively to the need for practical decision-making tools, particularly to the need to prioritize the costs and benefits of policy alternatives that cannot be purchased in the market place (i.e. noise pollution, travel costs, human lives). It is the responsibility of the decision maker to exercise care in interpreting the findings of any cost–benefit analysis.

Techniques of cost–benefit analysis

The purpose of cost–benefit analysis is to compare the benefits and costs of a project, to determine its feasibility, and to compare it to other projects in order to determine priorities. The steps involved in this undertaking are

1. Defining the project and alternatives;
2. Identifying, measuring and valuing costs and benefits of each alternative;
3. Calculating cost–benefit values; and
4. Presenting the results.

Step 1: Defining the project and alternatives

Answers to the following questions will help the analyst frame the project and make key assumptions. The assumptions may change throughout the project, but with a solid foundation at the beginning of the analysis, the entire process will be more efficient.

- What is the problem the project addresses?
- What are the intended benefits of the project?
- What will the project do and how will it be done?
- Who will do it and when?
- What is the purpose of the analysis?
  - Feasibility, prioritization or selection of projects

- What's the appropriate level of effort that should be invested in the analysis considering the expected payoff of the project?
- Who will receive the benefits?
- Who will bear the direct and indirect costs?
- What will happen if the project does not happen?
- How else could the expected benefits be achieved?
- When will costs be incurred?
- When will benefits be realized?
- What type of analysis should be used?
  - Cost–benefit ratio, net present value, internal rate of return, other basis
- What geographic areas will be affected by the project and its alternatives?
- What is the time horizon for the project?

Step 2: Identifying, measuring, and valuing costs and benefits of each alternative

Benefits are all of the effects of the project or programme, not only on the users of the project but also on society within the project area. The benefits of a proposed new highway might include reduced travel time, accidents, emissions and vehicle operating costs. Other benefits or costs (negative benefits) may also encompass induced travel, noise, construction delays, habitat and water quality impacts and other impacts upon the community. These are critical to making choices among alternatives.

The labour, real property, material and other inputs to a project are the costs. The simplest way to determine the cost of a project is to review the proposed budget. If a budget is not available, the analyst should look to comparable projects in similar areas for a reliable estimate of the costs. Costs are easy to measure because they are usually market goods and services for which a price is readily attainable.

Opportunity costs should be given careful consideration when determining the overall costs of a project. Opportunity costs are the benefits that could be derived if other alternatives are chosen. For example, if a city decides to allocate money to a new park instead of renovating the jail, the benefits that would be expected from a renovated jail are the opportunity costs. Opportunities are limited to only those projects that could be funded with the monies allocated for the proposed project.

Step 3: Calculating cost–benefit values

When performing a cost–benefit analysis, several types of measurements can be employed. This section reviews cost–benefit ratio, net present value, cost-effectiveness and sensitivity analysis. Other measurements such as internal rate of return, marginal analysis, and payback period are also useful tools that are taught in applied public policy analysis courses.

The *cost–benefit ratio* is the total of the discounted benefits divided by the total discounted costs. Future cash flows – costs or benefits expected after the initial year of a project – are discounted to determine their present value. The rate at which future cash flows are adjusted is known as the discount rate. A project with a cost–benefit ratio of more than one has positive net benefits, whereas a cost–benefit ratio less than one is an inefficient project that should not be pursued. Projects with higher benefits relative to costs will have a higher cost–benefit ratio. The cost–benefit ratio is calculated as follows:

$$\mathrm{CBR} = \frac{\sum_{i=0}^{n} B_i / (1+d)^i}{\sum_{i=0}^{n} C_i / (1+d)^i}, \text{ where}$$

n = the number of years over which benefits and costs are analysed;
B_i = the benefits of the project in year i, $i = 0$ to n;
C_i = the costs of the project in year i, $i = 0$ to n;
d = the discount rate.

A simple example to illustrate the cost–benefit ratio will lead to a better understanding of the technique. In this example, the government of Ascension Island, a British Overseas Territory, wants to bring in an outside expert for a period of 3 years to help residents of the island market their handicrafts to visitors. The only costs the government must bear are the annual salary and transportation costs for the outside expert, as the remainder of the project is being funded by an international NGO. The outside expert will relocate to Ascension for 3 years and will be paid a salary of $50,000 in the first year, $55,000 in the second year and $60,000 in the third year of the project. The transportation costs the government must pay are $10,000 in both the first and third years. Accordingly, total annual costs over the 3-year project are $60,000, $55,000 and $70,000. The benefits, in the form of new revenues generated from the sale of handicrafts are forecasted to be $100,000 in the second year and $150,000 in the third year. As the project gets ramped up, no revenue is expected to be generated during the first year. Using a 10 per cent discount rate, the calculation of the cost–benefit ratio for this example is:

$$\mathrm{CBR} = \frac{\left[\$0/(1+0.10)^0\right] + \left[\$100,000/(1+0.10)^1\right] + \left[\$150,000/(1+0.10)^2\right]}{\left[\$60,000/(1+0.10)^0\right] + \left[\$55,000/(1+0.10)^1\right] + \left[\$70,000/(1+0.10)^2\right]} = 1.28$$

This results in a cost–benefit ratio of 1.28. Since the ratio is greater than one, this project is efficient and should be considered.

Net present value is the total discounted costs subtracted from the total discounted benefits. In rational political decision-making, only projects with positive net benefits should be considered. A project with a higher net present value is more justifiable than a project with a lower net present value. Net present value can be calculated as:

$$NPV = \sum_{i=0}^{n} B_i/(1+d)^i - \sum_{i=0}^{n} C_i/(1+d)^i, \text{ where}$$

n = the number of years over which benefits and costs are analysed;
B_i = the benefits of the project in year i, $i = 0$ to n;
C_i = the costs of the project in year i, $i = 0$ to n;
d = the discount rate.

The net present value can also be determined using the previous example of marketing handicrafts on Ascension Island. The calculation is:

$$NPV = \{[\$0/(1+0.10)^0] + [\$100,000/(1+0.10)^1] + [\$150,000/(1+0.10)^2]\}$$
$$- \{[\$60,000/(1+0.10)^0] + [\$55,000/(1+0.10)^1] + [\$70,000/(1+0.10)^2]\}$$

$$NPV = \$47,025$$

Since the net present value of this project is positive it should be considered. The project should also be given priority over other alternatives with a lower net present value.

Cost-effectiveness enables comparison between a given amount of money and the non-monetized benefits that can be achieved. For example, if a municipality was adding a new runway at the airport, a cost effectiveness ratio would be the cost per additional airline passenger, or the cost per additional commercial flight. This tool is useful when compared to other alternatives and can be used even if the benefits cannot be monetized. Cost effectiveness is calculated as:

$$CER = \sum_{i=0}^{n} \frac{C_i/(1+d)^i}{B}, \text{ where}$$

n = the number of years over which costs are analysed;
B = the given benefit (not necessarily expressed in monetary terms);
C_i = the costs of the project in year i;
d = the discount rate.

The Ascension Island handicrafts marketing project is expected to yield a total of 15 jobs. Calculating the cost-effectiveness ratio of this project in terms of the number of jobs is done as follows:

$$CER = \frac{[\$60,000/(1+0.10)^0] + [\$55,000/(1+0.10)^1] + [\$70,000/(1+0.10)^2]}{15} = \$11,190/\text{job}$$

This estimate means that for each $11,190 invested in the project, one new job will be created. This number can be compared to estimates for other projects when deciding on alternatives. If the cost-effectiveness ratio for other projects in terms of jobs is higher, then this project should be pursued.

Sensitivity analysis examines how changes in inputs or assumptions affect the cost–benefit conclusions. Sensitivity analysis allows the analyst and decision maker to determine the likely range of outcomes for various alternatives and compare risky and less risky projects. Any assumption that goes into an analysis, including timing, geographic focus, discount rate, and others, can be adjusted to determine the magnitude of these elements on the project and whether these assumptions, once changed, would affect the prioritized ranking of various projects. The case study of this chapter includes a sensitivity analysis. Below are additional tourism-related examples of queries to be investigated using sensitivity analysis (Federal Highway Administration, 2002).

1. Estimates of patronage on a new light rail system vary from 4000 to 10,000 passenger-trips per weekday. Would the system be viable with the lower patronage?
2. There are two design alternatives for constructing a bridge over an ice-prone river. The cost of one is lower unless there is a very cold winter, in which case it will be considerably higher. Is it worth taking a chance with this alternative?
3. There are differences of opinion regarding the lifetime of a pavement project. Are the benefit–cost rankings of the project alternatives different for different lifetime assumptions?
4. Some in Ascension Island believe the handicrafts marketing project will cost 10 per cent more and generate 10 per cent less than what has been forecasted. Should the project still be pursued relative to other alternatives?

Step 4: Presenting the results

The ultimate purpose of a policy analysis is to assist in rational and responsible decision-making. To this end, the presentation of the report should be simple but informative for all interested parties, particularly the decision maker. The report should be succinct yet provide detailed clarity on the methodology and results so that the analysis can be scrutinized in order to satisfy critics. Even if the quality of the analysis is flawless, a presentation that is unclear will be useless. The report should highlight the following (Fuguitt & Wilcox, 1999):

- All assumptions made in the analysis;
- All value judgments embodied in the analytical technique;
- Any technical choice made when performing the analysis;

- Any biases or subjective influences that may affect the analyst's outcome; and
- Possible errors in analytical procedures or estimates.

Any opinions or judgement areas needed on the part of the analyst or decision maker should be justified and any associated advantages or disadvantages should be highlighted. Anything that cannot be included in the monetized costs or benefits should be discussed so that information can be considered by the one who must make the decision on the project. Above all, the analyst and the analysis must remain neutral.

Influencing political decisions with financial contributions

While progress has been made in terms of the tourism industry's political advocacy participation and because the industry has been on the fortunate side of economic changes, there is still opportunity for continued improvement. One strategy towards this objective is to increase the political contributions made by members of the tourism industry. As laid out in the discussion on public choice theory, political contributions are necessary in order to advance a political agenda when competing with many other industries and influences.

Elected officials are heavily influenced by special interest groups, which exist to influence specific areas of public policy. Examples of such groups include a multinational corporation taking a stand against international tariffs, an industry trade association seeking benefits for its members, trade unions advocating for minimum wage increases, senior citizens expressing concern about social security benefits, and family groups focusing on rating systems for video games. Within the US tourism industry, special interest groups include the Western States Policy Council, Conference of National Park Concessionaires, American Automobile Association and arms of private-sector firms such as Holiday Inns, Cendant Corporation and Marriott International. These groups influence public policy through regulatory bureaucracy, legal proceedings or swaying the opinions of legislators. The primary method of directly affecting the actions of elected officials is through financial contributions to their campaigns, which is the focus of this section.

Table 8.1 presents a rank order of political contributions to federal candidates and political parties in the United States given by individuals or political action committees (PACs) during the 2005–2006 election cycle. The numbers show how industry segments rank in total campaign giving as compared with more than 80 other industries. Specifically, the table

Table 8.1 2005–2006 political contributions by industry segments relative to tourism-related sectors in the United States

Industry segment	Rank	Total contributions (US$)	Contributions from individuals (US$)	Contributions from PACs (US$)
Lawyers/law firms	1	68,529,030	59,907,961	8,621,069
Retired	2	63,342,234	63,342,234	–
Real estate	3	40,845,073	34,909,760	5,935,313
Securities and investment	4	34,680,675	28,081,468	6,599,207
Health professionals	5	28,678,339	18,076,074	10,602,265
Candidate committees	6	25,581,260	51,205	25,530,055
Leadership PACs	7	21,899,444	388,759	21,510,685
Insurance	8	17,284,783	6,635,163	10,649,620
Commercial banks	9	14,599,075	7,622,523	6,976,552
Business services	10	14,274,866	13,204,325	1,070,541
Lobbyists	11	13,927,601	13,097,452	830,149
TV/movies/music	12	12,802,509	8,644,204	4,158,305
General contractors	13	10,561,001	8,624,436	1,936,565
Pharmaceuticals/health products	14	10,432,530	3,889,743	6,542,787
Oil and gas	15	10,161,359	6,142,602	4,018,757

(*Continued*)

Table 8.1 Continued

Industry segment	Rank	Total contributions (US$)	Contributions from individuals (US$)	Contributions from PACs (US$)
Tourism-related sectors				
Air transport	26	7,115,354	1,743,725	5,371,629
Retail sales	28	6,710,258	4,024,924	2,685,334
Casinos/gambling	30	6,466,961	2,038,252	4,428,709
Beer wine and liquour	33	5,599,987	2,313,312	3,286,675
Food and beverage	34	5,428,827	3,267,959	2,160,868
Indian gaming	NA	4,355,515	834,276	3,521,239
Bars and restaurants	NA	4,128,761	2,470,412	1,658,349
Lodging/tourism	52	3,027,839	2,478,414	549,425
Recreation/live entertainment	65	1,649,945	1,423,167	226,778
Airlines	NA	1,341,381	528,556	812,825
Cruise ships and lines	NA	254,350	119,100	135,250

Based on data released by the Federal Election Commission on Monday, 24 April 2006.
Source: Center for Responsive Politics.

lists the top 15 industry contributors and also the industry segments that encompass tourism.

None of the industry sectors that make up tourism are listed among the 25 largest political contributors. However, if the donations of those listed in the second half of Table 8.1 were combined, the resulting total of $46,079,178 would place third in 2005/06 behind those who list their occupation as retired, and above members of the real estate industry – two powerful political influencers. It may be that these industries have more money to give. This assumption raises the question: Do they give more money because they have more money or do they have more money because they give more money?

It is understood that the industry sub-segments presented in the table may have different agendas. For example, the food and beverage sector may be interested in issues associated with meat imports that might not interest the airlines, which may be concerned more with taxes on aviation fuels. However, a consolidated effort should help each segment accomplish its own mission while working for the good of the entire industry.

Based on the co-authors' conversations with legislators and lobbyists, the tourism industry is often viewed as fragmented, with hotels, restaurants, airlines and other tourism-related businesses pursuing their own agendas. This dilutes what may be a common message. Among other reasons, in the United States, this fragmentation is a result of the lack of a national government tourism office to coordinate such efforts. A better cooperative working relationship needs to be established.

In the United States, groups formed to raise and spend money to elect political candidates are known as PACs. PACs originated in 1944, when a labour union collected voluntary contributions from workers to support the re-election of Franklin D. Roosevelt for president. This was in response to the Smith Connally Act of 1943, which disallows political contributions to federal candidates from funds belonging to a labour union. Currently, United States federal law limits annual contributions by PACs to $5,000 to a candidate per election, $15,000 to a national party committee and $5,000 to another PAC. In terms of donations received, PACs can be given up to $5,000 from any individual, PAC, or party committee contributor per year.

In 2005–2006, 12 tourism-related PACs contributed a total of $342,425 to federal candidates in the United States, as shown in Table 8.2. This classification includes groups representing hotels, motels, resorts and travel agents.

For comparison purposes, the top 15 PAC contributors to federal candidates are presented in Table 8.3. When the 2005–2006 lodging and tourism PAC contributions are combined, they represent only 19 per cent of the largest single PAC contributor, illustrating how the tourism industries are severely lagging in political contributions. Once again, this is an opportunity missed, as money gains the attention of the political decision makers.

Table 8.2 2005–2006 lodging and tourism PAC contributions to national candidates in the United States

PAC name	Total ($)	Dems ($)	Repubs ($)
American Hotel & Lodging assn	67,200	14,500	52,700
American society of Travel Agents	47,000	22,500	24,500
Asian American Hotel Owners Assn	2,000	–	2,000
Auto Club of Michigan	4,125	3,000	1,125
Cendant Corp	84,500	21,500	63,000
Conference of Natl Park Concessioners	8,500	1,000	7,500
Gaylord Entertainment	8,500	1,000	7,500
Holiday Inns	29,500	5,000	24,500
Intl Assn Amusement Parks & Attractions	4,100	–	4,100
Marriott International	28,250	–	28,250
National Tour Assn	9,500	1,500	8,000
Sabre Inc.	49,250	28,750	20,500

Based on data released by the FEC on Monday, 29 May 2006.
Source: Center for Responsive Politics.

Table 8.3 2005–2006 top 15 PAC contributions to national candidates in the United States

PAC name	Total amount ($)	Dem (%)	Repub (%)
National Assn of Realtors	1,768,005	49	51
Intl Brotherhood of Electrical Workers	1,673,000	97	3
Assn of Trial Lawyers of America	1,626,000	96	3
National Beer Wholesalers Assn	1,607,500	26	74
AT&T Inc.	1,569,300	35	65
Credit Union National Assn	1,523,899	42	58
United Parcel Service	1,470,809	31	69
National Auto Dealers Assn	1,353,000	31	69
American Bankers Assn	1,310,374	35	65
Teamsters Union	1,275,175	90	9
Carpenters & Joiners Union	1,241,390	66	34
American Fedn of St/Cnty/Munic Employees	1,212,171	97	2
Operating Engineers Union	1,172,605	78	21
United Auto Workers	1,159,500	99	1
National Assn of Home Builders	1,157,000	25	75

Source: Center for Responsive Politics.

Giving is one half of the contribution equation; receiving is the other. If money is not donated strategically, its efficacy is diminished. There is only one sub-committee in the United States Congress specifically connected to tourism – the Trade, Tourism, and Economic Development Sub-Committee of the Commerce, Science, and Trade Committee in the United States

Senate. It provides the only clear target for tourism industry contributions. In addition to tourism, the committee is also responsible for the following:

U.S. Coast Guard; coastal zone management; communications; highway safety; inland waterways, except construction; interstate commerce; marine and ocean navigation, safety, and transportation, including navigational aspects of deepwater ports; marine fisheries; U.S. Merchant Marine and navigation; nonmilitary aeronautical and space sciences; oceans, weather, and atmospheric activities; Panama Canal and inter-oceanic canals generally, except the maintenance and operation of the Panama Canal, including administration, sanitation and government of the Canal Zone; regulation of consumer products and services, including testing related to toxic substances, other than pesticides, and except for credit, financial services, and housing, regulation of interstate common carriers, including railroads, buses, trucks, vessels, pipelines, and civil aviation; science, engineering, and technology research and development and policy; sports; standards and measurement; transportation; and transportation and commerce aspects of Outer Continental Shelf lands. Comprehensive study and review of all matters relating to science and technology, oceans policy, transportation, communications, and consumer affairs.

Tourism must compete with all of these other interests when trying to affect legislative decision-making.

Table 8.4 shows total political contributions for the years 2000–2006 by committee-related industries to members of the US Senate Commerce, Science, and Transportation Committee for the years 2000–2006.

Table 8.4 Political contributions to members of the US Senate Commerce, Science, and Transportation Committee

Rank	Industry	Total ($)
1	TV/movies/music	2,917,741
2	Insurance	2,690,764
3	Oil & gas	1,735,047
4	Air transport	1,524,187
5	Telecom services and equipment	1,250,854
6	Telephone utilities	1,234,249
7	Automotive	1,007,461
8	Transportation unions	990,540
9	Sea transport	783,060
10	Railroads	473,469
11	Lodging/tourism	440,630
12	Trucking	361,611
13	Recreation/live entertainment	233,076
14	Misc transport	153,502
15	Fisheries and wildlife	129,580

Source: Center for Responsive Politics.

Lodging/tourism ranks number 11 in this category, highlighting another opportunity for the tourism industry to increase its political contributions for strategic purposes. To compete effectively with other industries for the attention of those making the most relevant decisions to the tourism industry, more giving is required.

Members of the tourism industry should unite in strategic and focused contributions to political campaigns. This, along with providing better information to legislators, will increase the political power of the industry.

Conclusion

While tourism is apolitical, all decisions made by public officials, whether elected or appointed, are made in a political context. In order for the tourism industry to have a more powerful effect on tourism policy, and public policy in general, more support must be given to influence political decisions. As the chapter points out, two effective avenues of support are (1) through financial contributions to elected officials and political action committees and (2) by providing government officials with analysis that can be used to make informed choices among many policy alternatives.

About policy analysis, Fuguitt and Wilcox (1999) write, '... caution is urged along with appreciation of what has become a highly sophisticated analytical technique – one that can provide useful economic assessment yet is no substitute for the decision maker's grappling with competing objectives and political interests in a complex real-world context'. Regardless of its limitations, public policy analysis is critical and necessary.

Despite the growing popularity of cost–benefit analysis, its use is not widespread within the tourism community. Reasons for this are numerous, including the lack of human and financial resources to carry out the analysis and a general lack of understanding of the importance of, and techniques for, conducting policy analysis. This chapter is intended to introduce the important fundamentals of public policy analysis, applied to tourism issues, to a new generation of tourism industry practitioners.

The chapter also highlights opportunities for the tourism industry to expand its political influence, relative to other groups, by increasing its political contributions. As described herein, political decision makers act in ways beneficial to their own political interests. With well-planned giving, the tourism industry can have a significant impact upon its own political power. Without advances in policy analysis and political contributions, the tourism industry will continue to lag behind other industries in terms of political influence.

Case study 8

A COST–BENEFIT ANALYSIS FOR COORDINATING INTERNATIONAL VISITOR INFORMATION COLLECTION AND DISTRIBUTION IN THE UNITED STATES

Researched and Written by: Jason R. Swanson

Executive summary

The programme, which would be a coordinated system to collect information on the 46 million international visitors per year to the United States, works to solve the problem of inefficient data collection and distribution by multiple federal agencies. These efforts are separate and single-purpose, with only limited data being exchanged between agencies. If the information were to be analyzed for, and distributed to, organizations responsible for international tourism marketing, promotional campaigns would be significantly enhanced. The analysis programme has been proposed in conjunction with President Bush's proposed $5.9 billion American Competitiveness Initiative.

The $1.5 million programme would provide the following benefits:

1. Increased direct expenditures by international travellers to the United States;
2. Increased payroll generated by international travellers to the United States;
3. Increased taxes paid by international visitors;
4. Decreased tax burden of individual citizens;
5. Increased balance of trade for the nation;
6. Decreased fiscal expenditures by multiple federal agencies;
7. Increased employment;
8. Increased quality of life for host communities based on the short-term economic benefits;
9. Increased community pride as the local area develops into a quality destination;
10. Increased cultural exchange as international visitors interact with members of host communities.

The aim of the project is to increase the effectiveness of organizations that market to international visitors by providing enhanced access to, and analysis of, visitor data. This analysis can then be used for planning more effective marketing campaigns and should ultimately increase the amount of money international travellers spend in the United States during their visit.

Based on analysis using historical international visitor data, supplied by the Travel Industry Association of America (TIA), this project has the potential to provide a significant net present value if the analysis programme can supply enhanced efficiencies in international tourism marketing as measured by increases in international visitor expenditures. Because of the volume of international visitor expenditures ($74.8 billion in 2004) and the limited budget of the project ($1.5 million), the break-even point for the increase in international visitor expenditures is merely 0.001107 per cent, or one thousandth of 1 per cent. Although this project is a small investment out of the total proposed budget for the American Competitiveness Initiative, it is an investment with significant upside potential that should be funded.

Introduction

In 2004, international visitors to the United States spent an estimated $74.8 billion during their visits. This does not include spending on airfares by international travellers arriving on US flag carriers. Despite the significant economic impact of the tourism industry, the United States has suffered a loss of market share in international tourism in recent years (United Nations World Tourism Organization, 2006). In order for state and federal tourism marketing agencies to react to this loss of market share, better research regarding international visitors and their behaviour is critical.

Announced by President Bush in his January 2006 State of the Union Address, the American Competitiveness Initiative is designed to encourage innovation and strengthen the nation's ability to compete globally. Recognizing the importance of innovation to the nation's economic future, the President's FY 2007 proposed budget has committed $5.9 billion to "increase investments in research and development, strengthen education, and encourage entrepreneurship" in order to ". . . create more jobs, and improve the quality of life and standard of living for generations to come" (Bush, 2006).

The tourism industry can play an important role in reaching the objectives laid out in the American Competitiveness Initiative by increasing the industry's effectiveness in international tourism marketing. In order for the industry to increase its international marketing effectiveness, a coordinated effort is necessary to collect and distribute international visitor information (Brothers, 2006a,b).

The US tourism industries represented by trade associations, such as the TIA, the Southeast Tourism Society (STS) and several state tourism offices are seeking increased innovation and efficiencies in data collection and distribution of information related to international inbound travellers. The academic researchers at North Carolina State University recently released a white paper on the subject and the university's tourism programme has offered to serve as the research agency in charge of analyzing and disseminating the collected information (Brothers 2006a,b).

The problem

To date, information on inbound international visitors to the United States has been inefficiently collected and distributed. Several federal agencies, including Department of Commerce, Department of Homeland Security and the Center for Disease Control, among others, currently collect information from over 46 million overseas visitors to the United States each year. These are separate, single-purpose efforts with only limited data being exchanged between agencies. The data are being independently used for a variety of applications, ranging from immigration control and homeland security to the calculation of balance of trade and customs enforcement. This project will coordinate data collection efforts among federal agencies so that resources can be better utilized.

From a tourism marketing and product development standpoint, there are critical gaps in the information collected. For example, arrival information captured with the I-94 form does not provide for multiple destinations within the country or length of stay in the destinations. The current system has resulted in multiple data sets, which inherently leads to data management challenges and hinders the tourism industry from maintaining its competitive edge in the marketplace.

Proposed program

The programme would develop an innovative, efficient and effective data collection system which can be accessed by multiple federal agencies and the tourism industry in near real-time. The analysis programme will be designed so that disparate government agencies can work together towards this objective, allocating resources and allowing for information to be distributed in a timely manner. Furthermore, the improved research instrument will include valid questions meaningful to the tourism industry, such as destinations visited and length of stay in each destination.

The analysis programme will enhance efficiencies among federal agencies and, equally important, it will provide the tourism industry with better marketing research information. The data collected by a coordinated effort will first be disseminated to each federal agency to analyze according to its particular purpose. After personal information is removed, the data will be sent to the research team. This information can then be used by all tourism organizations that promote their product or destination to international travellers. Data will be available to public-sector organizations such as convention and visitors bureaus, state tourism offices and federal agencies that may market internationally (i.e. National Park Service, Department of Commerce, Bureau of Indian Affairs), as well as to private-sector businesses, including airlines, hotel companies, attractions and all other segments of the tourism industry.

Programme inputs and costs

Based on a budget supplied by the researchers at North Carolina State University, the initial cost of the analysis programme in 2007 (Year 0) is $1.5 million. After software is developed and hardware is purchased, costs in future years fall to roughly $1 million each year, except in Year 4 when new equipment would need to be purchased (Brothers, 2006a,b). To maintain the conservative nature of the analysis, costs have been increased by 5 per cent per year after the first year to account for marginal increases in costs of personnel and data acquisition. Table 8.5 presents the preliminary 5-year budget for the analysis programme. Following is a discussion of each line item of Table 8.5.

Software development

Software development will involve creating the interface between the user of the research (i.e. tourism marketing organizations) and the data warehouse server, which is described below. Users will be able to access a unique "homepage" that will allow for customization of data pertinent to their particular destination, organization or marketing strategy. It will be necessary to hire software programmers to develop the user interface; this cost is based on estimates from SAS.

Hardware for data warehouse

Hardware is necessary for storage of significant amounts of data, including historical visitation records from government agencies, airports, weather

Table 8.5 Preliminary 5-year budget

Costs	2007 Year 0 (US$)	2008 Year 1 (US$)	2009 Year 2 (US$)	2010 Year 3 (US$)	2011 Year 4 (US$)	2012 Year 5 (US$)
Software development	(300,000)	–	–	–	–	–
Hardware for data warehouse	(300,000)	–	–	–	(300,000)	–
Personnel for data analysis and management	(200,000)	(210,000)	(220,500)	(231,525)	(243,101)	(255,256)
Data acquisition	(700,000)	(735,000)	(771,750)	(810,338)	(850,854)	(893,397)
Total costs	(1,500,000)	(945,000)	(992,250)	(1,041,863)	(1,393,956)	(1,148,653)

services and secondary data sources. As new visitor data is collected daily, it will be stored on the servers. The data will be used for modelling, including GIS and data mapping, which will require additional storage capacity. Storing the data in a secure environment will add to the data warehousing cost.

Personnel for data analysis and management

The project will be staffed by at least two information technology professionals and one administrative assistant. The cost for personnel includes salary, payroll taxes and employee benefits, and is based on similar costs in the Raleigh, North Carolina area.

Data acquisition

Data acquisition costs include obtaining the information from international airports before flights and the distribution of the electronic mechanism to collect the information from airports overseas. These activities will supplement the technology that is already in place. Additional data acquisition costs involve obtaining the information from government agencies after personal information has been removed. Adding certain questions (regarding destinations visited and length of stay) to the existing surveys entails additional cost.

Benefits/outcomes

With targeted marketing campaigns, based on analysis of richer and more complete data, the $74.8 billion export could be significantly enhanced, resulting in increased international travel expenditures (money spent in the United States by international visitors), and subsequent gains in jobs, taxes and other economic multipliers. Successful implementation of the project can also be expected to bring about such non-economic benefits as improved quality of life and increased community pride. These benefits and outcomes are summarized in Table 8.6.

Monetized benefits

Increased direct expenditures by international travellers to the United States: This includes new revenue for local entrepreneurs serving visitors, such as hotels, restaurants, accommodations, shops, gas stations, transportation companies and tour guides, and others. Beyond direct beneficiaries, those who supply the retail businesses, including farmers, manufacturers and local craftsmen, share in the gain from increased international tourism.

Table 8.6 Historical international tourism data

	1999	2000	2001	2002
International travel expenditures in the United States	$74,800,000,000	$82,400,000,000	$71,900,000,000	$66,500,000,000
Payroll generated by international travel in the United States	$19,345,000,000	$21,365,000,000	$20,943,000,000	$19,584,000,000
Jobs generated by International Travel in the United States	938,600	991,300	944,500	878,900
Taxes paid by international travellers in the United States	$12,099,000,000	$13,402,000,000	$11,879,000,000	$10,868,000,000

Source: TIA.

Increased payroll generated by international travelers to the United States: In 2002, approximately 878,900 jobs were generated by international inbound tourism, generating employee earnings of roughly $19,584,000,000.

Increased taxes paid by international visitors: Local and state taxes are paid by all international travellers. In many communities, taxes include sales taxes on retail purchases, restaurant taxes on meal expenditures, and occupancy taxes on lodging, a portion of which may be remitted to the state in which the expenditure occurs. Additional federal, state and local tax revenue arises from the payroll taxes of tourism industry employees.

Other monetizable benefits

For the sake of this analysis, only the three previously described benefits are being monetized. This is so for two reasons. First, the economic impact of tourism at the national level, beyond direct expenditures and employment, is difficult to assess accurately, and secondly, it is important to provide a conservative estimate of the net present value of the analysis programme. Other benefits that could be monetized but are not considered in this analysis include: (1) *Decreased tax burden of individual citizens:* The overall tax burden of individual citizens should decrease as the tax base is increased because of the taxes paid by international travelers. (2) *Increased balance of trade for the nation:* With additional travel expenditures paid by international visitors, exports should increase. This assumes that other import and export activities do not change significantly. (3) *Decreased fiscal expenditures by multiple federal agencies:* Increased efficiency, as a result of reducing the current duplication among data-collecting federal agencies, should positively affect agency budgets. For the sake of this analysis focused on tourism, calculating such a figure would be cumbersome and unnecessary.

Benefits that cannot be directly monetized

There are other benefits of increased tourism that are difficult to monetize. These include increased employment, increased quality of life for host communities based on the short-term economic benefits, increased community pride as the local area develops into a quality destination and increased cultural exchange as international visitors interact with members of host communities. Once again, to add to the conservative nature of the analysis, these benefits are not included.

Forecast of expected benefits

To provide a reasonable and conservative forecast of the economic impact from international tourism to the United States, data from 4 years

(1999–2002) were averaged. There is a time lag of data in tourism research, and 2002 is the most recent year in which complete data are available for all figures used in this analysis. These data, supplied by the Office of Travel and Tourism Industries/International Trade Administration/Department of Commerce, are summarized in the paragraphs to follow.

The average international travel expenditures in the US for this period are $73,900,000,000. This figure is used as the historical baseline for the remainder of the analysis. Averaging these numbers accounts for volatility in the tourism industries and also considers future market uncertainty. For example, while 1999 and 2000 showed growth in international visitation, arrivals and economic impact in 2001 and 2002 were significantly lower because of terrorism in the United States.

As presented above, the primary output of this project is better data that can be used for more efficient marketing research, which can then be used to plan and implement more effective marketing campaigns. The simple premise of this analysis is that better information leads to better research, more effective marketing and, ultimately, to increased international traveller expenditures, US jobs, tax revenues and other economic multipliers.

The amount international travel expenditures will increase due to enhanced visitor information collection and distribution is subjective. There is limited information on the true effects of marketing research in tourism; however the general belief among researchers and academics is that marketing plans should be based on research. And the better the data on which the research is based, the more successful the marketing plan should be. In other words, the more effective the marketing research, the more effective the marketing campaign and greater the economic impact resulting from the marketing campaign. The subjective nature of the marketing research effectiveness percentage is addressed in the "Sensitivity Analysis" section of this case.

To determine the potential visitor expenditures, the baseline visitor expenditure figure is multiplied by the marketing research effectiveness percentage. When the potential visitor expenditure is subtracted from the baseline historic visitor expenditure, the result is the incremental visitor expenditure. For example, a 5 per cent increase in international traveller expenditures, using the baseline of $73,900,000,000, results in an incremental increase in expenditures of $3,695,000,000.

This estimate is then used to calculate the expected increase in payroll and taxes based on historic ratios relative to the baseline expenditure. These ratios are summarized in Table 8.7. Based on historical data, for every $1 spent by international visitors, an additional $0.28 is generated in payroll and an additional $0.16 is generated in taxes. For every $78,651 spent by international travelers, one additional job is created.

Table 8.7 Performance ratios based on historical baseline

	Average	1999	2000	2001	2002
Payroll/expenditure	$0.28	$0.26	$0.26	$0.29	$0.29
Expenditure/job	$78,651	$79,693	$83,123	$76,125	$75,663
Taxes/expenditure	$0.16	$0.16	$0.16	$0.17	$0.16

Using a conservative estimate of an increase in historical baseline marketing results (traveller expenditures) of 1 per cent after implementing the proposed programme, the result would be an incremental increase in international traveler expenditures of $739,000,000. This is used to calculate further benefits of increased payroll and taxes based on the ratios presented in Table 8.7. Table 8.8 shows this calculation for six years. The figures are not increased in future years to account for future market uncertainty and to be conservative. Although any increase in marketing effectiveness is subjective, a one percent increase will be used for the sake of this analysis.

Net present value of the analysis program

Based on the numbers generated for a one percent increase in effectiveness, or a one percent increase in international tourism expenditures, the project returns a net present value of $4,581,105,575. This would create an additional 9,396 jobs. The net present value is calculated using a discount rate of 8 per cent and a period of 5 years. Table 8.9 summarizes the discounted cash flow with a 1 per cent increase in marketing effectiveness.

Sensitivity analysis

To aid in decision-making, the first sensitivity analysis that is presented calculates the break-even point for the percentage increase in marketing effectiveness. A one percent increase was used in the discounted cash flow presented in Table 8.9; however, the rate that causes the project to break even is 0.001107 per cent, as summarized in Table 8.10. This means that the project must have a return of one-thousandth of 1 per cent to be a worthwhile investment. Under this scenario, an additional 10 jobs would be created, tourism expenditures would increase by $818,146, payroll would increase by $225,743, and an additional $133,571 in taxes would be generated in each year of the projection.

Table 8.8 Incremental increases in benefits – 1 per cent increase in effectiveness

	2007	2008	2009	2010	2011	2012
International travel expenditures in the United States	$739,000,000	$739,000,000	$739,000,000	$739,000,000	$739,000,000	$739,000,000
Payroll generated by international travel in the United States	$203,905,392	$203,905,392	$203,905,392	$203,905,392	$203,905,392	$203,905,392
Jobs generated by International Travel in the United States	9,396	9,396	9,396	9,396	9,396	9,396
Taxes paid by international travellers in the United States	$120,649,346	$120,649,346	$120,649,346	$120,649,346	$120,649,346	$120,649,346

Table 8.9 Discounted cash flow – 1 per cent increase in effectiveness

Costs	2007 Year 0	2008 Year 1	2009 Year 2	2010 Year 3	2011 Year 4	2012 Year 5
Software development	(300,000)	–	–	–	–	–
Hardware for data warehouse	(300,000)	–	–	–	(300,000)	–
Personnel for data analysis and management	(200,000)	(210,000)	(220,500)	(231,525)	(243,101)	(255,256)
Data acquisition	(700,000)	(735,000)	(771,750)	(810,338)	(850,854)	(893,397)
Total costs	(1,500,000)	(945,000)	(992,250)	(1,041,863)	(1,393,956)	(1,148,653)
Monetized benefits						
International travel expenditures in the United States	739,000,000	739,000,000	739,000,000	739,000,000	739,000,000	739,000,000
Payroll generated by international travel in the United States	203,905,392	203,905,392	203,905,392	203,905,392	203,905,392	203,905,392
Taxes paid by international travellers in the United States	120,649,346	120,649,346	120,649,346	120,649,346	120,649,346	120,649,346
Total monetized benefits	1,063,554,738	1,063,554,738	1,063,554,738	1,063,554,738	1,063,554,738	1,063,554,738
Net benefits	1,062,054,738	1,062,609,738	1,062,562,488	1,062,512,876	1,062,160,783	1,062,406,085
Discounted cash flow						
Net benefits	1,062,054,738	1,062,609,738	1,062,562,488	1,062,512,876	1,062,160,783	1,062,406,085
Present value of net benefits	1,062,054,738	983,897,906	910,976,070	843,456,977	780,719,884	723,055,730
Net present value	4,581,105,575					

Table 8.10 Discounted cash flow – 0.001107 per cent increase in effectiveness

Costs	2007 Year 0	2008 Year 1	2009 Year 2	2010 Year 3	2011 Year 4	2012 Year 5
Software development	(300,000)	–	–	–	–	–
Hardware for data warehouse	(300,000)	–	–	–	(3,00,000)	–
Personnel for data analysis and management	(200,000)	(210,000)	(220,500)	(231,525)	(243,101)	(255,256)
Data acquisition	(700,000)	(735,000)	(771,750)	(810,338)	(850,854)	(893,397)
Total costs	(1,500,000)	(945,000)	(992,250)	(1,041,863)	(1,393,956)	(1,148,653)
Monetized benefits						
International travel expenditures in the United States	818,146	818,146	818,146	818,146	818,146	818,146
Payroll generated by international travel in the United States	225,743	225,743	225,743	225,743	225,743	225,743
Taxes paid by international travellers in the United States	133,571	133,571	133,571	133,571	133,571	133,571
Total monetized benefits	1,177,460	1,177,460	1,177,460	1,177,460	1,177,460	1,177,460
Net benefits	(322,540)	232,460	185,210	135,598	(216,495)	28,807
Discounted cash flow						
Net benefits	(322,540)	232,460	185,210	135,598	(216,495)	28,807
Present value of net benefits	(322,540)	215,241	158,788	107,642	(159,131)	19,605
Net present value	0					

Using further sensitivity analysis, it is helpful to determine the break-even percentage at which the project must perform if the investment was doubled to $3,000,000. Quite simply, the break-even percentage doubles when the investment doubles. The corresponding percentage is still a low 0.002214 per cent. It may be that if the costs can be justified, the analysis programme's budget should be increased.

Summary and conclusions

While improving the results of a marketing campaign by 1 per cent seems reasonably possible, the resulting $4.5 billion yield on a $1,500,000 investment, as shown in the net present value (Table 8.9), does not seem as rational. There are several concerns with this analysis. First, tourism marketing is undertaken by many organizations and it is therefore difficult to assume that all marketing campaigns would benefit from enhanced data collection. However, it still may be reasonable to assume that the overall marketing effectiveness could be enhanced by 1 per cent based on those organizations that do use the information.

Secondly, it is difficult to know what marketing research is currently being conducted by various international tourism marketers and how more reliable data would enhance their current efforts. Finally, not all international tourism is spurred by marketing. State tourism organizations only spend roughly $20,000,000 per year on international marketing. While there are other monies spent on international marketing, much of the demand for international travel to the United States may be attributed to factors beyond marketing, such as an inherent desire to visit the United States or ease of entry into and access to the nation for most of the world's citizens.

To determine the effectiveness of current marketing campaigns, improved research is necessary on the efficacy of tourism marketing, and the motivations of international travellers. As an added benefit, these two areas will be addressed in the project.

To make the analysis more conservative, the discounted cash flow presented does not account for other benefits that could be monetized such as the decreased tax burden of individual citizens and decreased fiscal expenditures by multiple federal agencies collecting duplicate information. This would further inflate the net present value of the project. Once again, the analysis does not increase the value of benefits over time, which adds conservatism to the analysis. In reality, tourism expenditures have grown at a compound annual average rate of roughly 2.4 per cent over the past 10 years (TIA, 2006). It is therefore likely that the net present value would be higher in reality if the benefits were projected to grow.

There is demand for this project as many tourism industry professionals are calling for better research on international visitors (Brothers, 2006a,b). Given what we know about marketing research and tourism marketing, better analysis is warranted, and if implemented well, this project is likely to have an impact far greater than the break-even percentage of 0.001107 per cent at the $1,500,000 funding level. Also, considering the relative size of this programme compared with the President's proposed $5.9 billion American Competitiveness Initiative, this programme should be funded. With the current state of international tourism and the image of the United States abroad almost any investment in facilitating international travel to the United States is a good investment.

References

Barbara, J. (2006) Tisch to Hoteliers: Get Involved in Fed Policy. *Commercial Real Estate News and Property Resource*. Retrieved June 6, 2006 from GlobeSt.com.

Brothers, G. (2006a). *International Visitor Information Collection and distribution: A Tourism Industry Perspective*.

Brothers, G. (2006b). *Personal Interview*. April 7, 2006.

Buchanan, J.M. and G. Tullock (1962). *The Calculus of Consent*. Univeristy of Michigan, Ann Arbor, MI.

Bush, G.W. (2006). *Letter on American Competitiveness Initiative*. February 2, 2006.

Carlile, W.H. (1994). *States Are Closing Firms' 'Candy Store': Laws Tighten Incentives, Seek Accountability for Subsidies*. The Arizona Republic, July 24.

Epstein, M.J. (1994). *Viewpoints: A Formal Plan for Environmental Costs*. New York Times, Section 3, April 3, 1994.

Federal Highway Administration (2002). *Status of the Nation's Highways, Bridges, and Transit: 2002 Conditions and Performance Report*. Available at fhwa.dot.gov/policy/2002cpr/ch10.htm.

Fuguitt, D. and S. Wilcox (1992). *Cost–Benefit Analysis for Public Decision Makers*. Quorum Books, Westport, CT.

Little, I.M. and J.A. Mirrlees (1974). *Project Appraisal and Planning for Developing Countries*. Heinemann Educational Books, London.

O'Toole, R. (1998). *Reforming the Forest Service*. Island Press, Washington, DC.

Shaw, J. (2002). Public Choice Theory. *The Concise Encyclopedia of Economics*. Retrieved June 5, 2006 from http://www.econlib.org/library/Enc/PublicChoice Theory.html.

Squire, L. and H.G. Van der Tak (1975). *Economic Analysis of Projects*. Published for the World Bank. Johns Hopkins University Press, Baltimore, MD.

Swanson, J. (2003). *Does Policy Matter? The Connection Between Tourism Policy and Economic Input*. Cornell University, Ithaca, NY.

Travel Industry Association of America (TIA). Retrieved November 1, 2006 from http://www.tia.org/researchpubs/itnl_tourism_world.html.

UNIDO (United Nations Industrial Development Organization) (1972). *Guidelines for Project Evaluation*. United Nations, New York.

United Nations World Tourism Organization (UNWTO) (2006). Retrieved November 1, 2006 from http://www.world-tourism.org/statistics/index.htm.

9

Strategic tourism planning

Before he sets out, the traveller must possess fixed interests and facilities to be served by travel.

George Santayana (1863–1952)

Just as the traveler must prepare himself with information (through learning about the destination's environs) to get the optimum value from his travel, so must the community/destination plan well for the future success of their tourism programmes. One popular tourism planning mechanism is 'strategic planning'. Strategic tourism planning is a process aimed to optimize the benefits of tourism so that the result is a balance of the appropriate quality and quantity of supply with the proper level of demand, without compromising neither the locale's socioeconomic and environmental developments nor its sustainability. Any discussion of strategic tourism planning must take into account economic, environmental and socio-cultural factors and their relationship to overall sustainable tourism goals and objectives. Thus, strategic tourism planning is a framework designed to provide direction for any tourism organization or destination, and it emphasizes quality, efficiency and effectiveness.

The mandate for effective tourism planning, as accepted throughout most of the world today, is to integrate stakeholders' concerns, effective management, efficient development and innovative marketing and community interests within the destination's tourism product. The process of tourism planning takes into account that a destination must be able to adjust to new trends, changing markets and a competitive market environment. Destinations that have planned well for tourism usually have a competitive edge in the marketplace. The planning effort aimed at the future sustainability of tourism will assure consistent quality of the tourism product(s) and yield the most benefits to the community/destination. In addition, good planning will override short-term goals aimed solely at profit motivations and emphasize many of the important future attributes that are more positive for the entire community.

Managing sustainable tourism, recognized as an important aspect of tourism planning, is now receiving even greater attention. In *Managing Sustainable Tourism: A Legacy for the Future* (2006), Edgell explains the importance of planning and management in developing sustainable tourism goals and objectives. 'In general, most studies have found that a well-researched, well-planned, and well-managed tourism program that takes into account the natural and cultural environment has a good chance of improving the local economy and enhancing the quality of life of residents'. In brief, tourism planning is essential to sustainability in the future and must foster the conservation of the resources that tourism is dependent on and improve the quality of life for most local residents.

Tourism planning in the past did not receive the same kind of attention considered necessary today. There are numerous examples of tourism areas and destinations that deteriorated and failed. Much of this decadence can be traced to haphazard planning and development, motivating modern tourism managers to insist on more careful planning. Even today, with the emphasis on organized planning, one need not travel far to see the negative impact of unplanned tourism development projects.

Good tourism planning gives a destination many advantages, five of which are listed below:

1. There is a close relationship between policy and planning; tourism planning strengthens an area's tourism policy. Goeldner and Ritchie (2006) discuss in detail the interrelationship of tourism policy and planning.
2. Tourism planning is a highly organized effort of rational thinking, concentrated on the goals and objectives of a given locale.
3. Tourism planning contains many steps, initiating from inventorying an area's tourism product to providing the blueprint for development. It is a highly integrative process.

4. Tourism planning balances economic goals with the need for conserving the environment and improving the quality of life for local residents.
5. Strategic tourism planning emphasizes quality, efficiency and effectiveness throughout the process.

Defining strategic tourism planning

Those who work in the tourism field are accustomed to seeing myriad variations of the strategic planning concept. The co-authors of this book have often used different approaches to strategic tourism planning depending on the circumstances, the destination and the community. One strategic plan may focus on organizational capacity, while another aids in building the appropriate supply. A strategic tourism plan may focus on visitor research, another may work toward developing stakeholder involvement and another may recommend ways to spend the marketing budget. A comprehensive strategic tourism plan will incorporate all of these elements.

Strategic planning in the tourism industry is usually a policy/planning/management tool to assist the tourism entity (national tourism office, destination, local community) in organizing to accomplish its desired goals, while focusing on available resources for obtaining the greatest benefits. In effect, it is a blueprint to help shape and guide the entity in reaching its future goals. A good example of a strategic tourism planning document is the Canadian strategic tourism plan mentioned in the case study at the end of this chapter.

When defining strategic planning, the reader must first look at the etymology of these two words. *Strategic,* from the word 'strategy', a plan of action relating to a goal, and *planning*, a method of doing something to reach a goal (Webster's II New College Dictionary, 2001). Both include the concept of a goal. In tourism, the goal is the basis for the entire strategic planning process.

Today, many strategic tourism planners include several steps in the process: develop a 'vision' (usually a single sentence), a 'mission statement' that explains the vision (usually no more than two sentences), and then goals, objectives, strategies and tactics. Some organizations also build into the process a 'situational analysis' (*or* needs assessment), a 'competitive analysis', a 'monitoring device', an 'evaluation', built-in 'performance measures' and 'research' (to improve the process). Early in the planning process is the time to form a team of interested individuals and groups. It may include, for example, a tourism director, the planning and research departments, marketing and sales departments, managers of hotels and resorts, associates from the airlines and the public transportation department and

others impacted by the outcome. In addition to tourism industry professionals, community leaders must also be involved. It is very important
to be generous in involving a large number of the key organizations and
individuals that have the ability to affect the success at accomplishing the
tourism planning goals and objectives.

Setting down the vision is the first step of the strategic tourism planning
process. Composed of just a few words, the vision will set the stage for an
intelligent foresight of the future of a tourism destination, a community
or place. It provides a common ideal or dream that all the stakeholders
can endorse. When penning a vision, the 'vision authors' need to have a
thorough understanding and knowledge of the destination or area and the
desired plans for future development and promotion. There are a number
of different techniques that can be used in preparing a vision. It might
evolve from a simple brainstorming session, where the stakeholders gather
to discuss their ultimate goals for the project. In some circumstances, it
makes sense to use focus groups to share a wide range of different opinions
to build the vision. This may also be a good time to utilize the services of an
experienced strategic marketing consultant who can help with developing
the vision and branding of the tourism product.

The mission statement is an important second step, in that it supports
the vision by defining the method(s) to obtain the vision, dictating the
pathway(s) to accomplishment. Unlike the vision, the mission statement is
generally a little lengthier in that it outlines 'how to get there' – much like a
road map. The mission statement is goal-oriented and designed to inspire
people to make decisions and take actions. Like the vision, there needs to
be a wide range of people involved in preparing the mission statement.

Following the vision and mission statement, the strategic tourism plan
includes goals and objectives. Repeated from Chapter 1 is the diagram
(Figure 9.1) 'Goal-oriented tourism planning', which provides a guiding
outline defining the pathway of goal(s), objective(s), strategy (strategies)
and tactic(s). Developing goals, objectives, strategies and tactics is vital to
the entire process.

The goal(s) are the driving force of what the plan intends to achieve in
the strategic tourism planning process and, therefore, needs careful craft-
ing to be effective. For most tourism-related projects, there may often be
several goals, which represent the aim or purpose intended by the stakeholders when the decision to develop the tourism project is initially crafted.
The project may have short-term goals (1 year or less), medium-term goals
(2–4 years) and/or longer-term goals (4 years and beyond). It is helpful
towards achieving the goals if they are measurable. For example, 'In two
years, we expect to have the tourism destination fully constructed and
operational' or 'Upon completion of the destination, we anticipate visitation levels to increase by 20 per cent per year' or 'By the fifth year, we
expect more than one million visitors will have come to this destination.'

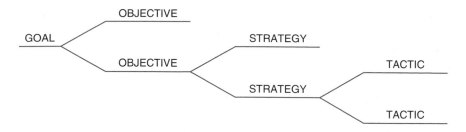

Figure 9.1 Tree diagram: goal-oriented tourism planning

Objectives go hand in glove with the goal(s); they are stepping stones to the goal and are concrete, real, practical steps or intentions that define expected achievements in the project. Objectives are goal-oriented targets of the organization that can be implemented and made operational in achieving the tourism plan. Generally, the objectives are in priority order such that the available resources earmarked to achieve the highest priority objectives are named first. The idea is to think about the overall objectives, the big picture, and to keep our minds fresh and free to encourage creative thinking.

Strategies relate to actions and operations that are necessary to meet the objectives included in the strategic tourism plan. In some circumstances, the strategy may include the development of new products or special programs for implementing the objectives. The strategy should also identify key target audiences that are a part of the overall planning process. One strategy might be to provide the leadership necessary to accomplish the objectives or set the criteria for measuring the quality of the tourism project. Strategies also involve identification of funding needs and sources, as well as review of existing resources related to the objectives of the plan. Furthermore, a strategy might include forming a partnership or collaborating with other interested entities or introducing new technology. The key is that the strategies, followed by the tactics, are aimed towards reaching the goals and objectives identified in the strategic plan.

The last item in the diagram is tactic(s). In the tourism planning process, the tactic is the short-term action (usually less than 6 months) implemented for immediate achievement of the overall goals and objectives. It is, in effect, the ways and means for securing the objectives designated by the strategy. Tactics are the day-to-day activities and details, whether setting the agenda for the stakeholders meeting or making arrangements to support the planning process, used to achieve the strategic planning goal.

The above-described parts of the strategic tourism planning process indicate how the success of a tourism destination depends on careful planning. There are other steps that are often included in designing the tourism plan. Some tourism plans include such categories as research, evaluation, monitoring, situational analysis and branding. A case in point is the strategic tourism plan for Canada, which the Canadian Tourism

Commission announced as the *2007–2011 Strategic Plan*, a classic example of positive strategic tourism planning.

Strategic tourism planning is a management tool meant to facilitate the user's skills towards meeting the desired purposes of the organization/destination, setting attainable goals and developing a methodology outlining the desired achievements in a responsible, sustainable fashion. It must be adaptable to the changing demand and supply of the tourism industry and the introduction of new tourism products. In addition, it must look to the future. Overall, the strategic tourism plan must be clear and concise, incorporating the given goals and objectives, all the while being responsive to the available resources of the organization plus the dynamic nature of the tourism industry.

This disciplined process calls for a certain order and pattern to keep it focused and productive. It should raise a sequence of questions to help planners examine the tourist's experience, test viable interpretations of certain data, incorporate information about the present and anticipate the organization's future impact on the tourism environment. Finally, the process must address fundamental decisions and actions as choices in order to answer the sequence of questions mentioned above. The strategic tourism plan is no more, and no less, than a set of decisions about what to do, why to do it and how to do it. The beauty of achievement, on finalizing a strategic tourism plan, lies in the knowledge that tough decisions have been made concerning the most important issues and that the entity can now move forward proactively.

Planning example

One of the co-authors of this book is currently working on a country strategic tourism plan. While the approach outlined above is used, additional steps are included. In his work, a *SWOT* (strengths, weaknesses, opportunities and threats) analysis is also applied. There are times when the order of the items in the analysis changes, as, for example, *OTSW* (opportunities, threats, strengths and weaknesses). In addition, in the goal-setting phase, the country plan includes *SMART* (specific, measurable, achievable, relevant and time-bound) goals. In other words, the strategic tourism planning approach taken is dependent on the conditions existing in the organization (in this case a country) and the marketplace. Commonly, the planner or leader will hold numerous brainstorming sessions to enable all stakeholders to reach a consensus on which tools are best for the strategic tourism planning process. As is the case for any planning instrument, the organization may have a wonderful plan, but if not carefully crafted, it will fail at the beginning of implementation. This supports the notion for continuously monitoring and evaluating, as dynamic processes may take place while the plan is being developed and implemented.

For any tourism organization to make sound decisions, the planning process must be based on solid and valid data considering both tourism supply and demand that incorporates scans of both the internal and external environments. The following lists outline research activities that can be included in a comprehensive strategic tourism plan.

Internal analysis

Internal analysis reviews the factors that characterize the destination. Characteristics may include interstate highway demand, heritage, sports facilities, outdoor recreation activities, the natural environment or proximity to major metropolitan areas, among many other factors that serve to drive tourism demand to the destination. Not only is it important to understand a destination's tourism product, or supply, it is equally important to identify the community's organizational structures that will influence tourism development. Steps that can be incorporated into the internal analysis of tourism strategic planning are the following:

A. Analyse the destination's natural environment

1. Assess the area's geography to identify opportunities and threats to tourism development.
2. Evaluate previous and predicted climate issues that could affect visitation to the area.
3. Gauge residents' attitudes towards tourism and tourism development by enabling community members to voice their views and concerns through either a 'town hall meeting' or a web-based survey.
4. Measure the general condition of service provided by the tourism industry workforce, addressing relevant training needs.
5. Identify meaningful elements of the area's culture that could be incorporated into the overall tourism experience.
6. Review the history of the area to maintain or revive critical characteristics important to heritage tourism.

B. Examine the assembled elements

1. Identify current mission, goals, objectives, strategies and tactics of key community and civic organizations; areas of concordance, overlap and conflict; and common and shared human and financial resources related to tourism development.
2. Review budgets and funding of comparable Destination Management Organizations (DMOs) as a benchmark to identify enhanced and sustainable funding opportunities for the Convention and Visitor Bureau (CVB) or other destination-related organization.

3. Identify specific tourism-related infrastructure needs or opportunities that may not meet visitor expectations and may detract from the destination's appeal.

4. Analyse the signage and transportation routes to and through the destination to ensure ease of access for visitors to the Welcome Centers, attractions and other tourism supply components.

5. Assess the use of technology by destination promoters in the areas of customer relationships, packaging, booking and travel planning, demographic information, promotion, communications and revenue management, among other areas.

6. Review quality, availability and distribution of visitor information about the destination.

7. Evaluate the community's existing crisis contingency plan to ensure it is proactive and can handle a wide array of incidents that could arise at any time.

C. Conduct extensive visitor research

1. Plan visitor research study by working with destination managers to establish and understand the survey objectives.

2. Design and test telephone, online, or paper-based visitor survey instruments to collect data from visitors.

3. Complete interviews with the general population who possess certain demographic characteristics as well as additional interviews with those who have visited the destination.

4. Prepare a summary report to include descriptive statistics of the data along with tests of the hypotheses stated in the original study design phase.

5. Identify existing and new market segments and decision patterns that will increase visitation to the region.

D. Investigate industry-operating sectors

1. It is necessary to inventory businesses in all tourism operating sectors (accommodations, meeting spaces, transportation, activities and entertainment, food services, outdoor recreation, visitor services and shopping) in order to determine quality and quantity.

2. Identify opportunities for improvement in all operating sectors.

3. Meet with selected tourism industry members, including supply operators, tourism managers and developers.

4. Conduct a web-based survey of local industry members to identify tourism development issues and concerns important to the stakeholders.

5. Gather information on new attractions and expansions that may be planned.

6. Examine the potential to repackage existing and develop new special events and niche tourism supply (convention centre, heritage, military, sports, nature, trails, agritourism and industrial activities, among others) that may bolster tourism in the shoulder and off-season months.
7. Evaluate the impacts of existing outdated facilities and inadequate supply, including the aesthetic appeal of architectural design standards, such as streetscape, gateway, signage and façade improvements.

External environmental scan

It is crucial for a destination to understand how it fits in the larger tourism industry and how various factors at all levels may have an impact on visitation at the local level. This is done by studying industry trends at the regional, state/provincial, national and international levels. Competitive analysis is also a vital activity when pursuing a sound tourism development strategy.

A. Explore details of larger tourism systems

1. Identify the 'outside' (non-destination) stakeholders and design an effective and efficient means of outreach to them. Outside organizations may include neighbouring DMOs and state/provincial tourism, economic development, environmental and transportation agencies, among other groups.
2. Review current and anticipated industry trends in terms of visitation, origin of demand, revenues, supply development, consumer preferences, safety and security and other indicators at the state/provincial, national and international levels.
3. Research trends in particular activities and industries important to the destination.

B. Perform competitive analysis

1. Examine competitive destinations in the region.
2. Determine the competitive position of the destination against similar areas in terms that may include current and historical visitation, tourism revenue, market segmentation, markets of origin, marketing expenditures and/or other pertinent data.

Strategic tourism planning recommendations should lead towards optimized tourism in the destination. Research should focus on determining the future of tourism in the region and how it can achieve its highest and best goal within the context of infrastructure and environmental constraints in the destination, and in accordance with the wants and needs of area visitors and community stakeholders.

Sustainable tourism's effect on planning

The natural and built environments are powerful motivators for travellers choosing to visit a destination. The point has been well made that today's most carefully prepared strategic tourism plans incorporate sustainable tourism practices and policies. Although sustainable tourism resources are vital ingredients of a destination's success, they are not usually under the control of destination planners. Therefore, the planning process must include scrutiny of an area's natural environment elements, embracing its geography, climate and residents, as well as the built environment featuring history, heritage and culture. Those areas with more diverse resources will have more to offer to a wider array of tourists; however, this diversity may make planning more difficult, mandating a complete inventory of an area's resources. As explained at the outset, and throughout this book, the core policies of overall planning strategy are those that facilitate the development of sustainable tourism by means of balanced approaches towards economic, environmental and social issues (Figure 9.2).

Strategic tourism planning is, in summary, a practical, intensive, idea-packed approach to improving a destination's opportunities for sustainability over a long period. A tactical system aims to stretch the available resources through careful planning, monitoring and evaluation. It is an action-oriented plan to benchmark and counter competitors' strategies with built-in performance measures. Strategic tourism planning proposes to develop a coherent strategy to build upon destination strengths and learn from the past while correcting for the future in order to increase

Figure 9.2   Miami is a complicated destination developed within a vibrant combination of natural resources, the built environment and cultural assets (Photo: J.R. Gast)

tourism's positive impacts upon the community. The overall goal is to match tourism supply and demand – to provide adequate and appropriate facilities, amenities, services and events (supply) after identifying what visitors want and need (demand). Successful implementation of good tourism development strategies will result in the creation of new jobs, additional visitor expenditures and increased tax revenue. Tourism development, if done well, can improve an area's quality of life, which will be appealing to new residents, companies and entrepreneurs (Figure 9.3).

Following this Section is a case study titled 'Canada: An Effective Tourism Policy'. The co-authors of this book reviewed numerous country tourism policies and, after due consideration, chose Canada as the country that best represented strategic tourism planning as advocated in this chapter. Certain attributes of Canada's tourism policy are of particular interest to the co-authors. We believe that in the future more countries will adopt the Canadian approach of a true partnership of government and business in tourism planning, development and marketing, which is the hallmark of the present Canadian tourism policy.

In order to explain the Canadian tourism policy, it was necessary to plunge briefly into the history of its development. Two of the co-authors

Figure 9.3 Machu Picchu from the top of Wayna Picchu, a well-planned and managed destination (Photo: Jane M. Allen)

tudy, Scott M. Meis and Stephen L.J. Smith, had already
sively about some of the developments in Canada's tourism
1996, 1997). Their information became the base of this case
study. ird co-author of the case study, David L. Edgell, Sr, reviewed
some of the earlier documents and included what he thought best met
the intentions of this chapter. Tom Penney, Vice President Planning and
Evaluation, Product Development, Emerging Markets, Canadian Tourism
Commission, provided numerous helpful documents, including the latest
Canadian strategic tourism plan.

Case study 9

CANADA: AN EFFECTIVE TOURISM POLICY BY: SCOTT M. MEIS, STEPHEN L.J. SMITH AND DAVID L. EDGELL, SR

Introduction

The Canadian Tourism Commission (CTC) report *Options for a Long-Term Funding Solution for the Canadian Tourism Commission* (31 August 2005) says that in 1995 CTC was established as a "special operating agency" within the federal government department of Industry Canada. It further states that in January 2001 the CTC became a Crown corporation, allowing it more independence from federal government departmental financial and administrative controls. "The mandate of the CTC is to:

- Sustain a vibrant and profitable Canadian tourism industry;
- Market Canada as a desirable tourist destination;
- Support a cooperative relationship between the private sector and government; and,
- Provide information about Canadian tourism to the private sector and to the governments".

The report further states: "Since its inception, the CTC has operated on a public/private sector partnership basis with core funding coming from the Federal Government and matching or greater contributions coming from other industry partners. In response to both the opportunities and challenges presented by the current global tourism environment, the CTC believes it is crucial that it increase its marketing and research investments as part of ongoing efforts to protect and grow Canada's global tourism market share, and to increase associated economic returns to both the public and private sectors".

Background

Government tourism policy in Canada has an interesting history. It formally began during the Great Depression in 1932 with the establishment of the Canadian Bureau of Tourism (CBT). The mandate of the CBT was to promote Canada as a hunting and fishing destination to Americans with the intent of generating new jobs and income. Tourism promotion continued as a minor federal activity until 1967, Canada's Centennial Anniversary. One of the key events of that year was the World's Fair, Expo '67, in Montreal, Canada. The phenomenally popular and critical success of Expo '67 put Canada on the world map as a tourist destination. Recognizing the potential of more aggressively competing in the global tourism market, the federal government created the Canadian Government Office of Tourism (CGOT) and expanded its role to include tourism research, planning, policy, product development as well as marketing. The CGOT became Tourism Canada in 1985. While the responsibilities of the federal government in tourism waxed and waned over the years, one constant has always been marketing. Another constant has been the complaints by industry that whatever agency was responsible for tourism marketing, it was (1) underfunded and (2) not responsive to the market.

In response to industry discontent, a series of governmental and industry task forces and reports explored alternative structures and the future of tourism in Canada. This began with the 1985 "Statement of Principles on Federal, Provincial, Territorial Roles and Responsibilities in Respect of Tourism", prepared at the 1985 Federal-Provincial-Territorial Conference of Ministers of Tourism. As the title suggests, this report focused on the respective responsibilities of the various senior governments in tourism marketing, research, policy, planning and development. One outcome of the agreement was that Tourism Canada would no longer conduct domestic marketing, leaving that function to the individual provinces and territories (a decision reversed with the creation of the CTC a decade later).

Between 1985 and 1995, there were numerous discussions, meetings and conferences, which took place in an effort to establish an effective tourism policy. One of the important discussion documents was the report submitted by the Tourism Industry Association of Canada (TIAC), *Prosperity Through Tourism* (1995). This report reviewed the state of the industry and recommended changes in legislation, product development priorities, promotion strategies and human resource development. One of the most significant recommendations was to replace Tourism Canada with a national tourism authority jointly funded by the government and private sector but whose decisions would be industry-driven. The prime minister and his cabinet accepted the advice and established the CTC on 1 February 1995. In October of the preceding year, the federal government already had approved and published the federal overall micro-economic policy of Canada, *Agenda: Jobs and Growth, Building a More Innovative Economy* (1994). This recognized for the first time the significance of tourism in contributing to the economic well-being of Canadians as an essential element of national economic policy and specifying the role of and focus the federal government's involvement in tourism and its relation to overall government micro-economic policy objectives of promoting innovation and employment. Later on 20 October 2000, the federal government's policy commitment to tourism was further formalized in legislation with the passing of Bill C25, the Canadian Tourism Commission Act establishing the Commission as an independent government "crown" corporation. In relation to government tourism organizations throughout the world at that time, this new partnership arrangement was truly revolutionary. Today, this model continues to be studied by many countries.

Organizational structure

The CTC is a true hybrid of the public and private sectors, industry-led, with a Board of Directors dominated by the private sector and a minority of Board members from federal, provincial and territorial governments. Purchasing and contract procedures and the terms and conditions of employment are governed by federal regulations for government corporations with the salaries of employees paid by the CTC from the annual allocations to the Commission for the approved programmes, supporting organization and associated human resources.

Marketing and programme policies, organizational planning and strategic management are established and directed by six marketing and two industry development committees (marketing committees are "Canada", "US Leisure", "Business", "Europe", "Asia/Pacific" and "Aboriginal Tourism"; industry development committees are "Industry Enhancement" and "Research"). A "Performance Measurement Committee" provides guidance on the development of evaluation criteria or performance indicators for each programme. Committee membership comes from both the private and public sectors, with one or more designated full-time professional staff members providing logistical support.

A private sector representative, working with an executive subcommittee, serves as a director on the Board of Directors, which oversees the management of the affairs and business of the Commission. These committees consult with industry to develop sub-programme strategies, goals and objectives and associated programme activities and budgets, such as the 1999 Research Program technical paper *A Research and Development Program for Improved Tourism Industry Decision Making* (CTC, 1999).

Formulated as a three-year medium-term strategy, they must be sent to the Board for approval. Once the Board has voted on the overall programme strategy such as the Strategic Plan 2002–2004: Overview (CTC, 2002) document, for example, and the proposal and resource allocations are in place, negotiations begin on tactics and implementation. Detailed annual work plans for each designated committee-led programme are developed through committee consultation and brought to the Board to ensure they are in line with the programmes and require approval in principle. The Board Subcommittee Chairpersons are responsible for presenting the plans to the Board and for overseeing the implementation of the plans, while staff programme directors are responsible for managing the actual implementation of the plans. Unique to the CTC, staff persons who may be officers, employees, agents and any technical advisers are accountable to their respective programme directors, and through them and the senior management hierarchy to the President and the industry-led Board of Directors.

Funding and partnerships

The budget of the CTC is drawn from federal, provincial and territorial governments as well as from the private sector. The goal, as set by the prime minister, is 50 per cent funding from the federal government and 50 per cent from all partners (both public and private sectors). This is an effort to have a true partnership between the government and private sector.

The issue of partnership and matching funds is integral to the operation of the CTC. The CTC conducts a variety of marketing, product development and research projects to achieve its goals, virtually all of which are conducted with one or more partners. The CTC does not function as a granting agency; thereby, an organization only approaches the CTC with a proposal expected to make a significant contribution to its implementation.

"Partnership" is an increasingly common term in many nations' tourism industries; however, it often lacks operational definition. Because the CTC requires that the federal contribution be matched by an equal partnership contribution, it became necessary to operationally define "partnership" and associated business processes and appropriate practices (CTC, 2005). For example, does an organization actually have to transfer cash to the CTC to be a partner? Could they not, instead, contribute to covering programme costs? What about contributing in kind, such as providing air tickets or lodging for persons travelling on CTC business? What about expenses incurred for programmes that managed independently of the CTC but are consistent and operated in parallel with CTC program initiatives?

To resolve this, the CTC defines partnership as "a commitment to share resources on common objectives to achieve mutually beneficial results". Allocations of resources including in-kind contributions by partners involving an explicit commitment to work towards common objectives that achieve desired mutual results counted as a partnership contribution. In-kind resources are valued at current retail price for purposes of measuring a partner's contribution.

Results

The initial creation of the CTC and the associated integration of tourism into the national micro-economic policy led to an initial three-fold increase in national federal funding for the national initiatives. Subsequent partnership funding from other levels of government and the private sector led to a further doubling of overall contributions to the organization's budget and programmes. In addition, the newly developed strategic and annual operational planning processes led for the first time to a fully coordinated public and private sector approach to national tourism marketing, research and industry development. The new planning, coordination and partnership funding and decision-making approaches have sustained the Canadian tourism sector equally throughout the relatively positive conditions of the general business environment of the late 1980s as well as the more turbulent period experienced after 11 September 2001.

Challenges

While the structure of the Canadian national tourism organization has changed over the past 70 years, more changes are likely in the future. CTC cannot sit idly by and expect the market to grow. CTC must be innovative and creative in meeting the demands and trends in the tourism market. Tourism is a dynamic industry, with changes in product, market, communications, competition and technology taking place frequently. The use of e-commerce tools in tourism is but one dynamic in our fast-changing technology world. Tourism products are always in a state of flux as tourists change their interests. New competition enters the market every day and challenges existing products and markets; if you do not have a good Internet presence or an effective Web site, marketing efficiency is likely to decline.

There are other challenges as well. CTC must find ways and means to get greater cooperation from small- and medium-sized firms to compete in the marketplace (another use of "coopetition" as mentioned earlier in the book). In addition, Canada's total land area of 9,976,140 square kilometres (3,851,809 square miles) makes it such a huge country that effective cooperation and joint marketing planning and actual marketing have potential for hindrance. Some questions as to marketing strategies raised: Is it better to use cluster marketing, geographical marketing, niche marketing or some other form? How to you approach branding the country better?

Financing is always a discussion topic. Does the government follow the private sector or vice versa? Which markets are most effective and need greater financial attention? How do you balance small, medium and large firms in the marketing strategies? Is it possible to switch the market budget to meet short- and long-term needs of the industry? How do you adjust to safety and security issues? Many such questions were asked and answered for Canada's tourism programme to be successful. Certainly, one concern is whether the CTC is flexible enough to meet such demands.

In the opinions of the authors, the CTC is probably better equipped to adjust to markets faster and more efficiently than most other government programmes around the globe. Stated another way, the CTC is better organized than many national government tourism programmes and the joint government–private sector approach is the best approach in the current marketplace (The legal "Act" to establish the CTC is included as an addendum to this case study).

The future

An important function of CTC is to conduct "Strategic Tourism Planning". CTC conducts short-term and long-term planning and frequently revises its strategic plan to be in tune with the trends of the tourism industry. For example, in September 2006, CTC released its *2007–2011 Strategic Plan: Moving Forward with Vision*. This "Plan" is a classic example of many of the principles outlined in this chapter. It has a vision, mission statement, goals, objectives and strategies, all pertinent to good planning. The following is a summary taken directly from the plan.

> **Industry Vision:** Canada will be the premier four season destination to connect with nature and experience diverse culture and communities. **Industry Mission:** Canada's tourism industry will deliver world-class culture and leisure experiences year-round while preserving and sharing Canada's clean, safe and natural environments. The industry will be guided by the values of respect, integrity and empathy.

The Strategic Plan 2007–2011 – *The Plan at a Glance*:

> *GOAL*: GROW TOURISM EXPORT REVENUES
>
> *OBJECTIVES*
>
> 1.   Convert high yield customers;
> 2.   Focus on markets of highest return on investments;
> 3.   Brand consistency; and
> 4.   Research new market opportunities
>
> *PRIORITIES*
>
> Developing one-to-one relationship with customers;
> Align market allocations for maximum return on investment;
> Differentiate Canada;
> Leverage partner investment;
> Leverage media exposure afforded by the Vancouver 2010 Winter Olympic Games
> Create demand for increased air access; and
> Organizational excellence
>
> *2011 **ULTIMATE OUTCOME***
>
> Export revenues increase to $19.8 billion
>
> *STRATEGIC OUTCOMES*
>
> Canada has moved up from #11 ranking on UNWTO's list
> Awareness levels of the Brand Canada have increased
> Market yield has increased to $120.40 per day
> Partnership ration maintained at 1:1
> Employee satisfaction remains constant and/or increased

Strategic tourism planning is a dynamic process. As global and domestic tourism markets, destinations, products, and economies change, tourism plans and programs will adjust accordingly. This was true yesterday, is true today, and will be true in the future.

Addendum to case study: Canada: an effective tourism policy

An Act to establish the Canadian Tourism Commission
[Assented to 20 October 2000]

PREAMBLE

WHEREAS the Canadian tourism industry is vital to the social and cultural identity and integrity of Canada;

WHEREAS the Canadian Tourism industry makes an essential contribution to the economic well-being of Canadians and to the economic objectives of the Government of Canada;

WHEREAS the Canadian tourism industry consists of mainly small and medium-sized businesses that are essential to Canada's goals for entrepreneurial development and job creation;

AND WHEREAS it is desirable to strengthen Canada's commitment to Canadian tourism by establishing a Tourism Commission that would work with the governments of the provinces and the territories and the Canadian tourism industry to promote the interests of that industry and to market Canada as a desirable tourist destination;

Now, THEREFORE, Her Majesty, by and with the advice and consent of the Senate and House of Commons of Canada, enacts as follows:

SHORT TITLE

1. This Act may be cited as the *Canadian Tourism Commission Act*.

INTERPRETATION

2. The definitions in this section apply in the Act.
    "Commission" means the Canadian Tourism Commission established by section 3.
    "Minister" means the Minister of Industry.

ESTABLISHMENT

3. There is hereby established a corporation to be known as the Canadian Tourism Commission.

STATUS

4. The Commission is, for the purposes of this Act, an agent of Her Majesty in right of Canada.

OBJECTS

5.   The objects of the Commission are to

   (a)   sustain a vibrant and profitable Canadian tourism industry;

   (b)   market Canada as a desirable tourist destination;

   (c)   support a cooperative relationship between the private sector and the governments of Canada, the provinces and the territories with respect to Canadian tourism; and

   (d)   provide information about Canadian tourism to the private sector and to the governments of Canada, the provinces, and the territories.

POWERS

6.   (1)   For the purpose of carrying out its objects, the Commission has the capacity and, subject to this Act, the rights, powers and privileges of a natural person.

   (2)   The Commission may not initiate or finance programs involving the acquisition or construction of real property, immovables or facilities related to tourism.

BOARD OF DIRECTORS

7.   The affairs and business of the Commission shall be managed by a Board of Directors.

8.   The Board consists of not more than twenty-six directors, including a Chairperson and a President.

9.   The Chairperson shall be appointed by the Governor in Council to hold office during pleasure on a part-time basis for a term of not more than five years.

10.   The President shall be appointed by the Governor in Council to hold office during pleasure on a full-time basis for a term of not more than five years.

11.   (1)   Up to sixteen private sector directors shall be appointed by the Minister, with the approval of the Governor in Council.

   (2)   The Board shall establish a committee that shall provide advice to the Minister on the appointment of directors under subsection (1).

   (3)   Of the directors appointed under subsection (1),

      (a)   up to seven shall be tourism operators appointed to represent the following regions in the following numbers:

         (i)   not more than two for the Provinces of Nova Scotia, New Brunswick, Prince Edward Island and Newfoundland,

    (ii)   one for the Province of Quebec,

    (iii)   one for the Province of Ontario,

    (iv)   one for the Provinces of Manitoba and Saskatchewan,

    (v)   one for the Province of Alberta, the Northwest Territories and Nunavut, and

    (vi)   one for the Province of British Columbia and the Yukon Territory; and

(b)   up to nine shall be private sector representatives.

(4)   The directors appointed under subsection (1) shall be appointed to hold office during pleasure on a part-time basis for a term of not more than three years.

(5)   The definitions in this subsection apply in this section.

    "private sector director" means a director who is a tourism operator or a privates sector representative.

    "private sector representative" means a tourism operator or a person with the expertise required to satisfy the Board's needs.

    "tourism operator" means an owner or a manager of a private sector tourism business.

12. (1)   The Minister, with the approval of the Governor in Council, shall appoint public sector directors in the numbers specified in subparagraphs 11(3)(a)(i) to (vi) to represent the regions set out in those subparagraphs.

    (2)   The directors who are to be appointed under subsection (1) shall be appointed from among persons designated by the provincial or territorial ministers responsible for tourism. Those ministers may designate deputy ministers, persons who are equivalent to deputy ministers or persons who are heads of provincial or territorial agencies.

    (3)   The directors appointed under subsection (1) shall be appointed to hold office during pleasure on a part-time basis for a term of not more than three years.

13.   The Deputy Minister of Industry is, *ex officio*, a director.

14.   A director is eligible to be re-appointed to the Board in the same or another capacity.

REMUNERATION AND FEES

15.   The President shall be paid the remuneration that the Governor in Council may fix.

16.   The Chairperson and the private sector directors, other than the President, shall be paid the fees that the Governor in Council may fix.

CHAIRPERSON

17. The Chairperson shall determine the times when and places where the Board will meet and shall preside at those meetings.

18. If the Chairperson is absent or incapacitated or if the office of Chairperson is vacant, the Board may designate any director appointed under section 11 to exercise the powers and perform the duties and functions of the Chairperson during the absence, incapacity or vacancy, but no director may be so designated for a period exceeding ninety days without the approval of the Governor in Council.

PRESIDENT

19. The President is the chief executive officer of the Commission and has supervision over and direction of the work of the Commission including the management of its internal affairs and the hiring and termination of its staff.

20. If the President is absent or incapacitated or if the office of President is vacant, the Board may designate any person to exercise the powers and perform the duties and functions of the President during the absence, incapacity or vacancy, but no person may be so designated for a period exceeding ninety days without the approval of the Governor in Council.

21. Subject to any contrary provision in any other Act of Parliament, the President may delegate to any person any power, duty or function conferred on the President under this Act or any other enactment.

MEETINGS

22. The Board shall meet at least twice a year.

BY-LAWS

23. The Board shall make by-laws respecting the management and conduct of the affairs of the Commission and the carrying out of the duties of the Boards, including by-laws establishing

    (a) a code of ethics for the directors and employees of the Commission;
    (b) committees of the Board, including an executive committee, a human resources committee, a committee for the purposes of section 11 and an audit committee; and
    (c) a contracting policy for the Commission.

HEAD OFFICE

24. The head office of the Commission shall be in the place in Canada that the Governor in Council may, by order, designate.

ACCIDENT COMPENSATION

25.   The Chairperson, the President, the private sector directors and the employees of the Commission are deemed to be employees for the purposes of the *Government Employees Compensation Act* and to be employed in the public service of Canada for the purposes of any regulations made under section 9 of the *Aeronautics Act*.

AGREEMENTS

26.   (1)   The Commission may enter into an agreement with the government of any province or territory to carry out its objects.
      (2)   If the agreement provides for the incorporation of a corporation or the acquisition of shares in a corporation or all or substantially all of the assets of a corporation, the Commission may, with the approval of the Governor in Council, do any of those things, either by itself or jointly with any person or the government of a province or a territory, in order to carry out the provisions of the agreement.
      (3)   A corporation mentioned in subsection (2) may carry out only activities that are consistent with the objects of the Commission, taking into account the restriction set out in subsections 6(2).

STAFF

27.   The Commission may engage any officers, employees and agents and any technical and professional advisers that it considers necessary for the proper conduct of its activities and may fix the terms and conditions of their engagement.

28.   When the Commission, outside Canada, engages persons referred to in section 27 to perform duties outside Canada, it shall engage them and establish their terms and conditions of employment or work, and the *Canada Labour Code* does not apply to those persons.

TRANSITIONAL PROVISIONS

INTERPRETATION

29.   The definitions in this section apply in this section and in sections 30 to 46.

"commencement day" means the day on which this Act comes into force.
"employee" means a person whose employment in the Department of Industry is terminated under paragraph 11(2)(*g*.1) of the *Financial Administration Act* and who is hired by the new Commission following an offer of employment made by the new

Commission as a result of the transfer of the work of the former Commission from the Department of Industry to the new Commission.

"former Commission" means the Canadian Tourism Commission established by Order in Council P.C. 1995-110 of January 31, 1995 and the associated Special Operating Agency created by decision of the Treasury Board.

"grievance" has the same meaning as in subsection 2(1) of the *Public Service Staff Relations Act.*

"new Commission" means the Canadian Tourism Commission established by section 3.

FORMER COMMISSION

30. (1) The former Commission is dissolved and its work is transferred from the Department of Industry to the new Commission.

     (2) For the purpose of section 40.1 of the *Public Service Superannuation Act*, the transfer of the work of the former Commission is deemed to be a transfer or divestiture, by Her Majesty in right of Canada, of the administration of a service to a person.

31. The person who holds the office of Chairperson of the former Commission immediately before the commencement day continues in office as the Chairperson of the new Commission for the remainder of the term for which the person was appointed Chairperson.

32. The person who holds the office of President of the former Commission immediately before the commencement day continues in office as the President of the new Commission for the remainder of the term for which the person was appointed President.

33. Each person who is a director of the former Commission immediately before the commencement day continues as a director of the new Commission for the remainder of the term for which the person was appointed as a director.

34. All property of Her Majesty in right of Canada that is under the administration and control of the Minister and used for the purpose of carrying out the objects of the former Commission is transferred to the new Commission to be held in the name of the new Commission.

35. All obligations and liabilities of Her Majesty in right of Canada incurred in respect of the former Commission are transferred to the new Commission.

36. Every reference to the former commission in a deed, contract or other document shall, unless the context otherwise requires, be read as a reference to the new commission.

37. (1) Any action, suit or other legal proceeding in respect of an obligation or a liability incurred in carrying out the objects of the former

Commission may be brought against the new Commission in any court that would have had jurisdiction if the action, suit or proceeding had been brought against Her Majesty in right of Canada.

(2) Any action, suit or other legal proceeding in respect of the former Commission that is pending in a court immediately before the commencement day may, on that day, be continued by or against the new Commission.

38. The amount outstanding on the commencement day in the accounts of Canada in respect of the carrying out of the objects of the former Commission shall be paid to the new Commission in the manner most appropriate to give effect to the purpose for which the moneys or property constituting or otherwise giving rise to that amount were given, bequeathed or otherwise made available to the former Commission.

39. Despite the period prescribed for submitting a corporate plan, an operating budget and a capital budget under the *Financial Administration Act*, the new Commission shall, within six months after the commencement day, submit to the Minister in accordance with that Act a corporate plan, an operating budget and a capital budget for its first financial year.

40. Any amount appropriated, for the fiscal year in which this section comes into force, by an appropriation Act based on the Estimates for that year for defraying the charges and expenses of the former Commission in carrying out its objects is an amount appropriated for defraying the charges and expenses of the new Commission.

HUMAN RESOURCES AND LABOUR RELATIONS

41. A competition being conducted or an appointment being or about to be made under the *Public Service Employment Act* in respect of a position within the Department of Industry, the duties and functions of which are assigned to a position within the new Commission, may continue to be conducted or made as if the new Commission were a department for the purposes of that Act.

42. An eligibility list made under the *Public Service Employment Act* in respect of a position within the Department of Industry related to the carrying out of the objects of the former Commission that is valid on the commencement day continues to be valid for the period provided for by subsection 17(2) of that Act, but that period may not be extended.

43. (1) An appeal made under section 21 of the *Public Service Employment Act* by any person against an appointment to a position within the Department of Industry the duties and functions of which are assigned to a position within the new Commission,

and not finally disposed of on the assignment, must be dealt with and disposed of in accordance with that Act as if the new Commission were a department for the purposes of that Act and the person continued to be an employee for the purposes of that Act.

(2) Any recourse commenced by an employee under the *Public Service Employment Act* that has not been finally dealt with on the employee's engagement by the new Commission must be dealt with and disposed of in accordance with that Act as if the new Commission were a department for the purposes of that Act and the person continued to be an employee for the purposes of that Act.

44. (1) Every employee who was considered to be on probation under section 28 of the *Public Service Employment Act* immediately before being engaged by the new Commission continues on probation with the new Commission until the end of the period established by the Public Service Commission by regulation for that employee or a class of persons of which that employee is a member.

(2) Subsection 28(2) of the *Public Service Employment Act* applies to an employee of the new commission who is on probation but the reference to deputy head in that subsection is to be read as a reference to the President.

45. (1) Any grievance commenced by an employee under the *Public Service Staff Relations Act* that has not been finally dealt with on the employee's engagement by the new Commission must be dealt with and disposed of in accordance with that Act as if the employee's employment in the Department of Industry had not been terminated.

(2) A final decision with respect to a grievance referred to in subsection (1) that provides for the reinstatement of or payment of money to a person must be implemented by the new Commission as soon as is practicable.

46. An indeterminate employee who was a member of the Executive Group in the Department of Industry and whose employment is terminated under paragraph 11(2)(*g*.1) of the *Financial Administration Act* is not eligible for benefits under the Treasury Board Executive Employment Transition Policy.

CONSEQUENTIAL AMENDMENTS

ACCESS TO INFORMATION ACT

47. **Schedule I to the *Access to Information Act* is amended by adding the following in alphabetical order under the heading "*Other Government Institutions*":**

Canadian Tourism Commission
Commission canadienne du tourisme

FEDERAL-PROVINCIAL FISCAL ARRANGEMENTS ACT

48. **Schedule I to the** *Federal-Provincial Fiscal Arrangement Act* **is amended by adding the following in alphabetical order:**
Canadian Tourism Commission
Commission canadienne du tourisme

FINANCIAL ADMINISTRATION ACT

49. **Part I of Schedule III to the** *Financial Administration Act* **is amended by adding the following in alphabetical order:**
Canadian Tourism Commission
Commission canadienne du tourisme

PRIVACY ACT

50. **The schedule to the** *Privacy Act* **is amended by adding the following in alphabetical order under the heading "Other Government Institutions":**
Canadian Tourism Commission
Commission canadienne du tourisme

COMING INTO FORCE

51. **This Act comes into force on a day to be fixed by order of the Governor in Council.**

References

Canadian Tourism Commission. (1999). *A Research and Development Program for Improved Tourism Industry Decision Making: A Technical Paper.* Canadian Tourism Commission, Ottawa.

Canadian Tourism Commission. (2002). *Strategic Plan 2002–2004: Overview.* Canadian Tourism Commission, Ottawa.

Canadian Tourism Commission. (2005). *Partnering Handbook: Partnering Business Processes.* Canadian Tourism Commission, Ottawa.

Canadian Tourism Commission. (2005). *Options for a Long-Term Funding Solution for the Canadian Tourism Commission.* Canadian Tourism Commission, Ottawa.

Canadian Tourism Commission. (2006). *2007–2011 Strategic Plan: Moving Forward with Vision.* Canadian Tourism Commission, Vancouver.

Edgell, Sr, David L. (2006). *Managing Sustainable Tourism: A Legacy for the Future*. The Haworth Hospitality Press, Binghamton, NY.

Goeldner, Charles A. and J.R. Brent Ritchie. (2006). *Tourism: Principles, Practices, Philosophies* (10th ed.). John Wiley and Sons, Hoboken, NJ.

Industry Canada. (1994). *Agenda: Jobs and Growth, Building a More Innovative Economy*. Minister of Supply and Services Canada, Ottawa.

Meis, Scott M. and Stephen Smith. (1996). 'The Transformation of Tourism Canada into the Canadian Tourism Commission', International Conference on Tourism. Institute of Tourism and Service Economics, International Center for Research and Education in Tourism, Vienna.

Ministry of State (Tourism). (1985). *Statement of Principle on Federal Provincial and Territorial Roles and Responsibilities in Respect of Tourism*. Minister of Supply and Services Canada, Ottawa.

Smith, S.L.J. and Scott Meis. (1997). The Canadian Tourism Commission. *Annals of Tourism Research*, 24, 481–483.

Webster's II New Riverside Dictionary, Revised Edition. (1996). Houghton Mifflin Company, Boston & New York, 522, 667.

10

Future world tourism policy issues

The road of life can only reveal itself as it is traveled; each turn in the road reveals a surprise. Man's future is hidden.

Source Unknown

According to most global forecasts, the future of the tourism industry will be one of change, vibrancy and growth. Tourism policy will be critical to economic prosperity, sustainable management and quality of life opportunities for most communities, destinations and countries of the world. A key to the prospective growth of tourism will be to ensure that careful planning and effective policies are in place. This chapter will introduce selected major tourism issues advocated by the co-authors that are important to an enduring tourism industry for the future. Each section identifies and briefly discusses an overarching tourism issue of important concern to the future.

Today's travellers demand high-quality tourism experiences, variety in their tourism products and a clean and healthy environment. This trend will certainly continue in the near future. Tourism policy will help to guide the planning functions and political goals in response to new trends as tourism grows. Without such guidance, tourism's future may not meet private and public expectations. Looking towards the future is an exercise in imagination and foresight. The American writer and humorist Mark Twain said, 'Prophecy is very difficult, especially with respect to the future'. The travel world of tomorrow will be different from what we know today and experienced yesterday.

Safety and security in tourism

The first item of universal concern is the relationship of tourism to terrorism or, in the larger context, safety and security. Safety and security in tourism will be the greatest challenge for tourism policy and planning for many years to come. Much of the discussion on safety and security is in response to terrorism. While terrorism has existed for a long time, the terrorism attacks in the United States on 11 September 2001 have been the rallying cry in terms of international and national tourism policies to counteract the impact of terrorism. The aftermath of this tragic event seemed to galvanize many nations to act together to meet the need for policy attention and action. The imprint of terrorism on tourism worldwide and subsequent terrorist acts has been devastating. Policy changes developed and implemented thus far are only the beginning. The global tourism industry will be facing the policy challenge of responding to the burden of terrorism on tourism for some time to come.

Safety and security, particularly from crime and terrorism, have been extremely important issues in the tourism industry for many decades. (Safety from disease and pandemics is also on the minds of travellers, and is discussed later in this chapter.) Since the 11 September 2001 terrorist attacks in the United States, there has been heightened awareness of the vulnerability of the global hospitality and tourism industry to the challenges of ever-changing world events. Data and research on tourism clearly support the adage, 'When peace prevails, tourism flourishes', but unfortunately, we are experiencing an increase of terrorism specifically targeting tourist destinations. Figure 10.1 shows the increasing trend of tourism as a terrorist target from 1970 to 2004. The peak of terrorism activity occurred in the early 1990s; and by 1993 there was a clear effort by the US Government and the private tourism sector to address this issue (See Appendix F). In this light, there are steps a destination can take to protect those who seek a peaceful visit.

Although major terrorist attacks in high-profile destinations such as New York, London, Madrid or Bali often receive the bulk of attention, such tragedies occur frequently in all parts of the world. Between 1970

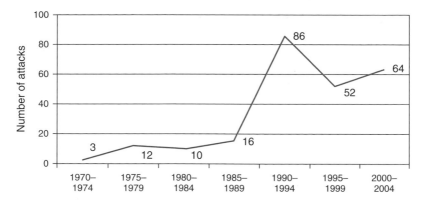

Figure 10.1 Terrorism attacks targeting tourism (1970–2004)
Source: Terrorism Knowledge Base (http://www.tkb.org)

and 2006, there have been 264 terrorism attacks, targeting tourism in 42 nations. Terrorists do strike in remote regions but, increasingly, terrorism occurs in popular tourist destination nations such as France and Spain, which rank worldwide as international tourism destinations and at the same time third and fourth in the number of terrorist occurrences during the past three decades. No area is invulnerable to the reach of terror, as shown in Figure 10.2.

General crimes against tourists such as robbery, murder and kidnapping are equally important concerns for destination planners. In many places, statistics regarding a victim's status as a resident or visitor are not regularly reported or collected by local police agencies. Nevertheless, when those crimes against tourists are featured in global media reports, the result is often detrimental to the overall image of the destination, despite the low-level of risk and number of actual offences (Figure 10.3).

To manage visitor safety and security and preserve the destination image, the South African government, for example, has created a National Tourism Safety Network, made up of key travel-related organizations. This stakeholder group has set a Tourism Safety Communication Strategy, which includes distributing tourism safety tips to visitors and handling crisis communications and management when incidents do occur. They also realize that terrorism activities in neighbouring countries can have a negative impact throughout the region or even throughout the continent.

Once seen as an encumbrance to travel, security measures are now endured, if not welcomed and demanded by travellers. Accordingly, safety and security must now be part of the destination development strategies for areas where the perception of terror and insecurity is indeed the reality in the mind of the visitor. The following list of important items to be included in a destination's security strategy is adapted from key points

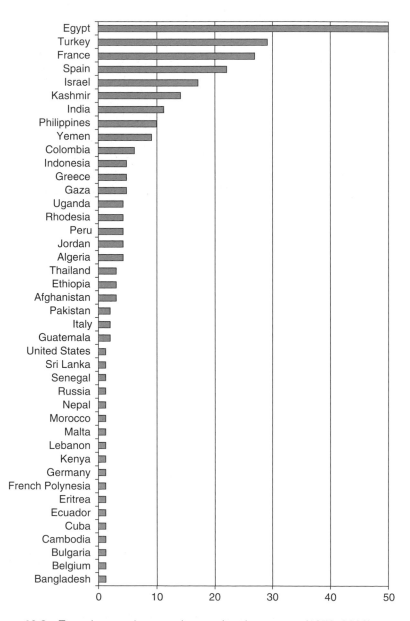

Figure 10.2 Terrorist attacks targeting tourism by country (1970–2006)
Source: Terrorism Knowledge Base (http://www.tkb.org)

Figure 10.3   Local police keep order in Cusco, Peru, during a protest by community members (Photo: Matt Schuttloffel)

proposed by Dr Peter Tarlow, a recognized expert on tourism and security concerns:

- Destinations and attractions must compete on their readiness to keep visitors safe and secure.
- Those destinations that provide sound security coupled with quality customer service will prosper.
- The lack of a comprehensive approach will create a false sense of security. For example, only having gas masks available for hotel guests may give false hopes if the hotel's water supply is poisoned.
- All members of the local tourism system should be included when developing a comprehensive tourism strategy.
- Media coverage of a local incident can spread the negative public relations effects to the entire continent.
- The safety development needs of all components of the visitor experience, including transportation infrastructure, accommodations, highway rest areas, food sources, should be assessed.
- Establish a place for visitors to turn to, if a terrorist attack were to occur, and openly communicate the location and purpose of the center in advance of any threats.

Global travel has increased despite the efforts of terrorists and criminals to disrupt the visitor experience. And while the attacks create obvious threats to the sustainability of any destination, safety and security issues can also create opportunities for destination planners; these come in the form of implementing strategies to add to the safety of an area with the hopes of mitigating future threats. Destinations able to leverage the power of tourism to offset the force of terrorism are those destinations where tourism will continue to flourish.

The impact of the world's economy on tourism

The world economy will have a major impact on the future of global travel. Individual country economies will continue to determine both domestic and international travel (discussed in detail in Chapter 4). With a vibrant world economy, more people will travel. In addition, if there is a greater individual country distribution of the country's wealth, more people will have the means to travel. Also related to the world economy is population growth. Accorded to the US Census Bureau 'World POPClock Projection', the world's current population is over 6.5 billion (accessed January 2007). The five most populous countries – China, India, the United States, Indonesia and Brazil – account for almost half of the world's population. If the economies of these five countries alone improve, as the estimates infer, global tourism will grow.

References show that tourism is a viable economic development tool and one that can be successfully used to alleviate poverty. Advancements in transportation eliminate some of the problems associated with reaching remote locations. Developing countries are cognizant of the added monetary incentives brought about by travel, and their economies are gaining these benefits. Lesser developed countries also recognize the important contributions the tourism industry makes, namely in the start-up of small, economically viable local industries, many of which employ women. The United Nations World Tourism Organization (UNWTO) highlights the 'added value' tourism offers such areas as the Iberoamerican countries and Africa as examples of developing and underdeveloped areas in addition to the Maldives, Nepal and Pacific island nations. 'The total tourist arrivals by region shows that by 2020 the top three receiving regions will be Europe (717 million tourists), East Asia and the Pacific (397 million) and the Americas (282 million), followed by Africa, the Middle East and South Asia. East Asia and the Pacific, South Asia, the Middle East and Africa are forecast to record growth at rates of over 5 per cent per year, compared to the world average of 4.1 per cent' (UNWTO, 2006). The following table is a projection by the UNWTO of international arrivals into the year 2020 (Table 10.1).

Tourism is often the first, second or third largest industry in many countries and nations; and its influence is felt not only in monetary measurements, but also in added non-monetary benefits. Summarily, tourism

Table 10.1 International arrivals into the year 2020

World	Base year 1995	Forecasts (million)		Market share (%)		Average annual growth rate (%)
		2010	2020	1995	2020	1995–2020
	565	1006	1561	100	100	4.1
Africa	20	47	77	3.6	5.0	5.5
Americas	110	190	282	19.3	18.1	3.8
East Asia and the Pacific	81	195	397	14.4	25.4	6.5
Europe	336	527	717	59.8	45.9	3.1
Middle East	14	36	69	2.2	4.4	6.7
South Asia	4	11	19	0.7	1.2	6.2

Source: UNWTO, Tourism 2020 Vision.

provides an avenue to foster broader cultural understanding, increases coopetition between the public and private sectors, boosts the economy of developing countries and can alleviate poverty and its associated conditions.

In a press release by the UNWTO on 2 January 2007, global tourism growth is expected to rise 4 per cent. UNWTO strongly encouraged tourism growth 'to the world's poorest countries to advance economic well being, social development and mutual understanding'. UNWTO also asked 'International Development Agencies – the World Bank Group, the Regional Development Banks and National Aid Agencies, to place tourism amongst their key priorities for infrastructure and entrepreneurial support'. In addition, if other regional organizations such as the Organisation for Economic Cooperation and Development, Organization of American States, Asia Pacific Economic Cooperation, Caribbean Tourism Organization and others will put economic development through tourism as a high priority, many countries' economies will be strengthened.

Managing sustainable tourism responsibly

The third key issue is managing sustainable tourism and doing so responsibly (see Chapter 6 for a broader discussion of sustainable tourism). The importance of sustainable tourism is paramount today and will be, also, tomorrow. Measures to educate the tourism enterprises, the host communities and travelling population about sustainable tourism must be continued as world populations increase. Respect for our natural and built environments today will be our historical legacy for future generations. Sustainable tourism has been an issue of concern for destination planning and regional and national policymaking for some time. This interest has produced many different ways of looking at sustainability in the tourism industry. In the last few years, there have been more books produced related to sustainable tourism than were available in the previous 25 years. There are dozens of conferences across the globe each year, with sustainable tourism as the central theme. These efforts will continue, and we can expect new and innovative approaches to planning with resulting policy changes in the field of sustainable tourism (Figure 10.4).

While there has been considerable attention given to the importance of sustainable tourism in a previous chapter of this book, the importance of managing the cultural, natural and social impacts of tourism cannot be overemphasized. Enhancing understanding among nations and promoting a culture of peace will assist in seeing that improved and sustainable tourism development can take place. In addition, the aspects of the environment and local culture will benefit as government revenues from tourism-related goods and services help visibly to restore monuments, open museums, make possible art galleries, increase local crafts and establish national parks.

Figure 10.4 Visitors to the volcano Villa Rica in Pucon, Chile, climb to the peak in a controlled and orderly fashion in order to balance visitor enjoyment with environmental protection (Photo: J.R. Gast)

As tourism grows, so does the need for tourism policy and planning to help guide the development of infrastructure. The building of new airports, roads, ports and sewage and water treatment plants improves the lives of the local people when implemented through well-planned policies and urban planning with sustainable tourism in mind. In brief, the concept of sustainable tourism development has become better understood as an outcome of viable policy and planning aimed at encouraging economic and social responsibilities for preserving and enhancing our cultural and environmental heritage through tourism.

Sometimes the presumption is that sustainable tourism's impact chiefly affects ecotourism, adventure tourism and other nature tourism-related activities. Certainly, these components of sustainable tourism have become important for many travelers, but they are only part of the larger concept of sustainable tourism. Throughout the world, many local destination managers and governments are acknowledging the monetary value of tourism, resulting in demands for new measures to support sustainable tourism practices. Can the destination feasibly support more people? Can the local populace provide the workforce and have access to affordable housing near their places of work. Can the infrastructure uphold an increase of usage? Fortunately, there is active dialogue occurring worldwide to address these and other questions, such as the discussions that have taken place in the **Destinations2006** summit. It is critically important to insure that the host population and the local tourism organization, as well as the tourist, are informed of the importance sustainable tourism provides the community. Adopting a 'good neighbor' policy may sound simplistic, but there is reasonable cause to do so.

At the country level, the UNWTO has provided many guidelines and directions for incorporating sustainability of tourism in an area's tourism programme. Likewise, the industry has explored numerous options for implementing sustainable tourism. Some global, private sector organizations, such as the World Travel and Tourism Council, Business Enterprises for Sustainable Travel-Education Network (BEST-EN) and others, have outlined effective strategies for sustainable tourism education and development. Universities worldwide have taken on the challenge and made sustainable tourism a major part of their higher education programmes, such as East Carolina University's 2006 announcement of the formation of a multidisciplinary 'Center for Sustainable Tourism', reporting directly to the Vice Chancellor for Research and Graduate Studies.

An imaginative, interesting example of sustainable tourism that will soon occur is that of Guilin, China. This beautiful and outstanding scenic destination is to be the location for the first UNWTO observatory to carry out a monitoring system for sustainable development of tourism. With support and guidance from UNWTO, the Guilin City Council and Zhongshan University will manage the project.

In sum, the tourism industry can ill afford to create further issues jeopardizing the environment. The global population is already contending with the negative consequences of misuse of our environment, unwise past public and private sector policies regarding energy resources and overpopulation. Sustainable destination management within the tourism industry can augment global societies and contribute to protection of tourism resources for future generations.

Tourism policy and strategic planning

Early in the book, tourism policy was defined as 'a progressive course of actions, guidelines, directives, principles, and procedures set in an ethical framework that is issues-focused and best represents the intent of a community (or nation) to effectively meet its planning, development, product, service, marketing, and sustainability goals and objectives for the future growth of tourism'. Tourism policy and strategic planning should ideally start at the local level and flow towards broad guidelines for use at different levels of government and for destinations and communities to improve the quality of life of the local citizenry (see Chapters 1, 2 and 9 for detailed discussions of tourism policy and planning). Issues of terrorism, however, global warming and other broad concerns will first need the attention at the country or global level before flowing to individual communities and destinations. Such policies should be research-based and lead to actions and solutions as applications become a reality throughout the tourism industry.

The global tourism industry faces many concerns over the coming decades, and quite certainly, tourism policy and strategic planning will drive many of the dynamics of tourism well into the future. We can expect to see a greater global focus on the tourism industry's potential for growth. In tandem, sustainable benefits of tourism for local communities will continue to grow in priority and importance. There will be greater efforts towards partnerships of the private and public sectors in facilitating tourism in combination with poverty alleviation, developing policies to combat negative impacts on tourism and supporting the economic, socio-cultural and environmental contributions of tourism for the benefit of world citizens.

In *Tourism Principles, Practices, Philosophies* (Tenth Edition) it states that 'Good policy and sound planning need to be conducted to ensure that a destination will be both competitive and sustainable. . . . It should be noted that the definitions and distinctions related to policy, strategy, goals, objectives, and planning are ongoing sources of debate in the management literature'. The key concept is that while policies generally reflect the 'big picture' and plans contain the detail, they both deal with the future development of tourism.

Developing new tourism projects, maintaining present destinations, and improving travel related facilities and services requires comprehensive policies and detailed plans that combine local needs, market competitiveness, and tourism sustainability. Those destinations, localities, and nations that prepare good policies and implement detailed strategic plans will reap the benefits for sustaining their tourism products in the future. When the policies and plans are multidisciplinary to include all aspects of tourism and foster the concept of coopetition, the opportunities for future success are greatly enhanced.

Utilizing e-commerce tools in tourism

Utilizing e-commerce tools in tourism is at the threshold in terms of its impact on the tourism industry. More than 50 per cent of travellers in the United States use the Internet in planning their travel and vacations. This phenomenon is growing globally. In addition, if a destination does not have a good Web site, it will likely miss tourism traffic. A positive feature in developing a destination Web site is that developers can find good Web sites that are similar to their destinations and copy the best features. 'Copy, copy, and copy' will be the protocol for Web site design in the immediate future.

As Internet access continues to increase in many nations, so will online travel revenues. The number of Internet users around the world is estimated to be 747 million in 2007, a 10 per cent increase over 2006. The bulk of this growth is attributed to the expanding economies of India (33 per cent), Russia (21 per cent) and China (20 per cent). In India, online travel revenues are projected to reach US $2 billion by 2010. This will represent an increase of over 270 per cent from 2005 revenues. To capitalize on this trend, Travelocity has expanded their operations by opening up a new office in India.

It is obvious that the use of e-commerce tools for tourism will continue to grow and occupy a high-level placement in tourism policy, planning and marketing discussions in the future. Several e-commerce tools equip tourism well for what surely will be a high-tech future. Information is a critical marketing tool for tourism destinations, and providing it to the traveller most effectively provides a strategic advantage. Tourism is an experience – a combination of products and services – the multimedia attributes of electronic commerce can be effectively applied to tourism in cutting-edge ways to increase destination attractiveness. Since a large part of tourism is marketing, tourism promoters who are technically savvy in interactive marketing will outpace less skilled competitors. Among emerging e-commerce tools, weblogs, podcasts and targeted Internet marketing are discussed below.

Weblogs

E-commerce tools not only connect consumers with suppliers but also create bridges among consumers and provides avenues for information exchange. Arguably, word-of-mouth travel accounts may be the best form of advertising for tourism businesses. Considering this, the global community of 'weblogs' ('blogs'), also known as the 'blogosphere', creates an opportunity and a challenge for tourism professionals to influence the perspectives of an increasingly interconnected consumer base.

In late 2006, there were more than 55 million blogs on the Internet – many of them containing visitor impressions about destinations worldwide. According to the Pew Internet & American Project (2006) survey, there are roughly 12 million bloggers in the United States alone. The median age is less than 30 years old, and approximately half live in suburban areas outside of major cities. A single visitor's unfortunate tourism experience can quickly be spread through sites such as vagabonding.com, globalwalk.org, hobotraveler.com, worldnomads.com, realtravel.com, and hundreds of others. Of course, the opposite is true as well – these virtual ambassadors often spread good will. Accordingly, in the light of an increasingly communicative and networked electronic travel landscape, the most important marketing expense may be money spent on quality assurance.

Blogs provide a new twist to the power of word-of-mouth travel information. Bloggers transform the communication landscape as Gutenberg and Marconi did centuries before in their development of the printing press and telegraph. In order to capitalize on this movement, tourism planners must be innovative in their promotion strategies. The possibilities include advertising on popular blogs, hosting key bloggers who write positively about travel, and even starting their own blogs to promote the destination.

Tourism businesses are using the Internet as an interactive medium. Starwood is taking advantage of this by sponsoring www.thelobby.com, where Starwood Preferred Guests can follow the latest travel trends. Several travel writers post daily travel-related blogs to which consumers can respond. The site supplies and solicits information.

Podcasts

A 'podcast' is a video or audio show that can be downloaded to a personal computer or iPod, Apple Computer's portable entertainment device. Not only are songs, books, movies and television shows available for download, but commercials for tourism destinations or visitor itineraries can be downloaded as well. Many destinations are also utilizing this medium by providing 'downloadable' narrative tours.

The initial tourism-related podcasts, distributed by such Web sites as http://journeypod.com, feature hip and trendy attractions in the popular destinations of Miami, Los Angeles, New York and Paris. The site also features restaurant reviews and secret 'hot spots' that may not be included in conventional itineraries but have been discovered by individual travellers. These activities and destinations match the demographics of the 'iPod generation'.

Similar to weblogs, some tourism podcasts can also be controlled by the consumer, instead of the destination management organization's marketing staff. This points out the importance of ensuring the overall quality of the visitor experience as information is disseminated beyond the control of destination marketers.

Internet marketing

The Internet has put large and small players on equal footing in many cases. Kamel and El Sherif (2001) researched e-commerce in Egyptian tourism and found that small- and medium-sized local, unaffiliated hotels are beginning to be able to compete on a global scale with multinational chains, such as Marriott or Sheraton. Used as a competitive tool, Internet marketing helped the King Hotel, a family owned 90-unit lodge in Cairo, capture additional demand from the United States, Hungary, Jordan and the United Kingdom. The hotel pursued this strategy because of global information diffusion, visibility generation, increasing responsiveness to customers, the ability to build a community of customers, cost reduction and improved profitability. In this case, the money invested by the hotel in the Internet marketing initiative was recovered within 3 weeks after launch through increased bookings. This is an example of the big power afforded to small tourism businesses competing in a global tourism marketplace.

Tourism marketing becomes personal via the Internet as Internet marketers use 'cookies' to personalize online advertisements. Cookies are small text files that stay in a computer's random access memory and are used by Web sites to store a user's preferences and have these selections open quickly when called upon in the future. Advertisers also use cookies to target ads based on users' interests as determined by their online habits. Based on Web users' previous choice of sites and online purchases, Internet advertisers can direct unique ads to all Web site users. Hypothetically, a person who participates in online gaming can be shown ads for

Atlantic City when visiting the New Jersey state tourism Web site. Or if a person has previously visited several sports-related Web sites, then ads for the Meadowland Sports Complex may be shown on the same New Jersey tourism Web site. These advertisements would be different although the two users would be viewing the same page on the same site (http://Webstreetstudios.com).

Although the interactions between business and consumer, or destination and visitor, are becoming less personal, tourism still exists in what might be called the relationship economy. While the Internet gives the power to the consumer, strategic advantages will be gained by those organizations who can effectively utilize technology to create and nurture relationships. As slow-movers catch up to fast-movers, new technological advances must be constantly pursued in order for any advantage to be maintained. The future will include increased use of content customization based on visitor research. A proactive e-commerce strategy is crucial for tourism businesses to enjoy sustained success.

Tourism education and training

Tourism education and training has blossomed as a tourism issue around the world (see Chapter 7 for a broader discussion of tourism education and training). Numerous innovations are taking place at some universities. For example, the University of the Balearic Islands (Majorca, Spain) has a Master and PhD in Tourism and Environmental Economics that is truly unique with students from many different countries. It is a well-designed global program offering a wide range of courses. More than 50 visiting professors from different countries with unique backgrounds teach in the programme. Globalization and innovation will be the hallmark of tourism education and training in the future.

Increased requirements and opportunities for education and training for individuals within the tourism industry are direct and critical responses to these growth trends. As noted in Chapter 7, many initiatives and changes are already taking place. New trends include collaborative organizations, which link traditional competitors (educators at various colleges and universities) while attempting to address the changing needs of the industry. BEST EN (Business Enterprises for Sustainable Travel – Education Network) is one example of this new affiliation – this one between tourism businesses and academic education institutions. This group holds annual international tourism and hospitality education 'think tanks', combined with research conferences, at various locations worldwide in which research is presented, sustainable tourism topics are addressed and a research agenda and curriculum modules for use in undergraduate education are developed. In the research sessions, participants present papers and identify knowledge gaps in the multiple sectors or fields of sustainable tourism that are in need of further investigation. The resulting curricular modules are designed for inclusion in existing traditional tourism and hospitality education courses and programmes around the world. This focus allows for the promotion and sharing of the latest best thinking and practices in tourism education. Outdated concepts can be retired quickly as educational leaders, through the BEST EN process, identify the declining use and viability of various models and readily share viewpoints and collaborate in the creation of sustainable best practices across all sectors. The results can then be included in education curricula and presented in classes to upcoming managers in the tourism and hospitality industry today and for the future.

Other important current and future trends in tourism education and training are closely tied to globalization and political stability. Bremmer (2006, p. 277) states, 'Openness enables change. Change is an essential ingredient in growth and prosperity. Only the free exchange of information, values, ideas, and people can build a sustainable global stability that enriches all who take part in it'. This can best happen with the continued reduction of barriers to the flow of international tourism education and training. Today's international students will be leaders of their countries tomorrow, and all will leave their host countries having contributed to and gained intercultural understanding and appreciation (Washington Post).

With 234 million international jobs today created through the provision of travel and tourism products and services, a highly educated workforce is essential to the global tourism industry's continued growth and success. Marriott International recently announced a major expansion in the global marketplace, with the addition of more than 30,000 new hotel rooms in countries such as India and China, along with 'tens of thousands of rooms added [through acquisitions] to its U.S. and Canada portfolio... China is expected to lead the world in tourism growth through 2016. Marriott International currently has 30 hotels in China' (Wilmeth, 2006, p. 23). An undisputed world leader in quality hospitality products and services, Marriott will also undoubtedly be investing millions of dollars in the education and training of its existing and newly recruited international workforce to meet this global growth strategy. 'The lodging industry is a global business and three factors dominate it: global wealth, demographics and trade', said Chairman and CEO J.W. Marriott, Jr (Wilmeth). To these factors, the co-authors would add a fourth – a world-class quality service workforce – and this requires a commitment to outstanding international tourism and hospitality education and training.

Emerging tourism markets

The seventh issue relates to emerging tourism markets. Two of the emerging tourism markets to watch in the near future are China and India which together account for about one-third of the world's population. Each country's economy is literally exploding, and at the same time, a greater segment of the population is sharing in the economic gains and anxious to travel. Both countries are emerging as important receiving and generating countries for tourism. Russia could also become an important player as a country generating and receiving tourists in the future (Figure 10.5).

In terms of arrivals and receipts, Europe continues to account for about one-half of the world's tourism market. Asia and the Pacific have been the fastest growing regional market, surpassing the Americas; and there is every reason to believe that this region's percentage growth will continue. The Americas market will still hold strong as far as international tourism receipts are concerned, largely due to the combined influences of the United States, Canada and Mexico. In terms of major generating (and receiving) countries, the United States and much of Europe will continue to produce millions of tourists each year.

One country recognizing that tourism will be a key economic driving force in the future is the United Arab Emirates (UAE). This small country traditionally has been economically dependent solely on its petroleum industry; but a few years ago, the UAE made the policy decision to launch one of the biggest efforts in the world to become a global tourism destination. The first major indoor ski slope became available in 2006, in Dubai, in line with that nation's stated intention to launch many new tourism products over the next several years.

Figure 10.5 With new inbound destinations emerging in India and other areas, careful planning must take place as old world traditions meet modern demands (Photo: J.R. Gast)

Another oil-rich nation turning to tourism is Gabon, Africa. Gabon's leaders also recognized that its economic future cannot depend only on oil and made the policy decision to develop ecotourism as an alternative to the petroleum industry. Their plan: 11 per cent of the country will become national parks with a heavy emphasis on outdoor-related tourism.

A continent that offers tremendous potential for future tourism development is South America. This region of the world, as far as tourism is concerned, is still largely undeveloped and its opportunities for tourism development abound. If strong policies and plans are put in place for sustainable tourism development, South America could emerge as an important tourism market.

Quality tourism products and experiences

As mentioned earlier in this book, tourists are demanding greater variety, flexibility and quality in their tourism products. Quality tourism experiences are, and will continue to remain, an important tourism issue for the future. Tourists are somewhat fickle, in that their demands for tourism products are constantly changing; however, quality in tourism experiences is usually high on their list.

One service category in travel that seems to receive large numbers of complaints in terms of quality is air travel. Air travel remains a contentious travel issue as far as quality is concerned. Mature travelers experienced higher quality airline services in the 1970s and 1980s and are not generally very happy with air travel today (although from an economic perspective, air travel is relatively less expensive today than it was in the 1970s and 1980s). This situation is manifesting itself in travellers' more frequently driving to destinations they formerly flew to visit.

In the future, the number and variety of new tourism products will change. Adventure travel (jungle tours, safaris, trekking and underwater exploration) to space travel is on the immediate horizon. (Figure 10.6.) There will be no shortage of activities for the active traveller. Planning for new or improved tourism products will be critical. India, for example, recognizes that health care is the fastest growing global industry and tourism, the second fastest, has developed hotel-style health care centres. The family of the patient (and sometimes the patient too) is able to stay in beautiful surroundings and encouraged to participate in tourism-related activities.

Tourists are expressing a desire for a clean environment, more nature-based tourism and cultural tourism. Tomorrow's traveller will be better informed than today's regarding tourism destinations as e-commerce

Figure 10.6   Ecological camps, such as this one in Peru, cater to higher-end adventure travellers interested in both quality and conservation (Photo: Matt Schuttloffel)

tools are used more effectively in the planning of travel. As a result, the future of tourism is going to be greatly dependent on the introduction of new quality tourism products and experiences. Destinations offering high-quality tourism products will reap the benefits.

Regarded as this century's newest tourism product, space tourism will grow dramatically as soon as the price becomes more reasonable. (Currently, a space trip package is priced at about US $20 million.) Dennis Tito, a US businessman, became the first tourist to outer space in 2001, travelling in a Russian space shuttle to the International Space Station. In 2002, Mark Shuttleworth, a South African Internet entrepreneur, paid US $20 million to Russia's space agency for a trip to the International Space Station on a Soyuz rocket. In 2005, US scientist and millionaire Gregory Olsen paid US $20 million to Russia for a 'space flight' (a term he preferred over 'space tourist'). The first female space tourist, US entrepreneur Anousheh Ansari, was accompanied by a US-Russian crew on the Soyuz TMA-9 capsule in 2006. She, too, paid US $20 million for the trip. Riding in a Russian Soyuz capsule in April 2007, Charles Simonyi, an American billionaire, paid US $25 million for a 2-week trip to the International Space Station.

In the not-too-distant future, Russia may begin offering trips around the moon for US $100 million. It appears thus far that Russia is the only nation with an effective 'space tourism policy' – e.g. for US $20 million dollars or more, you can join Russian cosmonauts on their journey to the International Space Station or perhaps beyond. The US government is more conservative in its approach to space tourism. If a private firm is willing to facilitate and accept all liabilities, policy legislation is in place that will allow it. As space tourism grows, the need for more defined tourism policy and planning will follow.

While space tourism is capturing current headlines, undersea tourism is emerging as a tourist market that likely will expand in the future. Exploring the oceans' bottoms is an expensive undertaking, although not as costly as space tourism. Undersea tourism will grow once new technology for exploration becomes available to mainstream tourists. (Again, it appears that Russia is leading the way in offering tourists underwater experiences.)

Another relatively new global tourism product that appears to be gaining great interest is 'volunteer vacations'. The year 2006 witnessed more than 6 per cent of the world's population undertaking a vacation to help less fortunate people or to support a humanitarian cause (Figure 10.7).

At the same time these new tourism products are appearing, traditional tourism products will continue to grow, provided they offer tourists what they want and maintain a certain quality standard. Five simple examples in the midwestern region of the United States making this special connection to tourism follow. The key to the future of these and other locations will be in maintaining and developing quality tourism products.

The community of Dubois, Wyoming, along the Wind River continues to be an appealing destination, especially for those who enjoy adventure, recreation, fishing, hunting and leisure travel. Each Fourth of July, the roads are blocked off (including the highway running through the middle of town) so that the community and visitors can enjoy a fun-filled day of special celebrations, parades, and good homemade food – cultural tourism at its best. The Rustic Pine Tavern, the Cowboy Café, and other

IIPT Credo of the Peaceful Traveler

Grateful for the opportunity to travel and experience the world because peace begins with the individual, I affirm my personal responsibility and commitment to:

- Journey with an open mind and gentle heart
- Accept with grace and gratitude the diversity I encounter
- Revere and protect the natural environment which sustains all life
- Appreciate all cultures I discover
- Respect and thank my hosts for their welcome
- Offer my hand in friendship to everyone I meet
- Support travel services that share these views and act upon them and,
- By my spirit, words and actions, encourage others to travel the world in peace

Source: **International Institute for Peace Through Tourism**

Figure 10.7 The IIPT Credo of the peaceful traveller

establishments in Dubois offer up fond memories for the visitors and town folk as well.

The farming community of Stockton, Kansas, is realizing that its economic survival depends on hunting and fishing tourism. Stockton goes out of its way to welcome hunters in the fall and winter as their expenditures on services, products, food, entertainment and accommodations help the community survive economically throughout the year. With several lakes nearby, fishing is likely to add to the economy of this farming village.

Kansas City, Kansas, is becoming a strong tourism destination, rivalling its bigger neighbour, Kansas City, Missouri. A few years ago, the community convinced NASCAR (National Association for Stock Car Auto Racing) to locate there and build a track with a seating capacity of 75,000 people. This was the impetus for many additional attractions, and the community is now one of the most visited in the Midwest.

Vandalia, Illinois, a community dependent in the past on agriculture-related industry, recognized that it needed additional products to survive economically. Its strong connection to the early history of the state as the first capital, and where Abraham Lincoln developed his political skills that carried him to the White House, now promotes its Lincoln connection. The State Capital building and grounds are a viable tourism product, expected to grow in the future.

An interesting and beautiful sustainable tourism destination is Green Lake, Wisconsin. While much of the tourism product is related to the attractive emerald colored lake, hence, Green Lake, with its abundant variety of fish and plant life, there are also tremendous opportunities for hiking, biking and bird watching. This tranquil setting of lush forests and exquisite flora and fauna make this area a true nature-based tourism product.

Partnerships and strategic alliances in tourism

Tourism-based partnerships and strategic alliances are an important and growing aspect of the tourism industry's future development and need to be addressed in policy and planning discussions. A form of partnership discussed earlier in the book and well suited to tourism is coopetition. Within the public–private partnership arena, new partnerships are occurring regularly, such as the one between the UNWTO and the Meetings Industry announced 28 November 2006, in which the United Nations Tourism Satellite Account will now measure the Meeting Industry's global economic contribution. Other partnerships are initiating the use of coopetition with good results, and the opportunities available are unlimited.

One recognizable form of coopetition is the rewarding of frequent travellers with 'points' for use with car rental companies, hotels, airlines and other components of the industry. Hotels that have a strategic alliance with certain airlines will give the visitor points for room nights spent at the hotel, which accumulate and are then redeemable for free airline tickets or upgrades, or for use in booking future hotel rooms. A major partner in the 'rewards' programme is the credit card companies that award points for each dollar spent (using their card) for tourism-related services. There appears to be no abatement in these programmes; in fact, most are growing even though there is a heavy administrative cost for the partners. These companies believe customer loyalty and marketing data generated are worth the involved costs.

Tourism partnerships are a form of cooperation to facilitate often competitive but nonetheless mutual interests. They occur on many levels – local, state/provincial, regional, national and/or international – and can be any combination of private and/or public sector entities. Two key words are 'responsibility' and 'collaboration', for it is through connectivity that advantages are gained, and successful partnerships are formed. These partnerships in turn leverage their power to exert forces in the travel and tourism market place.

A best practices example of tourism partnerships was initiated less than a month following the terrorist attacks in the United States on 11 September 2001. The World Travel & Tourism Council (WTTC) organized a *Declaration of Global Travel and Tourism Associations* of '... leading associations from around the world ... to form a global coalition for travel and tourism to work collectively to promote the interests of the global economy, our industry and the millions of people involved in travel and tourism. All of us ... collectively form one of the largest industries in the world and a major contributor to the global economy' (WTTC, 2001, para 4).

Such tourism partnerships can create and enhance products, public policy and the industry's image. Partnerships can lead to innovative thinking across tourism industry sectors, as its members seek to improve existing market conditions and meet demonstrated needs. In response to an upturn in the number of families accompanying business travellers, Loews Hotels and the Fisher-Price, Inc., toy company have partnered successfully to offer a travel package attractive to families with younger children, called 'Loews Loves Little Kids presented by Fisher-Price®'. The travel product created by this partnership highlights the under-10-year-old traveller and features age-appropriate gift toys upon arrival, early development play classes, the loan of necessary baby equipment and child-friendly in-room mini-bars. This partnership creates both a new product and new jobs.

The formation of strategic alliances comes about when tourism industry sectors connected by a common thread – such as a market opportunity or threat to market stability such as a war or terrorism event – recognize the need for joining for their mutual benefit. The participants are empowered as they move away from competing against one another to operating together for the benefit of the tourism-based strategic alliance itself and the overall national or local economy. Strategic alliances, just like tourism partnerships, can occur on many levels.

The Tourism Industry Association of Nova Scotia (TIANS) recognizes the power of such alliances and has on its Web site, http://www.tians.org, information on three strategic alliances formed by Nova Scotia's tourism operators:

1.   The Adventure Tourism Association of Nova Scotia
2.   The Campground Owners Association of Nova Scotia
3.   The Nova Scotia Bed and Breakfast Association.

TIANS goes on to say, 'These groups play a necessary and important role in developing a strong business sector within the larger tourism industry. TIANS assists these groups by providing secretariat duties, meeting facilitation, advocacy support, and membership development'.

Through strategic alliances in tourism, the tourism industry can maximize its usage of outsourcing, especially in the areas of cost effectiveness/reduction and brand loyalty. Outsourcing can provide the means to provide up-to-the-minute information on flights, weather, availability, crisis management or whatever service or information demand the travelling customer may have. Interactive, multilingual communication offered 24/7 assists the space tourist of the future as well as the family planning a weeklong trip to a national park. In other words, partnerships and alliances in the tourism industry assist in the creation of alternative companies and service providers. Coopetition can fuel competitive yet cooperative relationships encouraging both new companies and well-known, established organizations to explore growth and expansion of industry-driven tourism products and services.

The impact of health issues/natural disasters/climate change on tourism

The volume ends with discussions of global health issues, natural disasters and climate change as extremely critical and worrisome issues in their potential impact on tourism. Fortunately, there is a substantive and growing body of literature forthcoming from numerous experts on these topics such that our discussions here need serve only as signposts to the future.

Health issues and tourism

With respect to health concerns, most travellers avoid areas that have high health risks. In addition, the likelihood that travellers can spread epidemics of certain diseases is a constant concern. Policymakers across the globe are concerned about the potential disastrous effects that avian flu could produce.

It is well documented that diseases spread more rapidly due to travel, especially through international aviation. Reports released by Harvard Researchers indicate the flu virus is spreading more rapidly due to international business and leisure tourism, and especially air travel. With the potential and lethal spread of avian or bird flu into pandemic levels now of global concern, international travel and tourism's public, private and non-government organizations must take leading roles in the development and support of tourism health measures and safeguards.

Fear of disease reduces travel demand. AIDS was originally brought to the United States and Canada by a flight attendant, who contracted the disease in Africa. Other examples include SARS, which spread rapidly throughout Asia and Canada, and foot and mouth disease that spread from the UK to continental Europe. Due to the SARS scare (which came on the heels of terrorism and a war), the hotel occupancy rate across Hong Kong plummeted to 5 per cent, in contrast to the usual 82 per cent. Following the outbreak of SARS and subsequent travel advisories from the World Health Organization (WHO), four Asian destinations suffered in particular – China, Hong Kong, Vietnam, and Singapore. 'The impact of SARS on these countries has been four or five times the impact of September 11 [2001] in the States', says Rick Miller, vice-president of research and economics at the WTTC (Clark, 2003, para 5). When an outbreak of foot and mouth disease occurred in the UK, it was estimated that the tourist sector lost between £2.7 and £3.2 billion in 2001, due to postponement and cancellation of trips (Watkiss, 2002, p. 1).

Policymakers now need to react to health crises in their own countries as well as to formulate strategies to react and provide support to the WHO and individual nations recommending restricted travel to affected countries. This will pose new challenges as disease-related issues may quickly negate costly marketing campaigns needed to generate a positive response. This also creates a quandary for tourism officials, who must protect their guests while generating or maintaining positive views on the affected destination's safety. A troubling case underscores the gravity of adequate coordination between international tourism policy and planning and global health issues. Andrew Speaker, a 31-year-old lawyer from Atlanta, Georgia, USA, was permitted to travel worldwide on commercial flights while infected with what at the time was thought to be extensively drug-resistant tuberculosis (XDR-TB). This deadly form of TB, declared a global emergency in fall 2006 by the World Health Organization, and other common and highly contagious diseases such as polio, syphillis, measles, and cholera are making a comeback in infection rates worldwide in part due to the growth of international transportation, a major sector in global tourism.

On the other side of the health issue, destinations are now promoting the health benefits of travel. According to survey results, '95 million visits are made to spas in the United States annually generating $5 billion in revenues. Spas generate more in revenue than ski resorts ($3.1 billion) and only slightly less than box office receipts ($7.5 billion)' (Lanier, 2006, para 1). 'The U.S. spa industry generated an estimated $11.2 billion in revenues in 2003. On average, half (52 per cent) of a spa's revenue is derived from treatment rooms. Resort/hotel spas, despite the size of the segment, account for an impressive 41 per cent of industry revenue while the largest segment, day spas, accounts for just under half – 49 per cent' (Locker, 2004, para 7). In other words, health tourism consumers are attracted to the relaxation, rejuvenation and quasi-medical treatments they receive and, in many cases, to significant cost savings over similar healthcare expenses for comparable services in their own countries of origin.

In another rapidly growing industry, countries all over the world are touting their surgical centres, particularly those providing cosmetic surgery. Aimed at combining surgery and a long, often exotic vacation, travellers return home looking younger and refreshed. According to the American Society for Plastic Surgeons, complex issues surround medical treatments in non-native countries. Difficulty in assessing surgeons' credentials, potential complications (arising from infection, haematomas, patient dissatisfaction and combining surgery with travel) and follow-up care and monitoring are the main concerns (http://www.plasticsurgery.org/news_room/Cosmetic-Surgery-Tourism-Briefing-Paper.cfm, 2005).

As more countries strive to attract this lucrative health tourism business, tourism professionals will need to partner with other government workers to plan courses of action addressing the development and implementation of health tourism policies.

Effects of natural disasters on tourism

The environment today is, and will continue to be, a primary focus for the tourism industry. Natural disasters have always had large and often devastating impacts on the tourism industry. People avoid travel to affected regions, which, in turn, precludes the recovery of the industry suffering major long-term infrastructure damage. Once this occurs, there is limited opportunity to use tourism as an economic engine to restart the economy or to obtain much-needed new currency to reinvest in the locale, in the tourism and hospitality industry and in the well-being of local people.

Airline disruptions caused by storms effect delays and cancellations in weather-affected locations. To add to these problems, affected airlines suffer further negative economic impacts as delays and groundings cause air-planes to be misallocated for the start of the next round of flights. 'US Air-ways alone had more than 11,000 flights delayed during the last two weeks of June because of bad weather. That represented 40 per cent of its opera-tions. Weather has presented the most challenging operations that we have had since 2004', said spokesperson Phil Gee (Wilkening, July 2006, para 2).

Two major storms in recent history – Hurricane Katrina in Southeast-ern United States and the tsunami in the Asia Pacific region – caused mass disruptions in domestic and international tourism. 'Prior to Hurri-cane Katrina, tourism and the cultural economy were $10.4 billion indus-tries in the State of Louisiana. Since the hurricanes, the New Orleans tourism and hospitality industry has lost $15 million per day due to lack of tourism arrivals, while Lake Charles and its surrounding areas lost some $1.5 million in daily revenue' (Davis, 2006, p. 3). The tsunami resulted in huge losses and significant downturns in tourism in Asia. Phuket arrivals were down (international and domestic travel) minus 44.7 per cent after the first 4 months. Tourism to the Maldives was down 52 per cent (PATA, 2005, p. 3). New Orleans and Phuket slowly continue to rebuild. Yet with insufficient tourism products and services, they now struggle with which should come first – investments in the tourism products to entice visitors to return or the return of the visitors, which will entice financing and reconstruction of tourism products and services.

Other types of natural disasters also have lasting impacts. Mudslides generate huge clean-up costs, disrupt business enterprises and destroy landscapes. Venezuela suffered severe mudslides in the late 1990s. 'Accord-ing to government statistics, tourist arrivals in Venezuela fell by more than 25 per cent in 1999, with the sharpest decline coming at the end of the year, normally the busiest period here' (Rohter, 2000, p. 3).

Lessons learned from these natural disasters mandate the need to develop quick responses to coordinate relief and to reinvigorate the tourism industry. Much depends on the ability of various agencies to work together to meet the new challenges. At these times, there is a tremendous need for financial capital. Creative approaches beyond international aid are required. 'Catastrophe bonds were started in the 1990s, and have largely been issued by private companies to cover losses from natural disasters. Taiwan is the only other government (besides Mexico) that has issued such a bond against a quake, but it covers damages from losses' (Malkin, 2006, p. 4).

As the tourism industry evolves and grows, new public policy tools and best practices need to be developed that respond to natural disasters. Travellers need transportation systems and alternative accommodations, access to telephones or other communication devices and places to stay should their current lodging be destroyed or damaged. Safety concerns for consideration include clean drinking water and the physical safety of tourists. Furthermore, tourist organizations need to review contingency and continuity plans for workers. Are there contingency plans for getting workers to and from work? Will enough workers be available to maintain the continuity of business operations? Or will they need to stay home to take care of their families?

Longer-term infrastructure concerns must also be addressed. Can the lodging withstand high winds, earthquakes or flooding? Are communication systems being devised and implemented, which will facilitate contacting employees or travellers contacting loved ones and travel agents for necessary arrangements? Policy formulation will need to be three-pronged to address the immediate needs of the industry and guests, long-term recovery and rebuilding and, lastly, prevention and/or impact minimization.

Climate change and tourism

Another rapidly emerging trend of international importance for tourism policy is climate change and its impact on tourism. Global warming continues to be a highly debatable subject and is a growing concern for travellers. In the face of mounting evidence of climate change, environmentalists from local to international levels are injecting greater urgency and momentum into the process of driving down global emissions of greenhouse gases. At a recent United Nations climate conference, delegates from the 165-member nations of the 1997 Kyoto Protocol approved a schedule of talks aimed at setting new quotas on carbon dioxide and other emissions before the Kyoto pact expires in 2012. Australia and the United States are two of the major industrial countries to reject the accord. Fast developing nations such as China and India, growing energy consumers, have long resisted early talks in which they and other poorer economies might be pressured to accept mandatory cutbacks until they see similar acceptance by the United States and other major powers (Hanley, 2006, p. A15).

Tourism administrators must undertake a paradigm shift away from overuse of natural resources toward environmental stewardship. Protecting natural tourism assets must become a primary focus in tourism policy and planning. In doing so, land changes will be less susceptible to problems such as mudslides, wildfires, and other ecological disasters. Switzerland recently started building a dam to protect a mountain tourist town from a potential catastrophe. The permafrost-covered mountainside was experiencing a base temperature increase (attributed to greenhouse gases), and scientists forecasted mudslides as the permafrost melted and shifted (Foulkes, 2001, para 1). Six percent of Switzerland is covered by permafrost, with 300 ski resort chairlifts anchored in permafrost rather than bedrock (Foulkes).

Recently published research by the World Wildlife Fund further documents the 'ecological footprint' of human activities around the world, many of which are embodied in international travel and tourism. Results indicate that the world's ecosystem is being degraded by humans at an unsustainable rate that risks causing 'irreversible damage' to the planet as well as triggering population declines of about 31 per cent in land animals since 1970, freshwater creatures by 28 per cent and marine animals by 27 per cent. Consumption exceeds by about 25 per cent the Earth's capacity to provide resources and absorb waste (Washington Post News Service, 2006, A10).

This report also cited the biggest users are residents of the UAE, the United States and Finland, with the Afghans, Somalis and Bangladeshis using the least. One hope is that the lessons learned and best practices developed and implemented by knowledgeable tourism industry professionals today – through sustainable tourism policies and strategic destination planning – can help put change management processes in place to make a difference for the future. 'There is still time to avoid the worst impacts of climate change, if we act now and act internationally', said Nicholas Stern in a recent report issued by the British government forecasting that the impact of climate change, uncurbed for even one more decade, could spawn environmental devastation that could cost 5–20 per cent of the world's annual gross domestic product (Eilperin, 2006, A18). Stern's call is for collaboration fostering research and innovation rather than adopting federal emission restrictions. The rich complexity of the travel and tourism industry, with its multiple products and service sectors, provides a strong platform for innovation and adaptation to changing economic, socio-cultural and physical environments. For this reason, the tourism industry can provide great leadership in pursuit of these goals.

Additionally, as global warming comes to the forefront in environmental concerns, tourism managers will need to stay attuned to forecast changes. Recent projections by the Pew Research Center indicate global warming will cause major shifts in tourism with locations that have higher altitudes and latitudes becoming the 'winners' while warmer countries experience declines by up to 20 per cent. The biggest winners: Canada, which they predict will experience a 220 per cent increase in international arrivals by 2100, Russia (174 per cent), and Mongolia (122 per cent). The biggest 'losers' of inbound tourism: Mauritania, where international arrivals are predicted to drop by 60 per cent, Mali (minus 59 per cent) and Bahrain (minus 58 per cent). 'Currently, popular destinations that are high up there include Macau (minus 48 per cent), Aruba (minus 42 per cent), and Jamaica (minus 39 per cent)' (Morin, 2006, para 4).

Individual regions need to address their potential climate changes and the effects on international inbound travel. Warm locations can expect declines during their current prime tourist season due to higher temperatures; however, current shoulder seasons could become the new high season. Coastal areas in France and the State of Florida in the United States stand to gain in the new, longer warm seasons. Britain will gain favour as the warmer weather improves their summer season. Other areas, mainly Caribbean and Mediterranean islands, are projected to lose their tourist seasons altogether as it becomes too uncomfortably hot to consider these destinations for a relaxing beach vacation (McGuire, 2006, paras 1–4).

Unfortunately, climate change can cause a circularity of responses or ripple effect in tourism. For example, climate change will affect which tourists visit certain locations and at what times of year. This shift in traveller patterns and travel periods then can have an impact on travel destinations *ldots*, which in turn affects the environment . . . , which in turn changes when visitors desire to come. Further environmental impacts will surface – from fossil fuel power and oil generation that support various modes of transportation – from accompanying greenhouse gas production. The resulting combination of changes is well illustrated in seasonal impacts, particularly on winter sports.

Mountain recreation areas often respond to warmer weather with artificial snow production. Mega ski resorts and international ski corporations, such as Intrawest, use snowmaking machines to protect the economic viability of their industry; however, this type of response is not viable for other winter tourism industries. Snowmobilers in Canada and the United States spend over $27 billion on snowmobiling each year (Klim, 2006, para 1). Snowmaking simply cannot cover the distances required for Nordic skiing or snowmobiling. The continued growth of the snowmobiling industry could, in fact, be significantly contributing to its own decline. Certain snowmobiles can produce, on a per-passenger-mile basis, as much pollution as 39 automobiles or 11 snow coaches. One snowmobile produces about 98 times more hydrocarbons and 36 times more carbon monoxide than one automobile, or about 31 times more hydrocarbons and 9 times more carbon monoxide than one snow coach (which holds a small group of people) (Sharpless, 2001, p. 55). These emissions contribute incrementally to the affects of global warming, leading to warmer temperatures and less snowfall. In the past, the snowmobile industry focused primarily on noise pollution reduction. Today, greater attention to tourism policies focused on emissions reductions is occuring. Forward-looking public policy managers should consider policies that include examination of all forms of pollution related to the tourism industry and of economical and sustainable means for greenhouse gas reduction.

Airlines, recognized as one of the major contributors to global warming through their exhaust emissions, are also attempting to take an industry-wide voluntary approach. Virgin Atlantic Airways' CEO Richard Branson has put his weight behind creating an industry-wide forum to address environmental concerns. He has contacted 'leaders at other *airlines* as well

Figure 10.8 Climate change and global warming may be caught in action as a chunk of Grey Glacier falls into Lago Grey in the Patagonia region of Chile (Photo: Matt Schuttloffel)

as manufacturers, asking them to join an "industry forum" to help brainstorm ways to tackle *global warming*' (Virgin Atlantic Airways, 2006, p. 68).

While scientists and politicians debate global warming's validity, tourism managers need to seek information proactively and take the lead in creating responses to projected changes. Tourism industry segments and sectors must consider creation of long-term policies to protect their environments and their livelihoods. Local tourism managers and politicians must focus on environmental issues to enhance their own tourism industry and prevent or reduce possible radical changes to their economies by anticipating projections for shifting environments and weather patterns (Figure 10.8).

Conclusion

It is our hope that the understanding gained from yesterday's and today's tourism policy and planning will set the stage for future world tourism policy. The world is increasingly characterized by complex interdependence and, as such, needs to be cognizant of both the differences and similarities of peoples and cultures as we plan for the future of tourism. Policies that include beneficial global codes of ethics as is expressed in the following case report help foster greater peace and prosperity to the world, leading to a higher quality of tourism and travel experiences.

Case report 10

UNITED NATIONS WORLD TOURISM ORGANIZATION GLOBAL CODE OF ETHICS FOR TOURISM

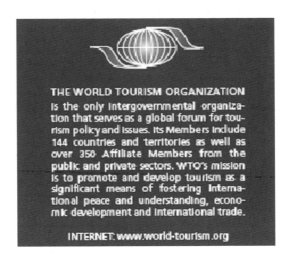

THE WORLD TOURISM ORGANIZATION is the only intergovernmental organization that serves as a global forum for tourism policy and issues. Its Members include 144 countries and territories as well as over 350 Affiliate Members from the public and private sectors. WTO's mission is to promote and develop tourism as a significant means of fostering international peace and understanding, economic development and international trade.

INTERNET: www.world-tourism.org

 ## ARTICLE 1
Tourism's contribution to mutual understanding and respect between peoples and societies

1. The understanding and promotion of the ethical values common to humanity, with an attitude of tolerance and respect for the diversity of religious, philosophical and moral beliefs, are both the foundation and the consequence of responsible tourism; stakeholders in tourism development and tourists themselves should observe the social and cultural traditions and practices of all peoples, including those of minorities and indigenous peoples and to recognize their worth;
2. Tourism activities should be conducted in harmony with the attributes and traditions of the host regions and countries and in respect for their laws, practices and customs;
3. The host communities, on the one hand, and local professionals, on the other, should acquaint themselves with and respect the tourists who visit them and find out about their lifestyles, tastes and expectations; the education and training imparted to professionals contribute to a hospitable welcome;

4. It is the task of the public authorities to provide protection for tourists and visitors and their belongings; they must pay particular attention to the safety of foreign tourists owing to the particular vulnerability they may have; they should facilitate the introduction of specific means of information, prevention, security, insurance and assistance consistent with their needs; any attacks, assaults, kidnappings or threats against tourists or workers in the tourism industry, as well as the willful destruction of tourism facilities or of elements of cultural or natural heritage should be severely condemned and punished in accordance with their respective national laws;

5. When travelling, tourists and visitors should not commit any criminal act or any act considered criminal by the laws of the country visited and abstain from any conduct felt to be offensive or injurious by the local populations, or likely to damage the local environment; they should refrain from all trafficking in illicit drugs, arms, antiques, protected species and products and substances that are dangerous or prohibited by national regulations;

6. Tourists and visitors have the responsibility to acquaint themselves, even before their departure, with the characteristics of the countries they are preparing to visit; they must be aware of the health and security risks inherent in any travel outside their usual environment and behave in such a way as to minimize those risks;

ARTICLE 2
Tourism as a vehicle for individual and collective fulfillment

1. Tourism, the activity most frequently associated with rest and relaxation, sport and access to culture and nature, should be planned and practiced as a privileged means of individual and collective fulfillment; when practiced with a sufficiently open mind, it is an irreplaceable factor of self-education, mutual tolerance and for learning about the legitimate differences between peoples and cultures and their diversity;

2. Tourism activities should respect the equality of men and women; they should promote human rights and, more particularly, the individual rights of the most vulnerable groups, notably children, the elderly, the handicapped, ethnic minorities and indigenous peoples;

3. The exploitation of human beings in any form, particularly sexual, especially when applied to children, conflicts with the fundamental aims of tourism and is the negation of tourism; as such, in accordance with international law, it should be energetically combated with the

cooperation of all the States concerned and penalized without conces-
sion by the national legislation of both the countries visited and the
countries of the perpetrators of these acts, even when they are carried
out abroad;

4. Travel for purposes of religion, health, education and cultural or lin-
    guistic exchanges are particularly beneficial forms of tourism, which
    deserve encouragement;
5. The introduction into curricula of education about the value of tourist
    exchanges, their economic, social and cultural benefits, and also their
    risks, should be encouraged;

ARTICLE 3
Tourism, a factor of sustainable development

1. All the stakeholders in tourism development should safeguard the
    natural environment with a view to achieving sound, continuous and
    sustainable economic growth geared to satisfying equitably the needs
    and aspirations of present and future generations;
2. All forms of tourism development that are conducive to saving rare
    and precious resources, in particular water and energy, as well as
    avoiding so far as possible waste production, should be given priority
    and encouraged by national, regional and local public authorities;
3. The staggering in time and space of tourist and visitor flows, par-
    ticularly those resulting from paid leave and school holidays, and a
    more even distribution of holidays should be sought so as to reduce
    the pressure of tourism activity on the environment and enhance its
    beneficial impact on the tourism industry and the local economy;
4. Tourism infrastructure should be designed and tourism activities pro-
    grammed in such a way as to protect the natural heritage composed
    of ecosystems and biodiversity and to preserve endangered species of
    wildlife; the stakeholders in tourism development, and especially pro-
    fessionals, should agree to the imposition of limitations or constraints
    on their activities when these are exercised in particularly sensitive
    areas: desert, polar or high mountain regions, coastal areas, tropical
    forests or wetlands, propitious to the creation of nature reserves or
    protected areas;
5. Nature tourism and ecotourism are recognized as being particularly
    conducive to enriching and enhancing the standing of tourism, pro-
    vided they respect the natural heritage and local populations and are
    in keeping with the carrying capacity of the sites;

ARTICLE 4
Tourism, a user of the cultural heritage of mankind and contributor to its enhancement

1. Tourism resources belong to the common heritage of mankind; the communities in whose territories they are situated have particular rights and obligations to them;
2. Tourism policies and activities should be conducted with respect for the artistic, archaeological and cultural heritage, which they should protect and pass on to future generations; particular care should be devoted to preserving and upgrading monuments, shrines and museums as well as archaeological and historic sites which must be widely open to tourist visits; encouragement should be given to public access to privately-owned cultural property and monuments, with respect for the rights of their owners, as well as to religious buildings, without prejudice to normal needs of worship;
3. Financial resources derived from visits to cultural sites and monuments should, at least in part, be used for the upkeep, safeguard, development and embellishment of this heritage;
4. Tourism activity should be planned in such a way as to allow traditional cultural products, crafts and folklore to survive and flourish, rather than causing them to degenerate and become standardized;

ARTICLE 5
Tourism, a beneficial activity for host countries and communities

1. Local populations should be associated with tourism activities and share equitably in the economic, social and cultural benefits they generate, and particularly in the creation of direct and indirect jobs resulting from them;
2. Tourism policies should be applied in such a way as to help to raise the standard of living of the populations of the regions visited and meet their needs; the planning and architectural approach to and operation of tourism resorts and accommodation should aim to integrate them, to the extent possible, in the local economic and social fabric; where skills are equal, priority should be given to local manpower;
3. Special attention should be paid to the specific problems of coastal areas and island territories and to vulnerable rural or mountain regions, for which tourism often represents a rare opportunity for development in the face of the decline of traditional economic activities;

4. Tourism professionals, particularly investors, governed by the regulations laid down by the public authorities, should carry out studies of the impact of their development projects on the environment and natural surroundings; they should also deliver, with the greatest transparency and objectivity, information on their future programs and their foreseeable repercussions and foster dialogue on their contents with the populations concerned;

ARTICLE 6
Obligations of stakeholders in tourism development

1. Tourism professionals have an obligation to provide tourists with objective and honest information on their places of destination and on the conditions of travel, hospitality and stays; they should ensure that the contractual clauses proposed to their customers are readily understandable as to the nature, price and quality of the services they commit themselves to providing and the financial compensation payable by them in the event of a unilateral breach of contract on their part;
2. Tourism professionals, insofar as it depends on them, should show concern, in co-operation with the public authorities, for the security and safety, accident prevention, health protection and food safety of those who seek their services; likewise, they should ensure the existence of suitable systems of insurance and assistance; they should accept the reporting obligations prescribed by national regulations and pay fair compensation in the event of failure to observe their contractual obligations;
3. Tourism professionals, so far as this depends on them, should contribute to the cultural and spiritual fulfillment of tourists and allow them, during their travels, to practice their religions;
4. The public authorities of the generating States and the host countries, in cooperation with the professionals concerned and their associations, should ensure that the necessary mechanisms are in place for the repatriation of tourists in the event of the bankruptcy of the enterprise that organized their travel;
5. Governments have the right – and the duty – especially in a crisis, to inform their nationals of the difficult circumstances, or even the dangers they may encounter during their travels abroad; it is their responsibility however to issue such information without prejudicing in an unjustified or exaggerated manner the tourism industry of the host countries and the interests of their own operators; the contents of travel advisories should therefore be discussed beforehand with the authorities of the host countries and the professionals concerned;

recommendations formulated should be strictly proportionate to the gravity of the situations encountered and confined to the geographical areas where the insecurity has arisen; such advisories should be qualified or cancelled as soon as a return to normality permits;

6. The press, and particularly the specialized travel press and the other media, including modern means of electronic communication, should issue honest and balanced information on events and situations that could influence the flow of tourists; they should also provide accurate and reliable information to the consumers of tourism services; the new communication and electronic commerce technologies should also be developed and used for this purpose; as is the case for the media, they should not in any way promote sex tourism;

ARTICLE 7
Right to tourism

1. The prospect of direct and personal access to the discovery and enjoyment of the planet's resources constitutes a right equally open to all the world's inhabitants; the increasingly extensive participation in national and international tourism should be regarded as one of the best possible expressions of the sustained growth of free time, and obstacles should not be placed in its way;

2. The universal right to tourism must be regarded as the corollary of the right to rest and leisure, including reasonable limitation of working hours and periodic holidays with pay, guaranteed by Article 24 of the Universal Declaration of Human Rights and Article 7.d of the International Covenant on Economic, Social and Cultural Rights;

3. Social tourism, and in particular associative tourism, which facilitates widespread access to leisure, travel and holidays, should be developed with the support of the public authorities;

4. Family, youth, student and senior tourism and tourism for people with disabilities, should be encouraged and facilitated;

ARTICLE 8
Liberty of tourist movements

1. Tourists and visitors should benefit, in compliance with international law and national legislation, from the liberty to move within their countries and from one State to another, in accordance with Article 13 of the Universal Declaration of Human Rights; they should have

access to places of transit and stay and to tourism and cultural sites
without being subject to excessive formalities or discrimination;

2. Tourists and visitors should have access to all available forms of com-
    munication, internal or external; they should benefit from prompt and
    easy access to local administrative, legal and health services; they
    should be free to contact the consular representatives of their countries
    of origin in compliance with the diplomatic conventions in force;

3. Tourists and visitors should benefit from the same rights as the citi-
    zens of the country visited concerning the confidentiality of the per-
    sonal data and information concerning them, especially when these
    are stored electronically;

4. Administrative procedures relating to border crossings whether they
    fall within the competence of States or result from international agree-
    ments, such as visas or health and customs formalities, should be
    adapted, so far as possible, so as to facilitate to the maximum freedom
    of travel and widespread access to international tourism; agreements
    between groups of countries to harmonize and simplify these pro-
    cedures should be encouraged; specific taxes and levies penalizing
    the tourism industry and undermining its competitiveness should be
    gradually phased out or corrected;

5. So far as the economic situation of the countries from which they
    come permits, travelers should have access to allowances of convertible
    currencies needed for their travels;

 ## ARTICLE 9
Rights of the workers and entrepreneurs
in the tourism industry

1. The fundamental rights of salaried and self-employed workers in the
    tourism industry and related activities, should be guaranteed under
    the supervision of the national and local administrations, both of their
    States of origin and of the host countries with particular care, given
    the specific constraints linked in particular to the seasonality of their
    activity, the global dimension of their industry and the flexibility often
    required of them by the nature of their work;

2. Salaried and self-employed workers in the tourism industry and
    related activities have the right and the duty to acquire appropriate
    initial and continuous training; they should be given adequate social
    protection; job insecurity should be limited so far as possible; and a
    specific status, with particular regard to their social welfare, should be
    offered to seasonal workers in the sector;

3. Any natural or legal person, provided he, she or it has the necessary
    abilities and skills, should be entitled to develop a professional activity

in the field of tourism under existing national laws; entrepreneurs and investors – especially in the area of small and medium-sized enterprises – should be entitled to free access to the tourism sector with a minimum of legal or administrative restrictions;

4. Exchanges of experience offered to executives and workers, whether salaried or not, from different countries, contributes to foster the development of the world tourism industry; these movements should be facilitated so far as possible in compliance with the applicable national laws and international conventions;

5. As an irreplaceable factor of solidarity in the development and dynamic growth of international exchanges, multinational enterprises of the tourism industry should not exploit the dominant positions they sometimes occupy; they should avoid becoming the vehicles of cultural and social models artificially imposed on the host communities; in exchange for their freedom to invest and trade which should be fully recognized, they should involve themselves in local development, avoiding, by the excessive repatriation of their profits or their induced imports, a reduction of their contribution to the economies in which they are established;

6. Partnership and the establishment of balanced relations between enterprises of generating and receiving countries contribute to the sustainable development of tourism and an equitable distribution of the benefits of its growth;

 ARTICLE 10
Implementation of the principles of the Global Code of Ethics for Tourism

1. The public and private stakeholders in tourism development should cooperate in the implementation of these principles and monitor their effective application;

2. The stakeholders in tourism development should recognize the role of international institutions, among which the World Tourism Organization ranks first, and non-governmental organizations with competence in the field of tourism promotion and development, the protection of human rights, the environment or health, with due respect for the general principles of international law;

3. The same stakeholders should demonstrate their intention to refer any disputes concerning the application or interpretation of the Global Code of Ethics for Tourism for conciliation to an impartial third body known as the World Committee on Tourism Ethics.

Source: http://www.world-tourism.org/code_ethics

References

American Society of Plastic Surgeons. (2005). *Briefing Papers: Cosmetic Surgery Tourism*, April. Retrieved 5 November 2006, http://www.plasticsurgery.org/news_room/Cosmetic-Surgery-Tourism-Briefing-Paper.cfm.

Bremmer, I. (2006). *The J Curve: A New Way to Understand Why Nations Rise and Fall.* NY: Simon & Schuster.

Clark, E. (2003). *SARS Strikes Down Asia Tourism*, 15 May. Retrieved 10 September 2006, http://news.bbc.co.uk/2/hi/business/3024015.stm.

Davis, A. (2006). *Louisiana Rebirth Restoring the Soul of America.* Retrieved September 12, 2006 from http://www.crt.state.la.us/LouisianaRebirth/TCIHousing/TCIHousing200603.pdf

Eilperin, J. (2006). 'Warming Called Threat to Global Economy,' *Washington Post*, October 3, p. A18.

Foulkes, I. (2001). *Village Pioneers Defences Against Global Warming.* Retrieved September 12, 2006 from http://www.swissinfo.com

Goeldner, Charles A. and J.R. Brent Ritchie. (2006). *Tourism: Principles, Practices, Philosophies (10th ed.).* John Wiley and Sons, Hoboken, New Jersey.

Hanley, C. (2006). 'Climate Talks End With Slow Timetable,' *Washington Post*, November 18, A15.

Impact of Global Warming on Tourism, Pew Research Center, 18 August. Retrieved 1 October 2006, http://pewresearch.org/obdeck/?ObDeckID=52.

Kamel, S. and El Sherif, A. (2001). The role of small and medium-sized enterprises in developing Egypt's tourism industry using e-Commerce, *Management of Engineering and Technology*, Vol. Supplement, Iss., 2001 pages: 60–68 vol.2.

Klim, E. (2006). *Snowmobiling is a $27 Billion Dollar Business.* 11 November, http://www.snowmobile.org/pr_bdbusiness.asp.

Lanier P. (2006). *Spa Industry Shows Incredible Growth.* Retrieved September 11, 2006 from http://www.familytravelguides.com/articles/health/spastudy.html

Locker, D. (2004). *The ISPA 2004 Spa Industry Study- Executive Summary.* Retrieved September 11, 2006 from http://www.experienceispa.com/ISPA/Media+Room/Press+Releases/2004+Industry+Study+Summary.htm

Malkin, E. (2006). Mexico is Offering Bonds to Cover a Major Quake. *New York Times*, 13 May, Business/Financial Desk, p. C4.

McGuire, B. (2006). *Holiday 2030: Climate Change to Drive Radical Changes in Global Tourism*, 1 September 1. Retrieved 10 November 2006, http://www.hbosplc.com/media/pressreleases/articles/halifax/2006-09-01-05.asp?fs=/media/press_releases.asp.

Morin, R. (2006). *The Surprising Impact of Global Warming on Tourism Book Your Mongolian Vacation Now.* Retrieved September 12, 2006 from http://pewresearch.org/pubs/52/the-surprising-impact-of-global-warming-on-tourism

PATA. (2005). *PATA Strategic Intelligence Centre_Tsunami Recovery Update*, 22 June, Retrieved 20 September, http://www.hospitalitynet.org/file/152002102.pdf.

Rohter, L. (2000). Travel Advisory: Correspondent's Report: Venezuelan Tourism Hit Hard by Flood *s. New York* Times, 7 May, Section 5, p. 3.

Sharpless, H. (2001). Environmental Impacts of Snowmobiles. *Natural Resources Year in Review,* May.

Tourism Industry Association of Nova Scotia (TIANS) (2006). *Strategic Alliances.* Retrieved 16 November 2006, from http://www.tians.org/alliances/.

United Nations World Tourism Organization. (21 November 2006). Tourism: An Instrument of development for Iberoamerica. News release retrieved 28 November 2006, from http://www.world-tourism.org/newsroom/Releases/2006/november/iberoamerica.htm.

United Nations World Tourism Organization. Tourism 2020 Vision. Retrieved 28 November 2006, from http://www.unwto.org/facts/eng/vision.htm.

United Nations World Tourism Organization. 'Increase Tourism to Fight Poverty' – New Year message from UNWTO. News release retrieved 5 January 2007, from http://www.unwto.org/facts/eng/vision.htm.

United Nations World Tourism Organization Executive Council. (21 November 2006). 'Tourism Fosters Trade and Development'. News release retrieved 28 November 2006, from http://www.world-tourism.org/newsroom/ Releases/2006/november/exe_council.htm.

US Census Bureau. (2007). Retrieved 5 January 2007, from http://www.cnesus.gov/ipc/wwwpopclockworld.html.

Virgin Atlantic Airways. (2006). *Aviation Week & Space Technology,* 2 October, 165:13, p. 68.

Washington Post News Service (2006). 'WWF Issues Caution On Earth's Ecosystem,' October 25, p. A10.

Watkiss, P., Pye S., Smith A., Arigoni Ortiz R,m Hunt A., Markandya A. et al (2004). *Strategies: Tourism Dawage and Disruption of Countryside Pursuits* retrived September 10, 2006 from http://www.defra.gov.uk/footandmouth/pdf/tourism_countryside_report.pdf.

Wilkening, D. (2006a). *Cruise Lines in Caribbean Scrambling to Avoid Tropical Storm.* 30 August. Retrieved 10 September 2006, http://www.travelmole.com/stories/109732.php?news_cat=&pagename= searchresult.

Wilkening, D. (2006b). *Summer Weather Creating Stormy Climate for US Airlines,* 13 July. Retrieved 10 September 2006, http://www. travelmole.com/stories/109732.php?news_cat=&pagename= searchresult.

Wilmeth, K. (2006). Marriot Announces Global Strategy. *The Examiner.* Retrieved October 20, 2006 from http://www.examiner.com/printa-353435~Marriott_announces_global_strategy.html

World Travel & Tourism Council. (20 October 2001). *Declaration of Global Travel and Tourism Associations.* Retrieved on 15 December 2006, from http://www.wttc.org/regProg/partners/pdf/Declaration%202nd%20Oct.doc.

Appendix A

EDUCATION AND TRAINING IN TOURISM:

AN HISTORICAL VIEW

Prepared by Dr Sheryl Elliott,
Associate Professor, Department of Tourism and
Hospitality Management, School of Business
The George Washington University
Washington, DC, USA 20052

Focus on skill development

The review of literature found that education and training studies are from the perspective of employee *skills development*, either to increase industry productivity or to improve tourism and hospitality school curricula. Most of these studies involved surveys that compared the perceptions of different groups of stakeholders (industry professionals, educators, employees, hospitality tourism alumni or current students) of skills they deemed *most important* for workers to have. There are too many studies to individually cite or discuss; however, key studies, illustrative of the literature, are presented in the following tables and discussed.

Characteristic of all the studies surveyed was an interest in both hard skill (conceptual and technical) and soft skill (human) development. Shaw (1995), Enz (1993) and LeBruto (1994) all conducted surveys of two or more population samples for comparison on the importance of skills for application in the hospitality industry. Of the combined 40 skills listed among all studies there was an overlap of 26 or 27%, and within this number, 22, or 55% dealt with "soft" (i.e. human) skills. The totally different population samples for each survey made comparison of the results difficult, except that all viewed "soft" skills as relevant, and personal communication as a particularly important skill. The importance of communication skills also ran true in studies by Breiter (1995), whose survey was limited to hospitality managers, as well as in Sheldon and Gee's (1987) and the earlier ones they cite in their review of literature (Ibid., 174). Breiter's list also included employee relations, training, and organization as important skills. In a study by Morton (1994), a different set of business skills emerged, which were found to be more important content areas for hotel and restaurant managers: marketing, human resources and finance.

A 1991 study by the National Restaurant Association is particularly relevant since it involved the same methodology used for this study, the Delphi survey. The NRA Delphi survey was conducted to determine skills food service managers would need in the year 2000 (Mills & Riehle, 1993). This survey involved a two round polling of panelists, of whom 120 responded in the second round. The panel members considered statements that were grouped into the following categories: administration, finance, human resources, facility maintenance, sanitation and food safety, service, marketing, food and beverage, working conditions, external issues, background and education, and industry needs and top educational priorities (Ibid., p. 158). The six areas viewed as education priorities were found to be communication, leadership, team building, training, motivation and supervision. Again, one observes the strong suggestion of the importance of soft skills, particularly communication. It was equally interesting to note which skill areas received the lowest educational priority for managers in the year 2000, "banking, off-premises or delivery, market research, menu design and policy/procedures were the ones least favoured by Delphi panelists" (Ibid., p. 157).

Several studies specifically addressed skill development for sub-sectors outside of the hospitality area, such as Grizzle's study (1992) which identified the most important skills needed by travel agents as being credit transactions, legal issues, marketing strategies and planning procedures. A study by Weilers (1993) of the skills most important to nature based tour operators included organization, leadership, motivation, entertainment, interpretation and resource management.

A seminal work, which assessed skills across tourism sectors was a study conducted by Sheldon and Gee (1987). Although limited to the state of Hawaii, that study was similar to the design of this research in that it considered a full spectrum of service areas in tourism, including accommodations, transportation, food service, travel agents, tour operators, attractions and entertainment. Its premise was also very similar that of this study: quality service depends upon the training and development of human resources. Sheldon and Gee surveyed employers and employees to determine gaps, or training needs, of the travel industry. The hypothesis was that gaps were the result of a difference between employers' and employees' *perceived* training needs (Ibid., p. 175). That study determined that there was agreement between both groups in the perceived benefits of training in the skill areas of communications, courtesy and human relations skills. The two groups also consistently ranked computer skills and a skill "Hawaiiana" as the lowest (Ibid., p. 177).

The major shortcoming of Sheldon and Gee's (1987) study was that no distinction was made between the various occupation levels. Were the agreed training needs as applicable for managers as they were for front line personnel across sectors? Another shortfall was what appeared to be an arbitrary and rather incomplete listing of skill areas: communications, courtesy, human relations, quality assurance, language, operations, salesmanship, computer skills and one entitled "Hawaiiana". If this study was to "provide guidelines for the future development undertaken of travel industry training" (Ibid., p. 181), a more comprehensive list of skills needed to be examined. An additional limitation of this study was that the difference between two sectors, attractions and entertainment, was unclear. Is a theme park considered an attraction or entertainment? That study is now 9 years old and was one of the first of its kind. It is an interesting benchmark to compare to a current employer assessment of education and training needs.

A number of observations can be made from all of the studies surveyed. First, the more specific the job (travel agent, tour guide, hotel comptroller), the more specific the articulation of skills found important. When the field broadened to general areas of hospitality, or the full tourism sector, skill development was stated in general terms (business skills, managerial skills, language skills) with a high degree of importance found in "soft" skill development (motivation, leadership and particularly, communication). Tas (1988) and Baum (1991) studies generated similar outcomes. Obviously, many of these broadly stated skill areas could imply different things to different professions. For example, communications was found to be an important central skill area, but does that finding, in and of itself, provide sufficient information to modify education and training curricula? Would it not be far more meaningful to know whether communication related to interpersonal verbal or written exchanges, ones requiring proficiency in another language (and if another language, what language)?

Although these skill development studies valuably sought to identify and describe the skills needed for successful current and future performance of workers on the job, almost all were limited to partial views of various industry segments which tend to compartmentalize thinking on education and training. The implication for education and training of all studies could be further questioned, as the surveys were mainly conducted in industrialized countries, and only attempted to determine whether skills were believed to be important. The studies failed to determine if they were also believed to be commonly lacking. In fact, no studies were found that scientifically investigated whether skills employees brought to the job were different from those needed on the job, across occupational levels and sectors.

One could contend that a skill suggested as important can be assumed as lacking. This, however, is arguably highly speculative, and hardly scientific. Furthermore, in industrialized areas, where the studies were conducted, there has been a large percentage increase in the number of students who seek degrees at the higher education level. (In the United States there was an increase of 15% in 1945 to 50% in 1995) (Council on Hotel. Restaurant and Institutional Education [CHRIE], 1995a, p. 6). Considering this, is there not a more qualified workforce available than in the past? Evans' (1993, p. 243) observation that there is an overproduction of tourism graduates for jobs available in the UK (Evans, 1993, p. 243), and that only 50% of those graduates are actually taking jobs in hotels, catering or related tourism activities (Parsons, 1991, p. 203), likewise suggests that there is a larger, more educated pool of workers on which to draw. If it can be validated that perspective workers often lack the skills needed today, does this not suggest a significant gap, considering that, in many countries today's workforce is a more educated one?

Focus on the role of government

The attainment of skills has been addressed by many studies as it relates to the organization of formal education and training provisions. Since the Sheldon and Gee (1987, p. 174) study closely parallels the proposed study, it was of interest to note that in their review of literature they found that, "Only a few governments have attempted to identify the training needs of the entire travel industry". The studies they listed included the 1981 Hong Kong Training Council study; the 1982 Hotel and Catering Industry Training Board (HCITB) study in the UK; a study by the Tourism Advisory Council of New Zealand in 1978 and the 1975 study of the Ontario Ministry of Colleges and Universities in Canada (Ibid., p. 174). A conspicuous omission from their list was a 1985 study by Lavery for the

English Tourist Board, to examine provisions of education and training courses in relation to tourism manpower needs (Lavery, 1988, pp. 167–170).

Since the Sheldon and Gee study, there have been additions, notably: The European Centre for the Development of Vocational Training (CEDEFOP) study, which was a survey in European Union countries to analyze job functions related to knowledge and skill requirements (Shepperd and Cooper, 1995, p. 16); the Travel Alberta study by the government of Alberta, Canada, which created the "Alberta Model" of tourism education and training to "enhance the efforts of educators and government agencies so as to better respond to industry needs"; (Pollock and Ritchie, 1990, pp. 568–585); the 1989 study of the National Economic Development Office (NEDO) of the UK, which compared education and training programmes in the UK with those in six other countries (Parsons, 1991, p. 197); and the US government funded CHRIE study for establishing National Voluntary Skill Standards (1995b).

A review of recent government studies showed a strong interest in finding better methods for developing human resources for work in the industry, and in particular, the use of competency based standards, or the comparability of qualifications, to improve the tourism education system output. Generally, government studies usually distinguish national practices and policies having to deal with vocational training from those having to deal with higher level or degree education.

Echtner (1995 pp. 32–41) refers to post secondary education as professional education, but since this might be confused with professional development or continuing education programmes, for the purpose of this discussion it will be referred to as higher or degree level education. Echtner (1995, p. 33) differentiates vocational training as largely for front line personnel and professional training as degree level education for managers. Admittedly, in a modern day context, arguments can be waged over what is vocational and professional learning.

Assessing or comparing different systems of vocational and higher education among countries is made complicated, if not confusing, by the differing regional terminology for diplomas and degrees, the differing emphasis countries place on vocational and degree level education, the multiple authorities and agents within countries who are involved in the process of validation for vocational and the degree level education, and degree of public and private sector involvement in education and training.

The UNWTO World Directory on Tourism Education and Training Institutions listed over 366 degree titles for programmes in *tourism and hotel management*. The list of degree titles more than quadrupled when the programmes of *catering management, travel and tourism, hospitality, tourism, leisure and recreation, and tourism planning and development* were added. Obviously, languages account for a substantial number of variations, however, if only using English language titles, degree titles for programmes in *tourism and hospitality management* totalled over 250. The large categorical areas for degree titles included associate degrees and associate diplomas, bachelor degrees, certificates and certificates of specialization, diplomas and graduate/post graduate diplomas, licenciado, master degrees and technical degrees (UNWTO, 1992a, index C).

In some countries, vocational training comes under the ministry of education, and the state provides institutions for such training (Lavery, 1988, p. 168), while in others the private sector has a predominant responsibility for vocational education and training and certification. Such is the case in many Latin American countries and the United States, while in Ireland a hybrid authority, the Council for Education Recruitment and Training (CERT) performs these functions (Ibid.).

Examining the specific context of skill attainment in the organization of formal education and training, a study was conducted by the English Tourist Board (Lavery, 1988, pp. 167–170) to identify shortfalls between education and training courses and the manpower needs of industry to manpower needs of industry and to suggest ways of eliminating these shortfalls (Ibid., p. 167). Like the Sheldon and Gee study, this study reported by Lavery was directed to assess education and training needs appropriate to a broad range of tourism services or sectors. "The study focused on the non-hotel sectors of the tourism industry because it was felt that the hotel and catering sector was well developed and that training in the tourist services sector is in a much earlier stage of development and has quite different manpower training requirements" (Ibid.). The study included a survey of educational institutions offering programmes in tourism education and training. The report provided an analysis of the different types of programmes offered among the institutions, along with the views of institutions directors as to what they judged to be the most critical education and training issues. The conclusion and findings were that there is a lack of experienced teachers, a lack of educator industry interface, a lack of professional development programmes, a lack of receptiveness by industry for tourism graduates and a lack of information about tourism industry requirements.

Although the English Tourist Board study provided a framework to examine tourism education and training by defining the principle venues for programme delivery – degree courses, business studies courses, technical courses – it did not appear to be able to make any analysis based its objective "to examine the existing provision of education and training *in relation to the manpower needs of the industry . . .* " In discussing the management implications of the study, Lavery did, however, suggest that any school planning to offer tourism courses should first consult with people in the industry to determine the industry's specific manpower needs and secure needed support.

In 1989, another study was conducted by the National Economic Development Office (NEDO) in the UK, to determine if declining tourism competitiveness in the country related to major differences in how education and training was provided at the higher education level. The study compared the UK system to ones in six other countries: Canada, Germany, France, The Netherlands, Switzerland and the USA. The NEDO findings as reported by Parsons (1991, pp. 197–207) indicated that "The approaches taken towards management education for the tourist industries vary considerably between – and often within – each of these countries" (Ibid., pp. 205–206).

This analysis is substantiated by others, such as Rutter (1991), who compared the French and British systems. Rutter found that, in higher education programmes for the tourism/hospitality sector, the French system presented a more sequenced path, with better built-in bridges for skill development and productivity (Ibid., p. 358). Nevertheless, while he argued that the more rigid central control of the French system, including a more rigorous examination process, produced students with "nationally assured academic standards," he contended that the timetables that go along with this system were not able to accommodate the out-of-the-classroom and practical learning experience usually deemed necessary in tourism/hospitality education. Rigidity of educational structures has been severely questioned in other studies, which argue that the dynamic process of tourism and hospitality require systems that are flexible and easily adaptable to industry changes (Pollack and Ritchie, 1990, p. 576).

Education and training systems vary widely between counties, but the NEDO study found that there were also many challenges common to all of the countries studied. In particular, the report observed a rapid expansion of high level degree programmes in tourism in each country. There was evidence in some of these countries that the rise of high degree level programmes resulted in the demise of intermediate level programmes, which had been an important source for skilled front line, supervisory and manager trainee workers. Although there were age differences among entry-level workers from one country to another, all of the countries in the study had systems for education and training at the intermediate level. For example, a Higher National Diploma (HND) was available in the UK, a Brevet de Technicien Superieur (BTS) in France and the associate bachelor degree programme in the United States.

Despite the increased production of graduates from high level degree programmes, evidence suggests that there is not uniform acceptance by industry of the value of such degrees. An analysis of the number of high level degree recipients who actually found employment within the industry in the UK was indicated only to be 50%, whereas in Germany, France, Switzerland and the United States the percentage was over 80%. Obviously, these percentages need to be weighed against other factors such as, the number of students entering who complete programmes, practical work components of school programmes and how these experience affect perceptions and desire to continue careers in the industry, the differing systems for pre-selection and admission into school programmes, as well as other labour dynamics, such as the presence and organization of unions, and variances in the performance of the economy in each country (Riley, 1993, pp. 47–59). The NEDO study also found that, with the exception of the United States, there is limited access to continuing management education or post-experience programmes, which were deemed critical.

While the English Tourism Board and NEDO studies raised a compelling set of issues in tourism education and training, later government studies have focused on the development of competency-based standards (notably in the UK and Canada) to assure a better match between education system outputs and industry needs. Initiatives in several countries have led to the development of actual skill and vocational standards and new approaches (such as industry- government councils) to better assess the full scope of the tourism industry and its employment needs. The development of such standards, though, is still in its infancy. To date, standards are only operative for a handful of occupations, mostly at the lower or the vocation level.

Headway was made in this effort in Europe in 1974, when the European Centre for the Development of Vocational Training (CEDEFOP), mandated by the European Council, developed a set of competency-based qualifications for various occupations or vocations (Cooper et al., 1994, p. 116). Prior to the existence of CEDEFOP, the UK's Industrial Training Act of 1964 established Industrial Training Boards, and in particular, the Hotel and Catering Industrial Training Board (HCITB), to ensure "the availability in the industry of the right number of trained people at the right time and place with the right skills" (Kelly, 1982, p. 22). During the next 20 years, the funding of these boards shifted between industry and government, and today the HCITB is organized as the Hotel Training Company. Kelly cites many problems the hotel and catering industry faced during this period, particularly in obtaining accurate data to predict the manpower needs of industry and in developing consensus between employers and educational institutions on education and training requirements. An additional body was thus formed, the Education and Training Advisory Council (ETAC), to provide "a forum for discussion and action on any matters which cross the boundaries between education and training, manpower and industry" (Ibid.). In 1986, the UK established a policymaking body, the National Council for Vocational Qualifications (NCVQ), to develop a framework for vocation qualifications on four levels of occupational competence (Ibid., p. 115). This organization is empowered to accredit qualifications offered by professional industry organizations.

The closest US counterpart to the NCVQ initiative was made possible by a 1993 grant from the US federal government to the CHRIE. The CHRIE initiative called for the establishment of the Hospitality and Tourism Skills Board, whose charge was to "develop and help implement national *voluntary* skill standards for our combined industry" (CHRIE, 1995b). CHRIE's research was directed at identifying tasks involved in certain occupations and the skills employees would need to perform those tasks competently. For example, the most important skills identified for a front desk clerk were: listening comprehension, oral expression and PC workstation keyboard operation. Necessary personal qualities were determined to be responsibility, self-esteem, sociability, integrity and self-management. The study was limited in three ways: it has, to date, assessed only eight positions, one occupation level (front line workers) and two sectors (food service and lodging). It was also designed only to set skill standards, and not to discern whether the majority of employees in those positions possessed or lacked the skills and qualities deemed needed.

In Canada, the development of occupational standards came out of the formation of the Tourism Industry Standards and Certification Committee and the Canadian Tourism Resource Council (CTRC) (Hawkins, 1996; Swedlove & Dowler, 1992, pp. 283–284). Two Canadian provinces, Alberta and British Columbia, have been particularly effective in developing the pioneer models, in which industry works with government to develop a "strategic infrastructure" for tourism education and training (Pollack and Ritchie, 1990). Although both provinces embarked on separate programmes with similar ambitions, the results led to models (the "Alberta Model" and the "British Columbia Model") that desegregated the tourism and hospitality sector in terms of component sub-sectors, occupation levels, and education and training needed at each port of entry. The Alberta and British Columbia models became crucial elements in the methodological structure of this study. The Alberta model included the delivery modes for education and training, identified by sectors, and occupation levels. It introduced career paths for entrants into the industry in terms of qualifications needed at each occupation level (as ascertained by degrees or diplomas earned). Models have now been implemented, with local adaptations, in all Canadian provinces.

Focus on issues for improving education and training systems

There is a growing realization in both industry and government that human resource and organizational development is the key to unlocking potential

tourism and hospitality growth opportunities to achieve a competitive advantage in companies and countries. There is also an emerging recognition that
competitive advantage begins in the classroom.

(Go, 1991, p. 1).

There is an ample supply of articles written by both educators and
professionals which have attempted to identify critical issues related to
improving education and training systems in the tourism and hospitality
field. In the post 11 September era, many important international conferences and meetings have brought tourism educators and professionals from the private and public sectors together to explore, identify and
prioritize issues related to the development of human resources for the
tourism industry. Key among these was the UNWTO- GW Tourism Policy
Forum in October, 2005, Washington, DC, described elsewhere in this volume. This is a strong historical trend for the industry. Between 1990 and
1995 alone, 65 conferences were held on tourism and education, with key
ones including PATA Human Resources Conference on Asia Pacific Travel
and Tourism: The New Workplace – Gearing Up for Growth, Vancouver,
1994; New Horizons Conference, the University of Calgary and the University of Surrey, Alberta, Canada 1991; Global Assessment of Tourism
Policy, The George Washington University, Washington, DC, 1990; Canada
CHRIE Regional Meeting: Bridging the Gap, University of Guelph, 1989.
The PATA conference was connected to a study commissioned by the
WTTC, *Gearing Up for Growth* (1994b). An underlying theme throughout is
a shift from educator-driven education and training systems to ones that
are more centred on industry needs. The wealth of ideas and recommendations generated from these conferences has been captured and distilled
in articles published by lead educators in the field, particularly, Cooper,
Ritchie, and Jafari. The industry also has shown an increased interest in
the subject, allocating resources for research on education and training
and human resource development in specific sectors and regions. It is
worth noting that recent studies have been commissioned by the WTTC
on education and training for careers in tourism. Their study, *Gearing Up
for Growth* (1994b) focused on the Asia Pacific region, and their 1996 study,
focused on Latin America and the Caribbean, were among the first, setting
the precedent for excellence in regional and global tourism workforce and
education research.

Unique among the findings and outcomes of professional meetings and
conferences, Ritchie (1993) used a conference format in 1991, which brought
together 200 educators from 25 countries (Ibid., p. 10). While issues were
identified and prioritized, the results were limited to the perspective of
educators, and not all tourism stakeholders. The Guelph University conference in 1992 polled 24 employers, educators, employees and students
for the purpose of evaluating and comparing in their perceptions and

expectations of one another (Haywood and Maki, 1992, pp. 240–248). The study showed there were significant gaps in the perceptions and expectations of employers, educators and employees, and concluded, "To the extent that employers or corporate executives realize the value that education, training and development can add to corporate strategy the greater the likelihood that the gaps facing all participants at the education and employment interface will be addressed and narrowed".

A world forum, held in 1990, which addressed global tourism policy (Spivack, 1991, pp. 1–16), produced a set of prioritized issues which included human resource development. The forum utilized a matrix approach for selecting participants or experts, to help ensure "the unbiased analysis of the complex issues" (Ibid., 3). The panel participants or Assembly for this forum included "a broad geographic representation of industry sector analysts, academicians, policy-makers, multinational business executives as well as managers of small enterprises and tourism related organizations" (Ibid.). By consensus, the Assembly produced 19 issues which need to be addressed by policy makers over the next decade. The development of human resources for tourism was one of the issues identified, and the major recommendations made are presented as follows:

One of the specific issues that must be addressed is the need for an enhanced development of the human resource base in tourism through education and training. In particular, we need to

- give a greater overall priority to effective tourism education and training programmes at all levels;
- encourage all sectors of the tourism industry to actively cooperate in the development of training and education programmes to ensure that training meets trends of a diverse workplace, particularly in relation to the special needs and areas of multiculturalism, gender and age;
- enhance the integration of tourism subjects in the public sector education system on a worldwide basis; and
- foster the training, education and placement of indigenous management and workers (Ibid., p. 11).

The broad recommendations from these conference forums reinforced conclusions from earlier studies and led to significant changes and improvements in human resource development as, indeed, a consequential element for the prosperity of the tourism industry in the years ahead.

A number of educators have examined literature in order to identify issues and develop recommendations for improving tourism education and training in respect to increasing industry relationships. Cooper (1993) suggests that not only should industry representatives come to education (involving themselves in school advisory boards, participating in the upgrading of practicum opportunities, and so forth), but educators must

Table A.1 Comparison of studies on skill development

Author (Year)	Population surveyed	Skill area considered most important
Shaw and Patterson (1995)	Hospitality and food service industry	Service quality, motivation, communication
Morton (1994)	Hospitality industry	Marketing, human resources, finance
Breiter (1994)	Hospitality manager	Communications, employee relations, training and organization
LeBruto (1994)	Hotel school faculty	Practical work experience
Weiler (1993)	Nature tour operators	Organization, leadership, motivation, entertainment, interpretation, resource management
Enz (1993)	Hotel school faculty, alumni and current students	Strategic planning, communications, managerial styles, leadership
Grizzel (1992)	Travel agents	Credit transactions, legal issues, marketing strategies planning procedures
NRA (1991)	Food service industry	Communication, leadership, team building, training, motivation and supervision
Sheldon and Gee (1987)	Tourism sector employers and employees	Communication, courtesy, human relations

do a better job of keeping in touch with industry trends and practices. Cooper offered a list of suggestions culled from other sources (Burton, 1988; Goodenough and Page, 1993; Ritchie, 1988). These have been added to by others and are summarized in Table A2. For analysis purposes, the suggestions were clustered into the areas of teaching, programme and curriculum design, faculty development and external educator development.

Cooper's important research viewed the partnership role as also including cooperative efforts between professional bodies, such as the HCIMA, and industry for improving tourism and education training. He cites a list by Messenger (1992) which is presented in Table A3. For the purpose of this study, the suggestions are organized into the areas of curriculum development, research and facilitation.

The issues and recommendations presented in the previous tables indicate that gaps suggested in the premise of this study are an outcome of an

Table A.2 Strategies for improving tourism education and training through industry–educator partnerships

Area	Strategy	Source
Teaching	Outside visits to public and private sector organizations	Goodenough and Page (1993)
	Series of seminars and visiting speakers	Goodenough and Page (1993)
	Role playing	Goodenough and Page (1993)
	Group presentations and projects which provide a convincing simulation of the real world, possibly undertaken at the workplace	Goodenough and Page (1993)
	Preparation of case materials for teaching	Ritchie (1988)
	Applied dimension in research projects	Ritchie (1988) and Burton (1988)
	Better qualified teachers	Parsons (1991)
	Use of industry for adjunct teaching	Burton (1988)
Program curriculum design	Peer group assessment	Goodenough and Page (1993)
	Problem solving with a formal framework	Goodenough and Page (1993)
	Contracted learning	Goodenough and Page (1993)
	Cooperative programming	Ritchie (1988), Burton (1988) and Parsons (1991)
	Portfolio programmes, credit for prior learning	Ritchie (1988) and Ritchie (1993)
	Intensive formats for course delivery	Burton (1988) and Parsons (1991)
	Work credit arrangements	Burton (1988)
	Practicum with intern contracts, log books and close academic supervision.	Parsons (1991)
	Arrangements that create student mobility between institutions and industry (including articulation agreements)	Parsons (1991)

(Continued)

Table A.2 Continued

Area	Strategy	Source
Teaching	Use of international programming mechanism	Parsons (1991) and Ritchie (1993)
	Adapting new technologies for teaching (university to work site, etc.)	Parsons (1991)
	More provision of post-experience and continuing management education	Parsons (1991) and Ritchie (1993)
	Serving on Boards of Directors of industry associations and private firms	Ritchie (1993) and Shepherd and Cooper (1995) Ritchie (1988)
Faculty development		
	Consulting	Ritchie (1988)
	Industry exchange programmes	Ritchie (1988)
Educator external	Feedback sessions	Goodenough and Page (1993)
	Practical experience before teaching	Burton (1988)
	Cooperation with the tourism industry	Goodenough and Page (1993) and Ritchie (1988)
	Use of industry advisory councils	Ritchie (1988) and Burton (1988)
	Developing as an academic community established through out-reach conferences and seminars	Shepherd and Cooper (1995)
	Supporting quality auditing through external organizations such as the WTO and ETEN	Shepherd and Cooper (1995)

Table A.3 Strategies for improving tourism education and training through government and industry partnerships

Area	Strategy
Program curriculum design	Provide institutions with information which will assist them in developing curricula
	Provide hospitality companies with information and advice on skills and knowledge requirements of managers working different sectors of the industry
	Provide information on the functions that hospitality managers perform at different levels and in different situations
	Provide content in environmental management
Research	Identify the education and training needs of managers in the European hospitality industry
	Provide information on how management roles may change in the future as a result of economic, social, technological and other changes
	Assess the extent to which the skills and knowledge required by hospitality managers are generic and may be transferable to different industries
Facilitation	Establish less rigid mechanism for access to higher-level courses

Messenger (1992)
Source: Cooper (1993)

embryonic discipline that is just beginning to engage in more expansive learning modes involving both industry and government in delivering education and training.

A foundation-setting industry-driven study, among the first ever to examine the education and training issues in the Asia-Pacific area, was conducted by the WTTC entitled, *Gearing Up for Growth*. This study included surveys of employers as well as 13 national tourism organizations regarding their perceptions at that time of education and training needs for the region (WTTC, 1994b).

The study attempted to present the major issues on tourism human resource development in the Asia-Pacific Area, drawing from both primary and secondary sources and relating them to the results of their survey. As Table A4 indicates, the problems identified in literature were confirmed by the results of the survey of employers. This survey found that employers were not satisfied with the workers produced by the then current education and training programmes, and that there was a need for more formal, quality-service oriented education and training containing greater "real world" applied relevancy.

The most serious limitation of the WTTC study was that there appeared to be no criteria for sector representation in the employers' survey, which

Table A.4 WTTC study on education and training in Asia-Pacific region

Major issues – secondary sources	*Major issues – survey results*
Lack of tourism education facilities	Need more qualified workers, particularly at the level
Lack of qualified instructors	Need for industries to reallocate training expenditure to include workers
Lack of standards and certification	Need better formal education and training programs
Lack of relevancy in education and training	Need more relevancy of formal tourism education to realities of the workplace
Lack of coordination in national training strategies	Need for education and training programmes to keep abreast of changes which affect industry
	Need for countries to address the issue of expatriate labour at unskilled and semi-skilled level, and also at managerial level
	Need to strengthen corporate training departments

Source: WTTC

resulted in selection bias toward the hotel and resort sector (68% of the respondents) (WTTC, 1994b, 8). Additionally, no definitions were provided for the occupational levels; thus, the results were difficult to relate to this study. For example, it was difficult to ascertain the difference between two of the four occupation levels – managerial and professional – in which data were collected.

Assessment of skill and training needs

Most studies and articles assessing education and training in tourism examined only hotels and food services. Furthermore, most of the articles and studies reviewed above fall into one of three general types:

1. Those that concentrate on skill development for improving industry performance;
2. Those that focus on the role of government for also improving industry performance and
3. Those relate to education systems for improving curricula and the output of these systems, with particular reference to increasing relationships with industry.

There is some overlap, with a number of studies fitting into one or more categories. Sheldon and Gee (1987) observe in assessing the education and training needs of the hospitality and tourism industry that most published articles dealt with hotels and catering services, mainly done "for the industry either by governments, or by educational institutions seeking to improve their respective curricula" (Ibid., p. 174). Thus, it would appear that today's education and training in tourism assessment literature has much in common with that of the last two decades.

References

Baum, T. (1991). The U.S. and the U.K.: Comparing Expectations of Management Trainees. *Cornell Hotel and Restaurant Administration Quarterlym,* 32(2) 79–84.

Breiter, D. (1995). *Hospitality Management Curricula for the 21st Century.* CHRIE Conference.

Burton, P. (1988). *Building Bridges Between Industry and Education,* University of Surrey, Teaching Tourism Into the 1990's Conference.

Cooper, C. (1993). An Analysis of the Relationship Between Industry and Education in Travel and Tourism. Teros International. Vol. 1(1).

Cooper, C. , Shepperd, R. and J. Westlake (1994). Tourism Hospitality and Education. The University of Surrey, Guildford.

Council on Hotel. Restaurant and Institutional Education. (1995). Building Skills by Building Alliances, Washington, DC.

Council on Hotel, Restaurant and Institutional Education, Washington, DC. (1995a). *A Guide to College Programmes in Hospitality and Tourism.*

Echtner, Charlotte M. (1995) Tourism Education in Developing Nations: A Three Pronged Approach. Tourism Recreation Research, 20 (2), 32–41.

Enz, C. (1993). Graduate-Level Education: A Survey of Stakeholders. *Cornell Hotel and Restaurant Administration Quarterly,* 34(4), 90–95.

Evans, J. (1993). Tourism Graduates: A Case of Over-Production. *Tourism Management,* August, 243–246.

Go, F. (1991). *New Horizons in Tourism and Hospitality Education, Training and Research (Conference Proceedings),* World Tourism Education and Research Centre, The University of Calgary.

Goodenough, R. and S. Page (1993). Planning for Tourism Education and Training in the 1990's: Bridging the Gap Between Industry and Education. *Journal of Geography in Higher Education,* 17(1), 57–72.

Grizzle, R. (1992). Continuing Education: Honing Your Management Skills. *ASTA Agency Management,* 61(9), 42–46.

Hawkins, D. (1996). *Investing in Human Resources: An Essential Sustainable Tourism Development Strategy for the Middle East and North Africa Region.* Presentation, Seminar on Sustainable Tourism Development in the Middle East and North Africa, Amman, Jordan.

Haywood, M. and K. Maki (1992). A Conceptual Model of the Education/ Employment Interface for the Tourism Industry. *World Travel and Tourism Review*, Eds. J.R. Ritchie, Donald Hawkins, et al. CAB International. 2, 237–241.

Kelly, T. (1992). Research into the Vocational Education and Training Requirements of the Hotel and Catering Industry in the UK. *Journal of Travel Research*, 21(2), 22–26.

Lavery, P. (1988). Careers in Tourism. *Tourism Management*, 9(2), 167–171.

LeBruto, Stephen M. (1994). The Educational Value of *Captive Hotels*. Cornell Hotel & Restaurant Administration Quarterly, Vol. 35 (4), pp. 72–79.

Messenger, S. (1992). The Implications of Competence Based Education and Training Programmes for the Hospitality Industry in the 1990's. *Tourism Management*, 13(1), 134–136.

Mills, S. and H. Riehle (1993). Foodservice Manager 2000. *Hospitality Research Journal*, 17(1), 147–159.

Morton, A. (1994). Education: Hospitality Schools Send the Industry Plenty of Workers Every Year . . . But Are They Ready? *Restaurant Business*, 93(3), 48.

Parsons, D. (1991). The Making of Managers: Lessons from an International Review of Tourism Management Education Programmes. *Tourism Management*, 12(3), 197–207.

Pollock, A. and J. Ritchie (1990). Integrated Strategy for Tourism Education/ Training. *Annals of Tourism Research*, 17(4), 568–585.

Riley, M. (1993). *Labor Market and Vocational Education. Human Resource Issues in International Tourism*, Eds. Tom Baum. Butterworth-Heinemann, Oxford: 47–59.

Ritchie, J. (1993). Educating the Tourism Educators: Guidelines for Policy and Programme Development. *Teros International*, 1(1), 9–24.

Ritchie J. (1988). *Alternative Approaches to Teaching Tourism*. Teaching Tourism into the 1990's, Conference Paper, University of Surrey.

Rutter, D. (1991). Catering Education and Training in France and Britain: Some Implications for Productivity. *Tourism Management*, 12(4), 356–360.

Shaw, M. and J. Patterson (1995). Management-Development Programmes: A Canadian Perspective. *Cornell Hotel and Restaurant Administration Quarterly*, 36(1), 34–39.

Sheldon, P. and C. Gee (1987). Assessment of Professional Education and Training in Tourism. *Annals of Tourism Research*, 14(2).

Shepperd, R. and C. Cooper (1995). Innovations in Tourism Education and Training. Tourism Recreation Research. 20(2), 14–24

Spivack, S. (1991). Assembly Report – Global Assessment of Tourism Policy: Policy Issues for the 1990's. The George Washington University, Washington, DC: 1–16.

Swedlove, W. and S. Dowler (1992). Competency-Based Occupational Standards and Certification for the Tourism Industry. *World Travel and Tourism Review*, 2, 283–291.

Tas, R. (1988). Teaching Future Managers. Cornell Hotel & Restaurant Administration Quarterly, 29(2), 41–43.

United Nations World Tourism Organization, Madrid, Spain. (1992a), *World Directory of Tourism Education and Training Institutions*.

Weiler, B. (1993). An Exploratory Investigation into the Roles of the Nature-Based Tour Leader. *Tourism Management*, 14(2), 91–98.

World Travel and Tourism Council. (1994b). *Gearing Up for Growth*.

Appendix B

AGREEMENT BETWEEN THE UNITED STATES OF AMERICA AND THE UNITED MEXICAN STATES ON THE DEVELOPMENT AND FACILITATION OF TOURISM

CONSIDERING that the United States of America and the United Mexican States share an extended border and have developed close neighborly and commercial relations;

RECOGNIZING that international cooperation and economic exchange should serve to foster man's development, to enhance mutual respect for human dignity, and to promote common welfare;

ACKNOWLEDGING that the promotion of tourism is considered a legitimate diplomatic and consular function;

CONVINCED that tourism, because of its socio-cultural and economic dynamics, is an excellent instrument for promoting economic development, understanding, goodwill, and close relations between peoples;

NOTING that a valuable structure for tourism, already existing between both countries, stands ready for further development;

The Governments of the United States of America and the United Mexican States (the Parties) agree to conclude a Tourism Agreement which, within their respective legal frameworks, will promote the objectives stated in the following provisions;

ARTICLE I
Government Tourism Offices and Personnel

1. In conformance with the laws, regulations, polities and procedures of the host Party, each Party;
   (a) May establish and operate official travel promotion offices in the territory of the other Party, and,
   (b) Agrees to accredit as members of a diplomatic or consular post tourism officials of the other Party.
2. Such tourism personnel shall perform traditional diplomatic or consular functions (e.g., the officials do not perform commercial transactions, including making airline or other travel arrangements or performing other similar services normally provided by travel agencies).

ARTICLE II
Development of the Tourism Industry and Infrastructure

1. The Parties, subject to their laws, will facilitate and encourage the activities of tourism service providers such as travel agents, tour wholesalers and operators, hotel chains, airlines, railroads, motor coach operators, and steamship companies generating two-way tourism between their countries.
2. Each Party will,
   (a) Permit air, sea and surface carriers of the other Party, whether public or private, to open sales agencies and to appoint representatives in its territory in order to market their services;
   (b) In accordance with the bilateral Air Transport Agreement, encourage the carriers of the other Party to develop and promote, through designated and authorized sales outlets in its territory, departures from their own territories with special or excursion fares designed to encourage reciprocal tourist travel;
   (c) Permit the sale of promotional transportation tickets for use in the territory of one Party by carriers of the other Party through authorized outlets in its territory;
   (d) Expedite, to the extent possible, the award to carriers of new air routes established under the bilateral Air Transport Agreement signed by both countries; and
   (e) In accordance with overall discussions and negotiations between the two countries, initiate substantive dialogue on motor carrier issues which impact on tourism.
3. To the extent that either Party is subject to statutes imposing duty on the entrance of ticket stock or sales materials of the carriers or tourism

enterprises of the other, that Party shall review those statutes with the objective of providing for the eventual duty-free entry of such materials on a reciprocal basis.

ARTICLE III
Facilitation and Documentation

1. The Parties will endeavor to facilitate travel of tourists into both countries by simplifying and eliminating, as appropriate, procedural and documentary requirements.
2. Each Party shall facilitate, to the extent permitted by its laws, the entry of performers and artists who:
    (a) Are nationals of the other Party; and
    (b) Have been invited to participate in international cultural events to be held in its territory.
3. Each Party shall take all necessary facilitative measures to encourage binational cultural events which would strengthen ties and promote tourism.
4. The Parties will consult on the opening of additional border crossing points and on the designation of such points as high priority based on the needs of touristic development of each area.
5. The Parties will encourage the training of personnel at ports of entry and elsewhere within their respective territories so that tourists' rights are respected and tourists of both countries are extended all appropriate courtesies.
6. The Parties shall consider, on the basis of reciprocity, and on official request, waiving applicable visa fees for the entry and exit of teachers and experts in the field of tourism.
7. Aware of the importance of automobile collision and liability coverage to automobile tourism between the two countries, the Parties shall publicize in the territory of the other, in accordance with applicable regulations in each country, the respective automobile insurance requirements, either by distributing information through their respective national tourist offices or by other appropriate means.
8. Both Parties recognize the necessity of promoting, within their respective facilities and administrative capabilities, the health and safety of tourists from the other country, whether traveling by automobile or any other means of transportation, and will either provide information about available medical services or encourage government and non-government organizations or agencies to do so as needed.
9. Both Parties recognize the need for promoting and facilitating, where possible, investment by Americans and Mexican investors in their tourism sectors.

10.   The Parties shall consult with each other, as appropriate, in their multi-lateral efforts to reduce or eliminate barriers to international tourism.

ARTICLE IV
Cultural and Tourism Programs

1.   The Parties regard it appropriate to encourage tourist and cultural activities designed to strengthen the ties between the peoples and to improve the overall quality of life of the inhabitants of both countries and will consider exchange programs which are consistent with the cultural heritage of each country.
2.   The Parties will consider it a priority to promote travel to developing regions which contain examples of the native culture of each country, and to develop and improve tourist facilities and attractions in those areas.
3.   The Parties will encourage the balanced and objective presentation of their respective historic and socio-cultural heritage and promote respect for human dignity and conservation of cultural, archaeological, and ecological resources.
4.   The Parties will exchange information concerning the use of facilities for shows and exhibitions in their countries.

ARTICLE V
Tourism Training

1.   The Parties consider it desirable to encourage their respective experts to exchange technical information and/or documents in the following fields;
     (a) Systems and methods to prepare teachers and instructors in technical matters, particularly with respect to procedures for facilitation, hotel operation and administration:
     (b) Scholarships for teachers, instructors, and students;
     (c) Curricula and study programs to train personnel who provide tourism services; and
     (d) Curricula and study programs for hotel schools.
2.   Each Party will encourage their respective students and professors of tourism to take advantage of fellowships offered by colleges, universities, and training centers of the other.

ARTICLE VI
Tourism Statistics

1.   Both Parties will do what is possible to improve the reliability and compatibility of statistics on tourism between the two countries, in both the border and interior regions.

2. The Parties agree to establish a technical committee on tourism statistics in which the appropriate agencies of both countries shall participate.
   (a) The committee shall address itself to the exchange and reconciliation of statistical data measuring tourism between the two countries and to the improvement of collecting such data.
   (b) The committee will consider the conduct of joint research studies.
   (c) The committee shall meet alternately in the United States and Mexico at least twice a year.
3. The Parties consider it desirable to exchange information on the size and characteristics of the actual and potential tourism markets in their two countries.
4. The Parties agree that the guidelines on the collection and presentation of domestic and international tourism statistics established by the World Tourism Organization shall constitute the requirements for such a data base.

ARTICLE VII
Joint Marketing of Tourism

1. Subject to budgetary limitations, the Parties shall consider the conduct of joint marketing activities in third countries.
2. Activities which shall receive consideration include joint operation of inspection trips for tour wholesalers and operators, and journalists from third countries, film festivals, travel trade shows and travel missions.

ARTICLE VIII
World Tourism Organization

1. The Parties shall work within the World Tourism Organization to develop, and encourage the adoption of, uniform standards and recommended practices which, if applied by governments, would facilitate tourism.
2. The Parties shall assist one another in matters of cooperation and effective participation in the World Tourism Organization.

ARTICLE IX
Consultations

1. The Parties agree that tourism and tourism matters shall be discussed, as appropriate, in bilateral consultations attended by representatives of their official tourism organizations. These meetings shall be held alternately in the United States and Mexico at least once a year.
2. Whenever possible these consultations will be held in conjunction with other meetings of the United States of America and the United Mexican

States. Both Parties will consider the possibility of establishing working groups to consider specific issues or articles of the Agreement.

3. The consultations to be undertaken under this Agreement constitute a part of the efforts to improve bilateral cooperation in the framework of the U.S.-Mexico Binational Commission. Therefore, both Parties shall report periodically to the Binational Commission on their programs, results and recommendations.

4. The United Mexican States designates the Tourism Secretariat as its agency with primary responsibility for implementing this Agreement for Mexico.

5. The United States of America designates the U.S. Department of Commerce as its agency with primary responsibility for implementing this Agreement for the United States.

ARTICLE X
Protocols

1. The Parties may implement this Agreement through protocols. Protocols may cover subjects such as cooperative activities to facilitate tourism, tourism training, joint marketing, development of tourism statistics, funding, procedures to be followed in such joint projects, and other appropriate matters.

2. The cost of all activities under this article shall be mutually agreed upon. These expenses for such activities will be borne subject to all applicable laws and regulations and to the availability of human and financial resources.

ARTICLE XI
Tourism Agreement of 1983 Superseded

This Agreement shall supersede and replace the Tourism Agreement between the Parties, signed April 18, 1983.

ARTICLE XII
Period of Effectiveness

1. Each Party shall inform the other by way of diplomatic note of the completion of necessary legal requirements in its country for entry into force of the present Agreement. The Agreement shall enter into force upon receipt of such notification by the second Party.

2. Upon entry into force, this Agreement shall be valid for a period of five years and will be renewed automatically for additional periods of five years unless either Party expresses objection in writing, through diplomatic channels three months prior to the expiration date.

3.   This Agreement shall be terminated ninety days after either Party transmits written notice of its intention to terminate to the other Party.

ARTICLE
XIII Notification

After entry into force, both Parties agree to notify the Secretariat General of the World Tourism Organization of this Agreement and any subsequent amendments.

DONE at Washington, DC this third day of October, 1989 in two originals in the English and Spanish languages, both texts being equally authentic.

Appendix C

B. TOURISM SERVICES
Article 1: Scope and Coverage

1. This Sectoral Annex shall apply to any measure related to trade in tourism services.

2. For purposes of this Sectoral Annex:

    tourism services include the tourism-related activities of the following: travel agency and related travel services including tour wholesaling, travel counseling, arranging and booking; issuance of travelers' insurance; all modes of international passenger transportation; hotel reservation services; terminal services for all modes of transport, including concessions; transportation; intercity tour operation; guide and interpreter services; automobile rental; provision of resort facilities; rental of recreational equipment; food services; retail services; organizational and support services for international conventions; marina-related services including the fueling, supply, and repair of, and provision of docking space to pleasure boats; recreational vehicle rental; campground and trailer park services; amusement park services; commercial tourist attractions; and tourism-related services of a financial nature;

tourism-related services of a financial nature means such services provided by an entity that is not a financial institution as defined in Article 1706; and

trade in tourism services means the provision of a tourism service by a person of a Party

(a) within the territory of that Party to a visitor who is a resident of the other Party, or

(b) within the territory of the other Party to a resident of, or visitor to, the other Party, either cross-border, through a commercial presence or through an establishment in the territory of the other Party.

Article 2: Obligations

1. This Chapter shall apply to all measures related to trade in tourism services, which measures include:

   (a) provision of tourism services in the territory of a Party, either individually or with members of a travel industry trade association;

   (b) appointment, maintenance and commission of agents or representatives in the territory of a Party to provide tourism services;

   (c) establishment of sales offices or designated franchises in the territory of a Party; and

   (d) access to basic telecommunications transport networks.

2. Provided that such promotional activities do not include the provision of tourism services for profit, each Party may promote officially in the territory of the other Party the travel and tourism opportunities in its own territory, including engagement in joint promotions with tourism enterprises of that Party and provincial, state and local governments.

3. The Parties recognize that the adoption or application of fees or other charges on the departure or arrival of tourists from their territories impedes the free flow of tourism services. When such fees or other charges are imposed, they shall be applied in a manner consistent with Article 1402 and limited in amount to the approximate cost of the services rendered.

4. Neither Party shall impose, except in conformity with Article VIII of the *Articles of Agreement of the International Monetary Fund*, restrictions on the value of tourism services that its residents or visitors to its territory may purchase from persons of the other Party.

Article 3: Relationship to the Agreement

Nothing in this Sectoral Annex shall be construed as:

(a)   conferring rights or imposing obligations on a Party relating to computer services and enhanced services as defined in Annex 1404(C), financial services as defined in Article 1706 and transportation services that are not otherwise conferred or imposed pursuant to any other provision of the Agreement and its annexes; or

(b)   affecting in any way the application of measures relating to the provision of tourism-related services of a financial nature.

Article 4: Consultation

The Parties shall consult at least once a year to:

(a)   identify and seek to eliminate impediments to trade in tourism services; and

(b)   identify ways to facilitate and increase tourism between the Parties.

Appendix D

MANILA DECLARATION ON WORLD TOURISM

The World Tourism Conference,

Held at Manila, Philippines, from 27 September to 10 October 1980, convened by the World Tourism Organization with the participation of 107 delegations of States and 91 delegations of observers, in order to clarify the real nature of tourism in all its aspects and the role tourism is bound to play in a dynamic and vastly changing world, as well as to consider the responsibility of States for the development and enhancement of tourism in present-day societies as more than a purely economic activity of nations and peoples,

Noting with satisfaction the addresses of His Excellency Ferdinand E. Marcos, President of the Republic of the Philippines, and Madame Imelda Romualdez Marcos, Governor of Metropolitan Manila and Minister of Human Settlements, as well as the messages of the Heads of State and of Government to the conference, the statements of delegations and the report of the Secretary-General of the World Tourism Organization,

Considering that world tourism can develop in a climate of peace and security which can be achieved through the joint effort of all States in promoting the reduction of international tension and in developing international cooperation in a spirit of friendship, respect for human rights and understanding among all States,

Convinced further that world tourism can contribute to the establishment of a new international economic order that will help to eliminate the widening economic gap between developed and developing countries and ensure the steady acceleration of economic and social development and progress, in particular of the developing countries,

Aware that world tourism can only flourish if based on equity, sovereign equality, non-interference in internal affairs and cooperation among all States, irrespective of their economic and social systems, and if its ultimate aim is the improvement of the quality of life and the creation of better living conditions for all peoples, worth of human dignity,

Agrees, in this spirit, to declare the following:

1. Tourism is considered an activity essential to the life of nations because of its direct effects on the social, cultural, educational and economic sectors of national societies and their international relations. Its development is linked to the social and economic development of nations and can only be possible if man has access to creative rest and holidays and enjoys the freedom to travel within the framework of free time and leisure whose profoundly human character it underlines. Its very existence and development depend entirely on the existence of a state of lasting peace, to which tourism itself is required to contribute.

2. On the threshold of the twenty-first century and in view of the problems facing mankind, it seems timely and necessary to analyse the phenomenon of tourism, in relation fundamentally to the dimensions it has assumed since the granting to workers of the right to annual paid holidays moved tourism from a restricted elitist activity to a wider activity integrated into social and economic life.

3. As a result of peoples' aspirations to tourism, the initiatives taken by States regarding legislation and institutions, the permanent activities of voluntary bodies representing the various strata of the population and the technical contribution made by specialized professionals, modern tourism has come to play an important role within the range of human activities. States have recognized this fact and the great majority of them have entrusted the World Tourism Organization with the task of ensuring the harmonious and sustained development of tourism, in cooperation, in appropriate cases, with the Specialized Agencies of the United Nations and the other international organizations concerned.

4. The right to use of leisure, and in particular the right to access to holidays and to freedom of travel and tourism, a natural consequence of the right to work, is recognized as an aspect of the fulfillment of the human being by the Universal Declaration of Human Rights as well as by the legislation of many States. It entails for society the duty of providing for its citizens the best practical, effective and non-discriminatory access to this type of activity. Such an effort must be in harmony with the priorities, institutions and traditions of each individual country.

5. There are many constraints on the development of tourism. Nation and groups of nations should determine and study these constraints, and adopt measures aimed at attenuating their negative influence.

6. The share tourism represents in national economies and in international trade makes it a significant factor in world development. Its consistent major role in national economic activity, in international transactions and in securing balance of payments equilibrium makes it one of the main activities of the world economy.

7. Within each country, domestic tourism contributes to an improved balance of the national economy through a redistribution of the national income. Domestic tourism also heightens the awareness of common interest and contributes to the development of activities favourable to the general economy of the country. Thus, the development of tourism from abroad should be accompanied by a similar effort to expand domestic tourism.

8. The economic returns of tourism, however real and significant they may be, do not and cannot constitute the only criterion for the decision by States to encourage this activity. The right to holidays, the opportunity for the citizen to get to know his own environment, a deeper awareness of his national identity and of the solidarity that links him to his compatriots and the sense of belonging to a culture and to a people are all major reasons for stimulating the individual's participation in domestic and international tourism, through access to holidays and travel.

9. The importance that millions of our contemporaries attach to tourism in the use of their free time and in their concept of the quality of life makes it a need that governments should take into account and support.

10. Social tourism is an objective which society must pursue in the interest of those citizens who are least privileged in the exercise of their right to rest.

11. Through its effects on the physical and mental health of individuals practicing it, tourism is a factor that favours social stability, improves the working capacity of communities and promotes individual as well as collective well-being.

12. Through the wide range of services needed to satisfy its requirements, tourism creates new activities of considerable importance which are a source of new employment. In this respect, tourism constitutes a positive element for social development in all the countries where it is practised irrespective of their level of development.

13. With respect to international relations and the search for peace, based on justice and respect of individual and national aspirations, tourism stands out as a positive and ever-present factor in promoting mutual knowledge and understanding and as a basis for reaching a greater level of respect and confidence among all the peoples of the world.

14. Modern tourism results from the adoption of a social policy which led to the workers gaining annual paid holidays and represents the recognition of a fundamental right of the human being to rest and leisure. It has become a factor contributing to social stability, mutual understanding among individuals and peoples and individual betterment. In addition to its well-known economic aspects, it has acquired a cultural and moral dimension which must be fostered and protected against the harmful distortions which can be brought about by economic factors. Public authorities and the travel trade should accordingly participate in development of tourism by formulating guidelines aimed at encouraging appropriate investments.

15. Youth tourism requires the most active attention since young people have less adequate income than others for traveling or taking holidays. A positive policy should provide youth with the utmost encouragement and facilities. The same attention should be provided for the elderly and handicapped.

16. In the universal efforts to establish a new international economic order, tourism can, under appropriate conditions, play a positive role in furthering equilibrium, cooperation, mutual understanding and solidarity among all countries.

17. Nations should promote improved conditions of employment for workers engaged in tourism and confirm and protect their right to establish professional trade unions and collective bargaining.

18. Tourism resources available in the various countries consist at the same time of space, facilities and values. These are resources whose

use cannot be left uncontrolled without running the risk of their deterioration or even their destruction. The satisfaction of tourism requirements must not be prejudicial to the social and economic interests of the population in tourist areas to the environment or, above all, to natural resources, which are the fundamental attraction of tourism, and historical and cultural sites. All tourism resources are part of the heritage of mankind. National communities and the entire international community must take the necessary steps to ensure their preservation. The conservation of historical, cultural and religious sites represents at all times, and notably in the time of conflict, one of the fundamental responsibilities of States.

19. International cooperation in the field of tourism is an endeavour in which the characteristics of peoples and basic interests of individual States must be respected. In this field, the central and decisive role of the World Tourism Organization as a conceptualizing and harmonizing body is obvious.

20. Bilateral and multilateral technical and financial cooperation cannot be looked upon as an act of assistance since it constitutes the pooling of the means necessary for the utilization of resources for the benefit of all parties.

21. In the practice of tourism, spiritual elements must take precedence over technical and material elements. The spiritual element are essentially as follows:

    (a) the total fulfillment of the human being,

    (b) a constantly increasing contribution to education,

    (c) equality of destiny of nations,

    (d) the liberation of man in a spirit of respect for his identity and dignity,

    (e) the affirmation of the originality of cultures and respect for the moral heritage of peoples.

22. Preparation for tourism should be integrated with the training of the citizen for his civic responsibilities. In this respect, governments should mobilize the means of education and information at their disposal and should facilitate the work of individuals and bodies involved in this endeavour. Preparation for tourism, for holidays and for travel could usefully form part of the process of youth education and training. For these reasons, the integration of tourism into youth education constitutes a basic element favourable to the permanent strengthening of peace.

23. Any long-term analysis of mankind's social, cultural and economic development should take due account of national and international tourist and recreational activities. These activities now form an integral part of the acknowledged values of tourism which are inseparable from it, the authorities will have to give more increased attention to the development of national and international tourist and recreational activity, based on an ever-wider participation of peoples in holidays and travel as well as the movement of persons for numerous other purposes, with a view to ensuring the orderly growth of tourism in a manner consistent with the other basic needs of society.

24. The States and other participants in the Conference, together with the World Tourism Organization, are strongly urged to take into account the guidelines, viewpoints and recommendations emanating from the Conference so that they can contribute, on the basis of their experience and in the context of their day-to-day activities to the practical implementation of the objectives set with a view to broadening the process of development of world tourism and breathing new life into it.

25. The Conference urges the World Tourism Organization to take all necessary measures, through its own internal machinery and, where appropriate, in cooperation with other international, intergovernmental and non-governmental bodies, so as to permit the global implementation of the principles, concepts and guidelines contained in this final document.

Appendix E

WORLD PEACE THROUGH TOURISM: THE COLUMBIA CHARTER

"The First Global Conference: Tourism – A Vital Force For Peace" (convened in Vancouver, British Columbia, Canada, October 23–27, 1988):

Observes that tourism is a worldwide social/cultural phenomenon involving people of all nations as hosts and guests;

Asserts that tourism is a fundamental human activity involving social, cultural, religious, economic, environmental, educational and political values and responsibilities;

Expresses the urgent reality that peace is an essential precondition for tourism and all other aspects of sustainable human growth and cultural development;

Acknowledges that tourism is growing more rapidly than other economic sectors;

Cautions that our global society has reached a critical crossroads in the earth's history demanding responsive strategies which address the political, social, economic and environmental problems facing humankind;

Promotes tourism which is in harmony with the world's natural and cultural resources;

Maintains that the monitoring, protection, preservation and wise use of the environment and ecological balance is essential to the future of tourism;

Encourages the funders and developers of tourism projects to support development which is consistent with the "social fabric" of the host community and reinforces local values, culture and the sustained vitality of the natural environment while providing equitable economic benefits to the local economy;

Seeks to advance the full exercise of human and civil rights as stated in the United Nations' Universal Declaration of Human Rights;

Recognizes that human understanding increases through face-to-face communication and positive interaction between people, especially at the community level;

Reinforces the hope that tourism will nurture conditions through which people can coexist, share their beliefs, appreciate each other's cultures and develop friendships;

Reminds that tourists are both teachers and students whose classroom is the world;

Advocates the development of educational systems both in institutions and in the community, in which everyone from industry leaders and government, to individual tourists, can learn the possibilities and the value of tourism as a force for peace;

Highlights the importance of accessibility to, and dissemination of, information concerning all peoples and regions of the world;

Calls for cooperative efforts between nations, private sector companies and volunteer organizations which foster and implement places for peace, twinning of cities and other exchange and connective programs;

Notes that government, academic and private sector leaders have identified and supported the potential of tourism as an influencing force for global peace through respect for human dignity, cultural diversity and the natural environment which supports all life;

Solemnly Calls upon all nations, governmental bodies, organizations and individuals to eliminate war, terrorism and injustices, stop the arms race, free hostages and shape new policies to guide public and private sector initiatives to build a world which works for everyone, and in which tourism:

- promotes mutual understanding, trust and goodwill;
- reduces economic inequities;

- develops in an integrated manner with the full participation of local host communities;

- improves the quality of life;

- protects and preserves the environment, both built and natural, and other local resources;

- contributes to the world conservation strategy of sustainable development

Resolves to implement the Conference recommendations and initiatives through responsible action undertaken:

- individually, through our interrelated roles as tourists, hosts and world citizens, guided by the "Credo of the peaceful Traveler;"

- collectively, through the International Institute for Peace through Tourism and the Columbia Club and through other such strategies required to reach the goal of "World Peace Through Tourism."

Appendix F

The following is a reproduction of the text of the May 24, 1993 letter signed by officials from the Travel Industry Association of America and the United States Department of Commerce regarding the Travel and Safety Security Initiative.

TRAVELER SAFETY AND SECURITY INITIATIVE

The United States Travel and Tourism Administration (USTTA) and the Travel Industry Association of America (TIA) have joined together to coordinate an industry-wide *Traveler Safety and Security Initiative*. The initiative is designed to bring together all elements of the U.S. travel and tourism product, consumers and suppliers alike, in pursuit of common approaches to traveler safety and security.

The *Traveler Safety and Security Initiative* will coordinate all elements of the U.S. travel and tourism industry–this includes public and private sector–to develop an action plan for suppliers to better inform travelers, thereby helping them to have a safer and more enjoyable travel experience. All private and public sector vertical organizations will be contacted so that current programs and practices in the area of traveler safety and security can be inventoried and catalogued. This material will be shared and distributed as widely as possible within the community of travel suppliers. The plan also would involve education and training for suppliers of the travel product on a sector-specific basis.

The *Traveler Safety and Security Initiative* will complement the *National Traveler Safety Campaign*, a major program launched earlier this year by a five-member coalition led by the American Hotel & Motel Association and including the American Automobile Association, the American Association of Retired Persons, the American Society of Travel Agents, and the National Crime Prevention Council. This coalition has a combined outreach potential to more than 100 million consumers.

USTTA and TIA believe that this supplier-and-consumer targeted initiative will achieve the desired effect of making the traveler better informed and, in so doing, making the USA travel experience more enjoyable.

David L. Edgell, Sr., Ph.D.
Acting Under Secretary of
Commerce for Travel and Tourism
USTTA

Edward R. Book
President
TIA

May 24, 1993

Index

Academy of Hospitality and
    Tourism: New York, 245
Access to Information Act: Canada,
    322–3
Accident compensation, 319
Accountability: aid usage, 268
Accrediting training, 235–8
Adventure tourism, 72, 341–2
Agreements, 142–3, 319, 383–9,
    391–3
Agritourism, 74, 121, 212–13
Aid coordination, 268, 349–50
Airline industry, 69–70
    aircraft technology, 103
    credit card use, 122
    demand, 107
    disruptions, 349
    global warming, 352–3
    quality experiences, 341
    safety, 156
Airports, 103, 267
Alabama, 261
Alaska, 185
Alex C. Walker Foundation, 202
American Competitiveness
    Initiative, 281–2, 295
Amoah, V., 243
Andorra, 238
Anthropological experts, 195
APEC (Asia-Pacific Economic
    Cooperation), 149–51
Appendices, 365–406
'Armchair' tourism, 185
Armstrong, Kate, 251
Arrivals: international, 100, 101,
    113, 331
Ascension Island, 271–3

Asia-Pacific Economic
    Cooperation (APEC), 149–51
Assamba, Aloun, 249
Australia, 83, 114
Automated Targeting System:
    security, 73
Avian influenza, 4, 156, 347

Balanced policies, 19–21
Bald Head Island: NC, 187
Bangalore, India, 104
Barcelona: Spain, 224
Battuta, Ibn, 41
Baum, T., 223–8, 232, 242–5
Beaches, 17–18, 81, 130, 153
Beeton, Sue, 251
Beirman, David, 249–50
Belize, 67–8
Berno, Tracy, 19
BEST EN *see* Business Enterprises
    for Sustainable Tourism
    Education Network
Biometric chips, 154–5, 171
Bird influenza, 347
Birding Trail: NC, 213
Black, Pamela, 205–6
Blogs, 336
Blueprint for New Tourism: WTTC,
    128, 145–6, 196
Boat travel, 40
Bonds, 79–80, 349
Brand image, 31–2, 49–51
Branson, Richard, 352–3
Brazil, 75–6
Break-even, 290, 294
Buchanan, James, 263
Budgets, 270, 284–5, 321
    see also Funding

Built environment, 182–3, 186,
    189–91, 196, 306, 332
Bull, P., 13
Bush Jr, George, 281–2
Business degrees, 233–4
Business Enterprises for
    Sustainable Tourism
    Education Network (BEST
    EN), 247–54
  modules, 247–8, 253
  think tanks, 247–54
  visioning, 253
Business travel, 107, 122
By-laws, 318

The Calculus of Consent (Buchanan
    and Tullock), 263
California: US, 201
Callahan Creek marketing
    agency, 26
Cambodia, 252
Canada:
  code of ethics, 135, 192–3
  integrating stakeholders, 243
  strategic planning, 301–2, 307–23
  tourism policy, 308–23
  training programmes, 241
  US-Canada free trade
    agreement, 391–3
Canadian Bureau of Tourism
    (CBT), 309
Canadian Government Office of
    Tourism (CGOT), 309
Canadian Tourism Commission
    (CTC), 16, 301–2, 315–23
  Act establishing CTC, 315–23
  challenges, 312–13
  funding, 311–12
  future, 313–14
  partnerships, 311–12
  results, 312
  structure, 310–11
Canoeing, 216
Cape Lookout National
    Seashore, 98
Capital budgets, 321

Cargo, 70
Caribbean Tourism Organization
    (CTO), 151–2
Carlsen, Jack, 251
Carrying capacity, 132–4, 184
Case studies:
  BEST EN, 247–54
  Canadian tourism policy, 307–23
  coastline tourism, 123–36
  cost-benefit analysis, 281–95
  ecotourism, 199–216
  Global Code of Ethics for
    Tourism, 354–61
  Kansas tourism, 20–32
  National Tourism Policy Act,
    51–62
  red wolf ecotourism, 201–16
  STPC, 165–80
  US visitor data, 281–95
  World Hotel Link, 82–93
Catastrophe bonds, 349
CBT (Canadian Bureau of
    Tourism), 309
Centre for Sustainable Tourism:
    NC, 240–1
Certification programmes, 227–8,
    235–6
Certification systems, 87, 89
CGOT (Canadian Government
    Office of Tourism), 309
Cheng Ho, 41–2
Child sex tourism, 70–1, 355–6
Chile, 112, 150, 182, 332, 353
China, 333
CHRIE (Council on Hotel
    Restaurant And Institutional
    Education), 229, 235–6
Clayton, Anthony, 252
Clean Air Act 1970: US, 266
Climate change, 252, 350–3
Coastline tourism, 104, 123–36
  best practice, 134–6
  congestion, 132–4
  cultural tourism, 130–3
  economic aspects, 123–36
  important characteristics, 136

measures of sustainability, 124–6
past and present, 126–7
sustainable tourism, 123–36
Codes of ethics, 64–5, 135, 192–3,
353–61
Collaboration *see* Coopetition
Colorado: US, 68, 76–7
Columbia: NC, 201, 204, 206, 215
Columbia Charter, 401–3
Commerce, Science and
Transportation
Committee, 279
Commercial tourism, 97–139
see also Economic aspects
Communication, 76–7, 82–93, 251
Comparative advantage, 109,
111–14
Compensation, 214, 319
Competition, 264–5
see also Coopetition
Competitiveness:
American Competitiveness
Initiative, 281–2
country strategic plans, 305
markets, 298, 313
pricing, 107
workforce development, 244–5
Comprehensive policies, 19–21
Congestion, 132–4, 184
Cookies, 337
Cooperation, 10, 19, 186
see also Coopetition
Coopetition:
Canadian tourism policy, 313
economic aspects, 103,
109–11, 129
partnerships, 344–6
red wolf ecotourism, 201–2
rural tourism, 120–1
Coordination:
disaster relief, 268, 349–50
stakeholders, 242–4
training, 239–42
US visitor data, 281–95
Cosmetic surgery, 348
Costa Rica, 239

Cost-benefit analysis, 280–95
conflicts/compromise, 267–9
decision-making, 265–9
political influence, 265–7
presentation of reports, 273–4
techniques, 269–74
US visitor data, 281–95
Cost-benefit ratio, 271
Cost-effectiveness, 272–3
Costs:
economic/non-economic, 18–19
red wolf ecotourism, 207–8
training programmes, 234–5
US visitor data programme,
284–8
Council on Hotel Restaurant and
Institutional Education
(CHRIE), 229, 235–6
Country strategic plans, 302–5
Credit cards, 122
Credos:
IIPT, 343
sustainable tourism, 198
Cresser, Hugh, 252
Crime, 326–7
Crises, 146, 248–54
Cruise ships, 67–8
CTC *see* Canadian Tourism
Commission
CTO (Caribbean Tourism
Organization), 151–2
Cuba, 221
Cultural (heritage) tourism, 27,
130–3, 195, 357
Cultural understanding, 157, 163–4
Cunliffe, Scott, 250, 253
Cusco: Peru, 148, 329

Data collection: US visitors, 281–95
Daye, Marcella, 250
Decision-making:
cooperation, 19
cost-benefit analysis, 265–9
policy, 13, 259–60
public choice theory, 263–5
stakeholders, 200

Demand, 15–16, 105–7
  economic development, 119–20
  strategic planning, 307
  workforces, 220–3
  see also Supply
Democracy, 148, 158–60
  see also Politics
Department of Hotel and Tourism
    Management (DHTM), 240
Department of Transportation:
    Kansas, 32
Destination Management
    Organizations (DMOs),
    303, 305
Destinations 2006 summit, 333
Destinations:
  global warming, 351–2
  management, 80–1, 86–7
  research, 191–2
  sustainability, 186
Destination Scorecards, 192, 196
Developing countries:
  boom effects, 251
  comparative advantage, 112
  cost-benefit analysis, 268
  economic aspects, 100–5, 123
  education, 225
  receipts, 104–5
  world economy, 330–1
  World Hotel Link, 83–93
Development:
  coastlines, 123–36
  community benefits, 17
  economic aspects, 119–20
  human resources, 225–8
  IDA, 77–9
  Kansas tourism, 32
  phase of policy, 67–8, 81
  strategic planning, 33–4
  supply, 109
  tools, 100–5
  US policy, 43–6
DHTM (Department of
    Hotel and Tourism
    Management), 240
Differentiation: SMTEs, 88–9

Disabled people, 230
Discounted cash flow, 290, 292–4
Discretionary income, 107
Diseases, 156, 247–8
DMOs (Destination Management
    Organizations), 303, 305
Domestic industries, 100
Drumm, A, 200
Dubai, 340
Dubois: Wyoming, 343–4
DuPont, 268
Dwyer, Larry, 251, 253
Dynamic processes, 314

East Carolina University, 240–1
Eco-labels, 252
E-commerce, 24, 84, 335–8
Economic aspects, 11–12, 97–139
  APEC, 149–51
  Canadian tourism policy, 310
  coastlines, 123–36
  commercial tourism, 97–139
  comparative advantage, 111–14
  coopetition, 103, 109–11, 129
  costs/benefits, 16–18
  crises, 251
  demand, 105–7, 119–20
  development, 100–5, 119–20
  employment, 114–15
  exporting tourism, 118–19
  global tourism, 100
  income, 115–16
  Kansas tourism, 26
  micro-economics, 310
  multiplier effect, 116–18
  OECD, 146–7
  policy research, 261
  red wolf ecotourism, 213–14
  supply, 108–9
  tourism information, 122
  world economy, 330–1
  World Hotel Link, 93
Ecotourism, 199–216
  definitions, 199–200
  global ethics, 356
  Kansas tourism, 27

Peru, 342
red wolves, 201–16
Edgell Sr, David L., 8, 34, 47, 51,
    100, 135, 182, 197, 298,
    308–23, 406
Education, 219–57
  accreditation, 235–8
  BEST EN, 247–54
  CHRIE, 229, 235–6
  coordination, 239–42
  credibility of programmes,
      233–4
  definitions, 221–8
  experiential learning, 242
  future issues, 338–9
  higher education, 224–8
  historical view, 365–82
  hospitality, 223–5, 227–31
  human resources, 231–45
  importance, 245–7
  modular approach, 247–8, 253
  overview, 219–20
  programmes, 240–1
  red wolves, 205–6, 209, 215
  Tedqual Certification, 237–8
  versus training, 225–8
  workforce supply/demand,
      220–3
Egypt, 39, 79, 337
Eisenhower, Dwight D., 44–6, 174
Elephant Orphanage: Sri
    Lanka, 161
Elliott, Sheryl, 220, 365–82
E-marketplace operators
    (MPOs), 84
Emerging markets, 340–1
Employees:
  Canadian Tourism, 319–22
  visitor data programme, 286
  see also Workforces
Employment, 9, 114–15
  generating, 287–8, 290–1
  multipliers, 117
  part-time/low skill, 231–2
'End Demand for Sex Trafficking
    Act of 2005' bill (US), 70–1

Entrepreneurs, 342, 360–1
Entry communities, 66–7
Environments:
  built, 182–3, 186, 189–91,
      196, 332
  environmental groups, 266
  'environmentally friendly'
      destinations, 185
  external scanning, 305
  global ethics, 358
  responsibility, 186–7
  stewardship, 350
  sustainable tourism, 181–3,
      186–91, 195–6, 332
  use/overuse, 18
  World Hotel Link, 92–3
  see also Natural environments
Epidemics, 4
Equality, 355
Ethics:
  business ethics, 64–5
  Canadian Tourism Industry,
      135, 192–3
  codes, 64–5, 135, 192–3, 354–61
  credos, 198, 343
  sex tourism, 70–1
  UNWTO, 64–5, 71, 354–61
Europe, 43–4, 229–30
Evaluating policy, 66–8
Exchange rates, 107, 117
Excursionists, 2
Experiential learning, 242
Experiential tourism, 29
Exploitation, 355
  see also Child sex tourism
Explorers, 40–2
Exporting tourism, 9–10, 100, 112,
    118–19
Exports, 116–17, 288
External environmental
    scanning, 305

Farmers' markets, 213
Farm products, 104
Fayos-Solá, Eduardo, 8
Federal agencies: STPC, 165–6

Federal government: Canada,
    309–10, 312
Federal Highway Program,
    169–70, 176
Federal Interagency Team on
    Public Lands Tourism:
    STPC, 166
*Federal-Provincial Fiscal
    Arrangements Act*: Canada, 323
Feedback from travellers, 87–9
Feeder industries, 11, 184–5
Festivals, 106, 190
Financial Administration Act:
    Canada, 323
Financial contributions: politics,
    274–80
Flint Hills: Kansas, 27
Flood, Joseph, 202–3, 205,
    207–8, 211
Florida, 153, 306
Food handling, 156
Foreign exchange receipts,
    115–16
Foreign investment, 100
Foreign policy, 141–80
    agreements, 142–3
    facilitating tourism, 154–7
    intergovernmental
        organizations, 143–53
    policies for peace, 158–64
    regional associations, 143–53
Forests, 167–8, 173, 176
Formative phase: policy, 66–7, 81
Forsyth, Peter, 251
Fragmentation of tourism
    industry, 277
Franchising: WHL, 86
Frangialli, Francesco, 237, 245
Fuentes, Gregorio, 226
Fulfillment: global ethics, 355–6
Funding:
    Canadian tourism policy,
        311–12, 321, 323
    Destination Management
        Organizations, 303
    hurricane relief, 179

Future issues, 325–63
    climate change, 350–3
    disasters, 348–50
    e-commerce, 335–8
    emerging markets, 340–1
    ethics, 354–61
    healthcare, 347–8
    partnerships/alliances, 344–6
    quality experiences, 341–4
    safety/security, 326–30
    strategic planning, 334–5
    sustainable tourism, 331–4
    world economy, 330–1

Gabon, 341
Gandhi, Mahatma, 69, 163
Gateway communities, 66–7, 168,
    171–2, 176
George Washington University,
    82–3, 241
Germany, 236
Gettysburg: Pennsylvania, 81
Global coalition: WTTC, 345
Global Code of Ethics for Tourism,
    354–61
    articles, 354–61
    business ethics, 64
    cultural tourism, 357
    entrepreneurs, 360–1
    implementation, 361
    liberty of movement, 359–60
    local communities, 357–8
    mutual understanding, 354–5
    right to tourism, 359
    stakeholder obligations,
        358–9
    sustainable tourism, 356
    UNWTO, 64, 144, 354–61
    value of fulfillment, 355–6
    workers, 360–1
Globalization: education, 339
Global markets, 87–9
Global tourism, 10–11, 48–9
Global warming, 350–3
Goal-oriented planning, 8, 300–1
Goeldner, Charles, 8, 135, 193–4

Government:
  Canadian organizations,
    309–10, 312
  ethics, 358–9
  history of education, 368–73
  revenue multipliers, 117
Grants, 80
Greeks, 39
Green Lake: Wisconsin, 344
Grey Glacier: Chile, 353
Grievances, 320, 322
Griffin, T., 225
Growth of tourism, 23, 33, 126–7
Guam, 79
Guilin: China, 333
Gulf War, 10
Gurtner, Yetta, 251

Hamilton, Marlene, 249
Hara, Tadayuki, 251
Hardware: visitor data
    programme, 284–6
Hawaii, 98, 184, 241
Hayle, Carolyn, 249
Healthcare, 71–2, 267, 347–8
Heritage (cultural) tourism, 28,
    130–3, 195, 357
Higher education, 224–8
Highways, 46, 169–70, 174, 176
Historic activities *see* Cultural
    tourism
Historical view of education,
    365–82
  assessment of needs, 380–1
  improvements, 373–80
  role of government, 368–73
  skills development, 365–8
Historic perspectives: tourism,
    37–42
Hohenschwangau Castle:
    Germany, 236
Homer: Alaska, 185
Home working, 244
Hong Kong, 240
Horizontal coordination, 242–4
Hospitality, 108, 223–5, 227–31

Hotels:
  accommodation, 105–6
  administration programmes, 119
  reservations, 234
  World Hotel Link, 76, 82–93
Human resources, 225–8, 231–45
  accrediting training, 235–8
  Canadian Tourism Commission,
    321–2
  changing world, 244–5
  coordinating training, 239–42
  credibility of programmes,
    233–4
  investment needs, 234–5
  misperceptions, 231–2
  training infrastructure, 239–42
  UNWTO, 235, 237–8
  workforce development, 244–5
Hurricanes, 168–9, 179, 250, 349
Hyde county: NC, 201–2, 216
Hyderabad: India, 190

IATC (Inter-American Travel
    Congress), 149
ICT (information and
    communication technology),
    76–7, 82–93
IDA (International Development
    Association), 77–9
IFWTO (International Federation
    of Women's Travel
    Organizations), 71
IIPT Credo of the Peaceful
    Traveler, 343
Illinois, 344
Image: US, 49–51
Immigration control, 156–7
Impacts of tourism, 14–15, 18,
    104, 130
Importance of tourism, 9–10, 262–3
Improvements: education, 373–80
Income, 107, 115–16
  see also Receipts
Income multipliers, 117
Independent travellers, 86
India, 68, 104, 190, 341

Information:
  Access to Information Act, 322–3
  economic aspects, 122
  strategic, 30–1
  US visitors, 281–95
Information and communication
    technology (ICT), 76–7, 82–93
Infrastructure:
  education, 239–42
  tourism, 100, 103, 333, 356
Initiatives: SMTEs, 88–9
In-kind resources, 312
Insurance, 72
Intangible goods, 4
Integrated chips, 154–5, 171
Integration: stakeholders, 19, 242–4
Inter-American Travel Congress
    (IATC), 149
Interdependency: feeder
    industries, 184–5
Intergovernmental organizations,
    143–53
International Development
    Association (IDA), 77–9
International Federation of
    Women's Travel
    Organizations (IFWTO), 71
International tourism:
  arrivals, 100–1, 113, 331
  definitions, 1–2
  receipts, 99–100, 102, 113, 115–17
  US, 43–6, 49–51, 281–95
International travel, 45–6, 52,
    171–2, 176
Internet, 335–8
  comparative advantage, 112
  coopetition, 110
  demand side, 106–7
  information, 122
  Kansas tourism, 28
  see also World Hotel Link
Interstate highways, 46, 169–70,
    174, 176
Investment, 73–4, 234–5
'Invisible' nature of tourism, 119
Iraq War, 251

Ireland, 243
Israel, 162

Jago, Leo, 252
Jamaica, 248–9, 252
Jobs *see* Employment
Jurowski, Claudia, 220, 248, 253

Kansas tourism, 20–32, 344
  development arguments, 33
  economic aspects, 23
  emerging issues, 26–9
  executive summary, 22–4
  future outlook, 31–3
  goals, 24
  objectives, 25
  opportunities, 22–33
  strategy, 25, 30–1
  tactics, 25
  transition, 24
Kansas Travel and Tourism
    Development Division
    (KTTDD), 24, 30–2
Kant, Immanuel, 159–60
Kauai: Hawaii, 184
Kayaking, 188, 216
Kenya Wildlife Service (KWS), 183
Khan, Herman, 223
Knowledge management, 246,
    249, 251
Krozer, Yoram, 250
KTTDD (Kansas Travel and
    Tourism Development
    Division), 24, 30–2
KWS (Kenya Wildlife Service), 183
Kyoto Protocol 1997, 350

Labour relations, 321–2
Lanai, Hawaii, 98
Land, 167, 170, 176, 186–7
Landino, Joe, 206–7, 209–10
Landowners, 209–10, 213–14
La Pederera Apartment:
    Barcelona, 224
Lash, Gail, 202, 205–9
Las Vegas, 5–6, 20, 230

Leadership: UNWTO, 237–8
Leakage, 109
Lebanon, 162
Leiper, N., 222–3
Liburd, Janne, 253–4
Loans, 79–80
Local communities:
  built environments, 190–1
  ethics, 357–8
  involvement, 134
  planning, 193
  red wolf ecotourism, 201–16
  stakeholders, 201–16
  sustainable tourism, 190–1, 193,
    197–8, 201–16
Location: knowledge of, 109
Logrolling, 264
Lost City of the Incas, 66
Low-skilled employees, 115, 231–2
Luggage inspections, 156

McDonald, Franklin, 252
Machu Picchu: Peru, 38, 40,
  66–7, 307
Majorca, 12, 133–4, 338
Managing Sustainable Tourism ...
  (Edgell), 182
Manila Declaration on World
  Tourism, 395–400
Maori culture, 188
Market access:
  OECD, 147
  WHL, 83, 86, 91
Marketing:
  Canadian tourism policy,
    309–10, 313
  defining policy, 7, 9
  developing countries, 83,
    86, 91–2
  ecotourism, 210–11
  Internet, 337–8
  Kansas tourism, 30–1
  online access, 83, 86, 92–3
  personal marketing, 337–8
  policy-making, 13

  sustainable tourism, 87–9, 198,
    210–11
  target marketing, 30–1
  visitor data programme, 289, 294
  World Hotel Link, 83, 86, 91–2
Markets, 298, 313, 340–1
Market segmentation *see* Target
  marketing
Marriot International, 339
Master of Tourism Administration
  (MTA) degree, 241
Measuring sustainability, 124–6
Medical tourism, 72
Medium-sized firms, 313, 315
Meis, Scott M., 308–23
Membership survey: STPC, 175–8
Memorandum of Understanding
  (MOU): STPC, 165–6
Mexico, 142–3, 383–9
Miami: Florida, 306
Micro-economics, 310
Misperceptions of policy, 262
Mission statements, 8, 32, 299–300,
  313–14
Mistilis, Nina, 251
Modern tourism, 42
Mongol empires, 39–40
Montana: US, 201
Montenegro, 79
Moore, A., 200
Morgan, Damian, 252–3
MOU (Memorandum of
  Understanding), 165–6
Mountain tourism, 352
Mozambique, 78–80
MPOs (e-marketplace
  operators), 84
Mt Airy, NC, 118
MTA (Master of Tourism
  Administration) degree, 241
Mudslides, 349, 350
Multiplier effect, 103, 116–18
Mutual Security Act 1957, 45
Mutual understanding, 354–5

National Association for Stock Car
Auto Racing (NASCAR), 344
National Geographic Traveler
articles, 124–5, 186, 191–2
*National Outdoor Recreation Policy
Act*, 172–3, 176
National parks: Canada, 192
National Park Service: US,
173–4, 176
National scenic byways program,
174–6
National Tourism Policy Act 1981,
47–9, 51–62
National Tourism Safety Network:
South Africa, 327
Natural disasters, 348–50
Natural environments:
ethics, 356
strategic planning, 303, 306
sustainable tourism, 181–3,
186–7, 189–90, 195–6, 332
Needs assessment: education,
380–1
Nelson, Bonalyn, 250–1
Net present value, 272, 290, 294
New York, 230, 245
New York-New York Hotel and
Casino, 230
New Zealand, 188
Niche marketing *see* Target
marketing
Non-credit programmes, 241–2
Non-destination ('outside')
stakeholders, 305
Non-economic benefits, 16–18
Non-economic costs, 18–19
North Carolina (NC), 98, 118,
120–1, 187, 201–16, 240–1
Nova Scotia, 346
Nutria, 214

OAS (Organization of American
States), 147–9
Ocracoke Island, North Carolina,
120–1

OECD (Organisation for Economic
Cooperation and
Development), 146–7
Old Havana: Cuba, 221
Online tourism, 76, 82–93
Operating budgets, 321
Operating sectors: tourism, 304–5
Opportunity costs, 270
Organisation for Economic
Cooperation and
Development (OECD), 146–7
Organizational planning, 310–11
Organization of American States
(OAS), 147–9
Organizations:
involved in tourism, 8–10
public sector, 16
Outdoor recreation, 175–8
Output multipliers, 117
'Outside' (non-destination)
stakeholders, 305

PACs (political action
committees), 274–8
Pakistan, 68
Palacio de Justicia: Lima, 75
Parks, 173–4, 176, 192–3
Partnerships, 344–6
Canadian tourism policy,
308–13, 317
coopetition, 110–11
global ethics, 361
Part-time employment, 231–2
Pavesic, D., 227
Payroll increases: US research,
287–93
Peace, 158–64
Columbia Charter, 401–3
democratic peace theory, 158–60
mutual trust/respect, 163–4
political stability, 160–2
reasons for peace, 160
tourism/peace diagram, 164
'Peaks and valleys' of demand, 106
People to People International, 46

Performance ratios: US research, 289–90
Perishable products, 2–3
Personal marketing, 337–8
Personnel *see* Employees
Peru, 38, 40, 66–7, 75, 148, 329, 342
Petroleum industry, 184
Phoenicians, 38–9
Pilgrimages, 37–8
Pisac: Peru, 15
Pizam, Abraham, 247
Planning, 4–7
   economic development, 120
   goal-orientated planning, 8
   impact of tourism, 130
   Kansas tourism, 23–4
   land, 186–7
   red wolf ecotourism, 208
   social impact, 190–1
   sustainable tourism, 182, 186–7, 190–1, 193–4, 208
   see also Policy; Strategic planning
Podcasts, 336–7
Points systems, 345
Policy, 4–9, 12–16
   balanced policy, 19–21
   Canadian case study, 307–23
   comprehensive policy, 19–21
   cost-benefit analysis, 265–74, 281–95
   current issues, 63–95
   definitions, 7–9, 65
   development diagram, 21
   evaluation stages, 65–9
   foreign policy, 141–80
   formulation diagram, 14
   future issues, 325–63
   influencing policy, 259–96
   Kansas tourism, 32–3
   past issues, 37–62
   political aspects, 141–80, 261, 265–7, 274–80
   STPC, 166–80
Political action committees (PACs), 274–8

Politics, 141–80, 274–80
   see also Policy
Polo, Marco, 40–1
Population figures, 330
Post-secondary education programmes, 233–4
Powell, Colin, 50
Preservation, 199–216
Press: ethics, 359
Pricing, 107–8
Privacy Act: Canada, 323
Private sector:
   cost-benefit analysis, 268–9
   Kansas tourism, 31–2
   partnerships, 308–11, 312–13, 317
   terrorism, 164
   WTTC, 145–6
Products used in tourism, 2
Project for Perpetual Peace (Kant), 159
Protecting environments, 189–90
Psychological aspects, 18–19
Publications: travel, 15
Public choice theory, 263–5
Public land, 170, 176
Public policy, 13, 69–70
Public relations, 31
Public sector, 16, 308–10
Public Service Employment Act: Canada, 321–2
Pucon: Chile, 332
Punta Arenas: Chile, 182

Qualified workers, 244–5
Quality:
   beaches, 17–18
   experiences, 341–4
   of life, 22, 63, 73, 263
   supply, 109
Quincy Library Group: California, 201

Raccoons, 214
Randall, Clarence B., 45
Ravinder, Ravi, 252

Real-estate values, 18
Receipts:
  developing countries, 104–5
  international tourism, 99–100,
      102, 113, 115–17
Recovery strategies: crises,
      249–50
Recreation, 126, 167–8, 172–8
Recreation Resource Advisory
      Committees (RRACs), 168
Red Wolf Coalition, 215
Red wolf ecotourism, 201–16
  benefits, 207–8, 214
  creating tourism, 212–13
  critical issues, 203
  education, 214–15
  future aspects, 216
  goals of meetings, 206–7
  group discussions, 203–4, 211–16
  presentation summaries, 207–11
  retaining revenue, 215–16
  stakeholders meetings, 202–16
  summaries of discussions,
      212–16
Redzepovic, Else, 250
Regional industry associations,
      143–53
Registered Traveler Program
      (RTP), 155, 171
Regulations, 69–70, 74
  see also Policy
Relationship economy, 338
Relief coordination, 268, 349–50
Religious pilgrimages, 37–8
Research, 5
  BEST EN, 253
  coastline tourism, 126
  education programmes, 233–4
  evaluating policy, 68
  hospitality sector, 230–1
  human resources, 232
  Kansas tourism, 23, 26–8, 30
  policy-making, 13–14
  sustainability, 191–2
  Swanson study, 261–2
  tourism impact graph, 178

  visitor data programme, 281–95
  World Wildlife Fund, 351
Ricardo, David, 111
Rice, Condoleezza, 50, 163
Rights: tourism, 359–61
Rio Petrohué, Chile, 112
*Risk Assessment and Cost-Benefit
      Analysis Act*, 266–7
Risk management, 248–54
Ritchie, J.R. Brent, 8, 135, 193–4
Roadways, 46, 169–70, 174, 176
Romans, 39
Rozga, Zachary, 76, 82, 84
RRACs (Recreation Resource
      Advisory Committees), 168
RTP (Registered Traveler
      Program), 155, 171
Ruf Strategic Solutions, 30–1
Rural tourism, 28–9, 120–1
Russia, 342–3
Ryu, Sarah, 250

Safety, 11, 72–3, 326–30
  BEST EN thinktank, 249
  facilitating tourism, 154–6
  policies for peace, 160–2
  Traveler Safety and Security
      Initiative, 405–6
Sahli, Mondher, 251
Sales multipliers, 117
SARS (Severe Acute Respiratory
      Syndrome), 4, 71–2, 156,
      251, 347
Scanlon, Nancy, 252
Scenic byways, 174–6
Schott, Christian, 252
Seasonality, 106
Sectoral annexes: US-Canada
      agreement, 391–3
Security *see* Safety
Segmentation:
  target marketing, 30–1
  tourism industry, 16
Selengut, Stanley, 189
Sensitivity analysis, 273, 290, 292–4
September 11th, 4, 48, 50, 67, 326

Services sector, 114
Severe Acute Respiratory Syndrome (SARS), 4, 71–2, 156, 251, 347
Sex tourism, 70–1, 355–6
Sheldon, Pauline, 249, 251, 253
SICTA (Standard International Classification of Tourism Activities), 222
Simonetti, Jill, 207, 210–11
Simonyi, Charles, 74, 342
Sirakayae, Ercan, 252
Skills, 115, 231–2, 365–8
Small businesses, 103–5, 118, 313, 315
Small-to-medium-sized tourism enterprises (SMTEs), 82–93
SMART goals, 302
Smith, Ginger, 247
Smith, Kay, 226
Smith, Stephen L.J., 308–23
SMTEs (small-to-medium-sized tourism enterprises), 82–93
Snowmobiling, 352
Social impacts, 18, 92, 191, 269
Software: US research, 284–6
South Africa, 327
South America, 105, 232–3, 341
Southeast Tourism Policy Council (STPC), 153, 165–80
 analysis of policy, 178–90
 future opportunities, 178–80
 membership survey, 175–8
 new policy categories, 177
 policy issues, 166–78
Southeast Tourism Society (STS), 152–3, 165–80
Space tourism, 73–4, 341–3
Spas, 348
Speaker, Andrew, 347–8
Special interest groups, 264–5, 274
Speciality tourism categories, 15
Spending, 107
Sports for youth, 16–17
Spurr, Ray, 251
Sri Lanka, 161–2

Staff *see* Employees
Stakeholders:
 APEC, 149–50
 coopetition, 111
 coordination, 242–4
 decision-making, 19
 ecotourism, 200–16
 global ethics, 358–9, 361
 Kansas tourism, 32
Standard International Classification of Tourism Activities (SICTA), 222
Standards: training, 235–8
Stear, L., 225
Stern, Nicholas, 351
Stewarding environments, 350
STPC *see* Southeast Tourism Policy Council
Strategic advantage, 30–1
Strategic alliances, 344–6
Strategic information, 30–1
Strategic planning, 297–324
 Canadian tourism policy, 308–23
 definitions, 299–302
 development flow chart, 34
 example, 302–5
 future issues, 334–5
 goals, 299–302, 314
 Kansas tourism, 23–4, 32
 objectives, 300–1, 314, 316
 red wolf ecotourism, 208
 sustainable tourism, 306–8
 tactics, 301
Strategies:
 definitions, 301
 policymaking, 7
 sustainability, 194–6
STS (Southeast Tourism Society), 152–3, 165–80
Sumerians, 38
Summative phase: evaluation, 68, 81
Supply, 15–16, 108–9
 comparative advantage, 111–12
 economic development, 119–20
 strategic planning, 307

Supply (*Continued*)
  workforces, 220–3
  see also Demand
Support systems, 155–6
Surgical tourism, 348
Sustainable tourism, 4–7, 9,
    181–218
  benefits, 196–7
  BEST EN, 247–54
  coastlines, 104, 123–36
  credo, 198
  current trends, 186–91
  ethics, 198, 356
  global impact, 191–3
  important precepts, 197–8
  Kansas, 27
  management, 181–218, 298,
    331–4
  OAS, 149
  planning, 182, 186–7, 190–4, 208,
    297–8, 306–8
  policy strategies, 194–6
  prescriptions for success, 125
  World Hotel Link, 85, 87–9
  see also Red wolf ecotourism
Swanson, J., 261–2, 281–95
Swan Valley group: Montana, 201
Switzerland, 350
SWOT analysis, 208, 302

Tabacon Hot Springs and Spa:
    Costa Rica, 239
Tallgrass Prairie National
    Preserve: Kansas, 27
Tangible goods, 4
Taputu, Meriana, 188
Target marketing, 30–1
Tarlow, Peter, 249, 329
Taxes, 77, 103, 287–94
Teamwork: planning, 299–300
Technology, 8, 100
  airport construction, 103
  e-commerce, 24, 84, 335–8
  hotel reservations, 119
  online tourism, 76–7
  rural interest, 93

September 11th, 67
US-VISIT programme, 155
virtual office, 244
visitor data programme, 284–6
World Hotel Link, 82–93
see also Internet
Tedqual Certification, 225, 237–8
TEP-TEI (Tourism Education
    Policy/Implementation)
    model, 243–4
Terrorism, 8, 11, 326–30
  foreign policy, 164–5
  policies for peace, 158
  September 11th, 4, 48, 50, 67, 326
Thailand, 70
Themis Foundation, 237–8
Themis Tedqual Practicum
    programme, 238
Think tanks: BEST EN, 247–54
Thurot, Jean-Maurice, 141, 157
TIAC (Tourism Industry
    Association of Canada),
    309–10
TIANS (Tourism Industry
    Association of Nova
    Scotia), 346
TIA (Travel Industry Association),
    51, 222, 282
Tisch, Jonathan, 260
Topography, 120
Tourism:
  definitions, 1–9, 221–5
  overview, 1–36
Tourism Canada, 309–10
Tourism Education
    Policy/Implementation
    (TEP-TEI) model, 243–4
Tourism Enriches campaign:
    UNWTO, 246
*Tourism in the European Recovery
    Program* (US white paper), 44
Tourism Industry Association of
    Canada (TIAC), 309–10
Tourism Industry Association of
    Nova Scotia (TIANS), 346
Tourists, 1, 23

Trade, Tourism and Economic
  Development Sub-Committee,
  278–9
Training, 240–2
  see also Education
Transaction multipliers, 117
Transitional economies, 123
Transportation department:
  Kansas, 32
Traveler Safety and Security
  Initiative, 405–6
Travel Industry Association (TIA),
  51, 202, 222
Travel publications, 15
The Travels of Marco Polo, 40–1
Tsunami: Asia Pacific region, 349
Tuberculosis, 347–8
Tullock, Gordon, 263
Tyrell county: NC, 201–2,
  205–8, 216

UAE (United Arab Emirates),
  340, 351
Undersea tourism, 343
Unemployment rates, 115
United Arab Emirates (UAE),
  340, 351
United Mexican States, 383–9
United Nations World Tourism
  Organization (UNWTO),
  144–5
  agreements, 142
  child sex tourism, 71
  congestion, 132
  defining tourism, 1–2
  ethics, 64–5, 71, 354–61
  Global Code of Ethics for
    Tourism, 354–61
  Guilin monitoring project, 333
  history, 42
  human resources, 235, 237–8
  SICTA, 222
  sustainable tourism, 127–8,
    194–5
  Tourism Enriches campaign, 246
  training accreditation, 235

US membership, 48–9, 51, 144
  world economy, 330–1
United States Fish and Wildlife
  Service (USFWS), 201–2,
  205, 209
United States Travel Service
  (USTS), 45, 48
United States Travel and Tourism
  Administration (USTTA),
  48, 51
United States (US), 43–62
  agreement with Mexico, 383–9
  Canada-US free trade
    agreement, 391–3
  Clean Air Act, 266
  economic impacts, 104
  employment, 114–15
  European travel, 43–4
  exporting tourism, 118
  history of hospitality, 229
  human resources, 232
  international tourism, 43–6,
    49–51
  Mexico, 142–3, 383–9
  Miami, 306
  National Tourism Policy Act,
    47–9, 51–62
  non-credit programmes, 241–2
  policy development, 43–6
  political contributions, 275–80
  reasons for policy, 49–52
  rural tourism, 120–1
  seasonality, 106
  space tourism, 342–3
  training programmes, 240–2
  Traveler Safety and Security
    Initiative, 405–6
  UNWTO, 48–9, 51, 144
  Venezuela, 142–3
  visitor data programme, 281–95
University of the Balearic
  Islands, 338
UNWTO *see* United Nations
  World Tourism Organization
US *see* United States

USFWS (United States Fish and Wildlife Service), 201–2, 205, 209
USTS (United States Travel Service), 45, 48
USTTA (United States Travel and Tourism Administration), 48, 51
US Visitor and Immigrant Status Indicator Technology (US-VISIT) programme, 155

Vandalia, Illinois, 344
Venezuela, 142–3, 349
Vertical coordination, 242–4
Villa Rica volcano: Chile, 332
Virginia, 78
Virtual office, 244
Visa Waiver Program (VWP), 154, 171
Vision, 8, 32, 204, 253, 299–300, 313–14
Visitor data programme, 281–95
  benefits, 286, 288–90, 294
  costs/inputs, 284–8
  five-year budget, 284–5
  historical data, 287, 289–90
  net present value, 290, 294
  problems, 283
  proposed programme, 283–4
  sensitivity analysis, 290, 292–4
Visitors, 1, 29, 281–95, 304
Volunteer vacations, 343
Vulcan Osorno, Chile, 112
VWP (Visa Waiver Program), 154, 171

War, 158
Ward, Colleen, 19
Warm locations, 351–2
Water management, 20
Weblogs, 336
Websites *see* Internet

Western Hemisphere Travel Initiative (WHTI), 143, 171
Wheeler, Kim, 215
WHL *see* World Hotel Link
WHTI (Western Hemisphere Travel Initiative), 143, 171
Wildlife, 126, 183, 201–2, 205, 209, 351
Wilkes-Barre, Pennsylvania, 109
Wisconsin, 344
Workforces:
  development, 244–5
  education, 339
  ethics, 360–1
  supply, 220–3
World Bank, 77–8, 89
World economy, 330–1
World Hotel Link (WHL), 76, 82–93
  ICT, 82–93
  implementation model, 84–5
  job stability, 85–6
  market access, 83, 86, 91
  policy implications, 91–2
  recommendations, 92–3
  scope, 89–91
  sustainable tourism, 87–9
  value chain diagram, 91
World Legacy Awards, 186
World Travel and Tourism Council (WTTC), 128, 145–6, 195–6, 222, 345
World War II, 43–4
World Wildlife Fund, 351
WTTC (World Travel and Tourism Council), 128, 145–6, 195–6, 222, 345
Wyoming, 343

Yorktown: Virginia, 78
Youth sports, 16–17

Zoning, 75–6, 81